Readings in American Politics and Political Marketing

Readings in American Politics and Political Marketing

FIRST EDITION

EDITED BY

Kenneth Cosgrove

cognella®

SAN DIEGO

Bassim Hamadeh, CEO and Publisher
John Remington, Managing Executive Editor
Anne Jones, Project Editor
Abbey Hastings, Production Editor
Asfa Arshi, Graphic Design Assistant
Trey Soto, Licensing Specialist
Natalie Piccotti, Director of Marketing
Kassie Graves, Senior Vice President of Editorial
Jamie Giganti, Director of Academic Publishing

cognella® | ACADEMIC PUBLISHING

3970 Sorrento Valley Blvd., Ste. 500, San Diego, CA 92121

CONTENTS

UNIT III

UNIT IV

INTRODUCTION

This book is about American political institutions, the way the United States deals with the rest of the world and the ways in which political communication have influenced both things. It looks at the current situation in which the country finds itself, the way its political institutions are organized and operate, the impact that political marketing has had upon them and the kinds of public policies that its government makes. Politics and public policy truly involve everything in American life, from the way in which the country deals with other countries, to the way its economy functions, to the way in which bourbon is produced and labeled. The world and the country have changed a great deal since the foundation of the United States, but the country's political system has remained relatively unchanged. What has changed are where and how Americans live, how they learn about politics and how politicians understand them and their concerns, and the number and complexity of issues that the national government deals with on their behalf. A volume like this is intended to show how the political system works and how it has changed since its long-ago foundation. By the end of it, the reader should have a good sense of the structures and forces that produce continuity and change in American politics.

Americans are more connected to national politics and politicians and to each other through social and electronic communication than they have ever been. On the other hand, it is very likely that they are less connected to the communities in which they reside and the people with whom they share a physical space than has ever been the case before something that the political scientist Robert Putnam noted in his important book *Bowling Alone* (2000). The transformation from a politics based on physical communities and local interests has profound consequences for the United States in terms of social cohesion and the tone of our politics because it has made it possible for Americans to live within their own electronic bubbles as the media scholar Joseph Turow argued would be the case in his book *Breaking Up America* (1998). The rise of niche politics has facilitated a personalized politics. We interact with others like us but not necessarily with the country as whole on a regular basis. This has produced a politics that is more polarized and less able to produce consensus policies than has been the case in a long time. We have a socially sorted country as Bill Bishop (2009) has noted and this has produced political super identities as Liliana Mason (2018) has noted. We will explore the way in which marketed, targeted politics work in a country that's really made up of a mosaic of niche identities. This book is structured into four sections. The first and last are shorter than the middle two units intentionally as these encourage you, the reader, to think about the big questions of

American politics, while the middle two sections focus more on the way in which the country's political institutions work and are structured, as well as the role that political marketing and advanced communications technologies has played in shaping the behavior of the institutions and the citizens.

Unit I will look at the way in which America's place in the world is changing. For the first hundred and thirty years or so of its existence, the United States was an internally focused nation that primarily focused on its expansion throughout North America not its place on the global stage. George Washington famously told his fellow citizens to "avoid entangling foreign alliances" and they took his word with a vengeance. The most significant military opponent Americans fought during this period was other Americans in an epic battle over human rights in the form of slavery and structurally in a struggle over the rights of the national versus state governments. This was primarily an agrarian country for most of its first hundred and thirty years or so. Industrialization changed all that, kicked off a wave of large-scale immigration and built great cities in the Northeast and Midwest dedicated to manufacturing and the primitive kinds of service industries that have blossomed in our era in which much of the population lived. While Theodore Roosevelt might have begun the process of building a global presence by sending the Great White Fleet around the world, it was Woodrow Wilson who put the United States on the global stage and tried to build global institutions in a way that most of his successors have never stopped trying to do. Wilson's entry into World War I set the stage for the American hegemony that would come at the end of the Cold War almost a century later (Suri, 2017). While Wilson didn't get the multilateral peace treaty and international institutions that he wanted, his Democratic successor Franklin D. Roosevelt (byname FDR) did. The world FDR and Truman shaped along with America's World War II allies as that conflict was winding down, began a process that made the United States into a global superpower. World War II and its aftermath transformed the United States into a global superpower and built a series of institutions that allowed it to exercise power domestically and abroad.

By the turn of the 21st century, the United States had won the Cold War against the USSR and become a dominant economic power. The national government took on responsibilities home and abroad that would have surprised the Framers. In addition to their many benefits, these policies had significant costs in blood and treasure. These costs made it possible for politicians like Ross Perot, Pat Buchanan, Barack Obama, and Donald Trump to talk about modifying the way in which the United States approached the world. This is easier said than done, as many of the events associated with these policies are beyond the American Government's ability to control. From the end of the USSR in 1991 until at least September 11, 2001, the United States was the world's dominant power, but the events of 9/11 set off a chain reaction that produced the world in which we now live. The country spent a lot of lives, time, and money on wars in Iraq and Afghanistan, while global rivals elsewhere were strengthening. Thus, the modern United States is a different strategic position and confronted with different challenges than it was during the Cold War and its aftermath. The United States is no longer the single great power, and some are questioning how an alliance structure like NATO and a multilateral world order that the United States helped to create at the end of World War II makes sense in the current world.

Unit II will look at the ways in which hard and soft power have been used and how the United States got into this situation in the first place. Americans have seen the downsides of being the dominant power from September 11, 2001 onward and the recent global pandemic showed them one of the downsides of the globalized world that had developed in the wake of the Cold War's conclusion. One of the biggest ways that the world order has been changed has been through the rise of China as a global power and competitor to the United States. Further, even though the Soviet Union might have gone, the Russian Federation remains a power capable of causing problems for America and its allies, and there are a host of other states like Iran with the capability of doing so as well. Much of the world became accustomed to an environment in which American forces and diplomats promoted security and American inspired institutions promoted stability but these arrangements were called into question in the current era. Donald Trump's election and administration positioned the United States differently on these issues than the United States had been positioned in a century.

What has not changed is the structure of America's political institutions. Congress and the Executive Branch still vie for power, the Courts still make rulings but there is a much bigger administrative state than there once was and many more interest groups trying to influence and media covering all of it. Section II looks at the battles that regularly take places between Congress and the President, how the Constitution still shapes those and how states too have considerable influence in the way in which public policy is made here. The Framers hoped that the branches would battle each other for supremacy because they thought doing this would prevent the development of a single majority faction capable of tyrannizing statistical minorities or the rise of a dictator prone to changing public policy on a whim. FDR made the Presidency into a central economic figure via his response to the Great Depression, the New Deal. His use of communications technology in the form of the radio transformed the President from a distant, cold, figure into a significant figure in the daily lives and culture of Americans. FDR is, in many ways, the progenitor of the Presidency as institution that we understand it to be today (Suri, 2017).

One of the questions that remains unsettled from the Founding is the relative strength of the states versus the national government in the political system. The question of federalism was the lesser cause of the Civil War because the Framers couldn't agree on the relative balance of state and national governmental powers themselves. This battle has taken many forms since the 1700s and the relative powers of both the federal government and the states have waxed and waned, but it is important to understand why such changes are even possible with a written constitution. The institutions are partly responsible for the kind of policy that the government makes, and the government makes policy about all sorts of things as the case of bourbon shows. While this seems like a trivial product, bourbon is a major American export because it can only be made in the United States following a specific set of procedures. No spirt made anywhere else can be called bourbon. Such standardization is common across many areas of American life at this point. The same kinds of definitions and regulations that can be applied to bourbon can be applied to many areas of American life.

Unit III will look at the impact of having consumer marketing techniques become so influential in politics. Changes in communications technology have made it possible for Americans and their leaders to be more in touch with each other than they ever were during the Founding era. There are more tools through which politicians can communicate. Indeed, the population itself has diversified in many ways, while the tools with which they can be understood and the platforms through which they can be reached are more precise and more extensive than they ever have been. We know more about a diverse country and how to reach a diverse country than has ever been the case before. Politics, rather than being a civic activity, has become something akin to a spectator sport in which American identify with one team or the other something that has consequences for the way in which our politics work and the way in which Americans relate to each other (Mason, 2018). American politics is an organized activity because of the way in which the Constitution structured the government, the multiple ways and places Americans live, and the model outlined by the 1960s African American Civil Rights Movement regarding the way to make an impact in this system and its example has been copied by all sorts of groups as Berry (1984) has noted. These groups lobby Congress and the President, work with political action committees, organizations that raise money and donate to campaigns, to help elect candidates and try to shape the choices that Americans are presented with in a variety of areas, including who gets to set on the Supreme Court.

Unit IV will end the book with a look at the way in which ideas fuel political movements. In the late 1980s philosopher Allan Bloom wrote a notable book entitled *The Closing of the American Mind*. Bloom argued that Americans were heirs to a specific intellectual tradition that was being wiped out by commercial and popular culture but also argued against cultural relativism. Bloom believed that some cultures really were superior to others. This is debatable topic and one that harkens back to a core debate in America about the existence and desirability of a single culture versus the benefits of a more multicultural orientation. Bloom's work argued against a kind of cultural relativism in favor of specific standards and values. Bloom might well have accelerated the nation's ongoing battle over culture, but he certainly accelerated the discussion of these topics in a way that resonates today in places far away from college campuses. What Bloom discussed, in many ways, was the template for the most recent era of American politics in which a lot of attention was paid to cultural issues but much less paid to economic issues. This is a trend that Teixeira and Halpin argue has limited the ability of progressive issues and candidates to resonate with White working-class voters. Such voters are a large part of the electorate, have shifted toward the Republicans in recent elections and voted for Donald Trump twice in big numbers. One can argue that Trump articulated a class-based politics in terms of style and presentation far more than do most progressives. Trump showed that a class-based appeal can work with these voters in ways that get them to support conservative causes. While White working-class voters are shrinking in size, they are strategically placed in terms of the electoral college and add numbers to a shrinking middle class professional Republican base as we saw will see in Section III's reading that deals with Donald Trump taking on upper middle-class professionals. The lesson of this article and the subsequent article is that class is an important but under examined way of thinking about politics. Issues and presentational styles that appeal to one class well may chase another one away from a political party or candidate, however, in this highly polarized, socially sorted country, creating specific appeals for specific audiences might work well for the marketer as a strategy because it sets up the customer base quite precisely. Having such structured and siloed politics might be great for winning elections, but it seems to be promoting a great deal of division in the process.

As Frank Dobbin notes, politics has become a profession not just a service or civic activity. Many people make a living by working for candidates, campaigns, interest groups, or other political entities. Many of them have very specialized skills. We see candidates presented in specific settings wearing specific clothing, using specific music, all aimed at reaching very specific subsets of the voting public. It is common to use marketing and commercial language to understand the electorate. Voters are consumers who make a purchasing decision in the form of a candidate during an election, public opinion can be seen as akin to an electoral market, and highly detailed databases of consumer behavior tell campaigns of all sorts who their audiences really are and what their issues of choice should be. Thus, the whole idea that political scientists have promoted of the logical voter seems to be under siege from the same kinds of emotional pitches that are used to sell a panoply of commercial products. Dobbin's key point is that politics can and does shift from a rational to an emotional actor model. This is an important insight in an age in which people seem to have both very strong feelings and very fixed identities about politics.

This volume provides a survey of American politics from the current situation facing the country, to the way in which its system developed, to how it influences policy outcomes, to the ways in which the system's structure influences behavior, to the ways in which technology has changed, to the ways in which people understand and interact with the system. By the end of this book, it is hoped that students have a good idea of the importance of these topics both in the life of the country and their own lives, a sense for the extent to which politics and public policy shape our daily lives and a good idea of why America came to occupy its current position in the world and why that is ever changing.

New Century, New Challenges and Opportunities

Unit I: Introduction

The world that the United States exists in has changed in dramatic ways several times during the last century. America's isolationism came to an end with its entry into World War I. Even though the country retreated for a time back into its more nationalist orientation, the onset of World War II meant that the country never left the global stage again. World War II led to the development of a permanent military and security state. Its existence was cemented by the onset of a long struggle between the United States and one of its World War II allies, the Soviet Union for global strategic, economic, and cultural supremacy. The so-called Cold War produced a clear identity among Americans and their allies and a strong sense of collective purpose that supported the development of international organizations like the World Bank and military alliances like the North Atlantic Treaty Organization (NATO). This world had the United States at its center and gave Americans themselves a sense of shared public purpose. The Cold War produced a sense of social harmony but also a sense that somebody was always watching and always presenting a threat to the country. Several generations of Americans grew up with the Cold War world being the only thing that they had known.

That world ended suddenly and unexpectedly as the Cold War gradually ended between 1989 and 1992. The end of the Cold War came about because of things that the United States and its allies did but also because of changes to the Soviet system itself. First, the older generations of Soviets, who remembered the Revolution and fought in World War II, gradually died off. They were replaced by Mikhail Gorbachev who stressed the need to change the Soviet system. Gorbachev, in addition to trying to reform the Soviet system in an effort to save it loosened the grip of Soviet control over its buffer states in Eastern Europe that it had held firmly since the end of World War II. The problem with having such buffer states and engaging with the United States and its allies on a global basis was that it was expensive and required that most of the USSR's economic output go to military spending instead of improving the living standards of average Soviet citizens. The military spending caused socioeconomic stagnation in the remainder of Soviet society and bred significant corruption and alcohol problems that Gorbachev's reforms aimed to solve. Second, America and its allies changed their emphasis from managing the Cold War to trying to win it. These allies took several obvious actions like upgrading weapons systems to do so but also subtle ones like trying to inspire a popular uprising in Poland and working with oil-producing countries to drive down the price of crude and weaken the oil-driven Soviet economy, thus limiting that country's ability to upgrade weapons systems or support its favored governments worldwide. Simply, fighting the Cold War became too expensive for the Soviets and too much of a limitation on the possibility for domestic reform that Gorbachev had bet would save the system. The Soviet buffer states in Eastern Europe were not in much better condition, meaning that when Gorbachev gave them a measure of autonomy, he inadvertently initiated a wave of pressure across Eastern Europe for market-oriented democratic reforms, nationalism, and ethnic battles rather than a movement to improve the Soviet system, not an improved version of the Soviet system[1].

While what looked like a wave of reform movements was cheered by the United States and its allies, they were not supported by the most pro-Soviet elements in the USSR and its buffer states, thus making them the focus of an internal struggle that made the situation even more unstable.

After a failed coup attempt in August 1991 and the rise of a new Russian Federation government, the USSR went out of business on Christmas Night, 1991 and the Cold War was over. While this was a good thing, it had a number of unanticipated consequences that the two articles in this section discuss in depth. First, it made the United States the world's only remaining superpower, meaning it was looked at as a kind of global police force. Second, it meant that the United States and its allies lost their central understanding of who they were and what they were advocating for because there was no obvious counterpoint as there had been during the Soviet period. Third, this made it more likely that the United States would become a target for extremists, which culminated in the attacks of September 11, 2001.

As Paul Bew notes in *The Eclipse of the West: Security and Order in a New Age of Isolation and Great-Power Rivalry*, Donald Trump's articulation of "America First" policies is nothing new in our history. For most of the first hundred and twenty years of the country, this was the dominant governing philosophy. As Bew shows, the real changes came with the United States getting involved in two World Wars then, after the second one, articulating internationalist policies that were frequently challenged at home. Especially after the Cold War ended, it became harder to justify the massive amounts of military spending and semipermanent war footing, especially as a slew of American Presidents complained about the unwillingness of NATO allies to fund the organization to the levels that they had promised thus putting the burden on American taxpayers. As Bew notes, by the time Barack Obama was in the White House there was widespread exhaustion with the wars and international battles that had raged since 1941, with a short break between the end of the Cold War and the onset of the War on Terror. Even during that period, Americans found themselves involved in either trying to mediate conflicts through diplomacy or through force that seemed to have no overarching theme and little relationship to the country's strategic interests. What Donald Trump did was articulate a skepticism about an elite consensus that had become more evident in the country and in both parties than it had been in a long while even if it went directly against established dogma in Washington.

It wasn't just Americans who weren't buying the Washington elite consensus Bew argues. The Russian and Chinese Governments had built up their own considerable power. In the Chinese case, the power was a mix of economic and military power, while in the Russian case, it was almost all military power. The United States and its allies might have argued that their soft or diplomatic power would carry the day, but this increasingly didn't seem to be the case. The People's Republic of China had developed economically and was creating military power to match, and the Russian Federation had reconstituted its ability to, at a minimum, cause problems for the Americans and their allies. Even more vexing, the alliance that defeated the Soviets was filled with nation states that had their own interests and their own domestic politics. The British vote to leave the European Union showed that institutions that had been set up to provide stability and unity in the face of a specific threat might themselves fall apart under the weight of differing national or regional interests. The results of America being the essential nation spoke for themselves: a swelling national debt, wide ranging international commitments and a government that seemed to lack basic capacities at home.

There had been other choices at the end of the Cold War, but the United States declined to make those. America, as Christopher Layne notes in *The Big Forces of History: Can the Era of America's Global Dominance Be Sustained?* could have scaled back its military and international commitments. Rather, it continued to pursue a strategy that kept it as the essential nation regardless of the cost to its citizens. Donald Trump's election, he argues, shows that Americans felt their country had declined in some ways and needed revitalization. Interestingly, Trump may have said all this but very little of what he did in office resulted in large-scale change. Trump was more of a symptom of fatigue with and a reflection of the decline of a status quo that had been in place for 70 years. Trump, as Layne argues, rhetorically spoke of change as his immediate predecessor had but substantively the broad outlines of the American approach remained unchanged since the end of World War II despite seismic changes in the world. One can argue that the ferocious response Trump and his proposed changes generated really showed the validity of President Eisenhower's warning about the growing power of the military–industrial complex in shaping the nation's affairs. The elites in both parties and in several institutions resented Trump's audacity in raising questions about the way in which these arrangements were working now and in calling out a series of failures by these institutions and the elites in both parties who populate them.

These two pieces show how policy commitments and institutional cultures can keep policies in place after they've outlived their usefulness to most of the citizens of the country. They show that the world that most Americans have known for their entire lives is not the only world that America has existed in and that the ability of the U.S. Government to control global events is more limited now than it once was. The problem, as the Trump experience shows, is that policy commitments and organizational cultures can take on a life of their own meaning that even though the surrounding world has changed, the institutions and individuals who have shaped the American approach to the world might be slow to recognize this reality and adjust accordingly.

Endnotes

1. For an in-depth discussion of this period see Baker and Glasser, 2020.

The Eclipse of the West

Security and Order in a New Age of Isolation and Great-Power Rivalry

By John Bew

To boldly go, on land and at sea: Statue of Liberty Enlightening the World (1886) by Edward Moran
Museum of the City of New York, USA/Bridgeman Images

John Bew, "The Eclipse of the West: Security and Order in a New Age of Isolation and Great-Power Rivalry," *New Statesman*, vol. 146, no. 5351, pp. 28-33, 35. Copyright © 2017 by New Statesman Ltd. Reprinted with permission. Provided by ProQuest LLC. All rights reserved.

In May 2015 Russia held its Victory Day parade in Red Square, Moscow, to celebrate the 70th anniversary of Nazi Germany's surrender at the end of the Second World War. The ceremony was boycotted by the country's former Western allies in protest at Moscow's interference in eastern Ukraine, though the military procession featured contingents from China and India. Addressing the crowd, President Vladimir Putin complained, "In the past decades, we have seen attempts to create a unipolar world"—by the United States, in cahoots with its allies. By the end of December 2016, with Russia claiming its version of success in the Syrian War and beginning to play kingmaker in Libya, Putin declared in an interview on Russian national television that Western efforts had failed. "We are already living in different times," he said. "The global balance is gradually restoring."

From Moscow to Beijing, there is no shortage of those ready to declare the "end of the American century". Yet what is striking is how much traction this notion has gained in the West. In European capitals, the long-held habit of griping about America's leadership in international affairs has been replaced by a growing concern about a world in which Washington's commitment to internationalism is diminished. In the US, meanwhile, there was a time when creeping pessimism about the nation's ability to shape the world would have seemed sacrilegious. Yet the post-mortems on the "age of unipolarity"—an era in which one power enjoyed a predominance of cultural, economic and military power in the international system—are coming thick and fast. There are trends at work that cannot be explained merely by the election of Donald Trump as president, though he is in part a beneficiary from them.

In *Making the Unipolar Moment*, Hal Brands describes what is happening as the natural passing of a phase in international affairs, brought about by the convergence of several historical forces, not least the implosion of the Soviet Union—America's greatest rival—in 1989. Another interpretation, by Michael Mandelbaum in *Mission Failure: America and the World in the Post-Cold War Era*, is that the diminution of US power is in part the consequence of overstretch and blowback from its misguided zeal to reshape the world in its image. In this version of events, nothing did more damage than the attempt to bring liberal democracy to Iraq in 2003, with all the blood and treasure that was spent in pursuing the cause.

The new vogue for self-examination should not be confused with any abandonment of Washington's aspirations to "primacy". Despite the undeniable creep of world-weariness, it is no easy task to wean the US off its habit of "leading from the front". In Trump's formulation, it is time for America to start "winning again". This does not imply a continuation of the humble retreat that began under Barack Obama. Yet there is no denying that a new narrative has taken hold. The rising power of China, the blunting of US power abroad and the stunting of growth at home have led to a realisation that "pre-eminence" cannot be taken for granted. It is for this reason that America's international commitments—from Nato to the UN—are about to undergo an audit. Those of us who have got used to operating in this orbit must be prepared to move faster on our feet.

Since the First World War, the question of "what America does next" has been more important to the security and health of the West than anything else. The truth, however, is that America has always been uncertain about the costs of the global leadership envisaged by President Woodrow Wilson and encapsulated in his "Fourteen Points", outlined in January 1918. For much of the past century, to borrow Henry Kissinger's formulation, it has been an "ambivalent superpower". On both left and right, there has been incessant grumbling against elites who were thought to be preoccupied with America's standing on the international stage to the detriment of the health of the republic at home.

The voices of the dissenters grew louder after the wars in Vietnam and Iraq, but they have been ever present in the debate. It is a mistake to see Donald Trump's victory as a wild aberration from the American national story; rather, it was the forthright expression of sentiments that have bubbled under the surface for more than a century.

The Obama world-view turned out to be more pessimistic, restrained and introspective than it first appeared

---

Trump's plea to put "America first" has a long lineage, and so does the unvarnished assertion of commercial aggrandisement as the guiding light of foreign policy.

The America First Committee, a vehicle for isolationist sentiments that opposed intervention in the Second World War, was dissolved in December 1941, four days after the Japanese attack on Pearl Harbor. Yet the sentiments that it expressed did not disappear. By the end of the war, as the US worked closely with the UK to create a new international system—fastened down through the Bretton Woods system, the creation of the United Nations and the building of Nato—there were many objections raised to the course of US foreign policy.

One was that Americans were picking up the bill for European security in a way that freed up the funds for a British experiment in socialism under the Labour prime minister Clement Attlee. Another, shared by many senior diplomats in the early stages of the Cold War, was that the British were taking advantage of the growing divide between the Soviet Union and the West to continue to pursue their imperial "great game" with the Russians in the Middle East and the eastern Mediterranean.

It was only after the triumph of foresighted American statecraft under the postwar secretary of state George Marshall that the US learned to take the long view and to come to terms with its superpower status. With leadership of the free world came a growing sense of the mission's gravity. For some, it was a gift bestowed by providence; for others, it was something of a cross to bear. Either way, generations of American elites were trained to assume these global responsibilities.

The people who hold these views have not disappeared in the space of one presidential campaign. Before Donald Trump's election, Washington was dominated by those who believed that America was the "indispensable nation". Among this cohort were many liberal internationalists who were concerned about a growing perception of American retreat under Barack Obama. If Hillary Clinton had won the presidency, they would now be in the ascendancy.

It is worth pausing for a moment to consider this alternate reality. Clinton believed that, under Obama, the United States had been too reticent in asserting itself and too complacent in letting the US-led order decay in the Middle East, eastern Europe and the Asia-Pacific region. "Don't do stupid shit"—Obama's mantra—was, in Clinton's view, an inadequate organising philosophy for a nation of this status and historical calling. That she served only one term as secretary of state gave her a chance to distance herself from aspects of Obama's foreign policy on Syria and Ukraine. Likely Clinton appointees, such as Michèle Flournoy, who was odds-on to be her secretary of defence, also stayed aloof during Obama's second term. This was partly because they were confident that they would be granted the opportunity to do it better.

Those who hung on in the hope that a more activist foreign policy would emerge (such as the then US ambassador to the United Nations, Samantha Power) looked increasingly forlorn. There was something pathetic, in the true sense of the word, about the sight of Power, who rose to prominence as an anti-genocide campaigner, chiding Russia at the UN for its actions in Syria while the nation that she represented opted to stay on the sidelines.

During last year's presidential election campaign, many of Hillary Clinton's critics warned that she was a "liberal hawk" and more likely to engage the US in conflict overseas than Trump. The American left was not galvanised by the prospect of a return to the business of policing international order under Clinton. Bernie Sanders raised the alarm at Secretary Clinton's interest in Henry Kissinger's latest book, *World Order* (published in 2014), and at the way that she called Kissinger her friend.

On the right, the cost of US hegemony also became a live issue during the primaries. The many Republican foreign policy experts who placed a premium on the continuation of US leadership on the world stage were alarmed by the prospect of a

Mr Trumputin
Anthony Garner

Trump presidency. Their concerns manifested themselves in the "Never Trump" letter, which was signed by some of the most influential figures in the Republican national security establishment. In both the Democratic and the Republican Parties, therefore, the champions of a US-led world order have found themselves locked out in ever-growing numbers.

This trend did not start with Trump, even if he has given it the fullest exposition. The Obama world-view—sprinkled with moral philosophy and the theology of Reinhold Niebuhr—appealed to many sophisticated minds in the West. However, it turned out to be much more pessimistic, restrained, introspective and centred on America than it appeared in those heady days in 2009 when he won a Nobel Peace Prize. The anti-Bush he may have been; yet a world healer he was not, nor did he pretend to be one.

At first glance, Obama and Trump could not be more different, but they share at least two core convictions. The first is that the US has been too intoxicated by the old way of thinking about its power: an obsession with maintaining "credibility" and acting as the guarantor of global peace and security. The second is that the US is paying too high a price for the privilege. Thus Obama was willing to break away from the "Washington playbook" when he resisted pressure to take military action against Bashar al-Assad's regime in Syria, after his "red lines" on the use

Sea change: the Japanese attack on Pearl Harbor on 7 December 1941, which brought the United States into the Second World War

US Navy/Interim Archives/Getty Images

of chemical and biological weapons were crossed. Those who despair that Trump respects no playbook must acknowledge that the one in the Oval Office was looking pretty dog-eared.

Of Trump's foreign policy pronouncements to date, what has caused most panic in Western capitals is his suggestion that Nato, in its current form, is "obsolete". Once again, however, we could do more to distinguish between the message and the messenger. America's exasperation at the failure of its Nato allies to pull their weight on defence spending has been growing for years. It was Obama who announced what he called the "anti-free-rider campaign", referring to the European nations that had grown lazy under the protection of the US security umbrella. Symptomatic of this, he hinted, was the poor performance of Britain and France in Libya following an intervention that they had pushed for in 2011.

As for the sanctity of Nato, there have been several senior European statesmen willing to play fast and loose with it long before Trump. Last year the French president, François Hollande, said: "Nato has no role at all to be saying what Europe's relations with Russia should be ... For France, Russia is not an adversary, not a threat. Russia is a partner." In Britain, the leader of Her Majesty's Opposition, Jeremy Corbyn, has stated that British troops stationed in Estonia are a provocation to Moscow and that Nato should have been wound up in 1990 along with the Warsaw Pact.

Since the Cold War, the West has lost its narrative about itself

---

Those who speak of the imminent decline of the West often view it through the lens of the growing power of Asia, or in terms of the US's declining competitiveness against new superpowers such as China and India. Yet the more immediate challenge is its internal fragmentation in the face of these pressures.

For Brexit Britain, access to new markets and centres of innovation in Asia is highly prized. Part of the rationale behind Brexit is that the EU lacks the requisite dynamism to wrap up quick deals. Even outside the EU, however, it is not so easy to escape entangling commitments. Under David Cameron, Britain was prepared to risk the wrath of the US in signing up to the China-led Asian Infrastructure Investment Bank. Given the importance of agreeing to a trade deal with the US, Theresa May's government will now have to think twice before attempting such a trick.

Such realpolitik calculations give our foreign policy a 19th-century feel. On the one hand, this may be a natural turning of the historical wheel. On the other hand, since the end of the Cold War, the West has lost a narrative about itself and a vision of how the world is supposed to work. This, in part, is an intellectual problem. The post-1945 international system was built on certain assumptions that reflected the views of the Allies who triumphed in the Second World

War. Chief among these was a version of historical development that held that economic and social progress would create the foundations for peace.

Many of these assumptions have been challenged in Western states by populations which reject the world-view that they imply. And they are fraying under the pressure of what the writer Pankaj Mishra, borrowing from Friedrich Nietzsche, calls the politics of *ressentiment*. Until a successor vision emerges for the management of global affairs, one that has a broad domestic consensus behind it, it will be our fate to deal with the moving parts—the changing alliances, porous borders and emerging threats—as they collide and splinter.

Much has been said about the internal crises draining the legitimacy of the Western elites, the ripping up of consensus and the quasi-revolutionary mood that is sweeping across nations. And yet, to an extent that has not been fully grasped, the crisis of the West has been tied to repeated failures in foreign policy.

Since the start of this century, the limits of Western power have been illustrated time and again—nowhere more so than in the Middle East. Compounding this, there has been a loss of appetite for lengthy and complicated foreign entanglements—in diplomacy as much as in war—and of the patience needed to see them through.

The Western way of war has become discredited in Afghanistan, Iraq and Libya. The fashion for counterinsurgency that characterised the past two decades partly grew out of a desire to evolve towards a more sophisticated, humane and more politically palatable use of force. *In extremis*, there was talk of campaigns being won—such as when British troops were sent to Helmand Province, Afghanistan, in 2006 to wrest control from the Taliban—without a shot being fired. Even in the rare cases of success, such as the US-led "surge" in Iraq, the political and financial costs of such lengthy campaigns are unsustainable. Not before time, rusty old concepts such as "deterrence" are being given a hearing again.

Over the past decades, we have lost the custom of thinking strategically

---

Blessed with decades of relative security, we have lost the custom of thinking strategically. Having enjoyed a preponderance of force and wealth, we have failed to grasp the changing nature of power in international affairs. Since 1989, from a position of strength, the West has evangelised about its capacity for "soft power", even attempting to quantify it as some sort of saleable commodity. Russia—a country with scandalously low life expectancy, haemorrhaging population levels and a sclerotic economy—has made a mockery of this. Moscow has not only deployed conventional "hard" power in Syria and Ukraine, but crafted its own version of "soft", or cultural, influence using instruments such as the media groups Sputnik and RT (formerly Russia Today).

Underpinning all of this is a loss of confidence in the merits of "Western civilisation" that would have seemed odd to our forebears in 1945. It is too easily forgotten that the vision of liberal internationalism was Western in inception, and it was based on a belief in the legitimacy and superiority of the Western way of government. Although imperfections were admitted, the organising philosophy was to apply these goods—such as the rule of law and the principle of self-determination—on an international scale.

By the same token, the linkage of our domestic political contracts to the ways in which our nations behave in their relationships with others is deeper than is sometimes understood. The foundation stone of the post-1945 world order was the Atlantic Charter of 1941–42. As Elizabeth Borgwardt explains in her wonderful book, *A New Deal for the World*, it can be understood as a globalised version of Franklin D Roosevelt's domestic New Deal politics and the broader conception of liberty contained therein.

It was in the same spirit that William Beveridge began his white paper of 1942 with the statement that a "revolutionary moment in the world's history is a time for revolutions, not for patching". In a series of newspaper articles, Beveridge interspersed his advocacy for its implementation on the home front with articles in support of what later became the UN. For the generation that fought the war, the two causes—domestic political renewal and the construction of a parliament of nations—were indivisible.

As last year's presidential election got under way, the Princeton foreign policy expert G John Ikenberry argued that Roosevelt had bequeathed the US a "centrist tradition of American world leadership", marked by a "strong bipartisan internationalist tradition". A radical conservative critique, he warned, was challenging "the progressive foundations of *Pax Americana*" by disparaging the New Deal foundations on which American internationalism was based.

There are those who would have us neatly separate the domestic and foreign into separate spheres. Yet there is a reason why a desiccated version of foreign policy realism or naked rationalism—the type of cultish obsession with the "national interest" that often emerges on the right in times of international flux—has never been pre-eminent among the West's leading states. For the past century at least, the practice of Western foreign policy has been tied to an organising philosophy, a larger vision of how the world should work, bolstered by myth.

This required both theologising and evangelicalism in the name of universal goals. An element of "sacred drama", as Conor Cruise O'Brien explained in his 1968 book on the United Nations, served a higher purpose. The risk has always been that sacred dramas are pushed too far—that the champions of international peace built their castles in the air, placing their faith in vapid utopianism that evaporates at the first sign of stress. And even though the post-1945 world order has lasted for more than 70 years, many of the myths around it have run their course.

The "rules" we often talk about are conceptual and moral as much as they are legally binding. In truth, the fate of Syria shows that, when it comes to maintaining certain international standards, it is the combination of political will and power that matters. Too often, the lawyerly emphasis on rules has ignored that they are unenforceable without order. It is a lesson that many liberal internationalists have found hard to stomach, to the detriment of their project.

Head of state: the bust of Churchill that George W Bush kept in the Oval Office and Obama removed

Tim Sloan/Afp/Getty Images

As with the Russian Revolution of 1917 or the fall of the Berlin Wall in 1989, watershed moments in international history can creep up on us without much warning. Since the Brexit vote and the election of Donald Trump, it has become fashionable to invest 2016 with a sense of great historical significance—as a year that future historians will look back on with sorrow and furrowed brows. This is before time.

A true historical sensibility should warn us against such fatalism. The Western world faces many challenges—none more pressing than its declining share of global wealth and population compared to Asia's leading states. Yet looking to the future with trepidation should not take the form of giving in to despair. To do so is to court a self-fulfilling prophecy.

Some of the most tumultuous years in history have been spurs to acts of great forward thinking and imagination. It was in 1933—which began with Adolf Hitler becoming the chancellor of Germany—that H G Wells published *The Shape of Things to Come*. Part novel and part "history" of the future, it tells an alternative story of humanity up to the year 2106. The world that the book depicts is one in which Franklin D Roosevelt fails to implement the New Deal and an economic crisis lasts for 30 years, punctuated by a second world war. (Wells predicts that it would begin in January 1940, sparked by a clash between Germany and Poland over Danzig.) There is no victor; the leading powers emerge exhausted, unable to prevent a plague that emerges in 1956—spread by a group of baboons that escape from London Zoo—and wipes out much of the world population.

Here Wells envisages a benevolent "dictatorship of the air", which takes shape at an international conference convened in Basra in 1965. The dictatorship goes on to attempt to eradicate the world's leading religions, but eventually melts away a century later, making way for a peaceful humanitarian utopia in which the struggle for material existence has ended, and a society that could therefore be governed by reason. The last recorded event in the book takes place on New Year's Day 2106, when there is a levelling of the remaining skeletons of the skyscrapers of New York.

As idiosyncratic as this may have been, it was the work of visionaries such as Wells that spurred the statesmen of the West to take hold of historical developments and to try to build a version of this world state. As much as anything, it was about ensuring the survival and adaptation of a beleaguered and near-bankrupt Western civilisation.

The first paragraph of *The Shape of Things to Come* describes a world experiencing a "confluence of racial, social and political destinies". With that, "a vision of previously unsuspected possibilities opens to the human imagination", which entails "an immense readjustment of ideas". Civilisation, as Wells puts it in words we could heed today, is "in a race between education and catastrophe".

Where today are the leaders or intellectuals in the West capable of offering a vision of the shape of things to come, around which their allies or populations might rally? In the short term, we have seen few front-line politicians since Tony Blair who have provided us with a view of the world around them (however disputed their vision might have been) and the nation's place within it. The great foreign policy speech seems to be a relic of the recent past.

If there is anyone looking to Donald Trump's White House for a vision of a "new world order", they will be disappointed. In his inauguration speech, there was no softening of his line and he wasted no time in reiterating that his priority was to put "America first". In the past 70 years, there have been few such unambiguous exhortations of this creed.

In the absence of an international vision, however, the burning question is whether Trump's foreign policy will follow a method; or, failing that, a pattern. An optimistic view of this has been ventured by the historian Niall Ferguson, who has suggested that Henry Kissinger, who is 93, has provided a script for the global rebalancing that may begin under Trump. The US president has sought Kissinger's counsel since his election, as did Hillary Clinton in the run-up to the vote.

There are rumours that Kissinger may be used in an attempt to reset relations for Russia. It was notable, too, that he was being feted in Beijing just as Trump was tweeting against China for its behaviour in relation to Taiwan and the South China Sea.

Will Trump's foreign policy follow Kissingerian grooves, in the form of some sort of triangulation of great-power diplomacy between Moscow and Beijing? Is there a strategic rationale behind the bombast, or could one emerge?

This is a possibility but nothing more. The first few days of the new presidency do not suggest that Trump the campaigner is about to give way to a statesman with foresight. Nonetheless, it is likely that US foreign policy will settle into a recognisable rhythm over the course of the year.

President Trump's propensity for slaying sacred cows is not shared by his nominees for secretary of state (Rex Tillerson, a former chief executive of the ExxonMobil oil company) or secretary of defence (General James Mattis). Both have stressed the importance of America's alliance network and their belief in the importance of Nato. The same applies to Nikki Haley, the governor of South Carolina and former Trump critic, who has been chosen as ambassador to the United Nations. The US state department and the Pentagon have grown used to acting in certain ways that suggest that a revolution on American foreign policy will not occur overnight.

The most important variable in second-guessing Trump's foreign policy is the extent to which he will seek to control it from the White House, continuing a trend of recent years, or leave his appointees to their work. If the Oval Office becomes the locus of action, the role of General Mike Flynn, Trump's controversial national security adviser, is likely to be of growing importance.

The key variable in second-guessing Trump's foreign policy is how much he will control it from the White House

---

For the past hundred years—but particularly since 1945—Britain has carved out a privileged place for itself by operating in the slipstream of US foreign policy. In that time, the UK's greatest strategic nightmare has been the prospect of an American retreat from its global responsibilities. There have been periods, as during the interwar years, in which the US preferred to mind its own business rather than engage in the business of world government. It is no coincidence that these were some of the most perilous years in British history.

Despite the hand-wringing that greeted Donald Trump's victory, these habits are deeply ingrained in our diplomatic and national security establishments and cannot easily be changed. Those arguing that it is time to break from the US and seize the opportunity for a new relationship with Europe, in which Britain plays the role of security provider, are both regurgitating an old argument and presenting a false dichotomy. Likewise, the idea that the leadership of the free world has passed to Angela Merkel's Germany is absurd.

The saga of the bust of Winston Churchill in the Oval Office—beloved by George W Bush, removed by Obama and brought back by Trump—has become a rather tired metaphor for the state of Anglo-American relations. In truth, the British delegation in Washington has engaged in catch-up since Trump's surprise victory but there are signs that the nettle has been grasped. As 2016 drew to a close, the British ambassador to the US, Kim Darroch, held his nose to deliver a speech at a US conservative think tank, the Heritage Foundation.

Grizelda.net

Speaking the language of "burden-sharing", he announced that one of the UK's two new super-carriers, *HMS Queen Elizabeth*, is scheduled to sail through the South China Sea on her maiden deployment in 2020, a restatement of the shared Anglo-American commitment to free navigation of the seas.

The Prime Minister has already managed to bump herself up the queue and is the first foreign leader to make the pilgrimage to the Trump White House. According to the *Sunday Times*, Bernie Sanders has expressed the hope that the UK might perform the function of a "moral conscience" in relation to the Trump administration's foreign policy. There will be developments in US foreign policy that will be hard to stomach, on matters from the Iran nuclear deal to climate change. Equally, the stakes are now so high—on trade and security—that Britain will have to pick carefully those issues on which it dissents.

In this new world, the choice facing Britain might seem stark. On further reflection, however, it is no choice at all. A rebalancing of the international system is about to begin, involving the world's major powers. The cosy "universalist" language to which we have grown used (and of which we are the foremost purveyors) may belong to another era. Britain can gripe from the sidelines and negotiate ourselves into irrelevance as the curator of the old order, or do its utmost to be present at the creation of the new.

A sprinkling of H G Wells might enliven our sense that there is a future to be grasped and an opportunity to contribute to a larger vision of how the world should work. Yet there has to come a time when we draw a line under the *fin de siècle* angst and get on with it.

The Big Forces of History

Can the Era of America's Global Dominance be Sustained?

By Christopher Layne

D onald Trump's presidential victory in November, a product of surging anti-establishment populism, has unnerved the U.S. foreign-policy establishment and its liberal-internationalist cousins abroad. They fear that under Trump's leadership the United States will disengage from the global leadership role it has played since 1945. And then, they solemnly warn, the prevailing post-World War II international order—*Pax Americana,* based on America's preeminent position upon the globe—will unravel.

On the other hand, Trump's triumph raised hopes among foreign-policy realists that he might engineer a major overhaul of U.S grand strategy, shifting the United States from its decades-long aim of pursuing global hegemony to a less interventionist strategy of geopolitical restraint and "offshore balancing" (relying on other states to maintain regional balances of power).

Both camps are wrong. As the new administration took shape and key foreign-policy players emerged, it seemed clear that neither the establishment's fears nor the realists' hopes will be realized during the Trump administration. Foreign-policy continuity, not a new direction, is the most likely approach of the new government, at least for the short term. Character issues or domestic politics may render some of Trump's choices for top national-security posts controversial. But in foreign-policy terms they are products of the establishment just as much as their post-1945 predecessors were—hawkish, internationalist, interventionist.

Still, it would be wrong to conclude that Trump has had no impact on the nation's foreign-policy debate. During the campaign, he promised to "Make America Great Again." Whether intended or not, the implication was that America had declined in important aspects: economically, culturally, and geopolitically. This is what realists have been arguing for years. The big forces of history, in this view, are reordering international politics, and American grand strategy must adjust accordingly. The question of grand-strategic adjustment is fundamental and hence will be the subject of ever more intensive debate in coming years.

This debate likely will be reminiscent of those various "great debates" about the U.S. world role that have erupted from time to time since America emerged as a great power at the beginning of the 20th century. These included the debates over whether to: annex the Philippines after the Spanish-American War; intervene in World War I (and, later, whether it had been a good idea); counter the rise of Germany and Japan as war engulfed Europe and threatened Asian stability; abandon the traditional U.S. policy of abjuring alliances in favor of constructing NATO; and fight in Vietnam and, if so, how to go about it. The nature of America's role in the Middle East has been the focus of another such great debate. Today we are poised on the edge of another great debate over such questions as: can the United States sustain its post-World War II strategy of global primacy? And, if not, what should be America's next grand strategy?

That this is a momentous time is reflected in the fact that the country's current grand strategy has guided its foreign relations for more than 70 years. Even as World War II gripped the globe, U.S. policy planners already were formulating U.S. postwar policy objectives. Washington's overriding goal was to ensure that the United States enjoyed a preponderance of power in the postwar world; that is, the U.S. sought an *imbalance* of power in its favor. American policymakers intended to use U.S. dominance to construct a stable international order—that so-called *Pax Americana*—that would ensure peace and prosperity. The prevailing distribution of military and economic power in the international system was propitious. Indeed, 1945 was America's *first* unipolar moment. The United States alone accounted for half of the world's manufacturing output, possessed two-thirds of the world's gold and foreign-exchange reserves, enjoyed a capacity to project more power more widely than any other nation; and, of course, held a crucial monopoly on atomic weapons. The United States leveraged these instruments of overwhelming power to build the military, economic, and institutional architecture of *Pax Americana*.

At the dawn of this new era, only the Soviet Union stood between the United States and uncontested global dominance. Then the Soviet collapse in 1989–91 removed that obstacle and unleashed a tsunami of American triumphalism, which was epitomized by Francis Fukuyama's "end of history" thesis and Thomas Friedman's celebration of peaceful "globalization" underwritten by America's "benign hegemony." Most American strategic thinkers believed the Cold War's end heralded a new era of international politics in which no geopolitical or ideological foe to the United States' global preeminence could emerge. Simply put, most U.S. policymakers and foreign-policy scholars believed the Cold War's end had ushered in the start of a long era of peace based on the spread of democracy, globalization, and international institutions—backstopped, of course, by the United States' hard military and economic power.

When America's superpower rival imploded, the country could have chosen to scale back the expansive (and expensive) security and leadership burdens it had borne during the Cold War. As political scientist Jeanne Kirkpatrick put it, the United States could have again become a "normal country in a normal time." But this did not happen. Rather than triggering a re-examination of the strategy of primacy, the Cold War's end served to reaffirm it. Instead of a grand-strategic downsizing, America's overseas commitments expanded both geopolitically (NATO expansion, the Middle East, and the Persian Gulf) and ideologically (the Clinton administration's strategy of "engagement and enlargement," and the George W. Bush administration's aim of transforming the Middle East and ending tyranny in our time).

Insisting on the imperative of "American leadership" (meaning, of course, primacy), the American foreign-policy establishment asserted that both the nation's prosperity and international peace required active engagement abroad to spread America's "universal" liberal values of democracy, human rights, and economic openness. (Has anyone in the foreign-policy establishment ever wondered why it is that, if our values are universal, the U.S. has to fight so many wars to get other people to accept them?) Seeing America as the world's "indispensable nation," U.S. policymakers believed the U.S. was obligated continually to flex its military muscles to preserve the liberal international order.

Events have demonstrated that the hopes fostered by post-Cold War triumphalism were illusory. America's second unipolar moment has been replaced by China's emergence as a peer competitor, the revival of Russian military power, and the European Union's multiple crises (Greece, Brexit, economic stagnation, uncontrolled immigration from the Middle East and North Africa). Further, the United States has been unable to extricate itself from the quagmires of Iraq and Afghanistan. Libya dramatized the limits of liberal interventionism. Syria has demonstrated the hollowness of U.S. pretensions to reshape the Middle East. It is apparent today that there are very real limits to U.S. power. Yet in official Washington, and the broader foreign-policy establishment, faith in primacy remains unshaken, impervious to the erosion eating away at the foundation upon which America's grand strategy of primacy was erected.

Has anyone in the foreign-policy establishment ever wondered why, if our values are universal, the U.S. has to fight so many wars to get others to accept them?

And then along came Donald Trump, probably the most unlikely presidential candidate in the country's history. Without demonstrating any discernible depth of understanding of foreign policy, he pressed forward forcefully in breaking with the internationalist, interventionist worldview that had been advocated by the American foreign-policy establishment since 1945. Trump contrasted himself with his rival, Hillary Clinton, who supported the use of American military power in Iraq, Libya, and Syria. Harking back to the period between the Fall of France and the Japanese attack on Pearl Harbor, from June 1940 to December 1941, he vowed to follow an "America First" foreign policy by defining U.S. security interests narrowly, and keeping the United States out of overseas conflicts that did not directly affect American security.

Trump broadly outlined what his America First foreign policy would look like. First, he said he would improve U.S. relations with Russia. Second, he vowed to review the relevance of NATO, even casting doubt over whether the U.S. should honor its treaty commitment to defend the Baltic States in the event they are attacked by Russia. Trump threatened to force South Korea and Japan to pay more for their own defense. He even linked the "burden sharing" issue with the question of whether South Korea and Japan should be allowed to continue sheltering beneath the U.S. "nuclear umbrella." Trump stated during the campaign that they should not and instead should acquire their own nuclear arsenals for protection against North Korea. With the exception of trade policy—notably his plan to slap a 45 percent tariff on Chinese imports—Trump had little to say about the great power dimension of the Sino-American relationship.

On the Middle East, Trump made two points during the campaign. First, ignoring the fact that President Obama was largely successful in keeping the United States from being sucked into the Syrian quagmire, he attacked the Obama administration for failing to eradicate the Islamic State (ISIS). He said he would solve the problem, quickly, by "bombing the hell out of ISIS," which the Obama administration already had been doing for two years. (Trump also suggested that cooperation between the United States and Russia could accelerate the Islamic State's defeat.) Second, he denounced the Iran nuclear accord, promising to work to dismantle it and adopt a more pugnacious stance toward Tehran.

Taken together, Trump's campaign statements about foreign policy did not add up to a new vision of American grand strategy. At best, they were impressionistic, a series of hints at what a Trump administration might do rather than a road map. Moreover, some of Trump's foreign-policy views were contradictory. How, for example, could he lead America out of the Middle East quagmire while demonstrating unrestrained bellicosity toward Iran?

But whatever Trump's jumbled foreign-policy pronouncements will add up to in policy terms, they did not signal a "neo-isolationist" foreign policy, as many of his critics have alleged. It's always wise to be skeptical when the "I" word is injected into debates about U.S. grand strategy; usually it signals a desire to stifle debate. In fact, America has always been deeply connected with the world economically and culturally, even when it chose to remain aloof from great power conflicts abroad.

So what really is meant when the term "isolationism" is invoked with respect to a specific set of grand-strategic proposals? University of Pennsylvania diplomatic historian Walter A.

McDougall expressed it well in his book, *Promised Land, Crusader State.* Isolationism is a term of opprobrium—"a dirty word that interventionists, especially since Pearl Harbor, hurl at anyone who questions their policies." It's still true today, when America Firsters of 1940–41 are lumped with Charles A. Lindbergh as either overt Nazi sympathizers or as fellow travelers. Susan Dunn's 2014 book, *1940: FDR, Willkie, Lindbergh, and Hitler—The Election Amid the Storm,* is an especially egregious example. In fact, most of those who believed in non-intervention in the European war in 1940–41 had sound strategic and national-interest reasons for doing so. Britain and the Soviet Union (with the help of U.S. economic support and war materiel) were tying down Nazi Germany. At the same time, geography and rapidly increasing American naval and air power effectively insulated North America from German attack. Of course, the received wisdom is that the United States was drawn into World War II because its "isolationist" policy failed. This is false. In fact, the U.S. became involved in the war because it was not isolationist enough. Far from taking a hands-off stance in 1940–41, the United States actively opposed Japan's ambitions to become the hegemon of its own region, East Asia. American policymakers knew full well that U.S. policies toward Japan—including a crippling oil embargo— could culminate in war between the United States and Japan. Washington nevertheless deliberately ran that risk. The result was Pearl Harbor. Thus can we see that sometimes, despite the pejorative name-calling, non-interventionism (restraint, offshore balancing, even neo-isolationism, if one wants to call it that) can be a good grand strategy that keeps the United States from spilling its blood and treasure in otherwise avoidable wars of choice.

Image 1.2.1

Will this be Trump's outlook and strategy? Apparently perceiving that America's "unipolar moment" is a thing of the past, he offered a tantalizing hint that America's "neo-isolationist moment" might be just around the corner. Specifically, his campaign comments at the least suggested that a Trump administration would recalibrate America's alliances in Europe and East Asia, pursue rapprochement with Moscow, and curtail U.S. involvement in the Middle East.

But this shouldn't be overblown. True, Trump's advisers want America's European and East Asian partners to pick up more of the slack with respect to defense. But this is a purely transactional concern—over who pays how much for defense. America's foreign-policy establishment has been wrestling with burden-sharing issues for decades, dating back almost to NATO's beginning. And Trump's foreign-policy team doesn't include people who seem inclined to fundamentally rethink America's alliance commitments. Nor is there any indication that Trump's senior appointees share his desire to heal Washington's relations with the Kremlin. On the contrary, they view Russia through a Cold War lens. Nor is there any reason to believe that any of his senior appointees will pick up on Trump's suggestion that South Korea and Japan should provide their own nuclear deterrence instead of relying on the American nuclear shield.

Far from disengaging from the Mideast quicksand, many key members of the Trump national-security team seem bent on plunging the United States even more deeply into the region. Indeed some, such as National Security Adviser-designate Michael Flynn, are champing at the bit to trigger a civilizational war between the United States and the Islamic world. By the same token, there is no sign that any senior Trump appointee dissents from the idea of American exceptionalism, or questions whether the United States is the world's "indispensable nation." In other words, the senior foreign- and defense-policy figures in the Trump administration are very much in the mold of the foreign-policy establishment types who have staffed every administration since FDR's.

There is a big reason why America's grand strategy under Trump probably will not break in any significant way with the establishment's post-1945 foreign-policy consensus. Even if Trump wanted to redirect U.S. grand strategy along the lines of offshore balancing and restraint, it would be nearly impossible for him to do so. Policy is decided by personnel, and there just aren't enough qualified non-interventionist realists to fill the key positions at the assistant secretary, deputy assistant secretary, and NSC staff levels of an administration.

For the non-interventionist realists to actually change America's grand strategic course, they must undertake the "long march through the institutions." This means developing a cadre of future foreign-policy officials who can think innovatively about U.S. grand strategy and challenge the foreign-policy establishment's foundational assumptions about America's world role. The Charles Koch Foundation is trying to help build a new generation of grand strategic innovators by supporting the creation of excellence in grand strategy at top U.S. universities. But it will take time before a "counter-establishment" of offshore balancers and restrainers can emerge to staff and help guide an administration committed to adopting a realist, non-interventionist grand strategy.

Meanwhile, big forces of history are re-ordering international politics, and American grand strategy eventually will have to adjust accordingly. The great debate is coming, forced into the consciousness of America's foreign-policy elites by big events and developments around the globe.

Trump's electoral victory elicited great anguish among the liberal foreign-policy elites, both here and abroad. Leading voices—Robert Kagan, Gideon Rachman, Philip Stephens—have voiced fears that Trump's presumed "neo-isolationism" will cause the crackup of the "rules-based international order." Indeed, *Pax Americana* is in trouble, but not because of Donald Trump. American primacy is in question because the foundations of the international order that the U.S. constructed after World War II are weakening. In macro-historical terms, the geopolitical and economic centers of gravity in the international system are shifting from the Euro-Atlantic world to Asia. New challengers to American power are rising (or, in fact, have risen), and old rivals are resurgent. These factors, not Trump, are generating doubt about the staying power of the post-1945 liberal-international order.

The United States and the international system are approaching an inflection point. The unavoidable question now is whether America can afford a grand strategy of primacy, and also whether public support for that strategy can be sustained. Indeed, there are increasing signs that Americans are suffering from hegemony fatigue. As the *Financial Times* reported, a recent poll by Survey Sampling International, the Center for the National Interest, and the Charles Koch Institute found widespread public opposition to U.S. military intervention abroad. Uncertainty about primacy bubbled to the surface during the 2016 presidential campaign, and also is receiving increased attention from the community of scholars in the field of security studies.

It isn't clear just how the Trump administration will respond to these tectonic economic and geopolitical shifts that are weakening primacy's foundations. First impressions based on Trump's team-building are not encouraging. But administrations—and presidents—change and evolve. And there are good reasons for the United States to rethink its alliance relationships that are more fundamental than mere burden sharing. Far from providing stability, U.S. alliances in Europe and East Asia are potential causes of instability—and even war (potentially nuclear). U.S. grand strategy needs to aim at burden *shifting,* not burden sharing—and, even more important, risk shifting. Those nations with the highest security stake should bear the greatest strategic risk, not the U.S. Instead of worrying about a trade war with China, Washington should be fearing a real war. The power dynamics in East Asia resemble all too closely those that culminated in the catastrophe of 1914. How will the United States accommodate the reality of China's rise? If Trump's decision to speak to Taiwanese President Tsai Ing-wen by phone is any indication, Trump could usher in a tumultuous era in Sino-American relations that dramatically heightens the risk of conflict. Rather than thinking of international politics as a morality play, the U.S. should relearn some of the fundamentals of great power politics, such as spheres of influence and the importance of power balance. If the United States wants to repair its relationship with Russia—and it should—Washington not only needs to re-examine its lingering Cold War narratives but also to recognize that, like all great powers, Russia long has had security interests in the regions that are geographically proximate to it. Finally, the U.S. needs to extricate itself from its disastrous involvements in the Middle East. That region is afflicted with its own serious maladies, and it is far beyond America's capacity to fix them.

Perhaps President Trump eventually will follow his "neo-isolationist" instincts (if, indeed, he has them) and become a grand-strategic change agent. As leading realist scholars of American foreign policy—George Kennan, Hans Morgenthau, Robert Osgood, Robert W. Tucker, and Kenneth Waltz—understood, the U.S. is safer when it follows a prudent, restrained grand strategy rather than an interventionist one. One can hope that eventually the Trump administration comes to understand this. In a world where the foundations of *Pax Americana* are crumbling, U.S. leaders must chart the path forward in a world that no longer is dominated by unrestrained American power.

Unit I: Post-Reading Questions

Directions: Refer to what you learned in this unit to respond to the questions and prompts below.

1. Layne uses the term "America's unipolar moment" and argues that Trump's election indicates a dawning recognition that it is coming to an end.

   a. What does this term mean and what does Bew think should be done in response to this environmental change?

2. Layne uses the term "Pax Americana."

   a. What does this term mean and how has the goal of creating such a thing been put into actions that the United States has taken since World War II?

3. According to Layne, what caused the end of the American unipolar moment and what could an effective response to its passage be?

4. John Bew argues that Donald Trump and Barack Obama had two commonalities in terms of their approach to the rest of the world.

   a. What are they and what is their significance in terms of understanding how the United States approaches the rest of the world in the current era?

UNIT II

American Institutions

Unit II: Introduction

T he United States and its position in the world have changed a great deal since the country's
founding. The country now stretches from coast to coast, has a highly developed and diverse
economy and a large, equally diverse population to match it. The United States today is not the
same country as the one in which the Framers wrote the constitution under which we are still
governed.

The people, country, and economy might have changed a lot, but in some ways the system
very much has not changed. It has evolved in some important ways to meet the needs of a
modern diverse nation, but these changes too have been the source of friction, much of which
was on display during the Trump Administration. John Haskell, Sara Grove, and Marian Currinder
in *Congress and the President: The Struggle over Directing Public Policy* note that the conflict that
took place during the Trump years was more of the climax of a long running battle over ideas
of which branch should govern, what the bureaucracy should do, and how the President should
do their job rather than a battle that was unique to it. The Framers themselves were not in
agreement about what they thought their new government should be structured like or what
it should do, and our current system very much reflects that. People often end up frustrated
by the government's action or lack of it because it set up more as a compromise itself than as
a coherent plan.

Our system was designed by socioeconomic elite who were familiar with the latest ideas
about what rights the people had and tried to build a system that reflected their understanding
of these new notions. As Glen Krutz and Sylvie Waskiewicz show us in *The Constitution and Its
Origins*, the Declaration of Independence and the constitution developed out of a philosophy
now known as liberalism. While the Democratic Party has been called liberal since the era of
Franklin Roosevelt and the New Deal, both parties embody the liberal values held by this founding
elite who are often called the Framers. The Framers framed our system, hence their name. They
were informed by their lived experience under a British Monarchy that they saw as repressive
and unrepresentative of their interest and values.

The Framers believed in what we would call human rights, but they called natural rights.
They set up a system designed to safeguard the people's natural rights. These rights were called
natural rights because the Framers thought that they were a naturally occurring phenomenon like
gravity or the weather, meaning that they wanted the government to be limited in what actions
it could take and keep it responsible to the public. Our system still has a strong emphasis on

individual rights and the government is very much responsible to the people, even if this does not always seem to be the case.

When Americans talk about their rights or raise questions about the government's powers, they are very much speaking the Framers' language. The United States Constitution itself is a tribute to the liberal philosophy in which the Framers believed. To cement the position of a rights-based liberalism in this country they added a list of ten major rights that people have at the end of the document. These 10 rights were added as amendments to the constitution and together make up what we know as the Bill of Rights.

As Cal Jillson remarks in *Federalism and American Political Development*, the Framers had lived under the first system of government that the United States tried after the Revolution, the Articles of Confederation. They thought the Articles too weak to supply security and develop a single strong, continent-wide country. They felt that the Articles created a system that prompted too much interstate rivalry and interstate relations that were too complicated, a hindrance to growth, and increased the chances that the British and other European colonial powers would return. The Framers were interested in a system that protected the rights of the individual and statistical minorities in the population because they were wealthy and well educated. They were afraid that, left to their own devices, states would not protect people like them or their interests. Future events in France in the 19th century and Russia in the 20th century showed that their concern was well founded. These class-based revolutions set to conditions under which people like the American Framers suffered and died.

The Framers' great failing was on the issue of slavery. Because they could not agree on a unified position on the topic, they compromised by counting slaves as 3/5ths of a person when it came to allocating seats in the House of Representatives but did not really deal with the issue in any other way. This compromise initiated a pattern that lasted up until the Civil War in which the question of slavery was either not dealt with at all or compromises were reached that allowed it to endure. The pattern reasserted itself after the end of the Civil War era. Reconstruction was undertaken in a way that allowed segregation and other forms of oppressive behavior against a racial minority to endure until at least the 1960s and some would say until our own time. This failing shows that the Framers were people of their time as much as they were the visionaries that they are sometimes made out to be.

The Framers sought to balance individual rights and government authority, as well as the powers of the state and national governments. While the Framers thought that the states had too much power under the Articles system, they thought states were an important safeguard of the citizens' rights. State governments are physically much closer to the people whom they represent than the national government, and they represent many fewer people than does the national government. In a state like New Hampshire, that has about 1.35 million citizens (about the population of Maine), there are 424 state legislators, a governor who serves a two-year term and a five-member executive board to represent the citizens. In a bigger state, like Massachusetts, that has about 7 million residents (about twice the population of Oklahoma), there are 240 legislators, a governor who serves a four-year term and an eight-member executive board. In most states, the ratio of citizens to representatives is much lower than the 535 legislators and one President for 330 million people that exists at the national level. In addition, states can deal with the specific problems facing them or raise these problems with their elected national representatives.

The Framers, most especially James Madison, thought that as Americans expanded westward, different interests would develop in different areas (1961). This diversity of region and interest could help preserve the Republic and the rights of the citizens. This situation has happened in the modern country just as regionalism or sectionalism had in the early Republic. The states become interested in issues that impact their populations directly. For example, there is no need for the state government of South Dakota to concern itself with the regulation of marine fisheries any more than there is for the state government of New Hampshire to concern itself with range land management policy. Instead, New Hampshire pays a lot of attention and asks for the help from the national government on the former, while South Dakota does so on the latter.

States also act as test beds for innovative ideas and, by trying them, let the rest of the country can see what would happen if something similar were done nationwide. Recent examples of policies that have become widespread after showing a promise at the state level include marijuana and sports gambling legalization. Given that the states have started these changes, different states have different policies, meaning that we can get a good sense for how even minor changes in a policy might affect its overall workings.

The above-noted case of race was but one area on which the Framers did not agree, meaning that they set up lots of ambiguities in the constitution. We can see the constitution as a negotiated settlement between the representatives of the states and between differing visions of who should rule: the Congress or the Executive Branch. The entire system can be understood as a negotiated deal that balances state, national, and ideological interests. As representatives of the states, the Framers created the national government and they set up ambiguities in the constitution because there were some things they did not agree on, to promote balance between the states and the national government, between the branches of national government, and between the power of the government and the rights of the citizens.

The Framers created a system that gave the national and state governments some of the same and some different powers. They thought that there were specific things each could do well but other things in which having them vie for dominance would serve the system and the citizens well and prevent tyranny. It is a federal system because power is likewise shared between the national and the state levels of government. Even the ways in which power is split between the states and the national government are continually subject to change caused by competitive pressure between the two levels. Examples of the way in which the relationship has changed include the New Deal that put the national government in charge of many things and the Reagan era devolutionary reforms that shipped many of these responsibilities back to the states.

The Framers believed in a national government capable of balancing different regional, cultural, and economic interests. They also wanted one strong enough to support the country's future development, its defense, and secure its place in the world. The Framers believed in balancing interests between the branches of the national government to ensure that the same kind of thing that they rebelled against the British over or that had happened in a couple of states did not develop in the country. They did not want dictators or self-interested parties running the show and set up a system aimed at preventing both from getting in charge while limiting what they could accomplish if they got power. Thus, they created a three-part national government that featured a President, a legislature, and a Supreme Court.

Two of the biggest tensions facing our country currently are that between the Presidency and the Congress but also between the people in elected positions who are supposed to pass laws versus unelected federal agencies that make public policy via rule. A second way this elected versus unelected tension plays out is in the role that courts play in shaping what our system does. The Framers believed that the constitution was subject to interpretation by the people living under it at any given time but because they were products of the English common law system believed that the constitution could be used to establish broad governing principles and its meaning could be interpreted by subsequent generations through an amending process.

Some Framers believed that the Constitution would be subject to interpretation by future generations and the judicial branch. Chief Justice John Marshall cemented this position into American law with the decision in case of Marbury vs. Madison. The Constitution is amendable, but it is not easy to do that. The Constitution has only been amended 27 times. Thus, the courts are the more frequent vehicle for changing the way in which rights are understood in the American system. Understanding the role that the courts and bureaucracy play in our system and how that differs from what they do in other kinds of federal systems is an important undertaking. While the Framers might have had questions about the power that Courts and bureaucracy have come to hold in the American system, many of them would have applauded how difficult it is to get things done in the system and some would have been pleased by the rise of the strong Presidency.

The Framers belief in balance between the national and the state governments and their distrust of unfettered democracy extended to the way in which both the United States Senate and the President were chosen. Senators were originally chosen by the votes of state legislatures (something that changed to direct election in the early 20th century with the passage of the

17th Amendment) and the President is still chosen by the votes of the Electoral College not those of the citizens. The system was created to supply balance between the states and the national government in several ways but also between the branches of the national government. The House and Senate have different and competing powers, but no law can be created without both bodies agreeing to it. In this separated system, it is extremely hard to get things done and policies that are made tend to stay in place, thus making the big structural change that both conservatives and liberals seek to accomplish difficult.

As Haskell et al. point out the public's expectations of what the national government should do and for whom it should do it have changed since the Framers wrote the constitution. This has impacted the relative powers of Congress and the Presidency as the two branches vie for dominance in the marketing to shape public policy. Presidents have significant tools at their disposal to shape public policy including a large White House staff, a slew of Executive Branch agencies, and a high public profile that assures ready media access. While Congress considers and passes legislation, the President too must act for a bill to become law. The Presidency has other tools that it can use to implement policy and those tools have grown (along with the power of the Presidency) as the country's history has unfolded. The President and winning the Presidency get so much attention in the American system now versus what the Framers thought that they would because the Presidency gained considerable power via a series of economic and security crises, as well as the increasing complexity and interconnectedness of the country's economy during the period since the Great Depression.

There is more to the American system than Congress and the Presidency. Courts play a significant role in the public policymaking process here and abroad. Looking at Courts in a variety of federal systems in *Comparing the Power of Courts in Federal Systems*, Christina Ruggiero finds varying levels of ambiguity and different approaches to the ways in which courts approach policy, using abortion policy as a case study. Ruggiero points out that courts and legislatures are engaged in an interplay in which each partly shape the other's actions. This is partly decided by the extent to which judicial review is established in a system and the extent to which the citizens' rights are developed and articulated. It is also partly determined by the federal system that exists in each authority. The places with more state autonomy are likely to generate more court cases and the places in which laws are written more specifically versus broadly will see more intervention.

This unit will close by looking at the way in which the interplay of the national government's branches, the bureaucracy, federalism, state rules, courts, and international treaties impact a commercial product. In this case, we will look at how these things have produced an extremely specific legal understanding of what constitutes bourbon. Bourbon is a distinctly American product, and its producers must follow some specific processes to legally sell it. The specificity around bourbon shows the power that the national government has gained over many aspects of

American life, the economic importance of participating in international agreements and bodies but also the powers that states continue to have.

Spirits companies from around the world would love to make bourbon, but none can legally do so because bourbon can only be produced in the United States, meaning that the solution for foreign producers eager to secure a steady supply of the stuff has been to buy a U.S. producer. As Brian F. Haara shows, bourbon gradually came to have a specific definition around the same time that the federal government began to regulate more areas of American economic activity, especially food products, in the name of public safety. Over time, bourbon came to have a specific definition of what it is that was created by the national and state governments. For example, Tennessee state law defines what that state's whiskey is and specifies an additional process for making that spirt beyond the one used to make bourbon. Thus, because of a state law, even though this product meets the federal legal definition for bourbon, it is not usually labeled as being bourbon. The way in which these products are produced, bottled, packaged, and then marketed around the world is the result of an interplay between producers and two levels of government, the way regulatory agencies have acted and bills that Congress has passed and Presidents signed that impacted many aspects of how bourbon came to be a uniquely American product. Some things are legally specified like the "Bottled in Bond" designation that means this product met specific production processes while others, like the terms "rare" or "small batch" are commercial terms aimed at differentiating one type of the product from another in a competitive global marketplace. What happened to bourbon happened to many other aspects of American life.

This unit has outlined the reasons why the American system developed as it did, how it operates, how it can change, and what the impact of the system has been to foster a unique policymaking environment, political culture, and how it has nurtured one American product into a global powerhouse.

Congress and the President

The Struggle over Directing Public Policy

By John Haskell, Sara Grove, and Marian Currinder

[W] e saw that for agencies of the government to do things, they need legal authority—authority that can come only from an act of Congress. Similarly, they need Congress to give them the funds to do the work they are authorized to do. And Congress relies on the implied power of oversight to encourage agencies to "do the right thing," at least as key members of Congress see it.

The interesting thing about our system of government is that these agencies and the officials who work in them do not for the most part answer directly to the legislative branch. The chain of command in the executive branch goes from the people in the agencies running federal programs on a day-to-day basis up to the top leadership of those agencies and departments (most of whom were appointed by the president, some requiring Senate confirmation) to the president himself. And to be clear: the president certainly likes to think of himself as having a say over the direction of federal policy.

And in fact, the president would be right—he has a good many tools to influence federal policy in any area, such as education, health, defense, transportation, space, and so on. It is most certainly *not* the end of the story when a law is passed. After all, Congress has to depend on an executive branch agency to implement that law.

Federal policy is most accurately thought of as the result of a struggle between the two political branches, with Congress as the board of directors pressing its case through lawmaking and oversight and the president maneuvering within the wide range of discretion he is given in law. Sometimes, when Congress passes a particularly far-reaching law or the president exercises his prerogatives in controversial ways, the federal courts are brought into the action either by people in the government or by interested parties in the public. [...]

Here, the focus is on the political branches. In the end, with regard to almost any issue— education, workplace, safety, land management, and all the rest—one can reasonably ask: which branch is more influential in setting the direction of policy as carried out by the agencies and departments of government? In short, who is the boss of those agencies? Is it the president, who literally *presides* over the executive branch agencies, or is it Congress, the institution that is the source of the authority by which the agencies act?

The answer is really: both. In some areas, one branch will have an advantage, at least for a time; in others, the other branch will. At the end of the [reading], we assess which branch might be said to have more lasting impact on the direction of policy. But first, we will look at the development of the relationship between the branches in directing federal policy. The history of the relationship involves a period in the middle decades of the 20th century when Congress delegated a great deal of authority to the president. Congress pushed back in the 1970s, reclaiming some of its prerogatives. We are at a time when, in domestic policy, the two branches each have the resources to influence policy in important ways, if those resources are exploited effectively.

The next section provides a review of what each branch has going for it in the struggle for control over public policy. Here we call them "toolkits,"[1] which are essentially those resources—or "power tools"—the branches have for influencing the direction of policy.

After that, we see how the struggle plays out in a couple of important areas of public policy. Two good examples of how the political branches employ the tools at their disposal are federal policy on regulating the financial sector of the economy and the nutritional components of federally subsidized school meals.

We finish the [reading] by looking at national security policy, where the relationship between the branches is different. For a long time, presidents have had the clear upper hand, dating back to the end of World War II. National security is a kind of exception to the rule that the branches struggle on a more or less equal basis over the direction of policy. But it is not true that presidents are entirely unaccountable in the pursuit of their policy aims in this realm. We will see the ways in which the law constrains presidents, even regarding covert operations such as the predator drone program conducted by the Obama administration.

THE RELATIONSHIP BETWEEN THE BRANCHES IN THE 20TH CENTURY: A HISTORY OF DELEGATION

Congress has always delegated authority to the president. But this tendency went to a new level with the 1921 Budget and Accounting Act, which created the Bureau of the Budget (BOB), later renamed the Office of Management and Budget.

Prior to this act, each agency of government went directly to Congress to appeal for money to fund its programs.[2] The president simply did not have the staff to manage the relationship between the agencies and Congress. Long-standing relationships had developed between agency personnel and members of Congress, often leaving the president out of the equation. In this way, it was Congress that had its hooks in the agencies, effectively driving policy through the power of the purse. This power dynamic generally held true even though presidents had the power to nominate agency heads who served at their pleasure.

Prior to 1921, the executive branch spoke with many voices, and to say there was a coherent presidential agenda was a stretch. This began to change with the creation of the BOB. Its charge was to provide Congress a comprehensive look at the federal budget every year—essentially bringing together all the agency requests into a coherent whole on behalf of the president. This gave the president the wherewithal potentially to press for an agenda, to have his branch of government effectively speak with one voice.

It is reasonable to wonder why Congress would willingly have provided the president this potentially powerful institutional tool, which could be wielded against it in the struggle over the direction of policy. But the federal budget was under great stress, and had been since the end of World War I in 1918. Debt had exploded because of the war effort and seemed uncontrollable. Congress was under tremendous pressure to do something about it. The idea to pass off some responsibility to the executive seemed appealing at the time.

The New Deal and the National Security State

Another crisis, in this case the Great Depression, drove calls for dramatic and rapid federal action. The election of Democrat Franklin Roosevelt and an overwhelmingly Democratic Congress in 1932 put in place the political conditions that made this possible. Given the severity of the Depression, Congress was moved to pass almost anything Roosevelt wanted. New agencies were created to address the banking crisis, the farm crisis, unemployment, and myriad other things. These agencies were often given very broad authorities to deal with the crisis at hand.[3]

The most notable example was the establishment of the National Recovery Administration in the National Industrial Recovery Act of 1934. Its charge: keep the economy from spiraling further out of control by regulating all sorts of economic activity, including wages, production levels, and prices in certain industries. By 1935 the so-called NRA codes, which spelled out the regulations, were under scrutiny in the courts. The Supreme Court ruled that year that congressional delegation of authority to executive branch agencies that were regulating production in the poultry industry was unconstitutional.[4] The Court said that regulating commerce in this way was tantamount to lawmaking and was the proper purview of Congress, not unelected agency officials. Under pressure in the next few years, the Court reversed course, permitting agencies to exercise these sorts of powers as long as they were rooted in some way in statutory authorities.[5] [...]

As the federal government assumed more and more responsibilities for the welfare of the citizenry as a response to economic hardship, the complexity of managing all the new programs and agencies became increasingly apparent. President Roosevelt was driven to ask for broad authorities to reorganize the executive branch. Included in his request was the need for more assistance at the White House in the form of an Executive Office of the President (EOP), essentially a layer of bureaucracy to help the president make sense of everything the government was doing. It would ideally give him the ability to deal with jurisdictional disputes and overlapping responsibilities among the agencies.

The Reorganization Act of 1939 gave the president much of what he wanted. The sprawling new government was rationalized to an extent under cabinet departments, and the EOP was formed.[6] Presidents were given the ability to reshuffle the agencies, with Congress able to weigh in only after the fact.

After World War II, presidential power was further enhanced by the National Security Act of 1947, which (especially after it was amended in 1949) gave the president the tools to bring together the big picture in foreign policy, military policy, and intelligence gathering. The National Security Council was created at the White House, and the armed forces were brought under one umbrella at the Department of Defense. We will look more at this development later in the [reading].

The Great Society

What had been created in the New Deal was a much bigger federal government, active in ways it had never been before in regulating the economy, providing social insurance, and directing agricultural policy. But the federal presence in other important aspects of American life—civil rights, the environment, education, health, sciences, and transportation—was still rather modest. But this changed, beginning in the 1950s and escalating in the mid-1960s.

The 1950s saw the development of the interstate highway system and the beginnings of major investments in science with the Space Act of 1958 that created NASA. But progressive forces saw their efforts come to full fruition in the mid-1960s, during Lyndon Johnson's Great Society. In 1964 the Civil Rights Act was passed into law, outlawing racial segregation and providing legal protections against discrimination based on race and sex; 1965 saw the Voting Rights Act, which led to a federal takeover of voter-registration policy in large swaths of the country to guarantee the right to vote to African Americans; and also in 1965 the federal government became a major player in education policy at all levels. In addition, Medicare and Medicaid were passed into law that year, giving seniors and the poor federally subsidized medical coverage. In the 1960s and into the early '70s, environmental and consumer protections were enacted, the National Endowments of the Arts and Humanities were created, and science funding skyrocketed. Pretty much any area of American life the federal government had not been involved in was federalized to a significant extent in that era.

The upshot of all this was an even bigger executive branch with ever more responsibilities, usually involving considerable delegation of authority to agency officials and by extension the president. Congress was rapidly being overshadowed. Its staff was overwhelmed keeping up with everything it had created, and presidents such as Democrat Lyndon Johnson (1963–1969) and Republican Richard Nixon (1969–1974) were more than happy to step into the breach and direct agencies according to their respective agendas.

The 1970s: Congress Pushes Back

Congress found itself in a tricky situation. While it was a practical necessity to delegate authority to the president if it wanted the government to do all the things it had put into law, members found themselves getting more and more communications from their constituents who were now virtually all touched profoundly by federal programs, seemingly on a daily basis. The members *had to be* more interested in the work of the agencies as their constituents pestered them for answers, but they did not have the resources to keep up.

The 1970s saw Congress trying to get back into the power game, to reinvigorate its ability to direct the work of the agencies as it, Congress, saw fit. After all, the members were the ones writing the laws and believed to a man and woman they had a right to direct the agencies.

Around this time, Congress appropriated itself resources for more staff, especially at the committee level, to keep track of the agencies. The House began requiring every committee to put together annual agency oversight plans. In addition, Congress began requiring agencies in law or in accompanying report language to update the committees of jurisdiction on the progress and performance of programs of particular interest. New laws scheduled legislative sunsets on agency authorities, essentially Congress forcing itself to reconsider what the agencies were doing. Congress put inspectors general into every agency and department in 1978 to report directly to Congress on waste, fraud, and abuse in the executive branch. The president's legal authority to reorganize agencies and departments was allowed to lapse. The Ethics in Government Act put in place a system that would give tremendous powers to independent counsels (sometimes called special prosecutors) to look into abuses of power in the agencies and the White House.[7]

One of the motivations of all of this was political survival: an enhanced capacity to monitor the executive branch would enable members to better serve their constituents. Some political scientists came up a more cynical interpretation, namely, that members could exploit the vastly complex government their branch had created by "saving the day" for constituents confused by red tape and at the same time scoring political points by chastising agency officials in public.[8]

Whatever the motivation, Congress felt itself at too great a disadvantage in the early 1970s and needed to bolster its ability to influence the direction of federal policy. In doing so, it made itself a more serious player in contending with the president over the direction of federal policy.

THE TOOLKITS OF EACH BRANCH

Congress's Toolkit

In the 21st century, both the executive and the legislative branches have considerable means to influence the direction of public policy. In virtually every imaginable area, particularly in the domestic realm, there is a struggle for the upper hand; today you could say it is a struggle between two fairly evenly matched heavyweights.

This [reading] is about Congress's powers vis-à-vis the federal agencies. What follows is a summary of the "power tools" available to the board of directors to shape policy. After that, we look at the president's toolkit. Then we see the power tools in action in two key areas of public policy. At the end of the [reading] we try to answer this question: which branch is more powerful in influencing the direction of federal policy?

Legislative direction. As we have seen, Congress may be as specific as it wants to be in legislation—authorizing or appropriations—in giving direction to agencies. *Particularly in appropriations bills* [...], Congress gives specific administrative instructions to the agencies. If the president signs the bill, he has for all intents and purposes agreed to Congress's micromanaging of a program.

Legislative sunsets. Whereas it was once common for Congress to give indefinite authorizations to federal programs, beginning in the 1960s it rarely did anymore.

Now, many agencies come up for reauthorization on a regular basis. [...] it is true that most expired authorizations apply only to the authorization of appropriations—the actual agency programs continue to be authorized to exist (and usually receive funding in spite of the expiration date on funding authorization). Even so, the fact that Congress sunsets agency authorizations gives them real or at least implied power to redirect what the agency does in law. Needless to say, agencies are wary.

Spending limitations. Congress is effective in directing agency policy by prohibiting the use of funds for certain purposes in what is called limitation language in appropriations bills. It also sometimes "fences off" portions of agency appropriations until the Committees on Appropriations sign off on a spending plan. This enables even a small subset of Congress—these committees—to have immense influence. [...]

Direction in report language. Appropriators exert their influence in nonstatutory ways as well, giving explicit direction to agencies, sometimes in very forceful language, in the committee reports and the joint explanatory statements that are attached to appropriations bills. Although agencies are not legally bound in these cases, ordinarily they follow these instructions to the letter, as they have to come back to the Appropriations Committee every year for money. It is unwise to make enemies of the members of that committee!

Investigative authority and threat of subpoena. The power Congress has to investigate wrongdoing in the agencies and issue subpoenas for testimony and documents [...] enables it to get executive branch officials' attention. Even just the idea that Congress can dig around in agency business, forcing the commitment of considerable resources, means that agencies have to pay attention to even informal suggestions made by key members of Congress, especially committee chairs and party leaders.

Hearings and using the media. Congress is in a position to draw attention to issues it cares about by holding hearings and planting stories in the media. Normally, agencies try to avoid controversy and will do their best to address the wishes of key members. For this reason, even the *threat* of a hearing—or the *threat* of legislative action, for that matter—can be an effective tool in directing public policy.

The fire-alarm system. [...] Congress attempts to monitor agencies through GAO audits, inspectors general reports, and regular reporting requirements. In addition, many interested parties with a stake in federal policy—academics, interest groups, and advocates of all stripes—have contacts on congressional staffs. And the media, especially investigative journalists, are a crucial resource. Taken together, this so-called fire-alarm system is a valuable tool, bolstering Congress's ability to keep tabs on executive branch agencies. When their constituents are affected, or when they can score points against the other party, or when a special policy concern is involved, chances are that some sort of action will be taken.

All in all, then, Congress has ways to influence agency policy even when it has given agencies wide latitude in the law itself. New laws can always be more specific, and especially annual appropriations bills can wield the all-important power of the purse for policy ends. But as often as not, it is the implied or threatened use of legislative tools that gives Congress the ability to affect public policy.

The Presidential Toolkit

This [reading] has not been about the executive branch explicitly, although the theme is that one cannot understand the two political branches in isolation. As a result, we have frequently touched on the agencies and the president in relation to the powers wielded by Congress. One thing we have stressed in this [reading]: the executive branch by necessity has been delegated a great deal of wiggle room in implementing the aims of legislation passed by Congress. *In fact, perhaps the most important thing to remember about any law passed by Congress is that it does not accomplish anything in the real world without subsequent action, which includes interpretation and implementation by executive branch agencies and sufficient appropriations provided by Congress.*

In short, crucial to understanding the direction of federal public policy is how the objectives of Congress are put in place by the agencies. The president, atop the executive branch, has a lot of power tools at his disposal to make a difference.

Executive orders. Perhaps more important than anything, presidents may issue executive orders to provide direction to agencies in the implementation of the law.[9] These orders may either require specific action by an agency official (usually a department secretary or agency head) or give that official broad authority to act as he or she sees fit. Laws normally lay out fairly broad objectives to, for example, make progress in cleaning the air or regulating a specific market. Within these confines, the president has a great deal of latitude to direct policy. Executive orders have legal force when the president has been given delegated authority in law, as noted above. Presidents can go further and "fill in the blanks" by issuing orders to agency officials in areas that Congress has not specifically legislated in. This can be controversial and may lead to congressional reaction. Presidents can go even further and provoke confrontation by issuing an order that could be construed as contradicting what the law says. In those situations, the federal courts are often asked to intervene and settle the matter.

Some areas of public policy shift dramatically from president to president, almost from day one of a new administration. For example, recently presidents have put forward dueling executive orders on US funding for international health groups that perform abortions. As the *Washington Post* reported in early 2009:

> President Obama yesterday lifted a ban on U.S. funding for international health groups that perform abortions, promote legalizing the procedure or provide counseling about terminating pregnancies.

Obama issued a memorandum rescinding the Mexico City Policy, also known as the "global gag rule," which President Ronald Reagan originally instituted in 1984, President Bill Clinton reversed in 1993 and President George W. Bush revived in 2001.

The memorandum revokes Bush's [executive] order, calling the limitations on funding "excessively broad" and adding that "they have undermined efforts to promote safe and effective voluntary family programs in foreign nations." In an accompanying statement, Obama said he would also work with Congress to restore U.S. funding support for the United Nations Population Fund "to reduce poverty, improve the health of women and children, prevent HIV/AIDS and provide family planning assistance to women in 154 countries."[10]

Appointment power. Presidents appoint thousands of agency officials, including the top tier of about 800 people subject to Senate approval. These people serve at the president's pleasure, which gives him a way to exert authority over the direction of policy.

Agency management. The day-to-day operations of the agencies are performed largely by career civil servants who cannot be fired by the president. These people have the experience and know-how to make the agencies work. However, they do answer to the top so-called political appointees who manage the agency in the service of the president's objectives.

The president's budget. [...] every year the Office of Management and Budget puts together a comprehensive budget for the entire government, detailing what the president would like to accomplish and what funding that would require. It is essentially a blueprint for federal public policy. Of course, Congress may choose to alter that blueprint legislatively, usually by funding different priorities. But the fact is the president has a significant tool as the "contractor," the guy who actually has people working for him who know all the details of the thousands of federal programs. Congress is comparatively *very* thinly staffed. To the extent Congress does not get into the details of government programs, the direction laid out in the president's budget carries the day.

Veto power. The veto power is the president's most effective tool in influencing what gets passed into law. But, if not handled deftly, it is a rather blunt one. Presidents cannot veto parts of bills; they have to accept the whole thing or nothing at all. It is, then, the *threat* of vetoing a bill (very few vetoes are overridden) that is the key to wielding power vis-à-vis Congress. The OMB's Statement of Administration Policy (SAP) is the official conveyance of a veto threat. It is used at different stages of the legislative process to signal to Congress what parts of a bill, if any, are unacceptable. The language in an SAP can be opaque. Sometimes presidents *suggest* that they will veto a bill because of a certain provision without saying it outright. Essentially, the veto power is the president's entrée into the legislative process, giving him the potential to influence the shape of legislation.

The Office of Information and Regulatory Affairs (OIRA). The executive branch's *rulemaking* process is managed by the Office of Information and Regulatory Affairs, an agency within the OMB. The rulemaking process is of paramount importance; essentially, it is the way agencies put legislative authority and direction into effect. Congress's typically broadly stated legislation gives authorities to executive branch agencies to do countless things, from securing the Internet to cleaning up rivers to ensuring the safety of air travel. To put the law into effect agencies develop regulations through the rulemaking process that companies, local governments, and private citizens have to abide by.[11] These regulations have the force of law, as they are rooted in statutes passed by Congress.

While the agencies themselves develop the regulations through processes that are open to public input, OIRA reviews those regulations before they are put into effect.[12] OIRA is headed by a presidential appointee, giving the president considerable leverage over the specifics of federal regulations, which might mean a more or less strict rule on land use or a more or less inhibiting regulation on what financial instruments a bank may use.

The bully pulpit. The president has an unequaled ability to draw attention from the media, giving him the potential to marshal public opinion in the interest of influencing the direction of legislation or policy more broadly. Also, unlike Congress, the president can speak with one voice. Congress can be a cacophony of voices that are not necessarily on the same page, a disadvantage when trying to influence agency policy.

PUTTING THE TOOLKITS TO WORK: TWO CASE STUDIES

In the words of a prominent congressional staffer:

> In American Government class I learned that when a major law was passed—say, to secure voting rights or to clean the nation's rivers—policies were immediately in place to make those goals happen. When I actually worked in government, I found out that it doesn't work that way. Laws have to be interpreted and implemented. Those things take time. And of course funds are needed to make them happen. In fact, the passage of a law is just the beginning of the fight.[13]

The development of public policy on any issue is ongoing. All three branches may get into the act; the executive and legislative always do. What follows are two examples that illustrate this staffer's point that the actual direction of public policy at any given moment is the result of a struggle between the branches. The first case is the implementation of the Dodd-Frank bill. After that we look at the National School Lunch Program after passage of the Healthy Hunger-Free Kids Act of 2010.

Financial Regulation

In the fall of 2008, following the demise of Lehman Brothers (a major investment banking firm), it appeared that the financial system was bound to implode without drastic action. Many firms had made a lot of bad bets, and some banks were so large that if they followed Lehman, the consequences would be a depression of a magnitude not seen since at least the 1930s. The Emergency Economic Stabilization Act proposed to bail out some of the nation's major banks—even and it seemed especially those that had not handled their assets responsibly. Although there was a lot of opposition, and passage wasn't easy, President Bush signed the bill into law on October 3, 2008. It set up the Troubled Asset Relief Program, which was authorized to bail out banks to the unprecedented tune of $700 billion.[14]

Politicians and policy experts were chastened by the experience as the economy began to recover ever so slowly from the financial crisis. What could be done to prevent repeating the mistakes made by financial institutions that had been deemed "too big to fail"? Ultimately, there was considerable momentum to restructure the entire federal regulatory apparatus for the financial system, particularly after Democrats won the presidency and padded their margins in the House and Senate in the 2008 elections.

The path to legislation was long, however, as the problems themselves were incredibly complex and the debate increasingly took on a partisan tone, with Republicans opposing what they regarded as reform ideas that would tend to hinder the free movement of capital. In the end, the Dodd-Frank Wall Street Reform and Consumer Protection Act (named after Senator Christopher Dodd of Connecticut and Representative Barney Frank of Massachusetts, both Democrats and the principal sponsors of the legislation) was signed into law by President Obama on July 21, 2010. It envisioned a strengthened Securities and Exchange Commission (SEC) and Commodity Futures Trading Commission (CFTC), both of which had seen dramatic reductions in key areas of funding in recent years. Broadly speaking, Dodd-Frank mandated that those agencies pursue "securities fraud, reviewing public company disclosures and financial statements, inspecting the activities of investment advisors, investments companies, broker-dealers and other registered entities, and [maintain] fair and efficient markets." The law also created the Consumer Financial Protection Bureau (CFPB)—an agency that would be part of the Federal Reserve and have funding independent of Congress—to have broad authority to police a wide range of lenders and debt collectors, as well as some activities of credit unions and banks.

The law gave wide latitude to these key agencies to put the broad objectives of the law into effect through the federal regulatory process. They were given one year to accomplish that. President Obama appointed heads of these agencies (Chairwoman Mary Schapiro at the SEC and Chairman Gary Gensler at CFTC, who lead five-person bipartisan commissions, as well as the single director of the CFPB, Richard Cordray), giving him some influence over the direction of the policies. All the agency heads, however, serve fixed terms, giving them substantial independence.

The problem for implementation: the regulatory process is long and involved, requiring agencies to give the public (especially the entities subject to regulation and consumer advocate groups) ample opportunity to weigh in on proposed regulations. Experts acknowledge that putting the law into effect through regulations that explain what is and is not allowed was simply impossible in such a complex area of policy in only one year's time. Furthermore, the agencies were simply not staffed sufficiently to be able to make it happen. At the end of 2012, two and a half years after passage, only one-third of the needed regulations were in effect, one-third were proposed and in the pipeline, and fully one-third were not even proposed yet.[15]

There are a lot of factors to consider, not just in the completion of the task but in the actual policies being implemented. Some were internal to the executive branch agencies. As mentioned, the agencies simply did not have the staffing to get the job done, and the process itself was cumbersome. Furthermore, the agencies themselves have not always agreed on what to do in keeping with the law and even which agency is meant to take the lead in particular areas. The so-called Volcker Rule, a requirement of Dodd-Frank that aims to restrict banks from doing anything too risky with their money, is supposed to be the product of the work of the Federal Deposit Insurance Corporation and other banking agencies, with the CFTC playing a role. The SEC, too, has seen fit to join the policy-making process.[16] At this writing, no final rule has been put forth.

Struggles like these attract attention from members of Congress. Those critical of the delays or the direction of proposed regulations will bombard the agencies with letters demanding answers. Those critical of proposed regulations will, for their part, work behind the scenes lobbying the regulators furiously to narrow their force. Senator Scott Brown (R-MA) made it clear in various ways to officials at the Federal Reserve that he would fight on behalf of financial firms in his state for broad exceptions to the Volcker Rule.[17] And regulators have to listen to the politicians on Capitol Hill—after all, what good is a regulation that proves to be such a lightning rod that its implementation is not funded or it is overturned by subsequent legislation? All the hard work would be for naught.

Key members of Congress, especially committee chairs, use various tactics to influence the direction of policy. In the case of Dodd-Frank, these members send letters to the agency heads as proposed regulations are publicized, making it clear what they intended when they passed the legislation. Most of the efforts are more subtle than that—calls from committee staffers to make sure agency officials know they are paying attention: "My boss (the senator) is starting to get anxious about the pace of your work."

In fact, two Senate committees (Banking and Agriculture—the two in that chamber most involved in Dodd-Frank) have conducted hearings on the severe liquidity problems and eventual bankruptcy of derivatives broker MF Global. These drew attention to the very problems Dodd-Frank was meant to address with the hopes of encouraging agencies not to water down regulations. The threat of new refined legislation is always in the background—or even an unpleasant hearing involving the regulators themselves.

For opponents of Dodd-Frank, the 2010 midterm elections were a boon. An antiregulatory Republican House gave these members much more leverage over the agencies' processes. They held hearings on the negative impact of the regulations, as they saw it, putting pressure on the regulators. More important, in the annual appropriations process Republicans had the newfound leverage to reduce the growth of the agencies, making it impossible to do everything they were required to do under the time constraints laid out in Dodd-Frank. Sometimes limitation language restricting the scope of regulations was added to the House version of the Financial Services and General Government appropriations bill. These almost never made it into law, but they were effective bargaining chips in negotiations with the Democratic Senate and the president—chips that were cashed in for cutting funding for the relevant agencies. Slowing the regulatory process can be part of a long-term strategy for legislation down the road to change or even repeal the law.

Healthy School Lunches ... with Tater Tots?

Congressional passage of the Healthy Hunger-Free Kids Act of 2010 gave the Food and Nutrition Service (FNS), an agency in the US Department of Agriculture, the tools to make systematic change to the National School Lunch Program, among other things. This bill was near to the Obama administration's heart, in fact a pet project of the first lady, Michelle Obama.

The School Lunch Program had been in place by one name or another since before the 1940s, even though it never had specific statutory authorization. Its aim was and is to ameliorate hunger among the nation's needy children. It was given full-fledged legal authorization in 1946 and was amended in the 1960s in part to update nutritional standards in the meals.

The 2010 act gave the FNS the new authorities it needed to bring school lunches, breakfasts, and other similar programs in line with the latest nutritional science—something private-sector experts and nonprofits had advocated since the last revision in 1995. As with the authorities given to the financial regulatory agencies in Dodd-Frank, the FNS was given a lot of running room to put forward regulations to improve school meals.

The FNS tapped into the expertise of the Institute of Medicine, a widely respected independent organization. The IOM had put out a report, "School Meals: Building Blocks for

Children," in 2009 that was an important source for the legal authorities provided in the 2010 Hunger-Free Kids legislation.[18] In 2011 the FNS made it known that it planned to put in place a new regulation pursuant to that law that would remove starchy vegetables, including corn, peas, lima beans, and potatoes, from school breakfasts and reduce them to one cup per week at lunch. In their place would be more fresh leafy vegetables and other nonprocessed foods.[19] This would go into effect in 2012. The evidence showed that the changes would improve the nutritional value of the federally subsidized meals in keeping with the spirit and letter of the law.

The oversight fire-alarm system went off in the halls of Congress in the fall of 2011—especially loudly in the office of Senator Susan Collins (R-ME). The lead outside group bringing attention to the issue appeared to be the National Potato Council. Collins went the floor of the Senate with an amendment to the agriculture appropriations bill to prohibit implementation of the new rule. In an interview with *Politico*, she said, "To improve the quality of school lunches and breakfasts is something I have always supported. But either my amendment becomes law, or the department will decide it needs to cut its losses and rewrite the rule without waiting for it to become law. At the end of the day, the result is going to be the same."[20]

The administration entered into negotiations with the senator almost immediately. FNS head Kevin Concannon said, "Our proposed rule will improve the health and nutrition of our children based on sound science. ... [W]e will work with Congress to ensure the intent of this rule is not undermined."[21]

Collins's opposition as publicly stated emphasized the considerable additional costs associated with preparing fresh vegetables in place of processed foods—french fries, tater tots, and so on. Of course, potatoes are an important product in Maine, which didn't escape her attention.

In the end, the administration put into effect its new rule in early 2012, and in fact the school lunch menus did undergo major changes.[22] But Congress had pressured the administration into considering its concerns. In this case, a single powerful senator forced the administration to negotiate with her.

CONGRESS AND THE PRESIDENT: DOMESTIC VERSUS NATIONAL SECURITY POLICY

[...] As we have seen, there are often serious disagreements between the branches because of their different outlooks and perspectives. When one branch is charged with *directing* the work of government, and the other charged with *doing* the work of government, there are bound to be differences of opinion in the interpretation of congressional intent, as expressed in law or otherwise. This tension was built into our system quite intentionally to serve as a check on the power of the federal government; it could be described as part of the normal relationship between the branches. Each branch was given the ability to invade, as it were, the sphere of the other branch in order to serve as a check on its power.

In national security policy and especially war powers, however, the system of checks and balances does not work in the same way. In the past several decades, presidents have resisted efforts by Congress to intervene in policy decisions in this realm (especially those involving the commitment of troops to battle and covert operations); in fact, presidents are frequently downright dismissive of legislative branch efforts in ways rarely seen on the domestic side of policy. The past half century and more has been a period of existential threat and vigorous activism by the United States in world affairs. The nation faced the possibility of full-scale nuclear war and attempted to contain the spread of Soviet-style communism; attempted to promote democracy, human rights, and capitalism around the globe; confronted international terrorism; and shouldered the host of responsibilities that went along with its position as, eventually, the world's only superpower.

Every post–World War II president has initiated or overseen some form of American military action abroad. In a number of administrations, foreign wars have been the dominant focus of attention. Over the same period in this area of policy, Congress has become increasingly less effective, sometimes seemingly to the point of complete subordination to the will of the president.

The relationship between the branches is extraordinary in the area of war powers in part because there is no consensus over the meaning and implications of the relevant constitutional language. What are Congress's prerogatives? What exactly are the president's? The debate has gone on without interruption ever since World War II, with no end in sight in the 21st century. In fact, the Iraq War highlighted the clash between the branches. Former senator Robert Byrd of West Virginia, a vigorous proponent of congressional prerogatives, succinctly summarized the presidential position on the matter in the days leading up to the beginning of that conflict in 2003: "The Bush Administration thinks that the Constitution, with its inefficient separation of powers and its cumbersome checks and balances, has become an anachronism in a world of international terrorism and weapons of mass destruction."[23]

The Constitutional Provisions

Congress has essentially the same sources of power in determining the national security policy of the nation that it has in all other policy areas—those provisions in Article I that give the institution the power to authorize and fund the actions of the government. However, there are four constitutional provisions that are at the heart of the continuing debate over the two branches' prerogatives in the specific realm of war powers.

The first is the power to declare war, granted, in Article I, Section 8, to Congress:

Congress has the power ... to declare war, grant letters of marque and reprisal, and make rules concerning captures on land and water; to raise and support armies, but no appropriation of money to that use shall be for a longer term than two years; to provide and maintain a navy; to make rules for the government and regulation of the land and naval forces.

The second provision, in Article II, Section 1, refers to the general grant of executive power to the president:

The executive power shall be vested in a president of the United States of America.

The third, in Article II, Section 2, gives the president the commander-in-chief power:

The president shall be commander in chief of the army and navy of the United States, and of the militia of the several states, when called in the actual service of the United States.

The fourth, also in Article II, Section 2, confers a more general power over foreign affairs to the president:

[The president] shall have power, by and with the advice and consent of the Senate, to make treaties, provided two thirds of the senators present concur; and he shall nominate, and by and with the advice and consent of the Senate, shall appoint ambassadors.

Many scholars and politicians believe that the framers of the Constitution placed the power to commit the country to war in the hands of Congress and Congress alone. They see this as the most logical reading of Article I, Section 8. This perspective maintains that the president's commander-in-chief power, or any other constitutionally granted executive powers, cannot usurp Congress's authority to decide whether to go to war. As such, the power to declare war is not a shared power except insofar as a declaration of war, to be legally in effect, requires the president's signature.

Those in favor of congressional prerogatives say that the framers of the Constitution placed the war power exclusively in the hands of Congress in direct reaction to the existing European model, which placed the war power exclusively with the monarch. According to scholar Louis Fisher: "The framers broke decisively with that tradition. Drawing on lessons learned at home in the American colonies and the Continental Congress, they deliberately transferred the power to initiate war from the executive to the legislature. The framers, aspiring to achieve the ideal of republican government, drafted a Constitution 'that allowed only Congress to loose the military forces of the United States on other nations.'"[24]

Following this line of thinking, some Congress partisans suggest that the president's commander-in-chief power does not kick in until war is declared. This idea is backed up by a literal reading of the Article II, Section 2, provision stating that "the president shall be Commander in Chief of the Army and Navy of the United States, and of the militia of the several States, *when called into the actual service of the United States*" (emphasis added). A declaration of war would constitute the most obvious "call into the actual service of the United States." Presumably, this interpretation might also mean that the president has to relinquish the commander-in-chief power when the war is over.

But declarations of war have gone out of fashion. The United States has had dozens of military engagements, both major and minor, since the last congressional declaration of war in 1942. Is Congress's constitutional claim on the power to commit the nation to war even relevant anymore?

The President and the War Power

By designating the president the "commander in chief," in Article II, Section 2, the framers empowered him to do at least two things: one, to conduct military operations pursuant to declared or authorized wars; and two, to repel attacks on the homeland. Beyond that, there is no consensus as to what the framers intended.

Recent presidents and some scholars certainly do wish to extend the president's powers beyond those basics. They believe that the commander-in-chief power requires no trigger from a congressional authorization or declaration of war to take effect—instead, they maintain, it is always in place. Furthermore, although no president has attempted to lay claim to the power to declare war, numerous presidents and proponents of presidential war power have pointed to the commander-in-chief clause in the Constitution as, at least in part, a legitimate basis for sending US forces into battle irrespective of any action by Congress.

The most expansive interpretations of presidential power in the past 60 years include the contention that the Constitution gives the president the authority to commence and conduct virtually any military action that he sees as being in the interest of the nation.[25] *Presidents of both parties, even when they have received or sought congressional authorization, now maintain that they do not need that congressionally granted authority to commit American troops.* What has caused this rather dramatic and consequential change from an often restricted view of the president's prerogatives to a greatly expanded view of his commander-in-chief role? And how is it justified?

World War II, Communists, and the Standing Army

World War II saw a massive mobilization of the nation's industry and populace for war. The nation, together with its allies, fought the three notorious dictators from Japan, Italy, and Germany on multiple fronts around the globe. The scale of it easily exceeded the mobilization efforts required for World War I.

For the Second World War, American forces were based on multiple continents, as they had been for World War I, but there was a major difference in the American posture in the years after the war. Instead of "standing down"—dramatically scaling back the armed forces at the end of a war—the United States retained an international posture by maintaining bases all over the world and, in effect, keeping all the branches of the armed services on ready alert.

The reason? It was recognized very soon after the end of the war that a US ally in World War II, the Soviet Union, might constitute a threat to the Western European allies, and perhaps even the United States itself. The Soviets had rapidly solidified their position by exerting control over much of Eastern and central Europe. This development—the establishment of what were called the Warsaw Pact or Eastern-bloc nations—concerned Western Europeans, who feared further Soviet expansion into their countries. With the prodding of Britain's Winston Churchill and under the leadership of President Harry Truman, a bipartisan consensus developed in the United States around the idea that the Soviet Union needed to be contained within its sphere of influence.

The Soviets, for their part, made little effort to hide their intention to exert influence on other continents. It appeared that the Soviet Communists were on the move, and the only conceivable obstacle to them would be the United States, which, despite the considerable sacrifice of its citizens during the war, was relatively intact and economically vital compared to its other allies. Politically, the containment of the Soviets became an imperative supported enthusiastically by most Democrats and Republicans alike. The 45-year Cold War had begun.

This became only more of an imperative when the Soviet Union tested its first atom bomb in 1949. The United States no longer had a monopoly on nuclear weapons. The race to build more and more lethal bombs began in earnest. The competition with the Soviet Union affected American politics and its institutions profoundly. By the late 1940s, covert operations to counter Soviet influence in Europe and, in fairly short order, across the globe had escalated. The United States did not dare scale back its military posture for fear of encouraging the Soviets' ambitions. American interests were considered threatened in Asia, the Middle East, Africa, Central and South America, and, of course, Europe.

Post–World War II America and the Commander in Chief

In earlier times, American presidents, even if they had wanted to, would have had a great deal of difficulty unilaterally and precipitously committing the nation to a major foreign entanglement. The nation did not maintain the type of military posture necessary for sustained, large-scale military ventures. Considerable mobilization, necessitating appropriations for the armed services and other actions of Congress to harness industry, would have been required.

After World War II, the president had a lot more to work with. As noted, he had armed forces positioned at far-flung bases that were easily deployable anywhere around the world. It would take longer to mobilize a force for a large-scale war, but such a force was available at bases in the United States. The president also had the ability to inflict massive damage anywhere on earth with the rapidly growing nuclear arsenal, over which he had unquestioned authority. Most important perhaps, postwar presidents had what amounted to explicit bipartisan support to do what needed to be done—to contain the spread of communism by any means necessary.

It was not a huge stretch for presidents to conclude that they could get away with acting unilaterally to engage American troops or conduct covert operations whenever and wherever American interests were threatened. In fact, every single president since the end of World War II, Democrats and Republicans alike, has claimed the authority to do so. But how did presidents justify this rather radical departure from the long-established constitutional interpretation that Congress has control over the decision to commit troops to battle?[26]

Truman's 1950 decision to send troops without congressional authorization into the Korean conflict, a major front in the Cold War, precipitated a series of justifications. In 1951 Secretary of State Dean Acheson, testifying before the Senate Foreign Relations and Armed Services Committees, said, "Not only has the president the authority to use the armed forces in carrying out the broad foreign policy of the United States and implementing treaties, but it is equally clear that this authority may not be interfered with by the Congress in the exercise of power which it has in the Constitution."[27] Notably, some years later, a Johnson administration State Department official, Leonard Meeker, stated, "The grant of authority to the president in Article II of the Constitution extends to the actions of the United States currently undertaken in Vietnam."[28]

Practically speaking, the argument was that Congress had spent the money to put the armed forces on ready alert all over the globe for a reason. And that reason was that our interests and our very existence were perceived to be threatened in the Cold War. To presidents, there was no longer any debate: the nation was in a precarious situation that constituted something like a permanent emergency. The commander in chief had the authority unilaterally to commit troops to war if need be.

BOX 2.1.1
The Curious Case of Executive Power

One of the most intriguing and controversial passages in the Constitution of the United States is the one right at the beginning of Article II: "The executive power shall be vested in a president of the United States of America." The framers did not define fully what they meant by that sentence, which may have been intentional. After all, they were dipping their toes into a touchy subject so soon after the nation escaped the yoke of the English monarch, and they needed to tamp down controversy in order to get the Constitution ratified.

(Continued)

Many of the framers believed that the executive, while kept in check for obvious reasons, needed to have much more power to act decisively and make the government work than the impotent one that was set up in the ill-fated Articles of Confederation. The articles were an overreaction, they thought. The Constitution would put in place checks, but the executive needed "energy" and needed to be able to act with "dispatch" and authority. One of the reasons they settled on establishing a single executive instead of an executive council was in the interest of "energy" and "dispatch."[1]

But the executive's powers were not defined in Article II at anywhere near the level of specificity that Congress's were in Article I. What were the limits of this "executive power"? The legislative powers "herein granted" were exhaustively listed, especially in Article I, Section 8. The *executive power* seemed to be a more general grant of authority. (Gouverneur Morris was the delegate who actually penned the document. It is widely believed, given his sentiments on the matter of executive authority, that he was responsible for making sure executive powers were not circumscribed in the way legislative powers were by the inclusion of the words *herein granted* in the first sentence of Article II.)

The issue of what executive power meant became a political football. An entire political party movement, the Whigs, was organized around the idea that the president should limit himself to simply executing Congress's wishes (except in the most dire emergency) in order that the office would not endanger the liberties of the people. Others, especially Thomas Jefferson and Andrew Jackson, felt that the Constitution permitted them to exercise more discretion if done in the interests of the nation. Teddy Roosevelt in particular was famous for asserting that the president should act aggressively in the national interest as the "steward" of the nation, as long as he did not run afoul of the Constitution or the laws passed by Congress. There were plenty of gray areas for presidents to exploit, he said, and he meant to do so.

But there has been, since the beginning, an even more expansive interpretation of "executive power" that has been used to bolster controversial unilateral presidential actions. John Locke, a 17th-century English philosopher, was the source of something called the *prerogative view* of executive power. Locke had written that the executive needed "to act according to [his] discretion for the public good, without the prescription of the law, and *sometimes even against it*."[2] What he meant was that the executive could or even should break the law if that was necessary to serve the public in a crisis.

---

[1] Alexander Hamilton, *The Federalist Papers*, No. 70.

[2] John Locke, *Second Treatise of Government* (1690) (emphasis added).

(Continued)

Abraham Lincoln seemed to have Locke's view in mind when he wrote a famous letter to A. G. Hodges in 1864, defending some of the actions he had taken as president in the period leading up to and during the Civil War:

> Was it possible to lose the nation, and yet preserve the Constitution? By general law life and limb must be protected; yet often a limb must be amputated to save a life; but a life is never wisely given to save a limb. I felt that measures, otherwise unconstitutional, might become lawful, by becoming indispensable to the preservation of the nation. Right or wrong, I assumed this ground, and now avow it.[3]

President Nixon used the same justification, citing Lincoln's letter, in defense of some of his actions—many of which were plainly illegal—to quell protests and infiltrate what he regarded as potentially subversive domestic groups during the Vietnam War.[4] Thomas Jefferson was familiar with Locke's arguments and seemed to subscribe to them as well.[5]

President George W. Bush was extremely assertive regarding the president's executive prerogatives. His Administration put forth the *unitary theory* of executive power, which argues for strict limits on Congress's power to encroach on the president's turf.[6] Specifically, adherents of this view maintain that the president must have full control over subordinate officers in the executive branch and that the Constitution, through the commander-in-chief and foreign-relations clauses as well as executive power, gives the president the authority to move unilaterally in the realm of foreign and military affairs. (One former high-ranking Bush administration official suggested that the president's assertions of prerogative provoked such a fierce reaction from the other branches that, ironically, the institution of the presidency was weakened while he was still in office.)[7]

The exact meaning of "executive power" will never be established to everyone's satisfaction. The Constitution is far too opaque on the subject for a final answer to be discerned. But certainly, presidents have occasionally relied on the idea of an "undefined residuum" of executive power to bolster their case for an expanded interpretation of the commander-in-chief role.[8]

---

[3] Lincoln's full letter can be found at http://showcase.netins.net/web/creative/lincoln/speeches/hodges.htm.

[4] Nixon publicly espoused this position in the famous Nixon-Frost interviews of 1977. The relevant passages can be found at www.landmarkcases.org/nixon/nixonview.html.

[5] Jack L. Goldsmith, *The Terror Presidency* (New York: W. W. Norton, 2007), 80–83.

[6] A full examination of the unitary executive theory can be found in Stephen G. Calabresi and Christopher S. Yoo's book *The Unitary Executive* (New Haven, CT: Yale University Press, 2008).

[7] Goldsmith, *The Terror Presidency*.

[8] William Howard Taft used the "undefined residuum." He was an opponent of the expansion of presidential prerogatives advocated by his contemporaries, Teddy Roosevelt and Woodrow Wilson.

Advocates of presidential prerogatives have grounded this power in more than the commander-in-chief clause in Article II. Rather, they put forth a broader argument rooted in all three of the Article II provisions noted earlier.[29] The president is said to be solely responsible for representing the nation in foreign relations based on the primary role that presidents are given in the Constitution in treaty negotiations and the receiving of ambassadors. The Supreme Court essentially took this position in 1936.[30] The Court has also cooperated by not standing in the way of executive agreements and other unilateral diplomatic actions taken by presidents. And most broadly, the executive power vested in the president in the very first words of Article II is said to give him the exclusive power to act in the interest of the nation during a time of crisis. The centuries-long debate over the interpretation of "executive power" is described in Box 2.1.1.

The argument from this perspective is that the modern-day need for quick action (or "dispatch," in the words of the framers) necessitates a change in the way we should think about the constitutional provisions affecting presidential power. In the Cold War period from the late 1940s to 1991, when the Soviet Union collapsed, the Soviets' intercontinental nuclear capability, as well as their incursions and influence around the world affecting American interests, put the nation's security permanently at risk.

After the Cold War, Presidents George H. W. Bush and Bill Clinton still viewed the world as a dangerous place for American interests. Bush, in particular, identified American economic and strategic interests in the Middle East as a reasonable justification for unilateral presidential action in the First Gulf War. (He got the authority in law to remove Iraq from Kuwait, but claimed that he did not need it to act, given the UN resolutions and the clear threat to American interests.) And Clinton went further, arguing that instability and human rights violations in south-central Europe, as well as North Atlantic Treaty Organization commitments, justified unilateral presidential actions in the Kosovo conflict. It is interesting that US membership in NATO and the United Nations explicitly *does not* legally commit it (or any other nation for that matter) to war. The charters of the organizations leave it up to member states to make that determination. Having said that, these two presidents' political case for committing American troops was surely bolstered by our participation in those bodies.

Clinton and his successor, George W. Bush, also faced the threat of international terrorism. Again, the need for speed was used to justify presidential action, even to the point of committing the nation to war.

Ultimately, the consensus view among presidents, if not among scholars or members of Congress, is that waiting for Congress to weigh in before any commitment of American troops is an antiquated and downright dangerous idea in this day and age. (Some would add that, on the international front, a nation has more flexibility with less formal mechanisms of committing its military to war—specifically, statutes authorizing the use of force.) The view is that, unlike in previous eras, the nation's vital interests are so extensive and, in many cases, vulnerable, and the capabilities of America's enemies so diabolical and sophisticated, that the requirement of dispatch legitimizes the invocation of, in effect, an umbrella of constitutional authority (encompassing the commander-in-chief clause, executive power, and the Article II, Section 2, provisions covering foreign relations) to commit the country to military and covert action irrespective of congressional authorization.

Two Key Dimensions of the Presidential Advantage

There is no doubt about who the winner is in the struggle between the branches over the direction of national security policy: it is the executive in a landslide. Simply put, over the past several decades, Congress has not exerted the same kind of influence over national security policy, especially committing the country to war, as it has over domestic policy. Even its vaunted "power of the purse" has a diminished impact when it comes to influencing the president in the conduct of war. There are a couple of principal, overarching, reasons for the ascendancy of the executive branch.

First, there is a very strong *political dimension* to Congress's inability to weigh in on foreign or military affairs as effectively as it does on domestic policy. A long tradition of depoliticizing foreign and defense policy is encapsulated in the saying that "politics stops at the water's edge." This notion, articulated by Republican senator Arthur Vandenberg in 1952, meant, in his words, that it is important "to unite our official voice at the water's edge so that America speaks with maximum authority against those who would divide and conquer us."[31] He said this in the particular context of the Cold War at a time when he and some other Republicans were working with Democratic president Harry Truman to present a united front. Such a viewpoint gives the president extra leverage, as he always speaks with one voice—something that is virtually impossible for Congress to do. Presidents become much harder for other politicians to challenge when they are understood to be speaking for the interests of the nation in foreign relations.

The president's political advantage has not, however, enabled him always to dictate what America's proper role in world politics will be. In fact, during the Vietnam War era the debate about war and foreign policy was extremely heated, and during the Reagan years Congress was unusually assertive in opposing the president's policies in Latin America. That said, in the spirit of Arthur Vandenberg, a tradition of bipartisanship and unity in support of the president generally dominates in the most relevant congressional committees (the Senate Foreign Relations Committee and the Armed Services Committees in both chambers). And certainly, it is politically difficult or impossible for members of either party to support pulling the plug on funding for an ongoing military operation.

The second reason Congress has become weak on national security policy is the *informational dimension*. Although it is true that Congress depends on information from the executive branch to exercise its authorizing, appropriations, and oversight powers in the domestic arena, the situation is more problematic in the defense sphere. Information related to national security is controlled to a greater degree by the executive branch. The president has a tremendous built-in advantage vis-à-vis Congress when troops are stationed in or patrolling potentially hostile territory or seas. Presidents are able to use their access to military intelligence to portray events in such a way as to make it very difficult for Congress to oppose decisions in the national security area, including the march to war, when time is of the essence.

Perhaps the most famous example of this sort of information management was the controversial Gulf of Tonkin incident, which led to Congress passing a resolution that granted a broad authorization for military activity in Southeast Asia. Two ambiguous engagements in Southeast Asian waters in 1964 between American destroyers and North Vietnamese torpedo boats were portrayed by the Johnson administration as unprovoked attacks on the American ships. Congress had no ability in this time of crisis to gain access to all the available information (in fact, it took decades for all of it to become public) and had little recourse other than to respond affirmatively and quickly to the president's request for action. The resulting authorization for war was, as Johnson said privately, "like grandmother's nightshirt; it covers everything."[32] It should be noted that only two members of Congress opposed that authorization, and they were both defeated for reelection in the next electoral cycle.

President George W. Bush's administration was also criticized for how it managed ambiguous information in 2002 and 2003 concerning Iraq's program for developing and acquiring weapons of mass destruction. Ultimately, Secretary of State Colin Powell made the case to the United Nations in early 2003 that the United States had irrefutable evidence of the program. The closely controlled information—much of it highly classified—was nearly impossible to challenge, giving a decided advantage to the administration in its case for war. The conventional wisdom a decade later: the Bush administration took the country to war with Iraq based on faulty or misinterpreted intelligence.

In a broader sense, access to information related to defense and national security is limited by the sheer volume generated by the Department of Defense, the armed services, the intelligence agencies, the Department of State, and all the other departments and agencies that have some level of involvement with national security policy (including the Federal Bureau of Investigation (FBI), the Department of Homeland Security, and the Energy Department). Members of Congress, their staffs, and the institution's support arms—the Congressional Budget Office, Government Accountability Office, and Congressional Research Service—simply do not have the staffing and other resources to access or analyze the vast quantity of information in a systematic way. Congress is at a distinct disadvantage.

Although there are areas of domestic policy where the sheer volume of information presents problems, there are some important differences in the national security area. First, much of the information is collected outside the United States. Second, information related to national security is analyzed, cataloged, and stored by the defense and intelligence agencies and is often not available in the public domain (as opposed to domestic policy areas, where stakeholders, reporters, and others can get access to the information and provide Congress "outside help"). And last, a significant portion of that information is always going to be classified or sensitive and therefore may not be shared on a regular basis with Congress. Although members of Congress automatically have top security clearance, most congressional staff do not, and practical limitations are placed on sharing classified or sensitive information even with the members themselves.

In fact, through a combination of laws, report language, and interbranch understandings, the president shares some intelligence information with just the so-called Gang of Eight, a group that includes the Speaker of the House, the House minority leader, the Senate majority and minority leaders, and the chairs and ranking members of the two chambers' Intelligence Committees.[33] Gang of Eight notifications are supposed to be limited to covert operations—an area where information is held especially tightly by presidents for fear of leaks or the exposure of potentially risky activities. Such exposure could put operatives overseas in immediate mortal danger and could also be highly embarrassing, both diplomatically and politically.

One example of an operation that came to light and created political fallout is the National Security Agency surveillance program, which stirred great controversy in 2006. The NSA, an intelligence agency under the auspices of the Defense Department, was collecting information on terror suspects via wiretapping and other methods. The program's legality was dubious, and its existence was shared only with the Gang of Eight. When a few details of the program were leaked, some in Congress asserted that its existence should have been shared with a much broader range of members.[34]

In general, Congress's efforts to assert its oversight authority over covert operations have been sporadic and often thwarted. And despite the establishment of a congressional oversight regime beginning in 1979 with the creation of the House Intelligence Committee—the first systematic congressional oversight of the intelligence agencies in the nation's history—it took only a few years before Congress was again left out of the loop by the president and the CIA director regarding important covert operations.[35] In such matters, *sharing information with Congress depends on the cooperation and good faith of the president.* Congress has a great deal of difficulty locating or gaining access to information it might want in a timely fashion if the president chooses not to share it.

The result of both the political and the informational dimensions is that presidents have the upper hand, given their control of the flow of information, and the political dynamics militate strongly in favor of congressional deference in national security policy. Members of Congress do not necessarily dislike this arrangement—after all, when left out of the loop, they may be in a position to avoid accountability for botched intelligence or military ventures that bog down and may even be in a position to score political points at the president's expense.

Congress and National Security Policy: Accountability Before the Fact

Just because the president can take the initiative and determine the direction of national security policy does not mean that Congress has stood idly by. In fact, presidents are held accountable in a variety of ways in the 21st century that did not pertain prior to the 1970s.

In the '70s, Congress's push against executive overreach included angling for some influence in national security policy. The first notable effort was the War Powers Act of 1973, a reaction to presidential warmaking in Southeast Asia. In it, Congress required presidents to inform them in a timely fashion when troops were put in harm's way and put in place a mechanism by which troops would have to be withdrawn from hostilities within 90 days absent congressional approval. The first provision has been generally heeded by presidents, the second not at all, as presidents have regarded it as an unconstitutional infringement on their prerogatives.

In addition, Congress instituted the aforementioned oversight regime over covert operations, with the institution of permanent intelligence committees in both chambers. Notably, the Foreign Intelligence Surveillance Act of 1978 put in place a mechanism of required judicial approval for domestic wiretappings and other methods of eavesdropping when espionage or plans for terrorist acts are suspected.

Jack Goldsmith, a Harvard scholar and former high-ranking official in the Justice Department during the George W. Bush administration, makes the case for what are essentially before-the-fact constraints on presidential action in national security:

> Presidents used to wiretap at will in the name of national security, but now they must comply with complex criminal laws and get the approval of a secret court. Presidents used to conduct covert operations without any accountability, but now they must comply with elaborate restrictions and report all important intelligence activities to Congress in a timely way. Presidents used to have carte blanche in interpreting or ignoring international human rights law and the laws of war, but now these laws are embodied in complex regulations and criminal statutes that touch on every aspect of military and intelligence operations. Presidents used to hide information easily, but now they must take extraordinary steps to maintain records and give the public broad access to internal

documents. Quasi-independent inspectors general that were viewed as unconstitutional during the Reagan revolution are now well-established auditing and investigatory thorns in the president's side.

There are many other examples, but perhaps the best indicator of the impact of law on the presidency is that the CIA has well over one hundred lawyers, and the Department of Defense has over ten thousand, not including reservists. These lawyers—and many tens of thousands of other lawyers in other agencies—devote their days and many of their nights to ensuring that the extravagantly regulated executive branch complies with the law and with numerous forms of ex post accountability—inspector general audits, congressional investigations and queries, reporting requirements, and testimony before Congress—that influence executive behavior before the fact.[36]

It is hard to exaggerate the increase in the legal restrictions on various military actions in this era. As Goldsmith points out, the National Defense Authorization Act in 1977 was 16 pages long; in the new century, these bills are many hundreds of pages.[37] And international law has changed, too, putting in place other restrictions. At literally every stage of military action, lawyers are there to sign off on commanders' decisions. This is especially true when the armed services engage in peacekeeping, humanitarian assistance, and enforcement of economic sanctions—which is much of what is done nowadays. These situations are much more delicate, and legally appropriate actions are more circumscribed than they are in combat.

The predator drone program has gotten a great deal of attention in recent years, as President Obama has dramatically increased attacks on suspected terrorist targets in Pakistan and other places. These unmanned aircraft, directed by pilots 7,000 miles away in places like Nevada and Virginia, have the capacity to pinpoint targets and deliver lethal blows. Military lawyers literally sit with the pilots to assess the potential collateral damage, including civilian deaths, that might have an impact on the legality of a particular strike.

In the highest-profile cases, things move up the chain of command. The targeted killing of Anwar al-Awlaki, an American citizen living in Yemen who was alleged to have planned the so-called underwear bomber's efforts to blow up an airliner with 289 people on board in late 2009, was signed off by lawyers at the very highest levels of the Justice Department. Al-Awlaki was killed in September 2011 by a predator drone.

These targeted killings are controversial for another reason. A long-standing executive order makes it illegal for the United States to carry out an assassination: "*No person employed by or acting on behalf of the United States Government shall engage in, or conspire to engage in, assassination.*"[38] As a result, it is incumbent on the administration to have a legal justification for targeted killings. The Bush and Obama administrations have balked from sharing their thinking in the interest of concealing methods used in highly sensitive covert operations. But as more publicity has surrounded the drone campaign, total avoidance has become impossible. The Obama administration has leaned on the 2001 Authorization for the Use of Force Against al-Qaeda, claiming that eliminating the leadership of the group—even its offshoots almost anywhere in the world—is sufficient justification.

* * *

As we have seen, Congress cannot conduct oversight in many aspects of national security policy as easily or as thoroughly as it can in the domestic sphere.[39] The amount of information is almost too vast to easily digest and can be next to impossible to extract. Furthermore, presidents have independent constitutional authorities in national security that they do not have in the domestic realm. With modern weapons systems as they are, the commander in chief can do a great deal before anyone even has a clear picture of what happened.

But, at the same time, the system of accountability that has developed is not insignificant. It is an imperfect system, to be sure, and barely constitutes "oversight" strictly understood,[40] but it is a far cry from the 1950s and '60s, when Congress had few mechanisms in place for monitoring executive actions in war and national security before or after the fact.

CONCLUSION: WHO'S THE BOSS OF THE FEDERAL AGENCIES?

The relationship between the president and Congress was constitutionally established to invite struggle.[41] It was meant to give each political branch the leverage to challenge the other's prerogatives in order to prevent either one from abusing its power. For the most part, the relationship between the branches involves a shared and relatively balanced exercise of power. Of course, the relationship has tensions built into it. This involves wrangling over the interpretation and implementation of authorizing and appropriations laws, with the federal judiciary sometimes adjudicating disputes.

As a result, the direction of federal policy is typically determined in a tug-of-war between the two political branches. The exception is in the area of national security policy, where the president has real advantages. Congress relies on a nebulous system of what we call "accountability before the fact" for influence. In the day-today formation of policy in this realm, Congress is normally reactive to presidential initiative taking.

It is an open question which branch has more influence over the direction of federal policy in the domestic sphere. In effect, this is a fight over who runs the federal agencies who must implement public policy.

In this chapter, we looked at the "power tools" at Congress's and the president's disposal. At first blush, the president appears to have the upper hand, especially in issuing executive orders to implement broad statutory guidance. Congress simply does not have the capacity to track regularly every area in which it delegates authority. And data indicate that Congress does not do anything to nullify the overwhelming majority of executive orders.[42] Furthermore, recent trends show an increased willingness on the part of Congress to delegate. Dodd-Frank aspires to regulate the financial industry in very ambitious ways. The Affordable Care Act gives great power to the secretary of the HHS to put in place broad-ranging reforms in health care delivery. Even in the relatively narrow area of earmarking specific spending, Congress has in recent years refrained from directing federal dollars to specific districts or states, instead giving the agencies and the president more latitude in deciding on specific projects.

However, arguably the foremost expert on rulemaking and regulatory policy in the agencies, Cornelius Kerwin of American University, has a different take, which stresses the strengths Congress has in directing federal policy:

> The question of who runs the bureaucracy is by no means settled; Congress and the president have long struggled to gain the hearts and minds of [agency officials]. Both have formidable powers at their disposal to influence the course of bureaucratic decision-making. The president prepares budgets, appoints senior officials, and issues executive orders that profoundly affect how agencies manage their work. Congress is the ultimate decision maker on budgets and appointments, conducts oversight and investigations, and engages in casework on behalf of constituents. In the battle for influence over the [agencies], congressional powers are at least as substantial as those of the president. Congressional power to define an agency's mission and fix its budget is more determinative than the transitory and fragmented sources of presidential influence. Therefore, when delegating the power to interpret and prescribe law, Congress does it in the secure knowledge that it retains sufficient power and opportunity to redirect [bureaucratic decision making] that go[es] astray.[43]

Which perspective—the commonly held one that presidents have the edge or Kerwin's view of congressional advantage—is right? There is no easy answer. In fact, the direction of federal policy may be influenced differently in one area than another depending on the priorities of presidents and members of Congress. For example, at this writing in 2013, President Obama has a great deal of running room in prescribing the direction of federal policy at the elementary and secondary school level due to acquiescent congressional committee leadership. But as far as the direction of space policy and federal land management, Congress is far more assertive and influential.

The fact is that Congress does not have the resources to keep up with everything, but when key members focus or when it can pass a law requiring a new direction, it can really be the driver. Congress put a lasting mark on the direction of health care with the passage of the Affordable Care Act (while also delegating a great deal to the executive at the same time) and in food safety with the Food Safety Modernization Act of 2010, for example. And there is the case noted earlier of Senator Susan Collins almost single-handedly changing federal policy on school meals in the fall of 2011. Even a single member, if her actions are strategic enough, may have a great deal of impact.

Congress is well within its rights to push for its views after it has given the executive wide statutory latitude. Obviously, it can always pass a new law to make policy clearer. But even when the executive is working within its legislative mandate—as was the case with the Food and Nutrition Service above—members of Congress may try to affect what happens in that space. They have the tools to prevail at least some of the time. After all, the agencies have to come to Congress for money every year; it is the power of the purse that gives it the most leverage. At the end of the day, it is Congress that has the direct electoral link to the sovereign public; members feel very strongly about keeping powerful *unelected* agency officials accountable to the people.

QUESTIONS FOR DISCUSSION

1. No one doubts that the president can act unilaterally to commit troops to combat if the nation is under imminent threat. But when there is time for full debate, should Congress or the president have the right to decide whether to commit troops to battle? More generally, should Congress assert itself in the area of foreign policy and war powers? Why or why not?

2. Pick an interesting area of federal domestic policy and try to identify whether it is the president or Congress that is currently more influential.

3. Whose power tools do you think are typically more effective, the president's or Congress's? Why do you take that position?

SUGGESTIONS FOR FURTHER READING

Cooper, Joseph. "The Modern Congress." In *Congress Reconsidered,* edited by Bruce Oppenheimer and Larry Dodd, 401–436. 10th ed. Washington, DC: CQ Press, 2013.

Goldsmith, Jack L. *Power and Constraint: The Accountable Presidency After 9/11*. New York: W. W. Norton, 2012.

Howell, William G. *Power Without Persuasion*. Princeton, NJ: Princeton University Press, 2003.

Kerwin, Cornelius. *Rulemaking*. 3rd ed. Washington, DC: CQ Press, 2003.

Endnotes

1. The "toolkit" metaphor is borrowed from phraseology used by William G. Howell in *Power Without Persuasion* (Princeton, NJ: Princeton University Press, 2003).

2. Allen Schick, *The Federal Budget,* 3rd ed. (Washington, DC: Brookings Institution Press, 2007), chap. 2.

3. A good overview of the politics surrounding New Deal legislation can be found in Stephen J. Wayne's *The Legislative Presidency* (New York: Harper Row, 1978).

4. *A.L.A. Schechter Poultry Corp. v. United States,* 295 U.S. 495 (1935).

5. The beginning of the end of restraint on Congress's powers to regulate commerce was in 1937. Legal scholars point to the *West Coast Hotel Co. v. Parrish,* 300 U.S. 379 (1937), case as a key turning point.

6. The White House Office itself, housing the president's closest advisers, and the Office of Management and Budget spearhead the Executive Office of the President. Other agencies in the EOP attempt to manage complex policy areas that span several agencies, including the Council on Environmental Quality, the National Security Staff, the Office of Science and Technology Policy, and several others.

7. Independent counsels were often highly controversial, especially Lawrence Walsh, who looked into wrongdoing in the Reagan administration, and Kenneth Starr, who led investigations concerning President Clinton. Eventually, both parties agreed that it would be wise to let the law that established the office expire. This happened in 1999.

8. The classic work on this topic is Morris Fiorina's *Congress: Keystone of the Washington Establishment* (New Haven, CT: Yale University Press, 1989).

9. See Howell, *Power Without Persuasion;* Phillip J. Cooper, *By Order of the President* (Lawrence: University Press of Kansas, 2002); and Kenneth R. Mayer, *With the Stroke of a Pen* (Princeton, NJ: Princeton University Press, 2002).

10. Rob Stein and Michael Shear, "Funding Restored to Groups That Perform Abortions, Other Care," www.washingtonpost.com/wp-dyn/content/article/2009/01/23/AR2009012302814.html.

11. Cornelius Kerwin, *Rulemaking,* 3rd ed. (Washington, DC: CQ Press: 2003).

12. Many independent regulatory agencies are given the authority in law to put forth regulations without OIRA review.

13. Interview with Cory Claussen, professional staff, Senate Committee on Agriculture, December 8, 2012.

14. The authorization was subsequently lowered to less than $500 billion, and this aspect of the bailout ended up costing taxpayers very little money once the banks got on their feet. The program was expanded to assist other entities.

15. Davis Polk, "Dodd-Frank Progress Report, January 2013," www.davispolk.com/files/Publication/7191edca-f4ed-4460-a514-01ca9d3cf8b9/Presentation/PublicationAttachment/63d52126-7e7f-477a-b47c-08e8acfe145e/Jan2013_Dodd.Frank.Progress.Report.pdf.

16. Danielle Douglas and Dina ElBoghdady, "Regulatory Criticized for Delay in Finalizing 2010 Volcker Rule," *Washington Post,* October 26, 2012, A15.

17. Ben Protess, "Behind the Scenes, Some Lawmakers Lobby to Change the Volcker Rule," http://dealbook.nytimes.com/2012/09/20/behind-the-scenes-a-lawmaker-pushes-to-curb-the-volcker-rule/.

18. See www.iom.edu/Reports/2009/School-Meals-Building-Blocks-for-Healthy-Children.aspx.

19. David Rogers, "Susan Collins Triumphs in Spud Fight," *Politico,* October 18, 2011, www.politico.com/news/stories/1011/66304.html.

20. Ibid.

21. Ibid.

22. This chart shows the pre-2012 and current school lunches as developed by the Food and Nutrition Service at the Department of Agriculture: www.fns.usda.gov/cnd/Governance/Legislation/cnr_chart.pdf.

23. Robert C. Byrd, "Preserving Constitutional War Powers," *Mediterranean Quarterly* 14, no 3 (2003): 2.

24. Louis Fisher, *Presidential War Power* (Lawrence: University Press of Kansas, 1995), 1, quoting Edwin B. Firmage, "War, Declaration of," in *Encyclopedia of the American Presidency*, edited by Leonard Levy and Louis Fisher (New York: Simon & Schuster, 1994), 1573.

25. In the past couple of decades, an argument has been made in some quarters that Congress's power to declare war means that Congress has the power to recognize the existence of a war already in progress. The argument is that the commander-in-chief power and other Article II provisions were always meant to give the president the power to assess the international situation and commit the nation to war and to have Congress follow up with an official "declaration." Taking this position is Albert Jenner, "Fixing the War Powers Act," *Heritage Lectures*, no. 529 (May 22, 1995), www.heritage.org/research/nationalsecurity/hl529.cfm.

26. David Gray Adler, "The Constitution and Presidential Warmaking: The Enduring Debate," *Political Science Quarterly* 103, no. 1 (1988): 1–36.

27. Quoted in Edward Keynes, *Undeclared War* (State College: Pennsylvania State University Press, 2004), 2.

28. Quoted in ibid.

29. John Yoo, *The Powers of War and Peace* (Chicago: University of Chicago Press, 2006).

30. See *United States v. Curtiss-Wright Export Corporation* (1936).

31. Quoted in Richard Benedetto, "Remember When Partisan Politics Stopped at the Water's Edge?," *USA Today*, November 18, 2005, www.usatoday.com/news/opinion/columnist/benedetto/2005-11-18-benedetto_x.htm.

32. Quoted in *The American Experience: The Presidents,* PBS special, www.pbs.org/wgbh/amex/presidents/36_l_johnson/l_johnson_foreign.html.

33. Alfred Cumming, "Statutory Procedures Under Which Congress Is to Be Informed of U.S. Intelligence Activities, Including Covert Actions," *Congressional Research Service,* January 18, 2006.

34. Ibid., 7–8.

35. Fox Butterfield, "Casey Said to Have Failed to Follow Arms Rule," *New York Times,* April 3, 1987, http://query.nytimes.com/gst/fullpage.html?res=9B0DE1D6103DF930A35757C0A961948260.

36. Jack L. Goldsmith, "The Accountable Presidency," *New Republic,* February 1, 2010.

37. See Jack L. Goldsmith's *Power and Constraint: The Accountable Presidency After 9/11* (New York: W. W. Norton, 2010), 129.

38. Executive Order 12333, first signed by President Ronald Reagan in 1981.

39. Jennifer Kibbe, in "Congressional Oversight of Intelligence: Is the Solution Part of the Problem?," *Intelligence and National Security* 25, no. 1 (2010): 24–49, does a great job of explaining why it is so much more difficult to conduct oversight on intelligence matters given the classified nature of much of the information.

40. E-mail exchange with Dickinson College political scientist Andrew Rudalevige. See his book *The New Imperial Presidency* (Ann Arbor: University of Michigan Press, 2006).

41. On the relationship between the branches in foreign policy, see Cecil Van Meter, *Invitation to Struggle: Congress, the President, and Foreign Policy,* 4th ed. (Washington, DC: CQ Press, 1992).

42. See Howell, *Power Without Persuasion,* chap. 5.

43. See Kerwin, *Rulemaking,* 30.

The Constitution and Its Origins

By Glen Krutz and Sylvie Waskiewicz

[Reading] Outline

INTRODUCTION

The **U.S. Constitution**, see Figure 2.2.1, is one of the world's most enduring symbols of democracy. It is also the oldest, and shortest, written constitutions of the modern era still in existence. Its writing was by no means inevitable, however. Indeed, in many ways the Constitution was not the beginning but rather the culmination of American (and British) political thought about government power as well as a blueprint for the future.

It is tempting to think of the framers of the Constitution as a group of like-minded men aligned in their lofty thinking regarding rights and freedoms. This assumption makes it hard to oppose constitutional principles in modern-day politics because people admire the longevity of the Constitution and like to consider its ideals above petty partisan politics. However, the Constitution was designed largely out of necessity following the failure of the first revolutionary government, and it featured a series of pragmatic compromises among its disparate stakeholders.

FIGURE 2.2.1 Written in 1787 and amended twenty-seven times, the U.S. Constitution is a living document that has served as the basis for U.S. government for more than two hundred years. (credit: modification of work by National Archives and Records Administration)

It is therefore quite appropriate that more than 225 years later the U.S. government still requires compromise to function properly.

How did the Constitution come to be written? What compromises were needed to ensure the ratification that made it into law? This [reading] addresses these questions and also describes why the Constitution remains a living, changing document.

2.2.1 THE PRE-REVOLUTIONARY PERIOD AND THE ROOTS OF THE AMERICAN POLITICAL TRADITION

Learning Objectives

By the end of this section, you will be able to:

- Identify the origins of the core values in American political thought, including ideas regarding representational government
- Summarize Great Britain's actions leading to the American Revolution

American political ideas regarding liberty and self-government did not suddenly emerge full-blown at the moment the colonists declared their independence from Britain. The varied strands of what became the American republic had many roots, reaching far back in time and across the Atlantic Ocean to Europe. Indeed, it was not new ideas but old ones that led the colonists to revolt and form a new nation.

Political Thought in the American Colonies

The beliefs and attitudes that led to the call for independence had long been an important part of colonial life. Of all the political thinkers who influenced American beliefs about government, the most important is surely John Locke (Figure 2.2.2). The most significant contributions of Locke, a seventeenth-century English philosopher, were his ideas regarding the relationship between government and **natural rights**, which were believed to be God-given rights to life, liberty, and property.

FIGURE 2.2.2 John Locke was one of the most influential thinkers of the Enlightenment. His writings form the basis for many modern political ideas.

Locke was not the first Englishman to suggest that people had rights. The British government had recognized its duty to protect the lives, liberties, and property of English citizens long before the settling of its North American colonies. In 1215, King John signed Magna Carta—a promise to his subjects that he and future monarchs would refrain from certain actions that harmed, or had the potential to harm, the people of England. Prominent in Magna Carta's many provisions are protections for life, liberty, and property. For example, one of the document's most famous clauses promises, "No freemen shall be taken, imprisoned … or in any way destroyed … except by the lawful judgment of his peers or by the law of the land." Although it took a long time for modern ideas regarding due process to form, this clause lays the foundation for the Fifth and Sixth Amendments to the U.S. Constitution. While Magna Carta was intended to grant protections only to the English barons who were in revolt against King John in 1215, by the time of the American Revolution, English subjects, both in England and in North America, had come to regard the document as a cornerstone of liberty for men of all stations—a right that had been recognized by King John I in 1215, but the people had actually possessed long before then.

The rights protected by Magna Carta had been granted by the king, and, in theory, a future king or queen could take them away. The natural rights Locke described, however, had been granted by God and thus could never be abolished by human beings, even royal ones, or by the institutions they created.

So committed were the British to the protection of these natural rights that when the royal Stuart dynasty began to intrude upon them in the seventeenth century, Parliament removed King James II, already disliked because he was Roman Catholic, in the Glorious Revolution and invited his Protestant daughter and her husband to rule the nation. Before offering the throne to William and Mary, however, Parliament passed the English Bill of Rights in 1689. A bill of rights is a list of the liberties and protections possessed by a nation's citizens. The English Bill of

Rights, heavily influenced by Locke's ideas, enumerated the rights of English citizens and explicitly guaranteed rights to life, liberty, and property. This document would profoundly influence the U.S. Constitution and Bill of Rights.

American colonists also shared Locke's concept of property rights. According to Locke, anyone who invested labor in the *commons*—the land, forests, water, animals, and other parts of nature that were free for the taking—might take as much of these as needed, by cutting trees, for example, or building a fence around a field. The only restriction was that no one could take so much that others were deprived of their right to take from the commons as well. In the colonists' eyes, all free white males should have the right to acquire property, and once it had been acquired, government had the duty to protect it. (The rights of women remained greatly limited for many more years.)

Perhaps the most important of Locke's ideas that influenced the British settlers of North America were those regarding the origins and purpose of government. Most Europeans of the time believed the institution of monarchy had been created by God, and kings and queens had been divinely appointed to rule. Locke, however, theorized that human beings, not God, had created government. People sacrificed a small portion of their freedom and consented to be ruled in exchange for the government's protection of their lives, liberty, and property. Locke called this implicit agreement between a people and their government the **social contract**. Should government deprive people of their rights by abusing the power given to it, the contract was broken and the people were no longer bound by its terms. The people could thus withdraw their consent to obey and form another government for their protection.

The belief that government should not deprive people of their liberties and should be restricted in its power over citizens' lives was an important factor in the controversial decision by the American colonies to declare independence from England in 1776. For Locke, withdrawing consent to be ruled by an established government and forming a new one meant replacing one monarch with another. For those colonists intent on rebelling, however, it meant establishing a new nation and creating a new government, one that would be greatly limited in the power it could exercise over the people.

The desire to limit the power of government is closely related to the belief that people should govern themselves. This core tenet of American political thought was rooted in a variety of traditions. First, the British government did allow for a degree of self-government. Laws were made by Parliament, and property-owning males were allowed to vote for representatives to Parliament. Thus, Americans were accustomed to the idea of representative government from the beginning. For instance, Virginia established its House of Burgesses in 1619. Upon their arrival in North America a year later, the English Separatists who settled the Plymouth Colony, commonly known as the Pilgrims, promptly authored the Mayflower Compact, an agreement to govern themselves according to the laws created by the male voters of the colony.[1] By the eighteenth century, all the colonies had established legislatures to which men were elected to make the laws for their fellow colonists. When American colonists felt that this longstanding tradition of representative self-government was threatened by the actions of Parliament and the King, the American Revolution began.

The American Revolution

The American Revolution began when a small and vocal group of colonists became convinced the king and Parliament were abusing them and depriving them of their rights. By 1776, they had been living under the rule of the British government for more than a century, and England had long treated the thirteen colonies with a degree of benign neglect. Each colony had established its own legislature. Taxes imposed by England were low, and property ownership was more widespread than in England. People readily proclaimed their loyalty to the king. For the most part, American colonists were proud to be British citizens and had no desire to form an independent nation.

All this began to change in 1763 when the Seven Years War between Great Britain and France came to an end, and Great Britain gained control of most of the French territory in North America. The colonists had fought on behalf of Britain, and many colonists expected that after the war they would be allowed to settle on land west of the Appalachian Mountains that had been taken from France. However, their hopes were not realized. Hoping to prevent conflict with Indian tribes in the Ohio Valley, Parliament passed the Proclamation of 1763, which forbade the colonists to purchase land or settle west of the Appalachian Mountains.[2]

To pay its debts from the war and maintain the troops it left behind to protect the colonies, the British government had to take new measures to raise revenue. Among the acts passed by Parliament were laws requiring American colonists to pay British merchants with gold and silver instead of paper currency and a mandate that suspected smugglers be tried in vice-admiralty courts, without jury trials. What angered the colonists most of all, however, was the imposition of direct taxes: taxes imposed on individuals instead of on transactions.

Because the colonists had not consented to direct taxation, their primary objection was that it reduced their status as free men. The right of the people or their representatives to consent to taxation was enshrined in both Magna Carta and the English Bill of Rights. Taxes were imposed by the House of Commons, one of the two houses of the British Parliament. The North American colonists, however, were not allowed to elect representatives to that body. In their eyes, taxation by representatives they had not voted for was a denial of their rights. Members of the House of Commons and people living in England had difficulty understanding this argument. All British subjects had to obey the laws passed by Parliament, including the requirement to pay taxes. Those who were not allowed to vote, such as women and blacks, were considered to have virtual representation in the British legislature; representatives elected by those who could vote made laws on behalf of those who could not. Many colonists, however, maintained that anything except direct representation was a violation of their rights as English subjects.

The first such tax to draw the ire of colonists was the Stamp Act, passed in 1765, which required that almost all paper goods, such as diplomas, land deeds, contracts, and newspapers, have revenue stamps placed on them. The outcry was so great that the new tax was quickly withdrawn, but its repeal was soon followed by a series of other tax acts, such as the Townshend Acts (1767), which imposed taxes on many everyday objects such as glass, tea, and paint.

The taxes imposed by the Townshend Acts were as poorly received by the colonists as the Stamp Act had been. The Massachusetts legislature sent a petition to the king asking for relief from the taxes and requested that other colonies join in a boycott of British manufactured goods. British officials threatened to suspend the legislatures of colonies that engaged in a boycott and, in response to a request for help from Boston's customs collector, sent a warship to the city in 1768. A few months later, British troops arrived, and on the evening of March 5, 1770, an altercation erupted outside the customs house. Shots rang out as the soldiers fired into the crowd (Figure 2.2.3). Several people were hit; three died immediately. Britain had taxed the colonists without their consent. Now, British soldiers had taken colonists' lives.

Following this event, later known as the Boston Massacre, resistance to British rule grew, especially in the colony of Massachusetts. In December 1773, a group of Boston men boarded a ship in Boston harbor and threw its cargo

FIGURE 2.2.3 The Sons of Liberty circulated this sensationalized version of the events of March 5, 1770, in order to promote the rightness of their cause; it depicts British soldiers firing on unarmed civilians in the event that became known as the Boston Massacre. Later portrayals would more prominently feature Crispus Attucks, an African American who was one of the first to die. Eight British soldiers were tried for murder as a result of the confrontation.

(a)

(b)

FIGURE 2.2.4 Members of the modern Tea Party movement claim to represent the same spirit as their colonial forebears in the iconic lithograph *The Destruction of Tea at Boston Harbor* (a) and protest against what they perceive as government's interference with people's rights. In April 2010, members of a Tea Party Express rally on the Boston Common signed a signature wall to record their protest (b). (credit b: modification of work by Tim Pierce)

of tea, owned by the British East India Company, into the water to protest British policies, including the granting of a monopoly on tea to the British East India Company, which many colonial merchants resented.[3] This act of defiance became known as the Boston Tea Party. Today, many who do not agree with the positions of the Democratic or the Republican Party have organized themselves into an oppositional group dubbed the Tea Party (Figure 2.2.4).

In the early months of 1774, Parliament responded to this latest act of colonial defiance by passing a series of laws called the Coercive Acts, intended to punish Boston for leading resistance to British rule and to restore order in the colonies. These acts virtually abolished town meetings in Massachusetts and otherwise interfered with the colony's ability to govern itself. This assault on Massachusetts and its economy enraged people throughout the colonies, and delegates from all the colonies except Georgia formed the First Continental Congress to create a unified opposition to Great Britain. Among other things, members of the institution developed a declaration of rights and grievances.

In May 1775, delegates met again in the Second Continental Congress. By this time, war with Great Britain had already begun, following skirmishes between colonial militiamen and British troops at Lexington and Concord, Massachusetts. Congress drafted a Declaration of Causes explaining the colonies' reasons for rebellion. On July 2, 1776, Congress declared American independence from Britain and two days later signed the **Declaration of Independence**.

Drafted by Thomas Jefferson, the **Declaration of Independence** officially proclaimed the colonies' separation from Britain. In it, Jefferson eloquently laid out the reasons for rebellion. God,

FIGURE 2.2.5 The presentation of the Declaration of Independence is commemorated in a painting by John Trumbull in 1817. It was commissioned to hang in the Capitol in Washington, DC.

he wrote, had given everyone the rights of life, liberty, and the pursuit of happiness. People had created governments to protect these rights and consented to be governed by them so long as government functioned as intended. However, "whenever any Form of Government becomes destructive of these ends, it is the Right of the People to alter or to abolish it, and to institute new Government." Britain had deprived the colonists of their rights. The king had "establish[ed] … an absolute Tyranny over these States." Just as their English forebears had removed King James II from the throne in 1689, the colonists now wished to establish a new rule.

Jefferson then proceeded to list the many ways in which the British monarch had abused his power and failed in his duties to his subjects. The king, Jefferson charged, had taxed the colonists without the consent of their elected representatives, interfered with their trade, denied them the right to trial by jury, and deprived them of their right to self-government. Such intrusions on their rights could not be tolerated. With their signing of the Declaration of Independence (Figure 2.2.5), the founders of the United States committed themselves to the creation of a new kind of government.

Link to Learning

Thomas Jefferson explains in the **Declaration of Independence (http://www.openstax. org/l/29DeclarationIn)** why many colonists felt the need to form a new nation. His evocation of the natural rights of man and his list of grievances against the king also served as the model for the **Declaration of Sentiments (http://www.openstax.org/l/29DeclarationSe)** that was written in 1848 in favor of giving women in the United States rights equal to those of men. View both documents and compare.

2.2.2 THE ARTICLES OF CONFEDERATION

Learning Objectives

By the end of this section, you will be able to:

- Describe the steps taken during and after the American Revolution to create a government
- Identify the main features of the Articles of Confederation
- Describe the crises resulting from key features of the Articles of Confederation

Waging a successful war against Great Britain required that the individual colonies, now sovereign states that often distrusted one another, form a unified nation with a central government capable of directing the country's defense. Gaining recognition and aid from foreign nations would also be easier if the new United States had a national government able to borrow money and negotiate treaties. Accordingly, the Second Continental Congress called upon its delegates to create a new government strong enough to win the country's independence but not so powerful that it would deprive people of the very liberties for which they were fighting.

Putting a New Government in Place

The final draft of the **Articles of Confederation**, which formed the basis of the new nation's government, was accepted by Congress in November 1777 and submitted to the states for ratification. It would not become the law of the land until all thirteen states had approved it. Within two years, all except Maryland had done so. Maryland argued that all territory west of the Appalachians, to which some states had laid claim, should instead be held by the national government as public land for the benefit of all the states. When the last of these states, Virginia, relinquished its land claims in early 1781, Maryland approved the Articles.[4] A few months later, the British surrendered.

Americans wished their new government to be a **republic**, a regime in which the people, not a monarch, held power and elected representatives to govern according to the rule of law. Many, however, feared that a nation as large as the United States could not be ruled effectively as a republic. Many also worried that even a government of representatives elected by the people might become too powerful and overbearing. Thus, a **confederation** was created—an entity in which independent, self-governing states form a union for the purpose of acting together in areas such as defense. Fearful of replacing one oppressive national government with another, however, the framers of the Articles of Confederation created an alliance of sovereign states held together by a weak central government.

Following the Declaration of Independence, each of the thirteen states had drafted and ratified a constitution providing for a republican form of government in which political power rested in the hands of the people, although the right to vote was limited to free (white) men, and the property requirements for voting differed among the states. Each state had a governor and an elected legislature. In the new nation, the states remained free to govern their residents as they wished. The central government had authority to act in only a few areas, such as national defense, in which the states were assumed to have a common interest (and would, indeed, have to supply militias). This arrangement was meant to prevent the national government from becoming too powerful or abusing the rights of individual citizens. In the careful balance between power for the national government and liberty for the states, the Articles of Confederation favored the states.

Thus, powers given to the central government were severely limited. The Confederation Congress, formerly the Continental Congress, had the authority to exchange ambassadors and make treaties with foreign governments and Indian tribes, declare war, coin currency and borrow money, and settle disputes between states. Each state legislature appointed delegates to the Congress; these men could be recalled at any time. Regardless of its size or the number of delegates it chose to send, each state would have only one vote. Delegates could serve for no more than three consecutive years, lest a class of elite professional politicians develop. The nation would have no independent chief executive or judiciary. Nine votes were required before the central government could act, and the Articles of Confederation could be changed only by unanimous approval of all thirteen states.

What Went Wrong With the Articles?

The Articles of Confederation satisfied the desire of those in the new nation who wanted a weak central government with limited power. Ironically, however, their very success led to their undoing. It soon became apparent that, while they protected the sovereignty of the states, the Articles had created a central government too weak to function effectively.

One of the biggest problems was that the national government had no power to impose taxes. To avoid any perception of "taxation without representation," the Articles of Confederation allowed only state governments to levy taxes. To pay for its expenses, the national government had to request money from the states, which were required to provide funds in proportion to the value of the land within their borders.

The states, however, were often negligent in this duty, and the national government was underfunded. Without money, it could not pay debts owed from the Revolution and had trouble conducting foreign affairs. For example, the inability of the U.S. government to raise sufficient funds to compensate colonists who had remained loyal to Great Britain for their property losses during and after the American Revolution was one of the reasons the British refused to evacuate the land west of the Appalachians. The new nation was also unable to protect American ships from attacks by the Barbary pirates.[5] Foreign governments were also, understandably, reluctant to loan money to a nation that might never repay it because it lacked the ability to tax its citizens.

The fiscal problems of the central government meant that the currency it issued, called the Continental, was largely worthless and people were reluctant to use it. Furthermore, while the Articles of Confederation had given the national government the power to coin money, they had not prohibited the states from doing so as well. As a result, numerous state banks issued their own banknotes, which had the same problems as the Continental. People who were unfamiliar with the reputation of the banks that had issued the banknotes often refused to accept them as currency. This reluctance, together with the overwhelming debts of the states, crippled the young nation's economy.

The country's economic woes were made worse by the fact that the central government also lacked the power to impose tariffs on foreign imports or regulate interstate commerce. Thus, it was unable to prevent British merchants from flooding the U.S. market with low-priced goods after the Revolution, and American producers suffered from the competition. Compounding the problem, states often imposed tariffs on items produced by other states and otherwise interfered with their neighbors' trade.

The national government also lacked the power to raise an army or navy. Fears of a standing army in the employ of a tyrannical government had led the writers of the Articles of Confederation to leave defense largely to the states. Although the central government could declare war and agree to peace, it had to depend upon the states to provide soldiers. If state governors chose not to honor the national government's request, the country would lack an adequate defense. This was quite dangerous at a time when England and Spain still controlled large portions of North America (Table 2.2.1).

TABLE 2.2.1 The Articles of Confederation suffered from many problems that could not be easily repaired. The biggest problem was the lack of power given to the national government.

PROBLEMS WITH THE ARTICLES OF CONFEDERATION	
WEAKNESS OF THE ARTICLES OF CONFEDERATION	**WHY WAS THIS A PROBLEM?**
The national government could not impose taxes on citizens. It could only request money from the states.	Requests for money were usually not honored. As a result, the national government did not have money to pay for national defense or fulfill its other responsibilities.
The national government could not regulate foreign trade or interstate commerce.	The government could not prevent foreign countries from hurting American competitors by shipping inexpensive products to the United States. It could not prevent states from passing laws that interfered with domestic trade.
The national government could not raise an army. It had to request the states to send men.	State governments could choose not to honor Congress's request for troops. This would make it hard to defend the nation.
Each state had only one vote in Congress regardless of its size.	Populous states were less well represented.
The Articles could not be changed without a unanimous vote to do so.	Problems with the Articles could not be easily fixed.
There was no national judicial system.	Judiciaries are important enforcers of national government power.

The weaknesses of the Articles of Confederation, already recognized by many, became apparent to all as a result of an uprising of Massachusetts farmers, led by Daniel Shays. Known as Shays' Rebellion, the incident panicked the governor of Massachusetts, who called upon the national government for assistance. However, with no power to raise an army, the government had no troops at its disposal. After several months, Massachusetts crushed the uprising with the help of local militias and privately funded armies, but wealthy people were frightened by this display of unrest on the part of poor men and by similar incidents taking place in other states.[6] To find a solution and resolve problems related to commerce, members of Congress called for a revision of the Articles of Confederation.

Milestone

Shays' Rebellion: Symbol of Disorder and Impetus to Act

In the summer of 1786, farmers in western Massachusetts were heavily in debt, facing imprisonment and the loss of their lands. They owed taxes that had gone unpaid while they were away fighting the British during the Revolution. The Continental Congress had promised to pay them for their service, but the national government did not have sufficient money. Moreover, the farmers were unable to meet the onerous new tax burden Massachusetts imposed in order to pay its own debts from the Revolution.

Led by Daniel Shays (**Figure 2.2.6**), the heavily indebted farmers marched to a local courthouse demanding relief. Faced with the refusal of many Massachusetts militiamen to arrest the rebels, with whom they sympathized, Governor James Bowdoin called upon the national government for aid, but none was available. The uprising was finally brought to an end the following year by a privately funded militia after the protestors' unsuccessful attempt to raid the Springfield Armory.

FIGURE 2.2.6 This contemporary depiction of Continental Army veteran Daniel Shays (left) and Job Shattuck (right), who led an uprising of Massachusetts farmers in 1786–1787 that prompted calls for a stronger national government, appeared on the cover of *Bickerstaff's Genuine Boston Almanack for 1787*.

Were Shays and his followers justified in their attacks on the government of Massachusetts? What rights might they have sought to protect?

2.2.3 THE DEVELOPMENT OF THE CONSTITUTION

Learning Objectives

By the end of this section, you will be able to:

- Identify the conflicts present and the compromises reached in drafting the Constitution
- Summarize the core features of the structure of U.S. government under the Constitution

In 1786, Virginia and Maryland invited delegates from the other eleven states to meet in Annapolis, Maryland, for the purpose of revising the Articles of Confederation. However, only five states sent representatives. Because all thirteen states had to agree to any alteration of the Articles, the convention in Annapolis could not accomplish its goal. Two of the delegates, Alexander Hamilton and James Madison, requested that all states send delegates to a convention in Philadelphia the following year to attempt once again to revise the Articles of Confederation. All the states except Rhode Island chose delegates to send to the meeting, a total of seventy men in all, but many did not attend. Among those not in attendance were John Adams and Thomas Jefferson, both of whom were overseas representing the country as diplomats. Because the shortcomings of the Articles of Confederation proved impossible to overcome, the convention that met in Philadelphia in 1787 decided to create an entirely new government.

Points of Contention

Fifty-five delegates arrived in Philadelphia in May 1787 for the meeting that became known as the Constitutional Convention. Many wanted to strengthen the role and authority of the national government but feared creating a central government that was too powerful. They wished to preserve state autonomy, although not to a degree that prevented the states from working together collectively or made them entirely independent of the will of the national government. While seeking to protect the rights of individuals from government abuse, they nevertheless wished to create a society in which concerns for law and order did not give way in the face of demands for individual liberty. They wished to give political rights to all free men but also feared mob rule, which many felt would have been the result of Shays' Rebellion had it succeeded. Delegates from small states did not want their interests pushed aside by delegations from more populous states like Virginia. And everyone was concerned about slavery. Representatives from southern states worried that delegates from states where it had been or was being abolished might try to outlaw the institution. Those who favored a nation free of the influence of slavery feared that southerners might attempt to make it a permanent part of American society. The only decision that all could agree on was the election of George Washington, the former commander of the Continental Army and hero of the American Revolution, as the president of the convention.

The Question of Representation: Small States vs. Large States

One of the first differences among the delegates to become clear was between those from large states, such as New York and Virginia, and those who represented small states, like Delaware. When discussing the structure of the government under the new constitution, the delegates from Virginia called for a **bicameral legislature** consisting of two houses. The number of a state's representatives in each house was to be based on the state's population. In each state, representatives in the lower house would be elected by popular vote. These representatives would then select their state's representatives in the upper house from among candidates proposed by the state's legislature. Once a representative's term in the legislature had ended, the representative could not be reelected until an unspecified amount of time had passed.

Delegates from small states objected to this **Virginia Plan**. Another proposal, the **New Jersey Plan**, called for a **unicameral legislature** with one house, in which each state would have one vote. Thus, smaller states would have the same power in the national legislature as larger states. However, the larger states argued that because they had more residents, they should be allotted more legislators to represent their interests (Figure 2.2.7).

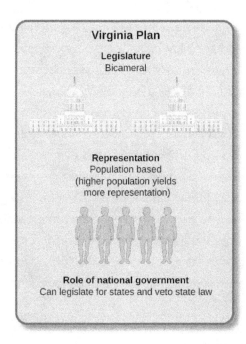

Virginia Plan

Legislature
Bicameral

Representation
Population based
(higher population yields
more representation)

Role of national government
Can legislate for states and veto state law

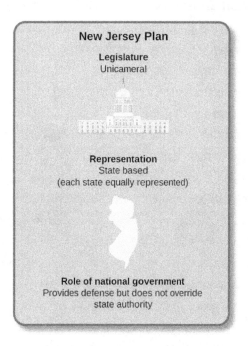

New Jersey Plan

Legislature
Unicameral

Representation
State based
(each state equally represented)

Role of national government
Provides defense but does not override
state authority

FIGURE 2.2.7 The Virginia Plan called for a two-house legislature. Representation in both houses would be based on population. A state's representatives in one house would be elected by the state's voters. These representatives would then appoint representatives to the second house from among candidates chosen by the state's legislature. The New Jersey Plan favored maintaining a one-house Congress with each state being equally represented.

Slavery and Freedom

Another fundamental division separated the states. Following the Revolution, some of the northern states had either abolished slavery or instituted plans by which slaves would gradually be emancipated. Pennsylvania, for example, had passed the Act for the Gradual Abolition of Slavery in 1780. All people born in the state to enslaved mothers after the law's passage would become indentured servants to be set free at age twenty-eight. In 1783, Massachusetts had freed all enslaved people within the state. Many Americans believed slavery was opposed to the ideals stated in the Declaration of Independence. Others felt it was inconsistent with the teachings of Christianity. Some feared for the safety of the country's white population if the number of slaves and white Americans' reliance on them increased. Although some southerners shared similar sentiments, none of the southern states had abolished slavery and none wanted the Constitution to interfere with the institution. In addition to supporting the agriculture of the South, slaves could be taxed as property and counted as population for purposes of a state's representation in the government.

Federal Supremacy vs. State Sovereignty

Perhaps the greatest division among the states split those who favored a strong national government and those who favored limiting its powers and allowing states to govern themselves in most matters. Supporters of a strong central government argued that it was necessary for the survival and efficient functioning of the new nation. Without the authority to maintain and command an army and navy, the nation could not defend itself at a time when European powers still maintained formidable empires in North America. Without the power to tax and regulate trade, the government would not have enough money to maintain the nation's defense, protect American farmers and manufacturers from foreign competition, create the infrastructure necessary for interstate commerce and communications, maintain foreign embassies, or pay federal judges and other government officials. Furthermore, other countries would be reluctant to loan money to the United States if the federal government lacked the ability to impose taxes in order to repay its debts. Besides giving more power to populous states, the Virginia Plan also favored a strong national government that would legislate for the states in many areas and would have the power to veto laws passed by state legislatures.

Others, however, feared that a strong national government might become too powerful and use its authority to oppress citizens and deprive them of their rights. They advocated a central government with sufficient authority to defend the nation but insisted that other powers be left to the states, which were believed to be better able to understand and protect the needs and interests of their residents. Such delegates approved the approach of the New Jersey Plan, which retained the unicameral Congress that had existed under the Articles of Confederation.

It gave additional power to the national government, such as the power to regulate interstate and foreign commerce and to compel states to comply with laws passed by Congress. However, states still retained a lot of power, including power over the national government. Congress, for example, could not impose taxes without the consent of the states. Furthermore, the nation's chief executive, appointed by the Congress, could be removed by Congress if state governors demanded it.

Individual Liberty vs. Social Stability

The belief that the king and Parliament had deprived colonists of their liberties had led to the Revolution, and many feared the government of the United States might one day attempt to do the same. They wanted and expected their new government to guarantee the rights of life, liberty, and property. Others believed it was more important for the national government to maintain order, and this might require it to limit personal liberty at times. All Americans, however, desired that the government not intrude upon people's rights to life, liberty, and property without reason.

Compromise and the Constitutional Design of American Government

Beginning in May 1787 and throughout the long, hot Philadelphia summer, the delegations from twelve states discussed, debated, and finally—after compromising many times—by September had worked out a new blueprint for the nation. The document they created, the U.S. Constitution, was an ingenious instrument that allayed fears of a too-powerful central government and solved the problems that had beleaguered the national government under the Articles of Confederation. For the most part, it also resolved the conflicts between small and large states, northern and southern states, and those who favored a strong federal government and those who argued for state sovereignty.

Link to Learning

The closest thing to minutes of the Constitutional Convention is the **collection of James Madison's letters and notes (http://www.openstax.org/l/29MadisonPapers)** about the proceedings in Philadelphia. Several such letters and notes may be found at the Library of Congress's American Memory project.

The Great Compromise

The Constitution consists of a preamble and seven articles. The first three articles divide the national government into three branches—Congress, the executive branch, and the federal judiciary—and describe the powers and responsibilities of each. In Article I, ten sections describe the structure of Congress, the basis for representation and the requirements for serving in Congress, the length of Congressional terms, and the powers of Congress. The national legislature created by the article reflects the compromises reached by the delegates regarding such issues as representation, slavery, and national power.

After debating at length over whether the Virginia Plan or the New Jersey Plan provided the best model for the nation's legislature, the framers of the Constitution had ultimately arrived at what is called the **Great Compromise**, suggested by Roger Sherman of Connecticut. Congress, it was decided, would consist of two chambers: the Senate and the House of Representatives. Each state, regardless of size, would have two senators, making for equal representation as in the New Jersey Plan. Representation in the House would be based on population. Senators were to be appointed by state legislatures, a variation on the Virginia Plan. Members of the House of Representatives would be popularly elected by the voters in each state. Elected members of the House would be limited to two years in office before having to seek reelection, and those appointed to the Senate by each state's political elite would serve a term of six years.

Congress was given great power, including the power to tax, maintain an army and a navy, and regulate trade and commerce. Congress had authority that the national government lacked under the Articles of Confederation. It could also coin and borrow money, grant patents and copyrights, declare war, and establish laws regulating naturalization and bankruptcy. While legislation could be proposed by either chamber of Congress, it had to pass both chambers by a majority vote before being sent to the president to be signed into law, and all bills to raise revenue had to begin in the House of Representatives. Only those men elected by the voters to represent them could impose taxes upon them. There would be no more taxation without representation.

The Three-Fifths Compromise and the Debates over Slavery

The Great Compromise that determined the structure of Congress soon led to another debate, however. When states took a census of their population for the purpose of allotting House representatives, should slaves be counted? Southern states were adamant that they should be, while delegates from northern states were vehemently opposed, arguing that representatives from southern states could not represent the interests of enslaved people. If slaves were not counted, however, southern states would have far fewer representatives in the House than northern states did. For example, if South Carolina were allotted representatives based solely on its free population, it would receive only half the number it would have received if slaves, who made up approximately 43 percent of the population, were included.[7]

The **Three-Fifths Compromise**, illustrated in Figure 2.2.8, resolved the impasse, although not in a manner that truly satisfied anyone. For purposes of Congressional apportionment, slaveholding

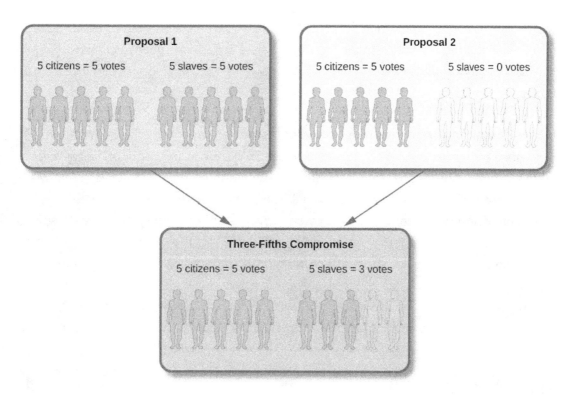

FIGURE 2.2.8 This infographic shows the methods proposed for counting slave populations and the resulting Three-Fifths Compromise.

states were allowed to count all their free population, including free African Americans and 60 percent (three-fifths) of their enslaved population. To mollify the north, the compromise also allowed counting 60 percent of a state's slave population for federal taxation, although no such taxes were ever collected. Another compromise regarding the institution of slavery granted Congress the right to impose taxes on imports in exchange for a twenty-year prohibition on laws attempting to ban the importation of slaves to the United States, which would hurt the economy of southern states more than that of northern states. Because the southern states, especially South Carolina, had made it clear they would leave the convention if abolition were attempted, no serious effort was made by the framers to abolish slavery in the new nation, even though many delegates disapproved of the institution.

Indeed, the Constitution contained two protections for slavery. Article I postponed the abolition of the foreign slave trade until 1808, and in the interim, those in slaveholding states were allowed to import as many slaves as they wished.[8] Furthermore, the Constitution placed no restrictions on the domestic slave trade, so residents of one state could still sell enslaved people to other states. Article IV of the Constitution—which, among other things, required states to return fugitives to the states where they had been charged with crimes—also prevented slaves from gaining their freedom by escaping to states where slavery had been abolished. Clause 3 of Article IV (known as the fugitive slave clause) allowed slave owners to reclaim their human property in the states where slaves had fled.[9]

Separation of Powers and Checks and Balances

Although debates over slavery and representation in Congress occupied many at the convention, the chief concern was the challenge of increasing the authority of the national government while ensuring that it did not become too powerful. The framers resolved this problem through a **separation of powers**, dividing the national government into three separate branches and assigning different responsibilities to each one, as shown in Figure 2.2.9. They also created a system of **checks and balances** by giving each of three branches of government the power to restrict the actions of the others, thus requiring them to work together.

Congress was given the power to make laws, but the executive branch, consisting of the president and the vice president, and the federal judiciary, notably the Supreme Court, were

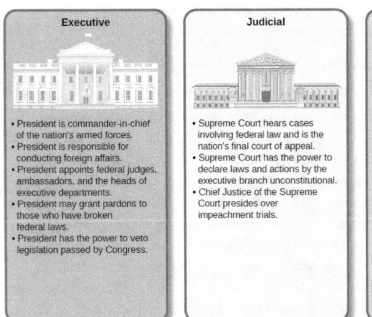

Executive
- President is commander-in-chief of the nation's armed forces.
- President is responsible for conducting foreign affairs.
- President appoints federal judges, ambassadors, and the heads of executive departments.
- President may grant pardons to those who have broken federal laws.
- President has the power to veto legislation passed by Congress.

Judicial
- Supreme Court hears cases involving federal law and is the nation's final court of appeal.
- Supreme Court has the power to declare laws and actions by the executive branch unconstitutional.
- Chief Justice of the Supreme Court presides over impeachment trials.

Legislative
- Congress has the power to pass legislation.
- Congress may declare war.
- Senate has the power to ratify treaties signed by the president.
- Senate must give its consent to the president's appointment of federal judges, ambassadors, and the heads of executive departments.
- Congress may impeach the president and remove him or her from office.
- Congress may establish the number of Supreme Court justices and regulate the Court's jurisdiction.

FIGURE 2.2.9 To prevent the national government, or any one group within it, from becoming too powerful, the Constitution divided the government into three branches with different powers. No branch could function without the cooperation of the others, and each branch could restrict the powers of the others.

created to, respectively, enforce laws and try cases arising under federal law. Neither of these branches had existed under the Articles of Confederation. Thus, Congress can pass laws, but its power to do so can be checked by the president, who can **veto** potential legislation so that it cannot become a law. Later, in the 1803 case of *Marbury* v. *Madison*, the U.S. Supreme Court established its own authority to rule on the constitutionality of laws, a process called judicial review.

Other examples of checks and balances include the ability of Congress to limit the president's veto. Should the president veto a bill passed by both houses of Congress, the bill is returned to Congress to be voted on again. If the bill passes both the House of Representatives and the Senate with a two-thirds vote in its favor, it becomes law even though the president has refused to sign it.

Congress is also able to limit the president's power as commander-in-chief of the armed forces by refusing to declare war or provide funds for the military. To date, the Congress has never refused a president's request for a declaration of war. The president must also seek the advice and consent of the Senate before appointing members of the Supreme Court and ambassadors, and the Senate must approve the ratification of all treaties signed by the president. Congress may even remove the president from office. To do this, both chambers of Congress must work together. The House of Representatives impeaches the president by bringing formal charges against him or her, and the Senate tries the case in a proceeding overseen by the Chief Justice of the Supreme Court. The president is removed from office if found guilty.

According to political scientist Richard Neustadt, the system of separation of powers and checks and balances does not so much allow one part of government to control another as it encourages the branches to cooperate. Instead of a true separation of powers, the Constitutional Convention "created a government of separated institutions *sharing* powers."[10] For example, knowing the president can veto a law he or she disapproves, Congress will attempt to draft a bill that addresses the president's concerns before sending it to the White House for signing. Similarly, knowing that Congress can override a veto, the president will use this power sparingly.

Federal Power vs. State Power

The strongest guarantee that the power of the national government would be restricted and the states would retain a degree of sovereignty was the framers' creation of a federal system of government. In a **federal system**, power is divided between the federal (or national) government and the state governments. Great or explicit powers, called **enumerated powers**, were granted to the federal government to declare war, impose taxes, coin and regulate currency, regulate foreign and interstate commerce, raise and maintain an army and a navy, maintain a post office, make treaties with foreign nations and with Native American tribes, and make laws regulating the naturalization of immigrants.

(a)   (b)

FIGURE 2.2.10 Reserve powers allow the states to pass intrastate legislation, such as laws on commerce, drug use, and marriage (a). However, sometimes judicial rulings at the federal level may supersede such legislation, as happened in *Obergefell* v. *Hodges* (2015), the recent Supreme Court case regarding marriage equality (b). (credit a: modification of work by Damian Gadal; credit b: modification of work by Ludovic Bertron)

All powers not expressly given to the national government, however, were intended to be exercised by the states. These powers are known as **reserved powers** (Figure 2.2.10). Thus, states remained free to pass laws regarding such things as intrastate commerce (commerce within the borders of a state) and marriage. Some powers, such as the right to levy taxes, were given to both the state and federal governments. Both the states and the federal government have a chief executive to enforce the laws (a governor and the president, respectively) and a system of courts.

Although the states retained a considerable degree of sovereignty, the **supremacy clause** in Article VI of the Constitution proclaimed that the Constitution, laws passed by Congress, and treaties made by the federal government were "the supreme Law of the Land." In the event of a conflict between the states and the national government, the national government would triumph. Furthermore, although the federal government was to be limited to those powers enumerated in the Constitution, Article I provided for the expansion of Congressional powers if needed. The "necessary and proper" clause of Article I provides that Congress may "make all Laws which shall be necessary and proper for carrying into Execution the foregoing [enumerated] Powers, and all other Powers vested by this Constitution in the Government of the United States, or in any Department or Officer thereof."

The Constitution also gave the federal government control over all "Territory or other Property belonging to the United States." This would prove problematic when, as the United States expanded westward and population growth led to an increase in the power of the northern states in Congress, the federal government sought to restrict the expansion of slavery into newly acquired territories.

Link to Learning

A growing number of institutes and study centers focus on the Constitution and the founding of the republic. Examples such as the **Institute for the American Constitutional Heritage (http://www.openstax.org/l/29Heritage)** and the **Bill of Rights Institute (http://www. openstax.org/l/29BillRightsIns)** have informative public websites with documents and videos. Another example is the **National Constitution Center (http://www.openstax. org/l/29NatlConstCtr)** that also holds programs related to aspects of the enduring U.S. Constitution.

2.2.4 THE RATIFICATION OF THE CONSTITUTION

Learning Objectives

By the end of this section, you will be able to:

- Identify the steps required to ratify the Constitution
- Describe arguments the framers raised in support of a strong national government and counterpoints raised by the Anti-Federalists

On September 17, 1787, the delegates to the Constitutional Convention in Philadelphia voted to approve the document they had drafted over the course of many months. Some did not support it, but the majority did. Before it could become the law of the land, however, the Constitution faced another hurdle. It had to be ratified by the states.

The Ratification Process

Article VII, the final article of the Constitution, required that before the Constitution could become law and a new government could form, the document had to be ratified by nine of the thirteen states. Eleven days after the delegates at the Philadelphia convention approved it, copies of the Constitution were sent to each of the states, which were to hold ratifying conventions to either accept or reject it.

This approach to ratification was an unusual one. Since the authority inherent in the Articles of Confederation and the Confederation Congress had rested on the consent of the states, changes to the nation's government should also have been ratified by the state legislatures. Instead, by calling upon state legislatures to hold ratification conventions to approve the Constitution, the framers avoided asking the legislators to approve a document that would require them to give up a degree of their own power. The men attending the ratification conventions would be delegates elected by their neighbors to represent their interests. They were not being asked to relinquish their power; in fact, they were being asked to place limits upon the power of their state legislators, whom they may not have elected in the first place. Finally, because the new nation was to be a republic in which power was held by the people through their elected representatives, it was considered appropriate to leave the ultimate acceptance or rejection of the Constitution to the nation's citizens. If convention delegates, who were chosen by popular vote, approved it, then the new government could rightly claim that it ruled with the consent of the people.

The greatest sticking point when it came to ratification, as it had been at the Constitutional Convention itself, was the relative power of the state and federal governments. The framers of the Constitution believed that without the ability to maintain and command an army and navy, impose taxes, and force the states to comply with laws passed by Congress, the young nation would not survive for very long. But many people resisted increasing the powers of the national government at the expense of the states. Virginia's Patrick Henry, for example, feared that the newly created office of president would place excessive power in the hands of one man. He also disapproved of the federal government's new ability to tax its citizens. This right, Henry believed, should remain with the states.

Other delegates, such as Edmund Randolph of Virginia, disapproved of the Constitution because it created a new federal judicial system. Their fear was that the federal courts would be too far away from where those who were tried lived. State courts were located closer to the homes of both plaintiffs and defendants, and it was believed that judges and juries in state courts could better understand the actions of those who appeared before them. In response to these fears, the federal government created federal courts in each of the states as well as in Maine, which was then part of Massachusetts, and Kentucky, which was part of Virginia.[11]

Perhaps the greatest source of dissatisfaction with the Constitution was that it did not guarantee protection of individual liberties. State governments had given jury trials to residents charged with violating the law and allowed their residents to possess weapons for their protection. Some had practiced religious tolerance as well. The Constitution, however, did not contain reassurances that the federal government would do so. Although it provided for habeas corpus and prohibited both a religious test for holding office and granting noble titles, some citizens feared the loss of their traditional rights and the violation of their liberties. This led many of the Constitution's opponents to call for a bill of rights and the refusal to ratify the document without one. The lack of a bill of rights was especially problematic in Virginia, as the Virginia Declaration of Rights was the most extensive rights-granting document among the states. The promise that a bill of rights would be drafted for the Constitution persuaded delegates in many states to support ratification.[12]

Insider Perspective

Thomas Jefferson on the Bill of Rights

John Adams and Thomas Jefferson carried on a lively correspondence regarding the ratification of the Constitution. In the following excerpt (reproduced as written) from a letter dated March 15, 1789, after the Constitution had been ratified by nine states but before it had been approved by all thirteen, Jefferson reiterates his previously expressed concerns that a bill of rights to protect citizens' freedoms was necessary and should be added to the Constitution:

> "In the arguments in favor of a declaration of rights, … I am happy to find that on the whole you are a friend to this amendment. The Declaration of rights is like all other human blessings alloyed with some inconveniences, and not accomplishing fully it's object. But the good in this instance vastly overweighs the evil. … This instrument [the Constitution] forms us into one state as to certain objects, and gives us a legislative & executive body for these objects. It should therefore guard us against their abuses of power. … Experience proves the inefficacy of a bill of rights. True. But tho it is not absolutely efficacious under all circumstances, it is of great potency always, and rarely inefficacious. … There is a remarkeable difference between the … Inconveniences which attend a Declaration of rights, & those which attend the want of it. … The inconveniences of the want of a Declaration are permanent, afflicting & irreparable: they are in constant progression from bad to worse."[13]

What were some of the inconveniences of not having a bill of rights that Jefferson mentioned? Why did he decide in favor of having one?

It was clear how some states would vote. Smaller states, like Delaware, favored the Constitution. Equal representation in the Senate would give them a degree of equality with the larger states, and a strong national government with an army at its command would be better able to defend them than their state militias could. Larger states, however, had significant power to lose. They did not believe they needed the federal government to defend them and disliked the prospect of having to provide tax money to support the new government. Thus, from the very beginning, the supporters of the Constitution feared that New York, Massachusetts, Pennsylvania, and Virginia would refuse to ratify it. That would mean all nine of the remaining states would have to, and Rhode Island, the smallest state, was unlikely to do so. It had not even sent delegates to the convention in Philadelphia. And even if it joined the other states in ratifying the document and the requisite nine votes were cast, the new nation would not be secure without its largest, wealthiest, and most populous states as members of the union.

The Ratification Campaign

On the question of ratification, citizens quickly separated into two groups: Federalists and Anti-Federalists. The **Federalists** supported it. They tended to be among the elite members of society—wealthy and well-educated landowners, businessmen, and former military commanders who believed a strong government would be better for both national defense and economic growth. A national currency, which the federal government had the power to create, would ease business transactions. The ability of the federal government to regulate trade and place tariffs on imports would protect merchants from foreign competition. Furthermore, the power to collect taxes would allow the national government to fund internal improvements like roads, which would also help businessmen. Support for the Federalists was especially strong in New England.

Opponents of ratification were called **Anti-Federalists**. Anti-Federalists feared the power of the national government and believed state legislatures, with which they had more contact, could better protect their freedoms. Although some Anti-Federalists, like Patrick Henry, were wealthy, most distrusted the elite and believed a strong federal government would favor the rich over those of "the middling sort." This was certainly the fear of Melancton Smith, a New York merchant and landowner, who believed that power should rest in the hands of small, landowning farmers of average wealth who "are more temperate, of better morals and less ambitious than the great."[14] Even members of the social elite, like Henry, feared that the centralization of power would lead to the creation of a political aristocracy, to the detriment of state sovereignty and individual liberty.

Related to these concerns were fears that the strong central government Federalists advocated for would levy taxes on farmers and planters, who lacked the hard currency needed to pay them. Many also believed Congress would impose tariffs on foreign imports that would make American agricultural products less welcome in Europe and in European colonies in the western hemisphere. For these reasons, Anti-Federalist sentiment was especially strong in the South.

Some Anti-Federalists also believed that the large federal republic that the Constitution would create could not work as intended. Americans had long believed that virtue was necessary in a nation where people governed themselves (i.e., the ability to put self-interest and petty concerns aside for the good of the larger community). In small republics, similarities among members of the community would naturally lead them to the same positions and make it easier for those in power to understand the needs of their neighbors. In a larger republic, one that encompassed nearly the entire Eastern Seaboard and ran west to the Appalachian Mountains, people would lack such a strong commonality of interests.[15]

Likewise, Anti-Federalists argued, the diversity of religion tolerated by the Constitution would prevent the formation of a political community with shared values and interests. The Constitution contained no provisions for government support of churches or of religious education, and Article VI explicitly forbade the use of religious tests to determine eligibility for public office. This caused many, like Henry Abbot of North Carolina, to fear that government would be placed in the hands of "pagans … and Mahometans [Muslims]."[16]

It is difficult to determine how many people were Federalists and how many were Anti-Federalists in 1787. The Federalists won the day, but they may not have been in the majority. First, the Federalist position tended to win support among businessmen, large farmers, and, in the South, plantation owners. These people tended to live along the Eastern Seaboard. In 1787, most of the states were divided into voting districts in a manner that gave more votes to the eastern part of the state than to the western part.[17] Thus, in some states, like Virginia and South Carolina, small farmers who may have favored the Anti-Federalist position were unable to elect as many delegates to state ratification conventions as those who lived in the east. Small settlements may also have lacked the funds to send delegates to the convention.[18]

In all the states, educated men authored pamphlets and published essays and cartoons arguing either for or against ratification (Figure 2.2.11). Although many writers supported each position, it is the Federalist essays that are now best known. The arguments these authors put forth, along

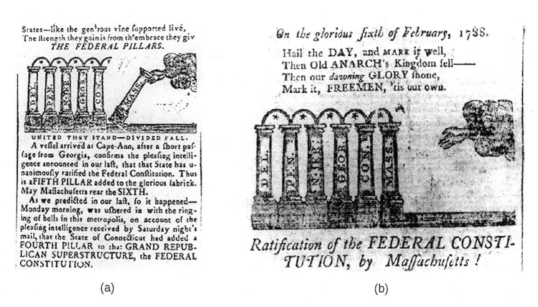

(a)   (b)

FIGURE 2.2.11 This *Massachusetts Sentinel* cartoon (a) encourages the state's voters to join Georgia and neighboring Connecticut in ratifying the Constitution. Less than a month later, on February 6, 1788, Massachusetts became the sixth member of the newly formed federal union (b).

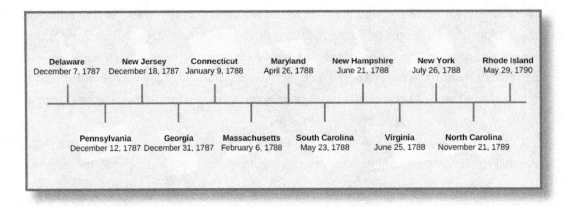

FIGURE 2.2.12 This timeline shows the order in which states ratified the new Constitution. Small states that would benefit from the protection of a larger union ratified the Constitution fairly quickly, such as Delaware and Connecticut. Larger, more populous states like Virginia and New York took longer. The last state to ratify was Rhode Island, a state that had always proven reluctant to act alongside the others.

with explicit guarantees that amendments would be added to protect individual liberties, helped to sway delegates to ratification conventions in many states.

For obvious reasons, smaller, less populous states favored the Constitution and the protection of a strong federal government. As shown in Figure 2.2.12, Delaware and New Jersey ratified the document within a few months after it was sent to them for approval in 1787. Connecticut ratified it early in 1788. Some of the larger states, such as Pennsylvania and Massachusetts, also voted in favor of the new government. New Hampshire became the ninth state to ratify the Constitution in the summer of 1788.

Although the Constitution went into effect following ratification by New Hampshire, four states still remained outside the newly formed union. Two were the wealthy, populous states of Virginia and New York. In Virginia, James Madison's active support and the intercession of George Washington, who wrote letters to the convention, changed the minds of many. Some who had initially opposed the Constitution, such as Edmund Randolph, were persuaded that the creation of a strong union was necessary for the country's survival and changed their position. Other Virginia delegates were swayed by the promise that a bill of rights similar to the Virginia Declaration of Rights would be added after the Constitution was ratified. On June 25, 1788, Virginia became the tenth state to grant its approval.

The approval of New York was the last major hurdle. Facing considerable opposition to the Constitution in that state, Alexander Hamilton, James Madison, and John Jay wrote a series of essays, beginning in 1787, arguing for a strong federal government and support of the Constitution (Figure 2.2.13). Later compiled as *The Federalist* and now known as **The Federalist Papers**, these eighty-five essays were originally published in newspapers in New York and other states under the name of Publius, a supporter of the Roman Republic.

The essays addressed a variety of issues that troubled citizens. For example, in *Federalist* No. 51, attributed to James Madison (Figure 2.2.14), the author assured readers they did not need to fear that the national government would grow too powerful. The federal system, in which power was divided between the national and state governments, and the division of authority within the federal government into separate branches would prevent any one part of the government from becoming too strong. Furthermore, tyranny could not arise in a government in which "the legislature necessarily predominates." Finally, the desire of office holders in each branch of government to exercise the powers given to them, described as "personal motives," would encourage them to limit any attempt by the other branches to overstep their authority. According to Madison, "Ambition must be made to counteract ambition."

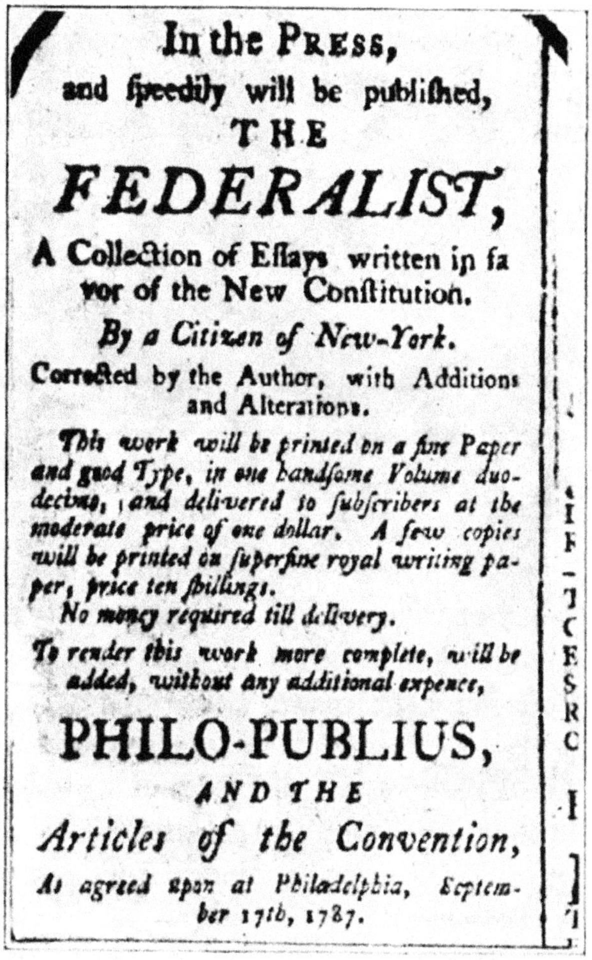

In the Preſs,
and ſpeedily will be publiſhed,
THE
FEDERALIST,
A Collection of Eſſays written in fa
vor of the New Conſtitution.
By a Citizen of New-York.
Corrected by the Author, with Additions
and Alterations.
This work will be printed on a fine Paper and good Type, in one handſome Volume duodecimo, and delivered to ſubſcribers at the moderate price of one dollar. A few copies will be printed on ſuperfine royal writing paper, price ten ſhillings.
No money required till delivery.
To render this work more complete, will be added, without any additional expence,
PHILO-PUBLIUS,
AND THE
Articles of the Convention,
As agreed upon at Philadelphia, September 17th, 1787.

FIGURE 2.2.13 From 1787 to 1788, Alexander Hamilton, James Madison, and John Jay authored a series of essays intended to convince Americans, especially New Yorkers, to support the new Constitution. These essays, which originally appeared in newspapers, were collected and published together under the title *The Federalist* in 1788. They are now known as *The Federalist Papers*.

Other essays countered different criticisms made of the Constitution and echoed the argument in favor of a strong national government. In *Federalist* No. 35, for example, Hamilton (Figure 2.2.14) argued that people's interests could in fact be represented by men who were not their neighbors. Indeed, Hamilton asked rhetorically, would American citizens best be served

(a)   (b)

FIGURE 2.2.14 James Madison (a) played a vital role in the formation of the Constitution. He was an important participant in the Constitutional Convention and authored many of *The Federalist Papers*. Despite the fact that he did not believe that a Bill of Rights was necessary, he wrote one in order to allay the fears of those who believed the federal government was too powerful. He also served as Thomas Jefferson's vice president and was elected president himself in 1808. Alexander Hamilton (b) was one of the greatest political minds of the early United States. He authored the majority of *The Federalist Papers* and served as Secretary of the Treasury in George Washington's administration.

by a representative "whose observation does not travel beyond the circle of his neighbors and his acquaintances" or by someone with more extensive knowledge of the world? To those who argued that a merchant and land-owning elite would come to dominate Congress, Hamilton countered that the majority of men currently sitting in New York's state senate and assembly were landowners of moderate wealth and that artisans usually chose merchants, "their natural patron[s] and friend[s]," to represent them. An aristocracy would not arise, and if it did, its members would have been chosen by lesser men. Similarly, Jay reminded New Yorkers in *Federalist* No. 2 that union had been the goal of Americans since the time of the Revolution. A desire for union was natural among people of such "similar sentiments" who "were united to each other by the strongest ties," and the government proposed by the Constitution was the best means of achieving that union.

Objections that an elite group of wealthy and educated bankers, businessmen, and large landowners would come to dominate the nation's politics were also addressed by Madison in *Federalist* No. 10. Americans need not fear the power of factions or special interests, he argued, for the republic was too big and the interests of its people too diverse to allow the development of large, powerful political parties. Likewise, elected representatives, who were expected to "possess the most attractive merit," would protect the government from being controlled by "an unjust and interested [biased in favor of their own interests] majority."

For those who worried that the president might indeed grow too ambitious or king-like, Hamilton, in *Federalist* No. 68, provided assurance that placing the leadership of the country in the hands of one person was not dangerous. Electors from each state would select the president. Because these men would be members of a "transient" body called together only for the purpose of choosing the president and would meet in separate deliberations in each state, they would be free of corruption and beyond the influence of the "heats and ferments" of the voters. Indeed, Hamilton argued in *Federalist* No. 70, instead of being afraid that the president would become a tyrant, Americans should realize that it was easier to control one person than it was to control many. Furthermore, one person could also act with an "energy" that Congress did not possess. Making decisions alone, the president could decide what actions should be taken faster than could Congress, whose deliberations, because of its size, were necessarily slow. At times, the "decision, activity, secrecy, and dispatch" of the chief executive might be necessary.

Link to Learning

The Library of Congress has *The Federalist Papers (http://www.openstax.org/l/29FedPapers)* on their website. The Anti-Federalists also produced a body of writings, less extensive than *The Federalists Papers*, which argued against the ratification of the Constitution. However, these were not written by one small group of men as *The Federalist Papers* had been. A collection of the writings that are unofficially called **The Anti-Federalist Papers (http://www.openstax. org/l/29AntiFedPapers)** is also available online.

The arguments of the Federalists were persuasive, but whether they actually succeeded in changing the minds of New Yorkers is unclear. Once Virginia ratified the Constitution on June 25, 1788, New York realized that it had little choice but to do so as well. If it did not ratify the Constitution, it would be the last large state that had not joined the union. Thus, on July 26, 1788, the majority of delegates to New York's ratification convention voted to accept the Constitution. A year later, North Carolina became the twelfth state to approve. Alone and realizing it could not hope to survive on its own, Rhode Island became the last state to ratify, nearly two years after New York had done so.

Finding a Middle Ground

Term Limits

One of the objections raised to the Constitution's new government was that it did not set term limits for members of Congress or the president. Those who opposed a strong central government argued that this failure could allow a handful of powerful men to gain control of the nation and rule it for as long as they wished. Although the framers did not anticipate the idea of career politicians, those who supported the Constitution argued that reelecting the president and reappointing senators by state legislatures would create a body of experienced men who could better guide the country through crises. A president who did not prove to be a good leader would be voted out of office instead of being reelected. In fact, presidents long followed George Washington's example and limited themselves to two terms. Only in 1951, after Franklin Roosevelt had been elected four times, was the Twenty-Second Amendment passed to restrict the presidency to two terms.

Are term limits a good idea? Should they have originally been included in the Constitution? Why or why not? Are there times when term limits might not be good?

2.2.5 CONSTITUTIONAL CHANGE

Learning Objectives

By the end of this section, you will be able to:

- Describe how the Constitution can be formally amended
- Explain the contents and significance of the Bill of Rights
- Discuss the importance of the Thirteenth, Fourteenth, Fifteenth, and Nineteenth Amendments

A major problem with the Articles of Confederation had been the nation's inability to change them without the unanimous consent of all the states. The framers learned this lesson well. One of the strengths they built into the Constitution was the ability to amend it to meet the nation's needs, reflect the changing times, and address concerns or structural elements they had not anticipated.

The Amendment Process

Since ratification in 1789, the Constitution has been amended only twenty-seven times. The first ten amendments were added in 1791. Responding to charges by Anti-Federalists that the Constitution made the national government too powerful and provided no protections for the rights of individuals, the newly elected federal government tackled the issue of guaranteeing liberties for American citizens. James Madison, a member of Congress from Virginia, took the lead in drafting nineteen potential changes to the Constitution.

Madison followed the procedure outlined in Article V that says amendments can originate from one of two sources. First, they can be proposed by Congress. Then, they must be approved by a two-thirds majority in both the House and the Senate before being sent to the states for potential ratification. States have two ways to ratify or defeat a proposed amendment. First, if three-quarters of state legislatures vote to approve an amendment, it becomes part of the Constitution. Second, if three-quarters of state-ratifying conventions support the amendment, it is ratified. A second method of proposal of an amendment allows for the petitioning of Congress by the states: Upon receiving such petitions from two-thirds of the states, Congress must call a convention for the purpose of proposing amendments, which would then be forwarded to the states for ratification by the required three-quarters. All the current constitutional amendments were created using the first method of proposal (via Congress).

Having drafted nineteen proposed amendments, Madison submitted them to Congress. Only twelve were approved by two-thirds of both the Senate and the House of Representatives and sent to the states for ratification. Of these, only ten were accepted by three-quarters of the state legislatures. In 1791, these first ten amendments were added to the Constitution and became known as the **Bill of Rights**.

The ability to change the Constitution has made it a flexible, living document that can respond to the nation's changing needs and has helped it remain in effect for more than 225 years. At the same time, the framers made amending the document sufficiently difficult that it has not been changed repeatedly; only seventeen amendments have been added since the ratification of the first ten (one of these, the Twenty-Seventh Amendment, was among Madison's rejected nine proposals).

Key Constitutional Changes

The Bill of Rights was intended to quiet the fears of Anti-Federalists that the Constitution did not adequately protect individual liberties and thus encourage their support of the new national government. Many of these first ten amendments were based on provisions of the English Bill of Rights and the Virginia Declaration of Rights. For example, the right to bear arms for protection (Second Amendment), the right not to have to provide shelter and provision for soldiers in peacetime (Third Amendment), the right to a trial by jury (Sixth and Seventh Amendments), and protection from excessive fines and from cruel and unusual punishment (Eighth Amendment) are taken from the English Bill of Rights. The Fifth Amendment, which requires among other things that people cannot be deprived of their life, liberty, or property except by a legal proceeding, was also greatly influenced by English law as well as the protections granted to Virginians in the Virginia Declaration of Rights.

Link to Learning

Learn more about the formal **process of amending the Constitution (http://www.openstax. org/l/29AmendProcess)** and view exhibits related to the passage of specific amendments at the National Archives website.

Other liberties, however, do not derive from British precedents. The protections for religion, speech, the press, and assembly that are granted by the First Amendment did not exist under English law. (The right to petition the government did, however.) The prohibition in the First Amendment against the establishment of an official church by the federal government differed significantly from both English precedent and the practice of several states that had official churches. The Fourth Amendment, which protects Americans from unwarranted search and seizure of their property, was also new.

The Ninth and Tenth Amendments were intended to provide yet another assurance that people's rights would be protected and that the federal government would not become too powerful. The Ninth Amendment guarantees that liberties extend beyond those described in the preceding documents. This was an important acknowledgment that the protected rights were extensive, and the government should not attempt to interfere with them. The Supreme Court, for example, has held that the Ninth Amendment protects the right to privacy even though none of the preceding amendments explicitly mentions this right. The Tenth Amendment, one of the first submitted to the states for ratification, ensures that states possess all powers not explicitly assigned to the federal government by the Constitution. This guarantee protects states' reserved powers to regulate such things as marriage, divorce, and intrastate transportation and commerce, and to pass laws affecting education and public health and safety.

Of the later amendments only one, the Twenty-First, repealed another amendment, the Eighteenth, which had prohibited the manufacture, import, export, distribution, transportation, and sale of alcoholic beverages. Other amendments rectify problems that have arisen over the years or that reflect changing times. For example, the Seventeenth Amendment, ratified in 1913, gave voters the right to directly elect U.S. senators. The Twentieth Amendment, which was ratified in 1933 during the Great Depression, moved the date of the presidential inauguration from March to January. In a time of crisis, like a severe economic depression, the president needed to take office almost immediately after being elected, and modern transportation allowed the new president to travel to the nation's capital quicker than before. The Twenty-Second Amendment, added in 1955, limits the president to two terms in office, and the Twenty-Seventh Amendment, first submitted for ratification in 1789, regulates the implementation of laws regarding salary increases or decreases for members of Congress.

Of the remaining amendments, four are of especially great significance. The Thirteenth, Fourteenth, and Fifteenth Amendments, ratified at the end of the Civil War, changed the lives of African Americans who had been held in slavery. The Thirteenth Amendment abolished slavery in the United States. The Fourteenth Amendment granted citizenship to African Americans and equal protection under the law regardless of race or color. It also prohibited states from depriving their residents of life, liberty, or property without a legal proceeding. Over the years, the Fourteenth Amendment has been used to require states to protect most of the same federal freedoms granted by the Bill of Rights.

The Fifteenth and Nineteenth Amendments extended the right to vote. The Constitution had given states the power to set voting requirements, but the states had used this authority to deny women the right to vote. Most states before the 1830s had also used this authority to deny suffrage to property-less men and often to African American men as well. When states began to change property requirements for voters in the 1830s, many that had allowed free, property-owning African American men to vote restricted the suffrage to white men. The Fifteenth Amendment gave men the right to vote regardless of race or color, but women were still prohibited from voting in most states. After many years of campaigns for suffrage, as shown in Figure 2.2.15, the Nineteenth Amendment finally gave women the right to vote in 1920.

FIGURE 2.2.15 Suffragists encourage Ohio men to support votes for women. Before the Nineteenth Amendment was added to the Constitution in 1920, only a few western states such as Wyoming gave women the right to vote. These women seem to be attracting a primarily female audience to hear their cause.

Subsequent amendments further extended the suffrage. The Twenty-Third Amendment (1961) allowed residents of Washington, DC to vote for the president. The Twenty-Fourth Amendment (1964) abolished the use of poll taxes. Many southern states had used a poll tax, a tax placed on voting, to prevent poor African Americans from voting. Thus, the states could circumvent the Fifteenth Amendment; they argued that they were denying African American men and women the right to vote not because of their race but because of their inability to pay the tax. The last great extension of the suffrage occurred in 1971 in the midst of the Vietnam War. The Twenty-Sixth Amendment reduced the voting age from twenty-one to eighteen. Many people had complained that the young men who were fighting in Vietnam should have the right to vote for or against those making decisions that might literally mean life or death for them. Many other amendments have been proposed over the years, including an amendment to guarantee equal rights to women, but all have failed.

Get Connected!

Guaranteeing Your First Amendment Rights

The liberties of U.S. citizens are protected by the Bill of Rights, but potential or perceived threats to these freedoms arise constantly. This is especially true regarding First Amendment rights. Read about some of these threats at the **American Civil Liberties Union (ACLU) (https://openstax.org/l/29AmCivLU)** website and let people know how you feel about these issues.

What issue regarding First Amendment protections causes you the most concern?

Endnotes

1. Nathaniel Philbrick. 2006. *Mayflower: A Story of Courage, Community, and War*. New York: Penguin, 41.
2. François Furstenberg. 2008. "The Significance of the Trans-Appalachian Frontier in Atlantic History," *The American Historical Review* 113 (3): 654.
3. Bernhard Knollenberg. 1975. *Growth of the American Revolution: 1766–1775*. New York: Free Press, 95–96.
4. Stuart Bruchey. 1990. Enterprise: *The Dynamic Economy of a Free People*. Cambridge, MA: Harvard University Press, 223.
5. Joseph J. Ellis. 2015. *The Quartet: Orchestrating the Second American Revolution, 1783–1789*. New York: Knopf, 92.

6. David P. Szatmary. 1980. *Shays' Rebellion: The Making of an Agrarian Insurrection.* Amherst, MA: University of Massachusetts Press, 84–86, 102–104.

7. U.S. Department of Commerce. Bureau of the Census. 1790. *Statistical Abstract of the United States.* Washington, DC: Department of Commerce.

8. U.S. Const. art. I, § 9.

9. U.S. Const. art. IV, § 2.

10. R. E. Neustadt. 1960. *Presidential Power and the Politics of Leadership.* New York: Wiley, 33.

11. Pauline Maier. 2010. Ratification: *The People Debate the Constitution, 1787–1788.* New York: Simon & Schuster, 464.

12. Maier, *Ratification*, 431.

13. Letter from Thomas Jefferson to James Madison, March 15, 1789, https://www.gwu.edu/~ffcp/exhibit/p7/p7_1text.html.

14. Isaac Krannick. 1999. "The Great National Discussion: The Discourse of Politics in 1787." *In What Did the Constitution Mean to Early Americans?* ed. Edward Countryman. Boston: Bedford/St. Martins, 52.

15. Krannick, *Great National Discussion*, 42–43.

16. Krannick, *Great National Discussion*, 42.

17. Evelyn C. Fink and William H. Riker. 1989. "The Strategy of Ratification." In *The Federalist Papers and the New Institutionalism*, eds. Bernard Grofman and Donald Wittman. New York: Agathon, 229.

18. Fink and Riker, *Strategy of Ratification*, 221.

19. "Charlotte Forten Grimké House," National Park Service, https://www.nps.gov/places/the-charlotte-forten-grimke-house.htm (June 1, 2021).

20. "Nine Poems by Charlotte Forten Grimké," Beltway Poetry Quarterly, https://www.beltwaypoetry.com/grimke-charlotte-forten/ (June 1, 2021).

Federalism and American Political Development

By Cal Jillson

Focus Questions: from reading to thinking

Q1 How did the meanings of the terms *federal* and *federalism* change over the course of the founding and early national periods?

Q2 What powers and responsibilities did the U.S. Constitution give the national government in relation to the states and to the states in relation to the national government?

Q3 How did the expansion and integration of the American economy shape the balance of governmental power and authority within the federal system?

Q4 What fiscal and political forces led to the change in American federalism called "devolution"?

Q5 Have the complexities of the twenty-first century rendered our government essentially national, or do state and local governments still have important roles to play?

THE CONSTITUTION TODAY

If Marijuana is Illegal, Why are They Selling It in California?

Article VI: "This Constitution, and the laws of the United States which shall be made in pursuance thereof … shall be the supreme law of the land."

Tenth Amendment: "The powers not delegated to the United States by the Constitution, nor prohibited by it to the states, are reserved to the states respectively, or to the people."

In 1970 the Congress passed and the president signed the Controlled Substances Act (CSA). The CSA declared marijuana, first made illegal in federal law in 1937, to be a Schedule I drug with a "high potential for abuse" and no legitimate medical use. The CSA is federal law to this day; yet new claims regarding the medical benefits of marijuana led California to enact a medical marijuana law in 1996. By 2017 medical marijuana was legal in twenty-five states and D.C. (Alaska, Arizona, Arkansas, California, Colorado, Connecticut, Delaware, Florida, Hawaii, Illinois, Maine, Maryland, Massachusetts, Michigan, Minnesota, Montana, Nevada, New Hampshire, New Jersey, New Mexico, North Dakota, Oregon, Rhode Island, Washington, and Vermont) and the Obama administration had instructed federal law enforcement officials not to enforce the CSA in those states. However, when the number of pot shops in California proliferated beyond apparent medical needs, federal authorities cracked down. By 2017, six states, California, Colorado, Massachusetts, Oregon, Nevada, and Washington, upped the ante when citizen referenda approved marijuana use by any citizen over 21. Can federal and state laws conflict like this and, when they do, is not federal law supposed to prevail over state law? Yes, well usually, but occasionally federalism, the topic of this [reading], is messier than we would like.

The question of the relative priority of federal versus state law plagued the Founders during the Constitutional Convention, was one of the central issues over which ratification was fought, and has surfaced time and again throughout American history. In the 1860s we fought a bloody Civil War over just this issue—national versus state authority within the federal system.

For most of American history, the claims of state officials that federal officials construed their powers too broadly and thereby infringed on the state powers protected by the Tenth Amendment were taken seriously in the federal courts. All of that changed during the "Great Depression," in 1937 to be exact. President Franklin Roosevelt moved aggressively to deal with the depression, but the Supreme Court resisted, striking down major parts of his agenda. FDR responded by trying to "pack" the court with new and more compliant members. The court blinked, almost wholly abandoning its traditional role of limiting government regulation of the economy in favor of a focus on civil rights and liberties. The federal government initiated expansive social programs and an aggressive regulatory agenda. Only in the mid-1980s did the court begin to challenge federal powers, but only occasionally on the basis of the Tenth Amendment.

How then can states push back against unwelcome actions by the federal government? One option is through nullification, the idea that states can render federal laws null and void within their boundaries if they believe the laws are unconstitutional—meaning touching matters beyond the scope of the Congress's enumerated powers. To understand this claim we must distinguish between formal and informal nullification. Formal nullification would involve a state government declaring an act of Congress void and the federal courts upholding that claim. The federal courts would have to declare that the federal action was an unconstitutional violation of the "reserved rights" of the states under the Tenth Amendment. The Supreme Court has done so only twice in the last half century. In the most notable case, *Printz v. U.S.*, the court struck down a provision of the Brady Handgun Violence Protection Act for requiring state officials to conduct background checks on persons seeking to buy a handgun.

Informal nullification, as with the case of medical marijuana or the broader marijuana use approved by Colorado and Washington, is more common and is well within the American traditions of political bargaining, popular democracy, and federalism. Informal nullification occurs in a variety of ways, most involving state and public reluctance to comply with a particular federal statute. State legislatures may pass contrary laws or decline to enforce federal mandates and public opinion and action might demonstrate an unwillingness to comply. If state authorities do not challenge federal authority directly, or do so carefully, federal authorities may react to the opposition by withdrawing the act or at least limiting enforcement.

FEDERALISM AND AMERICAN POLITICAL DEVELOPMENT

This [reading] completes our discussion of the origins of American political ideals and institutions and serves as a transition to our treatment of contemporary American politics. In this [reading] we explore the origins of the American federal system and ask how the federal structure has affected and been affected by political development and change within the broader American society.

TABLE 2.3.1 Strengths and Weaknesses of Federalism

STRENGTHS	WEAKNESSES
Limits concentrated national power	Leaves state power vulnerable
Encourages innovation by the states	Complex overlapping responsibilities
Encourages pluralism and citizen involvement	Lack of uniformity
National minorities may be subnational majorities	Encourages race to the bottom

A federal system divides political power and responsibility between national and subnational levels of government.[1] We describe how the nature of American federalism and the balance of power within it have evolved over time to address new issues and problems in a rapidly growing, increasingly complex, national and now international environment.

The Founders knew that the structure and character of the American government would affect the path of the nation's development. That is why they were so concerned about what kind of government they were creating: national or federal. Just as the Founders used separation of powers and checks and balances to allocate and limit executive, legislative, and judicial functions within the national government, they used federalism to allocate and limit political power and responsibility between levels of government. Some among the founding and later generations always wanted more power and initiative at the national level, others always wanted less. The struggle between and among national and state actors for the power and resources to define and address the dominant issues of American political life has been and remains the drama of American federalism.

As we shall see, twenty-first-century American federalism involves a complicated array of authorities and actors. The nation now spans a continent and contains more than 320 million citizens. These citizens are served, at most recent count, by 90,107 governments within the federal system. There is, of course, only one national government. There are fifty state governments. Within the states are 3,031 county governments, 19,519 municipalities, 16,360 towns and townships, 12,880 school districts, and 38,266 special districts that deliver all manner of services.[2] As you read this [reading] think about the tremendous growth and change that our nation has undergone over the course of its history. From small colonies scattered along the Atlantic seaboard, the U.S. is now a global economic and military powerhouse. Is the "social contract" that the founding generation struck and wrote into the Constitution still in force today? Has that social contract changed and, if so, when? How did the Constitution adapt to permit and even facilitate the evolution of our federal political structure? How healthy is contemporary American federalism and what are the system's prospects for effective governance in the twenty-first century?

Q1   How did the meanings of the terms *federal* and *federalism* change over the course of the founding and early national periods?

THE ORIGINAL MEANING OF FEDERALISM

Federalism is a very old idea. The word *federalism* and several closely related terms including *federal*, and *confederation* are drawn from the Latin root *foedus*, which means "treaty, compact, or covenant." The idea that people can establish lasting compacts or covenants among themselves by discussion and consent has been central to American political thought and development. Before the first Pilgrim stepped onto Plymouth Rock, the entire *Mayflower* company approved the famous Mayflower Compact to define the kind of society and government that they would have.

The great difficulty involved in thinking about government as resting on the ideas of compact or covenant is the obvious fragility of such an arrangement. Political scientist Samuel Beer remarked that, "Among the consequences of thinking of federal government as based on a contract was

Benjamin Franklin created this image of the separated serpent to convince his fellow colonists to unite, warning them to "Join or Die."

Library of Congress

the idea of secession, 'the idea of simply breaking a disagreeable contract whenever any pretext of bad faith on the part of any other party arose.'"[3]

Nonetheless, the best thinking of their day told the Founders that governments over large territories had to take one of two forms. One was a consolidated or **unitary government** like the empires of the ancient world and the monarchies of Europe. These centralized states were subject to the will of one man or woman who could wield his or her power both offensively and defensively. The other was a **confederation** of smaller republics. The confederal solution left the individual republics fully sovereign, fully in control of their own domestic affairs, but pledged to coordinate their foreign affairs and to assist each other if attacked. Not surprisingly, confederations, including our own Articles of Confederation, proved to be weak and unstable in times of crisis.[4]

What made the choice between consolidation and confederation seem so stark was the idea of sovereignty—that in any political system, ultimate or final political authority must rest somewhere specific. In English history, disagreement about whether the king or Parliament was sovereign resulted in almost fifty years of civil war between 1640 and 1688. In the American case, it seemed that sovereignty had to be located either in a national government or in individual states that might then confederate together. The Articles of Confederation allocated specific modest powers to the Confederation Congress, but unambiguously left sovereignty with the individual states. Article II read: "Each state retains its sovereignty, Freedom and independence, and every Power, Jurisdiction and right, which is not by this confederation expressly delegated to the United States, in Congress assembled." The powerful idea that several governments might operate in the same space and in relation to the same citizens if each was limited in its authority and jurisdiction was not yet widely understood or accepted.

The Constitutional Convention of 1787 set aside familiar names (confederation) and outdated assumptions (sovereignty) and let the problem that they were trying to solve guide their thinking in new directions.[5] Initially, James Madison and the supporters of the Virginia Plan called for a powerful national government capable of overriding the states where necessary. Madison's opponents rallied behind the New Jersey Plan's demand that the national government be grounded on the sovereignty of the states. Eventually, the Convention came to understand, if only vaguely, that neither old model applied well in the new nation and that a new understanding of federalism was required.

Q2 What powers and responsibilities did the U.S. Constitution give the national government in relation to the states and to the states in relation to the national government?

FEDERALISM IN THE CONSTITUTION

The Founders' most fundamental insight was that the apparent choice between a consolidated national government and a loose confederation of sovereign states was false. The ideas of constitutionalism and limited government laid open the possibility that within a single territory there might be two sets of governments and two sets of public officials assigned clear and specific responsibilities and powers through written constitutions.[6]

If political power derived from the people, why should the people cede sovereignty either to a consolidated national government or to loosely confederated sovereign states? James Madison gave the classic answer to this question in Federalist Number 51 [...]. Madison explained: "In the compound republic of America, the power surrendered by the people is first divided between two distinct governments, and then the portion allotted to each is subdivided among distinct and separate departments. Hence, a double security arises to the rights of the people." After this double security is in place, the Federalist concluded, "Every thing beyond this, must be left to the prudence and firmness of the people; who, as they will hold the scales in their own hands, it is to be hoped, will always take care to preserve the constitutional equilibrium between the General and the State Governments."[7]

The Constitution gave certain powers to the national government, barred the states from making policy in certain areas, offered them guarantees and assurances in other areas, and left still other areas open to the authority of both national and state governments. Despite Madison's assurances that the constitutional equilibrium between the national and state governments would be maintained by a watchful people, only occasionally has federalism been the target of popular tumult, as with the modern "Tea Party" movement. More commonly, the Congress, the Supreme

Court, and ever-watchful state and local officials have shaped American federalism. In fact, the American political system has been involved in one of its periodic reassessments of the balance of power and authority within the federal system since the mid-1990s.[8]

Enumerated, Implied, and Inherent Powers

James Madison arrived at the Constitutional Convention determined to strengthen the national government. The Virginia Plan envisioned a national Congress with both a broad grant of legislative authority and the right to review, amend, or reject acts of the several state legislatures. This strong national federalism, in which the states would play a decidedly secondary role, was rejected in favor of a national Congress wielding specifically listed or enumerated powers. The nationalists' disappointment was assuaged somewhat by the Convention's adoption of the **supremacy clause** in Article VI. Article VI read in part: "This Constitution, and the laws of the United States which shall be made in pursuance thereof; and all treaties made, or which shall be made, under the authority of the United States, shall be the supreme law of the land; and the judges in every state shall be bound thereby; anything in the Constitution or laws of any State to the contrary notwithstanding." Moreover, all state officials were required to take an oath "to support this Constitution."

The enumerated powers of Congress are laid out in Article I, section 8, of the U.S. Constitution. Article I, section 8, lists seventeen enumerated powers, including the powers to tax, to regulate commerce and coinage, to declare war, and to raise armies and navies. In theory, Congress is limited to making law and policy within its areas of enumerated power. But other language in the Constitution seems to give Congress **implied powers** that go beyond its specifically enumerated powers. The closing paragraph of Article I, section 8, grants Congress the power to "make all laws which shall be necessary and proper for carrying into execution" its enumerated powers. The "necessary and proper" clause, frequently referred to as the "elastic clause," suggests that Congress has a general authority beyond and in addition to its enumerated powers.

If the enumerated powers are fairly specific, and implied powers are somewhat broader but still must be a means to achieve enumerated purposes, the idea of inherent powers is only loosely related to specific constitutional provisions. Both Congress and the Supreme Court have accepted the idea, especially relating to the president and foreign affairs, that nationhood entails the right and necessity, without reference to specific language in the Constitution, to deal with other nations from a footing equal to theirs. In fact, these **inherent powers** of nationhood were what the Declaration of Independence referred to when it announced to the world: "That these United Colonies are, and of Right ought to be Free and Independent States; that … they have full Power to levy War, conclude Peace, contract Alliances, establish Commerce, and to do all other Acts and Things which Independent States may of right do."

One example of presidential initiative, taken in threatening circumstances, but with no narrow constitutional authorization, will suffice to clarify the nature of inherent powers. Early in 1861 President Lincoln took several steps in the immediate wake of the secession of the southern states, including calling up additional troops and spending substantial sums of money, even though Congress was not in session and had not previously authorized these actions. When critics complained Lincoln simply asked, "Was it possible to lose the nation and yet preserve the Constitution?" Lincoln assumed that the answer was "no" and that his actions required no further justification.

Concurrent Powers

The idea of **concurrent powers** was central to the Founders' conception of a complex republic in which national and state governments exercise dual sovereignty. Dual sovereignty suggests that in some fields, such as the power to tax and borrow, to regulate commerce, to establish courts, and to build roads and highways, the national and state governments have concurrent powers. Both levels of the federal system are authorized to act in these and similar areas of law and policy. Your tax bill is a good example of a concurrent power. In all but seven states citizens must fill out income tax returns for both the national and state levels (and sometimes the local level, too).

Powers Denied to the National Government

Article I, section 9, of the Constitution denied certain powers to the national government. Congress was forbidden to suspend normal legal processes except in cases of rebellion or grave public danger, to favor the commerce or ports of one state over another, to expend money unless lawfully appropriated, and to grant titles of nobility. Other limitations on national power have been added to the Constitution by amendment, but students should notice that this is a brief paragraph.

Powers Reserved to the States

In a course on American government, like this one, students often miss, [...] how important the states are and have always been. The fundamental logic of American federalism is that the states possess complete power over matters not delegated to the national government and not denied them by the U.S. Constitution or by their own state constitutions. As Madison explained in Federalist Number 39, the jurisdiction of the Congress "extends to certain enumerated objects only, and leaves to the several States a residuary and inviolable sovereignty over all other objects."[9] Nonetheless, widespread concern that the new national government might encroach upon the powers of the states and the rights of their citizens led many to demand that protections be added to the Constitution itself. The first Congress initiated a process that led to adoption of ten amendments to the Constitution—the Bill of Rights—in 1791. The Tenth Amendment reads as follows: "The powers not delegated to the United States by the Constitution, nor prohibited by it to the states, are reserved to the states respectively, or to the people."

Joseph Zimmerman has usefully divided the **reserved powers** of the states into three categories: "the police power, provision of services to citizens, … and creation and control of local governments."[10] The "police power" covers regulation of individual and corporate activities in order to protect and enhance public health, welfare, safety, morals, and convenience. States also provide services such as police and fire protection, road construction, and education. Finally, local governments are created and regulated by the states.

Powers Denied to State Governments

The Founders wanted to be very sure that the problems experienced under the Articles of Confederation, where individual states had antagonized dangerous foreign powers and tried to create economic advantages for their own citizens to the detriment of citizens of other states, were not repeated. Article I, section 10, of the U.S. Constitution forbids the states to enter into treaties or alliances either with each other or with foreign powers, to keep their own armies or navies, or to engage in war unless actually invaded. Foreign and military policy belongs to the

When President Obama sought to loosen immigration restrictions by executive order, a broad coalition of conservative, mostly Republican-led, states sued in the federal courts to stop him. Here, Congressman Ruben Gallego (D-AZ), center, and Dolores Huerta, long-time union and Hispanic activist, rally before the Supreme Court in favor of Obama's policies.
AP Photo/CQ Roll Call

national government. States are also forbidden to coin their own money, impair contracts, or tax imports or exports.

Federal Obligations to the States

The U.S. Constitution makes a series of explicit promises to the states. Most of these are found in Article IV, sections 3 and 4, and in Article V. The states are promised that their boundaries and their equal representation in the Senate will not be changed without their consent and that their republican governments will be protected from invasion and, at their request, from domestic violence.

Relations among the States

Article IV, sections 1 and 2, of the U.S. Constitution deal with interstate relations. Provisions require the states to respect each other's civil acts, deal fairly with each other's citizens, and return suspected criminals who flee from one state into another.

Full Faith and Credit. Article IV, section 1, of the U.S. Constitution requires that "Full faith and credit shall be given in each state to the public acts, records, and judicial proceedings of every other state." Stated most directly, "public acts are the civil statutes enacted by the state legislatures. Records are documents such as deeds, mortgages, and wills. Judicial proceedings are final civil court proceedings."[11] Through this simple provision, the Founders largely succeeded in creating a national legal system requiring the states to recognize and respect each other's legal acts and findings. Nonetheless, over the course of American history, social issues such as religious toleration, slavery, and, most recently, the decision by some states to permit gay marriage, have strained reciprocity and cooperation between the states.

Privileges and Immunities. Article IV, section 2, of the U.S. Constitution declares that "The citizens of each state shall be entitled to all privileges and immunities of citizens in the several states." The classic statement of the reasoning behind the privileges and immunities language was delivered by the Supreme Count in the 1869 case of ***Paul v. Virginia***. The court explained that citizens visiting, working, or conducting business in other states have "the same freedom possessed by the citizens of those States in the acquisition and enjoyment of property and in the pursuit of happiness; and it secures them the equal protection of the laws."

Extradition. Article IV, section 2, provides for a legal process called **extradition**: "A person charged in any state with treason, felony, or other crime, who shall flee from justice, and be found in another state, shall on demand of the executive authority of the state from which he fled, be delivered up, to be removed to the state having jurisdiction of the Crime."

Fundamentally, the Constitution left the states in charge of their own internal police and gave the national government responsibility for military and foreign policy. Yet, the Constitution also sought to lower trade and regulatory barriers among the several state economies to create a national economy, an American free trade zone, that would stretch from Maine to Georgia and from the Atlantic coast to the farthest edge of western settlement. Not surprisingly, the boundary line between the national government's supremacy within its areas of constitutional responsibility and the states' reserve powers has been fuzzy, contested, and shifting over the course of American history. In fact, it is fair to say that the principal point of tension in thinking about American federalism is how to balance federal power, grounded in the elastic clause and the supremacy clause, and the powers reserved to the individual states by the Tenth Amendment. As we shall see, these tensions arose early and remain with us today.[12]

DUAL FEDERALISM AND ITS CHALLENGERS

The view of American federalism that held sway from the founding period through the first third of the twentieth century was dual federalism. **Dual federalism**, often referred to as layer-cake federalism, sees the nation and the several states as sovereign within their areas of constitutional responsibility, but with little policy overlap between them. During the nation's early history and, to a lesser extent, throughout the nation's history, dual federalism had two challengers, one a nation-centered federalism and the other a state-centered federalism.[13] The national vision of federalism was championed by a long series of American statesmen including Alexander Hamilton, Chief Justice John Marshall, Senator Henry Clay, and President Abraham Lincoln. The fundamental idea was that the nation preexisted the states and in fact called the states into existence in June of 1776 when the Continental Congress instructed the colonies to sever ties to England.

Q3   How did the expansion and integration of the American economy shape the balance of governmental power and authority within the federal system?

A second set of American statesmen took a different view. Thomas Jefferson, John C. Calhoun, the South's great antebellum political theorist, and President Jefferson Davis of the Confederate States of America all believed that the states preexisted the nation and created it by compact among themselves. On this state-centered vision of federalism, the original parties to the compact, that is, the individual states, could secede from the Union if the national government violated the compact by encroaching upon the sovereign prerogatives of the states. Short of secession, states could nullify, or declare unenforceable, federal laws they believed fell outside Congress's Article II, section 8, enumerated powers.

The nation-centered and state-centered visions of federalism fought on even terms through the early decades of the country's history. However, as the industrial economy of New England outstripped the agrarian economy of the South during the 1840s and 1850s, state-centered federalism became increasingly isolated and strident. When Abraham Lincoln was elected president in 1860, the South seceded and two visions of American federalism faced off on the battlefields of the Civil War.[14]

Chief Justice John Marshall and National Federalism. As early as 1791, a federal court declared a Rhode Island state law unconstitutional, and in 1803 Chief Justice John Marshall, in the famous case of **Marbury v. Madison,** declared a section of an act of Congress, the Judiciary Act of 1789, to be unconstitutional. The broad result of the *Marbury* decision was to establish the Supreme Court as the final arbiter of what is and is not constitutional, and, hence, of the meaning, shape, and boundaries of American federalism.

The importance of the Supreme Court's role as arbiter of the meaning of the Constitution was highlighted by the Court's 1819 ruling in **McCulloch v. Maryland**. The issue in McCulloch, whether Congress could legitimately charter a bank, permitted the court to interpret the powers of Congress broadly and to limit state interference with them. No power to establish a bank appeared among the enumerated powers of Congress, so opponents of the bank, arguing from the state-centered or compact vision of federalism, denied

John Marshall, Chief Justice of the U.S. Supreme Court from 1801 to 1835, established the judiciary as a co-equal branch of the national government.
The Granger Collection, New York

that Congress had the power to create a bank at all. Chief Justice Marshall, writing from the nation-centered vision, rested the right of the Congress to establish and administer a bank on the "necessary and proper" clause. Marshall noted that Congress's enumerated powers include the power "to coin money" and "regulate the value thereof." He argued that the bank was an "appropriate," though perhaps not an "indispensable," means to this end. Marshall's classic interpretation of the "necessary and proper" clause made this point as follows: "Let the end be legitimate, let it be within the scope of the Constitution, and all means which are appropriate which are plainly adapted to the end, which are not prohibited, but consistent with the letter and spirit of the Constitution, are constitutional." This expansive interpretation of national power came at the expense of the Tenth Amendment "reserved powers" of the states.

A third decision completed Chief Justice Marshall's attempt to embed the nation-centered vision of federalism in the Constitution. The 1824 case of **Gibbons v. Ogden** dealt with the regulation of interstate commerce, that is, commerce conducted across state lines. While the court's interpretation of the commerce clause may seem arcane, even boring, it has been absolutely central to the expansion of congressional power from Chief Justice John Marshall's day to our own day. In fact, the broad interpretation of Congress's commerce power, just as much as the necessary and proper clause, has fueled and legitimated the expansion of national power in our federal system.

The issue in *Gibbons* was whether a steamship company operating in a single state was in interstate commerce and subject to the regulatory powers of the Congress. Advocates of the state-centered vision said no. Marshall, writing for the majority, held that the Congress's power to regulate interstate commerce applied to navigation, even in a single state, if any of the passengers or goods being carried on the steamship were engaged in a "continuous journey" that found or would find them in interstate commerce. Clearly, this was a very expansive ruling because it is almost inconceivable that not a single person or piece of cargo on such a steamship had been or would later be in interstate commerce. These decisions laid the foundation for the triumph of national federalism, though it would be another century before the structure was fully built. In the meantime, Marshall's opponents would have their century-long day in the sun.

Struggling Toward Democracy

In a letter to William B. Giles on December 6, 1825, Thomas Jefferson wrote, "I see, as you do, and with the deepest affliction, the rapid strides with which the federal branch of our government is advancing toward the usurpation of all the rights reserved to the States."

What do you think?

- In what areas, if any, do you think the states' ability to govern is being threatened by the federal government?
- Does the increased size of the country now compared to the founding make the role of the federal government more or less important?

Chief Justice Roger Taney and the States. Upon John Marshall's death in 1835, President Andrew Jackson named Roger B. Taney to be the new chief justice, an office he held until 1863. Chief

Justice Taney was a strong advocate of state-centered federalism and of a limited national government. A stronger advocate still was South Carolina senator John C. Calhoun. Senator Calhoun, convinced that the South was threatened by an overbearing northern majority, proposed "the doctrine of the **concurrent majority**," whereby each major region would have the right to veto national laws that threatened their fundamental interests. If the South was denied such security, Calhoun argued that the sovereign states could nullify illegitimate national laws and, as a last resort, secede from the Union. These ideas are occasionally still heard.

Chief Justice Taney's most infamous opinion was **Dred Scott v. Sandford** in 1857. Taney held that Congress had no right to prohibit a slave owner from taking his property, even his human property, into any state in the Union, even a free state, and holding that slave as property. The next year, in the Illinois Senate election of 1858, Senator Stephen A. Douglas argued that the deep American commitment to "popular sovereignty" meant that the citizens of individual states should be able to vote for or against slavery. Douglas's opponent, then a little-known former congressman named Abraham Lincoln, argued for the right of the national government to limit slavery to those states where it currently existed. Lincoln lost.

Roger Taney, author of the Dred Scott decision, is often seen as the Supreme Court's most infamous Chief Justice.
The Granger Collection, New York

The strong arguments by Taney and Douglas in favor of an expansive view of states' rights and the state-centered federalism helped set the stage for the Civil War. Northern opinion mobilized against the expansion of slavery and Lincoln rode that mobilization to the presidency in the election of 1860. The South seceded, the North resisted, and America went to war with itself over the nature of its federal Union.

FROM DUAL FEDERALISM TO COOPERATIVE FEDERALISM

Although the idea of the Constitution as a compact from which states might secede was a casualty of the Civil War, the idea of states' rights—a large and secure place for the states in the federal system—certainly was not. Congress did little to regulate state and local affairs until the Great Depression seemed to demand change in the broad character and basic structure of American federalism. After the 1930s American federalism was better described as cooperative federalism than as dual federalism.

The defining aspects of **cooperative federalism**, or marble-cake federalism as it is often called to highlight the sharing or mixing of national and state responsibility, have been nicely described by political scientist David Walker. Walker made two key points that distinguish cooperative federalism from dual federalism. In cooperative federalism, national, state, and local officials share "responsibilities for virtually all functions," and these "officials are not adversaries. They are colleagues."[15] Over time, however, concern about the national government's dominance of the federal system, usually by attaching mandates to federal funds provided to states and communities, has became a growing concern.

The Industrialization and Urbanization of America

Social change in America between the elections of Abraham Lincoln in 1860 and Franklin Roosevelt in 1932 was massive. During this period, the nation went from one mostly of small towns and isolated farms to one of burgeoning cities and large-scale industry. More important, the nation was bound ever more tightly into a web of commerce and communication that seemed to demand tending above the levels of states and communities. As the web of commerce expanded over the course of the nineteenth century and into the twentieth century, debate raged over the reach of congressional power channeled through the Constitution's commerce clause.

Consider two related developments: the rise of railroads and the telegraph. Prior to the arrival of railroads and the telegraph, businesses were local or at most regional. The size of a business was determined by the distance over which finished products could be distributed efficiently by wagon, barge, or boat. After the telegraph made it possible to order and advertise

---

Pro & Con

The Continuing Relevance of States' Rights

The language of the U.S. Constitution is ambiguous about the relative power of the national and state governments. Although Article VI suggests national supremacy ("This Constitution, and the laws of the United States which shall be made in pursuance thereof ... shall be the supreme law of the land"), the powers granted to Congress are enumerated rather than general. Moreover, the Tenth Amendment, adopted as part of the Bill of Rights in 1791, reads: "The powers not delegated to the United States by the Constitution, nor prohibited to it by the states, are reserved to the states respectively, or to the people."

Prior to the Civil War most discussions of the rights of the states in the new Union revolved around the ideas of nullification and secession. **Nullification** was the idea that a state could suspend within its borders the operation of an act of the national government with which it

(Continued)

disagreed. **Secession** was the idea that a state might actually withdraw from the Union if it disagreed deeply with the general pattern of policy activity of the federal government.

Although the Civil War destroyed both nullification and secession as practical ideas within the American political system, the broader idea of states' rights retained its importance. Some now believe that the fights against the racism and poverty of the 1960s and 1970s, important though they were at the time, left behind programs that no longer work and a federal government too large and intrusive for the needs of the twenty-first century. Therefore, many, mostly conservatives, believe that federal money and authority should be transferred back to the states, closer to the problems that need to be solved and to the people in the best position to know how to solve them.

Some others, mostly liberals, worry that the old states' rights arguments for the virtues of local control will once again be used by powerful local majorities to ignore the needs of weaker local minorities and that, as in the past, the most vulnerable (women, blacks, gays) will be among the first to suffer. The modern opponents of states' rights claim that fairness and justice require that national standards be set and maintained, not just in the obvious area of equal rights for minorities and women, but also in such diverse areas as health, welfare, and education. Absent such standards, they believe, some states will do much less than others to assist their neediest citizens.

When President Obama and Democrat majorities in Congress passed Obamacare, Democrats across the nation cheered. When the Supreme Court upheld Obamacare but declared that the states could not be required to implement it, conservatives did not know whether to cheer or cry. Although there are principled reasons to stand for states' rights or national uniformity, there is also a long national tradition that the party that dominates Washington is comfortable with uniformity while the opposition party looks for partial victories in friendly states.[16]

What do you think?

- What are the pros and cons of allowing each state to decide how they want to go on critical issues like health care, legalization of marijuana, abortion, guns, prayer in schools, and other hotly debated issues?
- Why might liberals or conservatives have conflicting views of state–federal powers depending on the policy issue?

PRO	CON
State differences are real	Natural standards for justice are critical
Problems should be addressed close to home	Many problems require national coordination
States' rights no longer about secession	Local minorities are still vulnerable

over long distances and railroads made it possible to deliver products quickly over long distances, businesses expanded rapidly. By the last decades of the nineteenth century, huge monopolies or trusts in basic service and product lines like banking, railroads, communications, steel, oil, and sugar dominated the nation's business landscape.

How could states, let alone localities, control and regulate a railroad that stretched across half a dozen states, or a steel, sugar, or tobacco trust that did business in every state in the Union? They simply could not. Yet, the Supreme Court declared in **U.S. v. E.C. Knight** (1895) that Congress's power to regulate interstate commerce did not reach manufacturing or production, only the transportation of goods across state lines. Hence, as the twentieth century dawned, the nation's largest businesses were beyond the reach of congressional and state regulation and control.

Knowing that changes are needed is not the same thing as knowing what changes are needed, much less knowing how to get political agreement to adopt and implement a particular set of changes. President Theodore Roosevelt threatened "trust busting" to encourage large private sector actors to accept more federal oversight. Future president Woodrow Wilson, still president of Princeton in 1908, urged a broader dynamic view of federalism. His *Constitutional Government in the United States* argued that the principles and institutions of government must adapt to serve an evolving society: "The question of the relation of the States to the federal government is a cardinal question of our constitutional system. ... It cannot, indeed, be settled by the opinion of any one generation, because it is a question of growth, and every successive stage of our political and economic development gives it a new aspect, makes it a new question."[17] Although the Progressive Era administrations of Theodore Roosevelt and Woodrow Wilson did establish a beachhead for the regulatory authority of government, the Roaring 20s saw a return to *laissez faire*. Not until Franklin Roosevelt rose to confront the Great Depression of the 1930s did the balance of American federalism begin a decisive shift of responsibility and authority to the national level.

In the early years of the twentieth century, state and local governments accounted for about 70 percent of total government spending in the United States, whereas the federal government accounted for about 30 percent (see Figure 2.3.1). However, in 1913, President Wilson proposed and the Congress passed the federal income tax. This meant that the national government could, for the first time in American history, raise large amounts of money by taxing the annual incomes of citizens and residents. As the national government moved to address each major crisis of the first two-thirds of the twentieth century, its share of spending rose markedly. When each crisis passed, the federal share of total spending fell back toward, but never all the way to, precrisis levels. Since the mid-1960s, the federal government has accounted for about 65 percent of all government expenditures while state

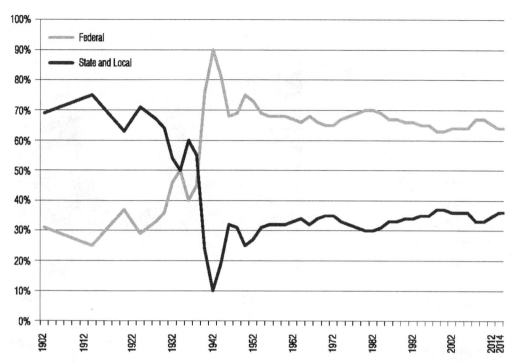

FIGURE 2.3.1   Percent of Government Expenditures by Level of Government, 1902–2014

Source: Historical Statistics of the United States, Colonial Times to 1957 (Washington, D.C.: U.S. Department of Commerce, 1960), 711, Series Y254–257, and 726, Series Y536–546. Post-1960 figures come from *Budget of the United States Government, Fiscal Year 2016*, Historical Tables (Washington, D.C.: Government Printing Office, 2016), Table 14.2, 350–351.

and local governments have accounted for the remaining 35 percent. Federal spending in 2009 jumped up to 68 percent in response to stimulus spending to combat the recession but has since fallen back to 65 percent.

The Great Depression

Nothing made the fact that the American economy had become an integrated whole more clear than its collapse in late October 1929. "The Crash," in which the stock market lost almost a quarter of its value in two days of panic trading, began a decade of deep economic depression and persistent unemployment. Just as the depression eased, World War II erupted.

The 1930s and 1940s were a period of national emergency. By the time Franklin Roosevelt assumed office early in 1933, the country had already been mired in depression for more than three years. The Depression was a national, even worldwide, economic collapse. The economy had declined by 40 percent from its 1929 high, and fully one-third of the workforce was unemployed. State and local governments were overwhelmed by the needs of their citizens. Roosevelt's dramatic response, known as the "New Deal" and initiated during his "first hundred days" in office, included "an extraordinary assumption of federal authority over the nation's economy and a major expansion of its commerce and taxing powers."[18] The Supreme Court, still committed to maintaining as much of the logic and operation of "dual federalism" as possible, declared virtually all of it unconstitutional.

Roosevelt threatened to ask the Congress to expand the size of the Supreme Court so that he could "pack" it with new members more favorably disposed to his vision of an activist role for the federal government. The Supreme Court blinked. Some members changed their votes, a few retired, and Roosevelt soon had a Supreme

In the depths of the Great Depression, unemployed men line-up for free coffee and donuts. The Depression struck deep into the working and middle classes, even the upper classes—note that some of the men in line are well-dressed.

Getty Images/Universal Images Group

Court that would bless a vastly expanded role for the federal government. By June of 1935, the court had approved several key economic programs including the National Labor Relations Act, the Railway Labor Act, the Farm Mortgage Act, and the Social Security Act. These decisions amounted to the end of "dual federalism" and the beginning of a period in which the national government would have the broad power to set and regulate economic activity in the states. The proportion of total government spending accounted for by the national government rose from 28 percent in 1927 to 50 percent in 1936.

Wickard v. Filburn shows how far the Supreme Court had moved by 1942. Roosevelt's program for rejuvenating agricultural prices, the Agricultural Adjustment Act (AAA), regulated the acreage that farmers could plant. Roscoe Filburn was authorized to plant 11 acres of wheat on his Ohio farm. He planted 23 acres, arguing that the wheat from only 11 acres would be sold and the other 12 would feed livestock. The Supreme Court, for decades a staunch defender of free markets and of a limited role for Congress in economic regulation, held that feeding the excess wheat to his own animals meant that he did not have to buy that wheat in the open market and that tiny effect on "interstate commerce" was enough to bring him under the purview of Congress's legitimate constitutional authority.[19] The balance between national and state authority within American federalism had shifted dramatically to the national level.

World War II drove the federal share of total government spending to 90 percent by 1944. When the war ended in 1945, the United States remained engaged in international politics, aiding in the rebuilding of the European and Japanese economies and constructing a military alliance to confront Soviet expansionism. Although the federal share of total government spending fell below 60 percent in 1950, the Korean War of the early 1950s drove it back up toward 70 percent. It has ranged between 60 and 70 percent for the past half century. Moreover, consolidation of political authority at the national level involved domestic policy as much as it did foreign and national security policy.

THE RISE OF FISCAL FEDERALISM

For most of American history, the limited congressional authority outlined in Article I, section 8, of the Constitution was understood to forbid national control of broad policy areas including education, health care, income and retirement security, and much more. Slowly, beginning with Theodore Roosevelt's "Square Deal" and picking up speed with Franklin Roosevelt's "New Deal," federal authorities highlighted the first clause of Article I, section 8, permitting Congress to "lay and collect taxes ... to pay the debts and provide for the common defense and general welfare of the United States." Especially during the "Great Depression," need in the nation's states and communities seemed to call for an activist federal government.

The reach of the national government within the structure of American federalism continued to expand during the 1960s and early 1970s. John Kennedy was elected president in 1960 on the promise to "get the country moving again" after the calm of the Eisenhower years. The fuel that would power this new movement was federal money. The favored device for delivering federal funds to states and localities was the **categorical grant**. Each categorical grant program offered state and local governments opportunities to receive federal funds if they would engage in a certain narrow activity and if they would do so in compliance with detailed federal mandates on eligibility, program design, service delivery, and reporting.

Only five categorical grant programs were in place in 1900 and only fifteen by 1930. Fifteen more were added during FDR's first two terms as president, but major transfers of funds from the national government to state and local governments did not begin until after World War II. Figure 2.3.2 shows that federal expenditures for grants to state and local governments rose dramatically and continuously from 1950 through the late 1970s.

Federal expenditures in constant 2009 dollars rose from more than $20 billion in 1950 to $275 billion in 1978. President Carter and the Congress reduced spending on grants to state and local governments modestly in 1979 and 1980, before the new Reagan administration slashed them by more than 20 percent in the early 1980s and then held them at that level through the remainder of the decade. Not until the early 1990s did federal grants to state and local

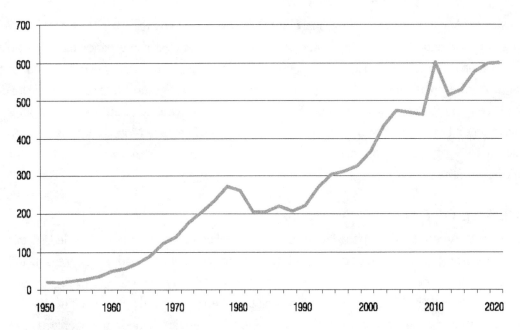

FIGURE 2.3.2 Federal Outlays for Grants to State and Local Governments, 1950–2020, in Billions of 2009 Constant Dollars

Source: Budget of the United States Government, Fiscal Year 2016, Historical Tables (Washington, D.C.: Government Printing Office, 2016), Table 12.1, 257–258. The numbers for 2015 to 2020 are official estimates from the same table.

governments begin to increase as part of the Clinton administration's aggressively domestic focus. Republican congressional majorities first elected in 1994 supported the devolution of federal authority to the states, but the Clinton administration resisted and then the Bush administration's homeland security initiatives dramatically increased federal transfers to state and local governments between 2002 and 2005 before they leveled off.

But national emergencies—whether they take the form of external threats, like World War II or 9/11, or economic catastrophes, like the Great Depression of the 1930s or the Great Recession of 2008 and 2009—invariably call out for concerted national action. Not surprisingly, then, the Obama economic stimulus program, passed just one month into the new administration, pumped tens of billions of new dollars into the states. Republican gains in the 2010 House elections led to initial cuts, but the struggling economy seemed to call for more stimulus. Obama administration projections, reflected in Figure 2.3.2, suggest a leveling off of federal transfers to the states, but skepticism is warranted.

LBJ: Creative Federalism and Grants-in-Aid

By the time John Kennedy entered the White House in early 1961, 132 categorical grant programs were in operation. During the five years that Lyndon Johnson was president, he and his overwhelmingly Democratic Congresses passed more than two hundred new categorical grant programs covering the full range of U.S. domestic policy initiatives. **Creative federalism** was the term used to describe the range and breadth of Johnson administration activities.

The "Great Society" initiatives of the 1960s were driven, not just by Democratic activism in the White House and the Congress, but also by a federal judiciary determined to end racial discrimination and segregation, protect civil liberties, reform criminal justice procedures, and afford new protections to rights of the accused and convicted.[20] Every new federal grant program passed and every expansive judicial decision handed down increased the federal bureaucracy's range of regulatory control. By the time LBJ left office early in 1969, his opponents had begun to refer to creative federalism as **coercive federalism**. In 1970, nearly one dollar out of every four spent by state and local governments came from the federal treasury.[21]

Nixon: Revenue Sharing and the First New Federalism

Republican President Richard Nixon's "New Federalism" was intended to enhance the discretion of the states in deciding how best to use the financial resources they received from the national government. President Nixon undertook two major federalism initiatives. The first, called **special revenue sharing (SRS)** or **block grants**, bundled related sets of categorical grants into a single SRS or block grant program. States and localities were permitted to decide how to allocate the money across the eligible program activities. The second Nixon initiative, called **general revenue sharing (GRS)**, provided $30.2 billion to the fifty states and approximately thirty-eight thousand local governments over a five-year period. Unlike categorical grants or even block grants, general revenue sharing funds had few strings attached. States could set their own priorities.

Nixon's New Federalism was purchased from the Democratic Congress at a high price. Congress exacted from President Nixon both increased expenditures and expanded regulation of state and local governments in other areas including civil rights, consumer protection, workplace safety, and environmental affairs. As a result, the late 1960s and early 1970s witnessed an historic expansion of federal regulation of state and local governments. Conservatives in Congress became increasingly concerned about the expense of federal mandates and regulations while many state and local officials complained about the complexity of application, administration, and reporting requirements. By the late 1970s, Democratic President Jimmy Carter began to trim federal transfers to state and local governments.

Not surprisingly, the rapid rise in federal spending and of federal transfers to the states over the past half century and more has sharpened the long-running conflict between nation-centered and state-centered federalism. In the 1960s and 1970s especially, the federal government used its financial resources to encourage state and local governments to follow their lead. In other policy areas, the federal government displaced state and local authorities altogether.

The modern version of the long-running historical battle between national federalism and states rights federalism is the battle between "preemption" and "devolution." **Preemption** is the power of the national government, based on the "supremacy clause" in Article VI, to preempt or push aside state law. Joseph F. Zimmerman, one of the nation's leading federalism experts, has written that Congress passed 678 preemption statutes between 1790 and 2011 in policy areas ranging from banking and commerce to health care and the environment.[22] Fully 70 percent of them were passed after 1970.

Alternatively, **devolution** stems from the idea that the Tenth Amendment to the U.S. Constitution guarantees the states against undue intrusion by the national government. Supporters of devolution call for returning both authority and financial resources to the states so that they can deal with the issues that seem most critical to them.

Reagan Turns Off the Tap: The Second New Federalism

Ronald Reagan came to the presidency early in 1981 with a view of American federalism unlike that of any president since Herbert Hoover. Reagan's first inaugural address declared his "intention to curb the size and influence of the Federal establishment and to demand recognition of the distinction between the powers granted to the Federal Government and those reserved to the States or the people."

The Reagan administration concluded that the national and state governments were doing too much and would do less only if they had less money. The Economic Recovery Tax Act (ERTA) of 1981 reduced the individual income tax rates by 25 percent over three years and reduced corporate income tax rates. The top bracket for individual income taxes was reduced from 70 percent to 50 percent in 1981 and reduced again by the Tax Reform Act of 1986 to 28 percent. Although tax rates were adjusted marginally upward during the late 1980s, federal revenue losses were massive.

Moreover, huge annual budget deficits put very heavy pressure on domestic spending in general and on transfer payments to state and local governments in particular. Strikingly, states were dropped from general revenue sharing in 1980 and the program was allowed to lapse in 1986. "[R]eal outlays to state and local governments fell by 33 percent between 1980 and 1987."[23] State and local governments were left to decide whether to pick up the slack or take the heat for program cuts.

Virtually all state and local governments, unlike the national government, are required, either constitutionally or by law, to balance their budgets each year. Declining federal support to states and communities makes them particularly vulnerable to economic downturns. When an economic downturn takes hold and revenues decline, the federal government can run a budget deficit but the states have to cut spending and, hence, programs and people feel it.

Q4　What fiscal and political forces led to the change in American federalism called "devolution"?

The Process of "Devolution" in Contemporary Federalism

Since 1980, only the first President Bush and Barack Obama were not governors before becoming president. Ronald Reagan, Bill Clinton, and the second President Bush all served as governors and all thought they knew how the national government should relate to the states. Ronald Reagan thought government, national, as well as state and local, was too big, too intrusive, and too expensive. He cut taxes at the national level and cut revenue transfers to the states so that government's role in American life would shrink.

Bill Clinton thought that government had an important role to play in American life, but that many problems were better addressed by people in their states and communities. He sought to redirect both financial resources and programmatic responsibilities to the states. After 1994, President Clinton's desire to produce a balanced budget joined with the Republican Congress's desire to shift primary responsibility for social welfare policy in the United States from the national to the state level to produce a dramatic overhaul of federal relations. In key policy areas like welfare, health care, job training, and transportation, Congress and the president rolled dozens of separate grant programs into a few large block grants. Each block grant gave the states greater flexibility in deciding how to spend the money allocated to them. However, the block grants often included only about 70 percent of what the federal government spent on the same programs when it administered them.

President George W. Bush accelerated the process of moving financial resources and policy responsibility to the states, especially in the areas of education, health care, homeland security, and electoral reforms. However, like Reagan, Bush also cut taxes, and the resulting budget deficits put new pressure on federal support for the states.[24]

Just as momentously, in a series of narrow 5–4 judicial decisions, beginning with *U.S. v. Lopez* (1995) and extending through *U.S. v. Morrison* (2000), the Supreme Court moved to limit the ability of the president and Congress to use the commerce clause to push states in directions that they did not wish to go. In *Lopez*, the court decided that the national government's prohibition on guns near schools was too loosely connected to regulating commerce to be justified. Similarly, in *Morrison*, the court held that the 1994 Violence Against Women Act was unconstitutional because its impact on commerce was too remote to displace the rights of the states to legislate as they see fit in this area. *Lopez* and *Morrison* were the first cases in more than 70 years, since

Wickard v. Filburn in 1942, in which the court struck down an attempt by Congress to regulate some realm of public activity under the commerce clause.

However, constitutional interpretation rarely goes in a straight line. In the 2005 case of *Gonzales v. Raich,* the Supreme Court upheld Congress's power under the commerce clause to make marijuana possession illegal. The court declared that regulating possession and use of marijuana fell "squarely within Congress's commerce power." The court's conservatives, led by then-Chief Justice Rehnquist, then-Justice O'Connor, and Justice Thomas, were dismayed. Justice Thomas argued that "if Congress can regulate this under the Commerce Clause, then it can regulate virtually anything, and the federal government is no longer one of limited and enumerated powers."[25]

A far larger battle broke out in 2010. The Obama health care program, passed in early 2010, was quickly challenged by twenty-six mostly Republican Attorneys General as an abuse of the commerce clause and an unconstitutional intrusion into the policy domain of the states.

Most close observers thought that there was at least an even chance that the Supreme Court would strike down all or most of Obamacare. Chief Justice John Roberts, writing for a divided court, surprised almost everyone, especially conservatives, by upholding most of Obamacare, not on commerce clause grounds, but under the federal government's power to tax. He did, however, acknowledge the role of the states in the federal system by holding that the national government could not pressure the states into expanding Medicaid as part of health care reform.

Struggling Toward Democracy

State governments receive more than one-third of their general revenue directly from the federal government. State officials claim that strings attached to the federal funds limit their ability to confront state and local problems as they think best.

What do you think?

- When the federal government sends money to the states, do they have the right to define how it can be used or not?
- Should the federal government withdraw its funding if states fail to comply?

Another line of cases decided since 1995 has strengthened the sovereign immunity of states against being sued in their own courts or the federal courts by state government employees or citizens.[26] Moreover, the findings limit the ability of Congress and the president to make federal law binding on state governments. So far, federal laws concerning worker rights, patent protection, and age discrimination have been struck down as they apply to state governments. In 2006, the

LET'S COMPARE

The Prevalence of Federal Systems in the World

Although the number of democratic nations in the world has grown dramatically over the past two hundred years, the number of federal systems is small and has grown slowly. Although all the nations that employ federal systems are democratic, it is certainly not the case that all democratic systems are federal. In fact, only about two dozen nations employ federal systems, and, as this sample shows, they have little in common except the fact that most are democratic and reasonably well-off by world standards.

The countries that have chosen to employ federal systems vary in geographical size, population, wealth, and ethnic and religious diversity. Most frequently, federal systems are chosen by the political leaders of countries who believe that some of the efficiency of centralization should be sacrificed to local and regional autonomy. In the United States, the claim is often made that federalism leads to bold experimentation and problem solving in the "laboratories of democracy" that are the fifty states.

NATION	POPULATION	AREA (SQ KM)	GDP PER CAPITA	ETHNIC DIVERSITY	RELIGIOUS DIVERSITY
Argentina	43,431,886	2,780,400	22,300	Low	Low
Australia	22,751,014	7,686,850	46,600	Low	Medium
Austria	8,665,550	83,870	46,600	Low	Low
Brazil	204,259,812	8,511,965	16,200	Medium	Low
Canada	35,099,836	9,984,670	45,000	Medium	Medium
Germany	80,854,408	357,021	46,200	Low	Medium
India	1,251,695,582	3,287,590	5,800	Medium	High
Malaysia	30,513,848	329,750	25,100	Medium	High
Mexico	121,736,809	1,972,550	18,000	Low	Low
Russia	142,423,773	17,075,200	24,400	Low	Low
Switzerland	8,121,830	41,290	58,100	Medium	Medium
United States	321,368,864	9,826,630	54,400	Medium	Medium

Source: Central Intelligence Agency, The World Factbook, *2016 (Washington, D.C.: U.S. Government Printing Office, 2016).*

U.S. Supreme Court rejected U.S. Attorney General John Ashcroft's attempt to intervene in opposition to an Oregon assisted-suicide law. The court noted that general regulation of medical practice traditionally had been a state responsibility. Nonetheless, the stark fact is that over the course of the twentieth century, the weight and focus of government in the United States shifted from the state and local levels to the national level.

Q5   Have the complexities of the twenty-first century rendered our government essentially national, or do state and local governments still have important roles to play?

THE FUTURE OF AMERICAN FEDERALISM

Federalism has been a part of American constitutionalism since several Puritan communities founded the New England Confederation in 1643. After more than 350 years of experience with federalism, one might think our commitment to it would be secure. It is not. Some wonder whether American federalism has been compromised, perhaps irreparably, by American political development and, more recently, by the globalization of the world communication, finance, and trade structures. They support the devolution of recent decades and call for more. Others believe that globalization of commerce, the serious threat of global warming, international terrorism, and the pandemic threats of Aids and bird flu require more national authority, not less.

Clearly, American political development—the progressive integration of our social, economic, and moral lives—has caused massive political change over the last 150 years or so. Hurricane Katrina highlighted the need to strengthen the abilities of local, state, and national forces to coordinate their efforts in dealing with natural disasters. Man-made disasters may confront us with worse in the future and our federal system must be prepared to respond.[27]

Social networks must be tended. Consider the nation's transportation infrastructure. There is a sense in which initially it built itself. Footpaths may not need to be managed, but roads are community projects. As a result, from the earliest days, New England villages elected town officers to monitor, improve, and extend roads and trails as growth and new settlements required. Highway systems, to say nothing of air traffic control systems, require management and integration above the level of towns, cities, and even states. Fundamentally, as societies and their economies grow and mature, more and more of their activities occur nationally and internationally.

For example, the North American Free Trade Agreement (NAFTA) signed by Canada, the United States, and Mexico in 1993 both permits free trade throughout North America and limits each nation's ability to manage its own internal trade and national labor markets. Similarly, the General Agreement on Tariffs and Trade (GATT), the worldwide trade agreement approved by virtually every nation in the world in 1994, restricts each nation's ability to protect and nurture its particular national industries. Finally, instantaneous satellite and Internet communications allow twenty-four-hour-a-day trading in every nation's stocks, bonds, and currencies. This makes each nation's financial markets much less subject to national control and management than they once were. These developments pose great challenges to American federalism. Once again, the resilience of the American federal system will be tested.[28]

CHAPTER SUMMARY

Federalism is a system of government that divides political power and responsibility between national and subnational levels of government. Initially, the distribution of political power described in the Constitution seemed to indicate that the national government would be responsible for dealing with foreign and military affairs and for economic coordination between the states and with foreign powers. The states would retain the power to deal with domestic affairs. The rights and liberties of the people would remain unfettered in broad areas where power had not been granted to either the national or subnational level of government.

TABLE 2.3.2   The Evolution of American Federalism

STAGES	EVENTS
National Federalism	John Marshall appointed Chief Justice (1800) *Marbury v. Madison* establishes judicial review (1803) *McCulloch v. Maryland* defines "necessary and proper" (1819) *Gibbons v. Ogden* defines "interstate commerce" broadly (1824)
State Federalism	Roger B. Taney appointed Chief Justice (1835) *Dred Scott v. Sandford* lets states define property (1857) U.S. Civil War (1861–65)
Dual Federalism	*U.S. v. E.C. Knight* limits federal commerce power (1895) *Plessy v. Ferguson* limits federal citizenship rights (1896) 19th Amendment approves federal income tax (1913)
Cooperative Federalism	FDR's New Deal (1935) *Wickard v. Filburn* expands federal commerce power (1941) LBJ's Great Society (1965) Nixon's Special Revenue Sharing (1972) Nixon's General Revenue Sharing (1974)
Devolution	Reagan's tax reform (1981) Clinton's welfare reform (1997) *U.S. v. Morrison* limits federal commerce power (2000) Obamacare approved; Medicaid expansion made discretionary (2012)

However, as the nation grew in size and complexity, many issues that had once seemed appropriate for state or local resolution, such as building and tending a transportation system, seemed to require support and coordination from the national level. As problems seemed to move within the federal system, power within the federal system had to be redistributed or realigned. After the founding there were two historical eras during which power was redistributed dramatically upward within the American federal system: the Civil War era of the 1860s and the Depression era of the 1930s.

Both the 1860s and the 1930s marked distinctive phases in the integration of the American economy and society. In the two decades before the Civil War and the two after, a national structure of communication and transportation was developed. Railroads and telegraph not only permitted goods and information to move nationally, but also permitted the businesses and corporations that produced these goods and information to become national entities. By the final decade of the nineteenth century, it had become clear that corporations dominating key sectors of an integrated national economy could be effectively regulated only from the national level. By the time FDR assumed the presidency in March of 1933, most Americans had become convinced by their experience with the Depression that federal regulation of the economy needed to be enhanced.

FDR's "New Deal" and LBJ's "Great Society" initiatives involved the federal government in almost every area of policymaking. Many of these areas, including education, job training, health care, and welfare, had traditionally been the exclusive responsibilities of state and local governments. Initially, states and localities were too eager to receive the federal funds to worry much about the rules and regulations that accompanied them. However, the rules and regulations that seemed reasonable when there were thirty categorical grant programs in the 1930s seemed unreasonable as the number of such programs passed four hundred in the 1960s, and by 1970 nearly one dollar in every four spent by state and local governments came as a transfer from the federal government. The complexity of applying for, administering, and reporting on all of these grants worked a hardship on state and local governments.

By the late 1980s and early 1990s the problems of fiscal federalism and of American federalism in general had been redefined. Ronald Reagan thought that government at all levels of the federal system was too big, demanding, and expensive. Reagan sought to scale back governments at all levels by denying them funds. Although Bill Clinton sought to restore federal assistance to states and localities, he and the Republican Congress that he faced through most of his administration agreed that federal responsibilities as well as funds should be devolved to the states where possible.

In the latter half of the 1990s, Congress moved to reconstitute the federal system by repackaging dozens of social programs into block grants, cutting the funds allocated to them by up to 30 percent, and returning primary responsibility for them to the states. This policy reversal, called "devolution," in which President Bush joined enthusiastically, was the largest reallocation of authority within the federal system since LBJ's "Great Society" and perhaps since FDR's "New Deal." Nonetheless, it was reversed, at least temporarily, when the "Great Recession" of 2008–2009 strained state budgets and the Obama administration offered help as part of its stimulus strategy. Today, the federal government supplies 30 percent of the dollars spent by state and local governments.[29] The struggle within the American federal system for authority and resources is unending.

Glossaries

unitary government   Centralized government subject to one authority as opposed to a federal system that divides power across national and subnational (state) governments.

confederation   Loose governing arrangement in which separate republics or nations join together to coordinate foreign policy and defense but retain full control over their domestic affairs.

supremacy clause   Article VI of the U.S. Constitution declares that the acts of the national government within its areas of legitimate authority will be supreme over the state constitutions and laws.

implied powers   Congressional powers not specifically mentioned among the enumerated powers, but which are reasonable and necessary to accomplish an enumerated end or activity.

inherent powers   Powers argued to accrue to all sovereign nations, whether or not specified in the Constitution, allowing executives to take all actions required to defend the nation and protect its interests.

concurrent powers   Powers, such as the power to tax, that are available to both levels of the federal system and may be exercised by both in relation to the same body of citizens.

reserved powers   The Tenth Amendment to the U.S. Constitution declares that powers not explicitly granted to the national government are reserved to the states or to the people.

Paul v. Virginia   (1869) This decision declared that the privileges and immunities clause of the U.S. Constitution guaranteed citizens visiting, working, or conducting business in another state the same freedoms and legal protections that would be afforded to citizens of that state.

extradition   Provision of Article IV, section 2, of the U.S. Constitution providing that persons accused of a crime in one state fleeing into another state shall be returned to the state in which the crime was committed.

dual federalism   Nineteenth-century view of federalism envisioning a federal system in which the two levels were sovereign in fairly distinct areas of responsibility with little overlap or sharing of authority.

Marbury v. Madison   (1803) Chief Justice John Marshall derived the power of judicial review from the Constitution by reasoning that the document was supreme and therefore the court should invalidate legislative acts that run counter to it.

McCulloch v. Maryland   (1819) The court announced an expansive reading of the "necessary and proper" clause, holding that Congress's Article I, section 8, enumerated powers imply unspecified but appropriate powers to carry them out.

Gibbons v. Ogden   (1824) This decision employed an expansive reading of the commerce clause, the doctrine of the "continuous journey," to allow Congress to regulate commercial activity if any element of it crossed a state boundary.

concurrent majority   South Carolina senator John C. Calhoun's idea for restoring balance between the North and South by giving each region the right to reject national legislation thought harmful to the region.

Dred Scott v. Sandford   (1857) The court declared that African Americans, whether free or slave, were not citizens of the U.S. Moreover, slaves were property and could be carried into any state in the union, even a free state, and held as property.

cooperative federalism   Mid-twentieth-century view of federalism in which national, state, and local governments share responsibilities for virtually all functions.

nullification   The claim prominent in the first half of the nineteenth century that states have the right to nullify or reject national acts that they believe to be beyond national constitutional authority.

secession   The claim that states have the right to withdraw from the Union.

U.S. v. E.C. Knight   (1895) The court held that Congress's power to regulate interstate commerce extended only to transportation of goods across state lines, not to manufacturing or production.

Wickard v. Filburn   (1942) The court rejected the narrow reading of the commerce power in *U.S. v. E.C. Knight* to return to the broader reading in *Gibbons v. Ogden* by which Congress could regulate virtually all commercial activity.

categorical grant   A program making federal funds available to states and communities for a specific, often narrow, purpose and usually requiring a distinct application, implementation, and reporting procedure.

creative federalism   1960s view of federalism that refers to LBJ's willingness to expand the range of federal programs to support state and local activities and to bring new, even nongovernmental, actors into the process.

coercive federalism   A pejorative term to describe the federalism of the 1960s and 1970s, suggesting that the national government was using its financial muscle to coerce states into following national dictates as opposed to serving local needs.

special revenue sharing   The Nixon administration developed block grants that bundled related categorical grants into a single grant to enhance state and local discretion over how the money was spent.

block grants   Federal funds made available to states and communities in which they have discretion over how the money is spent within the broad substantive area covered by the block grant.

general revenue sharing Program enacted in 1974, discontinued in 1986, that provided basically unrestricted federal funds to states and localities to support activities that they judged to be of highest priority.

preemption The Article VI declaration that national statutes are "the supreme law of the land" allows Congress to preempt or displace state authority in areas where they choose to legislate.

devolution The return of political authority from the national government to the states beginning in the 1970s and continuing today.

U.S. v. Lopez (1995) The court found that Congress's desire to forbid carrying handguns near schools was too loosely related to its power to regulate interstate commerce to stand. The police powers of the states cover such matters.

U.S. v. Morrison (2000) Citing *U.S. v. Lopez*, the court found that the Violence Against Women Act was too loosely related to Congress's power to regulate interstate commerce to stand.

Endnotes

1. G. Ross Stephens and Nelson Wikstrom, *American Intergovernmental Relations: A Fragmented Federal Polity* (New York: Oxford University Press, 2007), 2–6.

2. Department of Commerce and Bureau of the Budget, *Statistical Abstract of the United States, 2012* (Washington, D.C.: U.S. Government Printing Office, 2012), table 428, 267. See also "Government Organization Summary Reports" 2012, http://www2.census.qov/govs/cog/g12_org.pdf.

3. Samuel H. Beer, *To Make a Nation: The Rediscovery of American Federalism* (Cambridge, MA: Harvard University Press, 1993), 223–224. Beer quotes briefly from Patrick Riley, "The Origins of Federal Theory in International Relations Ideas," *Polity*, vol. 6, no. 1 (Fall 1973): 97–98.

4. Joseph F. Zimmerman, *Contemporary American Federalism: The Growth of National Power*, 2nd ed. (Albany, NY: State University of New York Press, 2008), 2–4. See also Raymond A. Smith, *The American Anomaly: U.S. Politics and Government in Comparative Perspective*, 2nd ed. (New York: Routledge, 2011), 34–37.

5. Vincent Ostrom, *The Meaning of American Federalism: Constituting a Self-Governing Society* (San Francisco, CA: ICS Press, 1991), 45.

6. David Brian Robertson, *Federalism and the Making of America* (New York: Routledge, 2012), 31–33.

7. Edward Meade Earle, ed., *The Federalist* (New York: Modern Library, 1937), no. 51, 339, no. 31, 193.

8. Edward A. Purcell, Jr., *Originalism, Federalism, and the American Constitutional Enterprise: A Historical Inquiry* (New Haven, CT: Yale University Press, 2007), 3–10.

9. Earle, ed., *The Federalist*, no. 39, 249.

10. Joseph E. Zimmerman, *Contemporary American Federalism: The Growth of National Power* (New York: Praeger, 1992), 35.

11. Zimmerman, *Contemporary American Federalism*, 146.

12. Robertson, *Federalism and the Making of America*, 34.

13. Bruce Ackerman, *We the People: Foundations* (Cambridge, MA: Harvard University Press, 1991), 40.

14. Edward S. Corwin, "The Passing of Dual Federalism," *Virginia Law Review*, vol. 36, no. 1 (February 1950): 4.

15. David B. Walker, *Toward a Functioning Federalism* (Cambridge, MA: Winthrop, 1981), 66.

16. David Brian Robertson, *Federalism and the Making of America* (New York: Routledge. 2012), 40, 151, 155, 171.

17. Woodrow Wilson, *Constitutional Government in the United States* (New York: Columbia University Press, 1908), 173.

18. Walker, *Functioning Federalism,* 68.

19. Theodore J. Lowi, *The Personal President: Power Invested, Promise Unfulfilled* (Ithaca, NY: Cornell University Press, 1985), 49–50. See also Adam Liptak, "At Heart of Health Law Clash, a 1942 Case of a Farmer's Wheat," *New York Times*, March 20, 2012, A1, A14.

20. Ross Sandler and David Schoenbrod, *Democracy by Decree: What Happens When Courts Run Government* (New Haven, CT: Yale University Press, 2003), 13–34.

21. Roberton Williams, "Federal, State, and Local Government Revenues," Tax Policy Center, July 2, 2007.

22. Joseph F. Zimmerman, *Congressional Preemption: Regulatory Federalism* (Albany, NY: State University of New York Press, 2005), 1–9; see also Zimmerman, "Congressional Preemption Trends," *The Book of the States*, 2012, vol. 44, 51–55.

23. Timothy Conlan, *New Federalism: Intergovernmental Reform from Nixon to Reagan* (Washington, D.C.: Brookings Institution, 1988), 153–154.

24. Jackie Calmes, "States Confront Fiscal Crisis," *Wall Street Journal*, December 18, 2003.

25. Linda Greenhouse, "Justices Say U.S. May Prohibit the Use of Medical Marijuana," *New York Times*, June 7, 2006, A15.

26. Linda Greenhouse, "States Are Given New Legal Shield by the Supreme Court," *New York Times*, June 24, 1999, A1. See also Anthony Lewis, "No Limit but the Sky," *New York Times*, January 15, 2000, A19.

27. Donald F. Kettl, *System under Stress: Homeland Security and American Politics*, 2nd ed. (Washington, D.C.: CQ Press, 2007), 102.

28. William T. Pound, "Federalism at the Crossroads," *State Legislatures*, June 2006, 18–20.

29. Roberton Williams and Yuri Shadunsky, "State and Local Tax Policy: What Are the Sources of Revenue for State Government," Tax Policy Center, May 7, 2013.

READING 2.4

Comparing the Power of Courts in Federal Systems

By Cristina M. Ruggiero

INTRODUCTION

This project generally asserts that high court power is shaped and conditioned by a number of institutional and political features, both intrinsic and extrinsic to high courts. [...] I posit three conditions under which such courts are likely to be powerful political actors: (1) A high degree of court policy comprehensiveness and specificity, (2) a high likelihood of court oversight/intervention in the policy process, and (3) a limited diffusion or overlap of legislative competencies between federal and sub-national governments. I find that particular institutional features, including the comprehensiveness and nature of constitutional rights guarantees, the structure of judicial review and the constitutional division of powers between the federal and sub-national governments enable these conditions. In addition, the following outlines the implications this analysis has for examining court power in other contexts and provides directions for future research. Lastly, I suggest how these concepts may apply to a more general approach to understanding institutional power.

HOW DO INTRINSIC INSTITUTIONAL FEATURES AFFECT THE QUALITY AND CONTENT OF COURT DECISIONS?

One argument this project has asserted is that the greater number of clear, uncontested institutional supports a court has, such as an extensively detailed guarantee of rights (both positive and negative) or unqualified judicial review, the more likely a court will provide policy directives (through its decisions) that are comprehensive, detailed and prescriptive. Conversely, if those features are absent or weak, a court is more likely to refrain from making comprehensive, detailed and prescriptive decisions. In addition, this study also finds that the courts with limited or constrained institutional supports are more likely to depend on court/legal rules and/or to 'defer' authority to legislative institutions in order to justify their interventions or non-interventions in the policy process. On these measures, the Canadian Supreme Court abortion decisions were the least comprehensive, detailed and proscriptive, while the German Constitutional Court's decisions were the most comprehensive, detailed and proscriptive.

The Canadian Supreme Court, with fewer independent institutional supports for the exercise of its authority as compared to the other two courts in this study, was the court that most often utilized legal rules such as mootness and standing in its decision-making. The Canadian Court was authoritative in its decision-making when reviewing lower court interpretations of the law, but restrained when exercising judicial review, particularly when the federal government was sending contradictory signals about whether the Court should 'interpose its friendly hand'. For example [...] the Court employed the 'mootness' standard to evade a charge of policy-making in *Borowski*, but chose to assert its judicial authority in *Daigle*. In *Daigle* the Court was resolving lower court conflicts regarding interpretations of civil and common law, whereas in *Borowski*, had the Court issued a ruling on the merits of the case, it would have had to review the acts of another branch of government.

In terms of comprehensiveness, the Canadian Supreme Court rulings were narrowly focused, often avoiding substantive questions such as where life begins and whether women have right to abortion. In regards to how or where abortions are to be performed, the Court decreed only that provinces may not use criminal sanctions to regulate abortions. Regarding rights issues, the Court did not address whether or not provincial health care services must provide and/ or pay for abortion services. It also consistently asserted that it was the federal government's responsibility to establish a new criminal law on abortion and refused to provide direction as to what reforms would pass constitutional muster. Overall, the Canadian Supreme Court's decisions were relatively restrained, narrow and not proscriptive.

Comparatively, the United States Supreme Court did not provide as much evidence of 'deference' to federal government actors in its decisions, but that is likely due to the fact that criminal law is largely a state matter within the US system. In addition, the United States federal government took little substantive action on abortion policies (during the time period examined in this study); therefore most of the legislative action on abortion occurred at the sub-national level. The US Supreme Court, while addressing more aspects of abortion policy than the Canadian Supreme Court, still left significant questions unresolved. The US Court only obliquely addressed the fetal life question. It provided a constitutional right for women to obtain abortions, yet weakened that right over time by replacing a specific test (trimester framework) with a broader and less specific one (undue burden). With a less stringent rule in place, states were encouraged to establish stricter abortion regulations.

Lastly, the German Constitutional Court specifically addressed the initial questions raised by abortion policy, evaluated abortion policy in detail and provided prescriptive, substantive directives for rewriting abortion regulations. If anything, over time, the Court's rulings on abortion became more proscriptive and comprehensive, rather than more diffuse, as what occurred in the United States. For example, as one commentator on the German Constitutional Court's *Abortion II* decision noted,

> Although the Court formally left the regulation of counseling to the legislature, its directives with respect to the "normative" contents of counseling do not leave much leeway. The Court itself has extensively "regulated" the content, procedure and organization of counseling held due for decriminalized, yet non-indicated early abortion by virtue of the *Grundgesetz*. (Walther 397)

This assessment was consistent with other court scholars estimating the impact of the of the Court's ruling on any future legislative revision of abortion policies. Court scholar Sabine Klein-Schonnenfeldpredicted, "the future [legislative debates] will be characterized by more or less detailed legal discourse on how to organize and control advice centers and the medical profession" (Klein-Schonnenfeld 132). Her prediction was accurate, [...] Bavaria passed complicated regulations limiting counseling centers and ability of doctors to provide abortions by mandating only a percentage of their income derived from performing abortions.

In comparison to the other two high courts, the German Constitutional Court established the limits of abortion policy and provided firm and detailed answers to the policy questions within those bounds. The US Supreme Court also determined both the parameters of abortion policy and some of the policy interior but not to the extent that the German Court did. The US Supreme Court left some policy areas untouched and provided only limited 'substance' in others. The Canadian Court provided the least amount of guidance on abortion policy, barely outlining abortion policy boundaries and leaves most of the interior policy terrain to be decided by other political actors.

Comparing across the cases presented, Germany's Basic Law was the most detailed and proscriptive regarding rights guarantees, providing both negative rights and positive guarantees that the state is obliged to uphold. Given the comprehensiveness and positive rights inherent in the Basic Law, as compared to the other two courts in the study, the German Constitutional Court had a stronger basis on which to base its decisions and to oblige state actors to conform to its interpretation of the Basic Law. In contrast, both the US and Canadian Supreme Courts started with constitutional documents that were less detailed and provided few (if any) positive rights guarantees requiring government intervention on the issue of abortion.

In regards to the nature of judicial review and its impact on court influence, this study confirms that abstract review significantly enlarges a court's influence and ability to intervene in the policy process. What is key, however, is not just the presence of such a procedure but that (1) multiple actors have access to this process and that (2) court decisions resulting from said review are to be binding on those actors. While both the Canadian and German systems provide for some type of 'abstract' review, in Canada that review may only be exercised by the ruling party in either the federal or provincial government. The opposition or minority faction in the Canadian parliament does not have access to the reference procedure as in Germany. In addition, in Canada, the 'reference' is only an advisory opinion that is not legally binding. In practice, the presence of the reference procedure actually inhibited the Canadian Supreme Court from making more substantive policy decisions in its concrete cases. Whereas, Germany's abstract procedure is definitive and legally binding; having such influence emboldens the German Constitutional Court to interject itself forcefully into the legislative process.

The Canadian government had the opportunity to make a 'reference' to the Canadian Supreme Court during the revision of the federal abortion law, but it chose not to do so. It sent contradictory messages to the Court on whether or not it wanted the Court to address the abortion issue. In its attempt to reform the criminal abortion law, the Mulroney government seemingly set itself up to fail, by allowing a free vote and too many amendments to its bill. In addition, government lawyers tried to make a 'mootness' claim in the *Borowski* case, when it should have asked for the case to be dismissed in the first instance. Lastly, the Prime Minister publically stated that the government would not take any further legislative action on abortion until after the *Borowski* ruling, which could have been interpreted as a 'deferral' to the Supreme Court. However, the Canadian Court did not see it that way.

It was never publically stated why the Canadian government chose not to make a reference to the Court, but as noted, the reference procedure is only an advisory opinion while an abstract review appeal (Germany) is binding on all governmental organs. Without the presence of a binding constraint, the reference procedure might not have provided enough political cover for the Mulroney government to decide to use the reference procedure. As Graber's asserts, judicial review can benefit elites when they can point "to their obligation to obey the law, while insisting that they disagree with the Court's holding" (Graber 1993: 43). Yet, without the binding constraint, the Mulroney government could not say 'we're amending the law in this way because the Supreme Court said so and we have to abide by its decision'. In other words, the Canadian government could not use the reference procedure to effectively 'defer' to the Canadian Supreme Court, insuring that the Court could be held responsible instead of the Mulroney government.

Conversely, since the government *did not* make a reference, the Court could have surmised that if it *had* made a substantive policy decision in *Borowski*, its legitimacy would be threatened if its decision was met with public opposition (which was likely to some extent given the controversy over the issue). The Mulroney government could have 'safely' criticized the Court for both an inappropriate exercise of judicial review and on the nature of the ruling itself. One could argue that the lack of the binding constraint of the reference procedure led *both institutions* to defer making a substantive policy decision.

Another background condition present in the Canadian case was that at the time the Canadian Supreme Court was not firmly established as a political actor equal to Parliament, as was the Constitutional Court in Germany. Early Canadian constitutional documents established limited independent authority of the Canadian Supreme Court. The Court had long operated under these conditions until the Charter of Rights and Freedoms, which had been in effect less for less than decade when the abortion debate took place in the Canadian Parliament. Therefore expectations of judicial review and constitutional supremacy were not as established at the time as it was in Germany. However, one could argue that these expectations have developed further over recent years, and perhaps if the Canadian Court was presented with such issues today, the Court would be less deferential in its decision-making.

Besides the binding nature of abstract review, the fact that more political actors may access the procedure in Germany has enabled its use, and by extension facilitated the Constitutional Court's intervention in the policy process. Alec Stone has argued that abstract review allows courts to act as 'third legislative chambers'. This was apparent in Germany, where the opposition had the opportunity to employ the abstract procedure, creating conditions under which legislative policies negotiated and passed by a majority could be overturned via a court's abstract review decision. However, in light of the Canadian case, if abstract review is an option but underutilized and/or is not sufficiently binding upon political actors, the presence of such review may inhibit a Court from issuing substantive policy decisions in *concrete* cases thereby diminishing the court's overall influence. Abstract review which results in only advisory opinions may also diminish the likelihood of its use and subsequently, the authority and influence of a high court. Therefore, both the level of access to and the binding nature of abstract review are significant determinants as to whether courts are empowered as 'third legislative chambers'. Future research comparing across high courts with varying 'types' of abstract review, in terms of the number of actors able to initiate such review and the 'finality' of said review, could confirm or refine this finding.

HOW DO THE EXTRINSIC FEATURES OF FEDERALISM SHAPE LEGISLATIVE RESPONSES TO COURT DECISIONS?

This project asserts that the distribution of both policy and legislative competencies between federal and sub-national governments significantly shapes whether and how governments advance their interests regarding abortion policy. Most notably, the determination of whether abortion is primarily a health or a criminal policy was a necessary but not sufficient condition in determining responsibility for abortion policy and how said government would legislate. In addition, whether or not sub-national governments were largely responsible for implementing federal abortion policies or establishing their own substantive regulations conditioned sub-national legislative responses to high court decisions. The *presence* and *nature* these features provided particular avenues in which legislative actors could act and shaped the conditions that facilitated or inhibited court oversight of such actions. Notably, sub-national governments who successfully avoided court challenges to their policies were those that strategically sought to enact their preferences by working within the policy and institutional competencies available to them. However, when sub-national actors exceeded either their policy or legislative (or both) competencies they were likely to face judicial review. Regardless of ideological or party affiliation, sub-national governments who avoided judicial oversight employed particular competencies, such as utilizing their fiscal authority or promoting their actions as falling clearly under sub-national policy authorities (such as health policy) thereby insulating their actions from legal challenge.

HOW DID THE FEDERAL LOGIC SHAPE THE INTERACTIONS BETWEEN THE FEDERAL AND SUB-NATIONAL GOVERNMENTS?

In Canada, the division of jurisdictional authority between the federal government and the provinces contributed to the competitive dynamic between the two levels of government. Since the Conservative Mulroney government did not reform the federal criminal law on abortion, the provinces, under the auspices of their authority to regulate health care policy, attempted to either enable or inhibit access to abortion. Alberta and Nova Scotia attempted to regulate out-patient clinics and billing procedures, which impacted abortion access. Under the leftist NDP government, Ontario provided travel grants and approved out-patient abortion clinics. When the Liberals gained control of the federal government, it attempted to coerce provinces to provide access to abortion through the Federal Health Act and withholding federal transfer payments to the provinces, however it did not seek to reform the federal criminal law on abortion (S.251). Had the Canadian federal government successfully revised S.251 of the criminal law, there still may still have been conflicts between the federal government and provinces, due to constitutional authority of provinces over health policy. If the federal policy was in conflict with the policy interests of particular provinces, such provinces may have imposed convoluted and complicated health regulations, 'deinsured' abortion to prohibit access, or determined that abortion was not a 'medically necessary' health procedure.

Conversely, in the United States, the most significant legislative act (during the time period examined) by the federal government was to *withhold* the distribution of federal funds to the states by prohibiting the use of Medicare monies to fund abortions, effectively limiting access to abortion for poor women. In addition, since criminal law is primarily under the jurisdictional authority of the states, the majority of legislative activity on abortion occurred within the states. Given this distribution of jurisdictional authority, there was little evidence of a competitive dynamic between the federal government and the states. In this case, the federal government seemed to 'wave the flag' of federalism in order defer the issue of abortion onto the states and the Supreme Court (through its review of state abortion legislation). [...] this is consistent with both Mark Graber's and Keith Whittington's observations regarding federalism as a condition which supports judicial review and influence.

However, if the US federal government passes legislation outright banning all abortions or prohibiting the regulation of abortions, this could lead to conflicts between the federal government and the states. It is not clear on what constitutional basis the federal government could take such action. Recently, the US federal government passed the Partial Birth Abortion Act (2003), prohibiting the use of a late term abortion procedure. Five years later in *Gonzales vs Carhart (2007)* the United States Supreme Court upheld the federal law. This legislation mirrored statutes that had been in effect in about half of the states in the US. The constitutional justification for the exercise of Congressional authority in order to pass the law was based nominally on the commerce clause (said justification was not addressed by the court). One could raise the argument, based on Supreme Court's own federalism jurisprudence (see *Lopez, Morrison),* that there is not a significant enough connection between late term abortions and interstate commerce in order to justify the law. Conversely (and somewhat ironically), since access to late term abortions has declined within states due to increased state regulations (enabled by Supreme Court decisions), this condition has de facto made abortion an 'interstate commerce' issue since women are more likely to travel across state lines in order to obtain an abortion.

In Germany, since the Constitutional Court was interjected relatively early into the policy debate over abortion through abstract review and subsequently issued detailed, proscriptive and comprehensive decisions, which were largely complied with by Parliament. Since the criminal law is the province of the federal government in Germany and the Länder do not have significant jurisdictional authorities which conflict with the federal government, there was not much of the policy area left for the Länder to exercise control over. As noted previously, Klein-Schönfeld's prediction that what would be 'left' after Constitutional Court's *Abortion II* decision were details about counseling centers and the medical profession was accurate. Both Bavaria and North Rhine

Westphalia created legislation that addressed the former, while Bavaria also addressed the latter. By attempting to limit the amount of income doctors could garner from performing abortions, Bavaria attempted to restrict the number of abortion performed in the Land.

In summary, while these cases revealed that the division of jurisdictional policy authority between the federal government and sub-national government conditioned legislative responses regarding abortion policy, this division was not always sufficient in determining which level of government would play a more significant role in establishing abortion policy. In Canada, the federal government had clear responsibility over criminal law, but chose not to exercise that authority, effectively leaving abortion regulation to the provinces through their authority over health policy. In the United States, the federal government could have easily deferred the responsibility of abortion regulation to the states, since criminal law is largely under state jurisdiction. In Germany, there is limited diffusion of legislative competencies between the federal government and the Länder. The federal government is largely responsible for criminal law and most other substantive policy areas, whereas the Länder are responsible for administering or implementing said federal laws, leaving few areas where the Länder have sole jurisdiction to establish substantive policies. Future research could examine additional federal cases, such as Brazil, Australia and even the European Union to further understand how different divisions of legislative authority in federal systems impacts the responses of legislative actors to high court decisions and subsequently court influence.

COMPARING COMPLIANCE ACROSS SUB-NATIONAL CASES

All three 'liberal' sub-cases (Ontario, Oregon and North Rhine-Westphalia), generally complied with the Court decisions on abortion and at various points utilized their own finances to ensure or promote access to abortion services. All three also took actions that were within their legislative and jurisdictional competencies, and generally did not pass legislation or take other actions that were highly controversial or could lead to a substantive legal challenge. When Ontario was ruled by the NDP (New Democratic Party) government it provided provincial funds supporting counseling and outpatient abortion services. In Oregon, the state government (through the Governor) chose to use its own funds to support counseling centers when federal funds were to be withheld. North Rhine-Westphalia provided subsidies to counseling centers that provided both social and medical counseling, ensuring such counseling centers would remain available to women. North Rhine-Westphalia was also careful to mimic both the language in the federal criminal abortion regulations and the Constitutional Court's abortion decisions in its regulations.

These activities contrast with the legislative actions taken in three of the 'conservative' sub-national cases of Nova Scotia, Utah, and Bavaria, where abortion regulations were eventually struck down by high courts. Nova Scotia attempted to prohibit the establishment of out-patient abortion clinics by attaching a criminal sanction to the regulation. Canadian courts struck down this criminal sanction as infringing upon the federal authority over the criminal law. Utah attempted to regulate abortions beyond the constitutional standards set out by previous US Supreme Court decisions. Bavaria attempted to limit the amount of income doctors could receive from performing abortions and to impose convoluted regulations of abortion counseling procedures. The US and Canadian Supreme Courts, in their review of the legislative policies of Utah and Nova Scotia respectively, avoided addressing substantive issues regarding abortion regulation, whereas the German Court did address these to some extent in its decision reviewing Bavaria's abortion regulations. However, the major justifications for the German Court's decision were based on some issues not directly related to the nature of abortion policy; the constitutional 'right to free employment' and the division of legislative competencies between the federal and state governments.

Why did the conservative states/provinces/Länder test the boundaries of their authority by passing controversial legislation? In Utah and Bavaria it appeared that these states passed their respective regulations in part they believed that the high courts would support them based upon the previous decisions by these courts. The Utah legislature passed a law that was unconstitutional as a response to Supreme Court decisions that essentially invited states to enact stricter abortion regulations. Similarly, the Bavarian government believed that its regulations were more consistent with the dictates of the Constitutional Court's *Abortion II* decision than the federal parliament's revision of the criminal abortion law. Both sub-national governments were vociferous that their actions were in compliance or at least consistent with previous court decisions. However in both cases courts eventually struck down these legislative actions.

In Canada, Nova Scotia was comparatively less confident in the constitutionality of its legislation as it attempted to 'shore up' the constitutional justifications for its regulations by passing supplemental legislation that fell under its authority to regulate hospital policy. Alberta chose a different route in evading compliance with the Canadian Supreme Court decisions on abortion. Alberta was consistent in casting its attempts to restrict abortion within its provincial authority to regulate health policy. Alberta also refrained from taking actions that appeared to impose criminal sanction. However, because of the jurisdictional overlap between the federal government and the provinces, the Canadian federal government was able to provide some oversight by withholding federal transfer payments to Alberta, eventually forcing the province to back down on its attempts to deinsure abortion.

These sub-national cases suggest that regardless of political orientations, sub-national governments who seek to exceed their competencies, are likely to have their actions reviewed by courts and those that take actions clearly within their competencies may insulate themselves from court oversight. This finding is both consistent with and extends arguments made by 'strategic scholars' by providing empirical evidence of the role "institutional arrangements play in structuring choices made by strategic actors." (Epstein et al. 2004: 171). In this case, jurisdictional authority helps determine what actions sub-national actors might take and also help us understand under which conditions they are likely to be successful or unsuccessful in evading court oversight. As Epstein et al. note,

> Policy formation. ... emanates not from the separate actions of the branches of government but the interaction among them. Thus it follows that for any set of actors to make authoritative policy—be they justices, legislators, or executives—they must take account of this institutional constraint by formulating expectations about the preferences of other relevant actors and what they expect them to do when making their decisions. (Ibid: 174)

What this research adds to that observation is that formulating expectations about what courts might do is necessary but not sufficient (as seen in the cases of Utah, Nova Scotia and Bavaria). Such actors must also be aware of other institutional structures which enable institutional interaction and subsequently may impact their ability to enact their preferred policy.

GENERAL THEORIZING, INSTITUTIONAL INTERACTION AND 'COMPLEX INTERDEPENDENCE'

As this project has demonstrated, one must consider the multidimensional structuring and 'complex interdependence' of institutional relationships in order to understand high court power and the responses of sub-national actors to court decisions. Based upon the cases presented this study posits that there are three conditions that significantly contribute to the influence of high courts in federal systems (1) a high degree of court policy comprehensiveness and specificity, (2) a high likelihood of court oversight/intervention in the policy process and (3) a limited diffusion or overlap of legislative competencies between federal and sub national governments. Future research may find that these conditions apply to predicting the influence of non-judicial institutions. Given these factors, we then may be able to compare across institutions to determine when and how institutions may exert influence. For example, the nature and degree of institutional integration or interaction may be a more reliable indicator of influence or power than whether compliance is dictated by a particular type of institution (i.e., a court or by a legislature). It may not be the functional differences (e.g., the lack of enforcement powers of courts) as much as the 'institutional matrix' in which these various institutions operate which provides incentives and disincentives for particular responses. Therefore we must continue to examine the complex interdependence among institutions and between levels of government, noting not just the preferences of other actors but the institutional structures which will hinder or enable their ability to make authoritative policy.

References

Epstein, L., J. Knight, and A. Martin. (2004). "Constitutional Interpretation from a Strategic Perspective" in *Making Policy, Making Law: An Interbranch Perspective,* ed. M. Miller and J. Barnes. Georgetown University Press.

Graber, M. A. (1993). "The Nonmajoritarian Difficulty: Legislative Deference to the Judiciary." *Studies in American Political Development* 7:35–73.

Klein-Schonnenfeld, S. (1994). "Germany" in *Abortion in the New Europe: A Comparative Handbook,* ed. B. Rolston and A. Eggert. Westport, CT: Greenwood Press 119–138.

Walther, S. (1993) "Thou Shall Not (But Thou Mayest): Abortion after the German Constitutional Court's 1993 Landmark Decision", *German Year Book of International Law.* (36) 391.

American Law Defines Bourbon

By Brian F. Haara

The question "What is bourbon?" is a bit more complicated than might be anticipated, with thanks again to laws. "What is whiskey?" is a broader question and a little easier to answer. Whiskey is essentially, in its most basic form, a spirit distilled from grain. The type of grain(s) used, the location of distillation, and nature of aging, along with many other factors, then dictate the *type* of whiskey (or whisky), including broad categories such as Scotch, Irish, Canadian, or Japanese and innumerable subcategories.[1]

Whiskey, or *whisky*, as a general term, is defined by law in the United States as "an alcoholic distillate from a fermented mash of grain produced at less than 190° proof in such manner that the distillate possesses the taste, aroma, and characteristics generally attributed to whisky, stored in oak containers (except that corn whisky need not be so stored), and bottled at not less than 80° proof, and also includes mixtures of such distillates for which no specific standards of identity are prescribed."[2]

Bourbon is a type of whiskey, and many distillers remind us that "all bourbon is whiskey, but not all whiskey is bourbon." In order to be bourbon, the whiskey must be made in the United States and must strictly meet these criteria:

- made from fermented mash of not less than 51 percent corn;
- distilled to not more than 80 percent alcohol by volume (abv) (160 proof);
- stored at no more than 62.5 percent abv (125 proof);
- stored in charred new oak containers; and
- because it is "whisky," bottled at no less than 40 percent abv (80 proof).[3]

Importantly, the word *bourbon* cannot be used to describe any whiskey not produced in the United States.[4] Other countries have acknowledged this territorial naming right as well through several agreements, including the North American Free Trade Agreement, the United States–European Union Agreement on Nomenclature of Distilled Spirits, and the United States–Australia Free Trade Agreement, which all recognize bourbon whiskey as a distinct product of the United States.[5]

That does not mean, however, that corporate ownership must be American. Indeed, the major American bourbon distillers represent a global cross section of ownership. The very American-sounding Wild Turkey was owned by the French company Pernod Ricard sa until 2009, when it was acquired by the Italian company Davide Campari Milano S.p.A.[6]

A darling of bourbon enthusiasts over the past decade, Four Roses, has been owned by the Japanese company Kirin Company, Ltd., since the Canadian spirits giant the Seagram Company fell apart. Another Japanese company, Suntory, acquired Beam, Inc., in 2015, creating Beam Suntory, and Takara Shuzo Company owns the Ancient Age brands produced by Sazerac-owned Buffalo Trace. World spirits giant British-based Diageo owns the wildly popular Bulleit brand, along with the legendary Stitzel-Weller Distillery in Louisville, and in March 2017 opened its new distillery in nearby Shelby County, Kentucky. Brown-Forman remains as the only United States–based publicly traded bourbon distiller. Privately held Heaven Hill Brands is America's largest private, family-owned producer of bourbon, and St. Louis–based Luxco, Inc., Lexington, Kentucky–based Alltech, Inc., and New Orleans–based Sazerac, Inc., round out the privately held American-owned major distillers.

While legally strict, the prerequisites to qualify as bourbon do *not* include many "rules" popularly believed to be law. One popular misconception (despite every Kentucky distillery tour guide's correction) is that bourbon must be produced in Kentucky. In fact, bourbon can be produced in any state in the union, even Alaska or Hawaii—it just so happens that thanks to history and due to its perfect conditions, Kentucky is responsible for 95 percent of the nation's bourbon. A large share of the remaining 5 percent is distilled just across the Ohio River border in southeastern Indiana, which shares many of Kentucky's geographic characteristics.

There was a time, however, when bourbon was considered to be a Kentucky-only whiskey, as documented by court cases from the early twentieth century. In *United States v. 50 Barrels of Whisky* evidence was presented that any spirit labeled "Bourbon Whisky" must be distilled "from a fermented mixture of grain, of which Indian corn forms the chief part," and be "distilled in the state of Kentucky."[7] Other courts recognized this early limitation too.[8]

Grain percentages have varied over time and from distiller to distiller. One article in 1905 claimed that bourbon is made from 60 percent corn and 40 percent "small grains": "Bourbon whisky is made from corn, rye and barley malt in the proportion 60 per cent corn and 40 per cent small grains, either 30 per cent rye and 10 per cent malt, or 25 per cent rye and 15 per cent malt."[9] Still today, although the 51 percent corn rule is well-known, there is occasionally some confusion about the use of grains other than corn. Legally, however, the type of secondary grain used—after at least 51 percent corn—does not matter. Court decisions through the mid-twentieth century tended to mention rye and malted barley as secondary grains after at least 51 percent corn and also recognized the required use of new charred oak containers.[10]

True enough, the most-used secondary grain in bourbon is rye. But some of the most popular brands today use wheat as the secondary grain, and distillers sometimes experiment with other secondary grains. Most distillers also use a small percentage of malted barley as part of the mash bill. Bourbon with wheat as the secondary grain is often referred to as "wheated bourbon," but that phrase has no distinct legal definition. Similarly, bourbon using rye as the secondary grain is often referred to as "high-rye" or "low-rye," depending on whether the amount of rye grain exceeds somewhere around 15 percent, but again, there is no distinct legal definition, so today, Sazerac produces so-called high-rye bourbon containing less rye grain than the low-rye recipe used by Four Roses.

Storage in a "charred new oak container" has historically been a *barrel*, but the word used in the law is *container*. If a distiller chose to do so—and could make it watertight—bourbon could be aged in a charred new oak box, bucket, cone, or tetrahedron. Additionally, contrary to popular belief, *American* oak or *white* oak are not required; any type of oak will do under the regulation, but American white oak tends to provide the best seal and flavor (red oak is a popular choice for the rick structure inside aging warehouses because termites typically avoid red oak). The size of the oak container is also left to the discretion of the producer, but the standard in the industry is fifty-three gallons. Many craft distilleries use smaller barrels, and Heaven Hill recently released a special edition bourbon aged for fifteen years in sixty-five-gallon barrels. The keys are *new*, *charred*, and *oak*.

Another false rule is minimum aging. An uncountable number of weekend whiskey fans have proclaimed that bourbon must be aged a minimum of two years (some publications with sloppy authors and editors have helped spread this belief). Regrettably, the Supreme Court of Kentucky recently promoted this myth too.[11] To the contrary, a charred new oak container could be filled with bourbon distillate and stored for any length of time, even just momentarily, and the distillate magically becomes "bourbon." The source of the two-year belief is probably that if bourbon is aged in compliance with its rules for two or more years, it becomes "straight bourbon."[12]

Even the word *age* has legal restrictions—producers can only count the period of time that bourbon is stored in charred new oak containers.[13] A statement of age is not always required on a label either, but many consumers view higher age statements as a sign of quality. Age statements are only required if a bourbon has been aged less than four years. Conversely, any bourbon without an age statement has been aged for at least four years.[14] If an age statement is used (whether involuntarily, because it contains bourbon aged less than four years, or voluntarily, because the label makes a reference to age or maturity for marketing purposes) and the bourbon is a blend of different-aged barrels, a label must state the age of the youngest bourbon in the blend.[15] Producers also have the option of listing the respective ages of each of the barrels used in a blend, on a percentage basis of the final product.[16]

Bourbon rules also get a little more complicated because of what is not referenced in the general definition. For example, straight bourbon and any bottled in bond bourbon (which by definition will already be a straight bourbon) cannot contain coloring, flavoring, or other additives. Regulatory agencies have not always provided clear guidance regarding additives. For example, the Alcohol and Tobacco Tax and Trade Bureau (ttb) is the federal agency charged with promulgating regulations regarding labeling of distilled spirits and other alcoholic beverages, and it also reviews and preapproves distilled spirits labels to ensure compliance with applicable laws. The ttb has interpreted the regulations to prohibit additives in non-straight bourbon, but the actual regulations arguably provide this restriction only for straight whiskies.[17] This disconnect, of course, sometimes leaves consumers wondering whether a bourbon that does not use the word *straight* might contain added artificial flavoring.

It could also lead a well-funded spirits producer to use additives in non-straight bourbon, arguing that a literal reading of the regulations allows it: "(i) such harmless coloring, flavoring, or blending materials as are an essential component part of the particular class or type of distilled spirits to which added, and (ii) harmless coloring, flavoring, or blending materials such as caramel, straight malt or straight rye malt whiskies, fruit juices, sugar, infusion of oak chips when approved by the Administrator, or wine, which are not an essential component part of the particular distilled spirits to which added, but which are customarily employed therein in accordance with established trade usage, if such coloring, flavoring, or blending materials do not total more than 2½ percent by volume of the finished product."[18] However, ttb's interpretation is that the phrase "customarily employed therein in accordance with established trade usage" prohibits the use of additives because, since the late 1800s, bourbon producers fought hard to prohibit additives. So, now it is not "customary" for *any* bourbon to contain coloring or flavoring additives.

This fight to establish customary standards for bourbon in the late 1800s and early 1900s was led by producers of straight whiskey against blenders and rectifiers of what Col. E. H. Taylor Jr. called "imitation whisky." The blenders and rectifiers fought back, claiming that their product was actually purer, and due to its substantially lower price, they captured a majority of the market share.[19]

Purity and the definition of bourbon were addressed by the Pure Food and Drug Act of 1906.[20] In *United States v. 50 Barrels of Whisky*—a case enforcing the Pure Food and Drug Act—the court used whiskey to tackle the far-reaching constitutional issue of federal authority over the transportation of goods in interstate commerce.[21] This case established the applicability of the new federal law to the transportation of spirits between states.

In that case, pursuant to the Pure Food and Drug Act, federal authorities seized fifty barrels of distilled spirits being transported from New Orleans to Baltimore. The court held that those barrels were misbranded as "Bourbon Whisky" because they really contained "a distillate of molasses with a slight infusion of sulphuric acid."[22] While *50 Barrels of Whisky* helped end false branding and labeling, producers and rectifiers of grain distillate continued to use *whisky* and *straight whisky* on their labels.

The question "What is whisky?" was finally answered by President William Howard Taft in 1909, in a declaration known as the "Taft Decision." President Taft had already served as U.S. Sixth Circuit Court of Appeals judge from 1892 to 1900, before his single term as president (1908–12), and later he served as U.S. Supreme Court chief justice (1921–30). While he served on the Sixth Circuit, President Taft gained some bourbon law experience in a case in which he found that James E. Pepper had been buying bourbon from other distilleries for years and had been mislabeling it as his own, all the while guaranteeing to the public that it was distilled by him as genuine and unadulterated Old Pepper.[23] This experience helped guide President Taft sixteen years later when he was called upon, as commander in chief, to clarify the Pure Food and Drug Act by defining "straight," "blended," and "imitation" whiskey in the so-called Taft Decision.[24]

President Taft ruled that both sides could use the word *whisky*, but rectifiers had to call their product "blended whisky."[25] "Straight whisky" was protected for Col. E. H. Taylor Jr. and other distillers who made what we know today as bourbon. President Taft railed against the rectifiers who complained that his ruling would hurt their sales by saying that he "only insists upon the statement of the truth of the label" and it was no problem if "they lose their trade merely from a statement of the fact."[26] President Taft's goal was to inform the public "exactly the kind of whisky they buy and drink. If they desire straight whisky, then they can secure it by purchasing what is branded 'straight whisky.' If they are willing to drink whisky made of neutral spirits, then they can buy it under a brand showing it; and if they are content with a blend of flavors made by the mixture of straight whisky and whisky made of neutral spirits, the brand of the blend upon the package will enable them to buy and drink that which they desire."[27]

The question "What is bourbon?" is very well defined today, but in the American way there are a number of legally defined subcategories and non–legally defined marketing terms. *Bottled in bond* adds an additional set of requirements on top of those already existing for straight bourbon, but *craft* and *small batch* seem to have taken more of a foothold with consumers. The basic question of whether a spirit is bourbon should safely be answered on the label, but consumers should know the meanings of various label phrases.

Not all whiskey is bourbon. Some bottles of brown spirits in the whiskey aisle are not bourbon. Labels that do not contain the word *bourbon* (and more specifically, *straight bourbon*, which should be the goal) are not bourbon. Even looking solely for the word *bourbon* is dangerous because "Whiskey Distilled from Bourbon Mash" is not bourbon. One brand in particular bottles something called "sour mash whiskey" and "American whiskey"; those are not bourbon either. The worst offender may be 2018's Crown Royal Bourbon Mash Blended Canadian Whisky, which gained ttb approval despite the apparent violation of the rule against using the word *bourbon* to describe a whiskey not produced in the United States. Crown Royal withdrew its label after an outcry from bourbon enthusiasts.

TASTING NOTES

Willett

Bardstown, Kentucky

Pure Kentucky XO, Kentucky Straight Bourbon Whiskey

Age: Unstated

Proof: 107 proof

Cost: $30.00

Notes: A sourced whiskey and part of Willett's Small Batch Boutique lineup, Pure Kentucky xo is an excellent example of an elegant, complex bourbon. Flavors of corn pudding, caramel, coconut, oak, leather, black pepper, and distinct malt round out this sleeper among high-proof brands.

Look for straight bourbon. Straight bourbon is bourbon that has been aged a minimum of two years, with no additives other than pure water.[28] The term *straight whiskey* came into existence just before the Civil War to distinguish natural barrel aging from artificially coloring and flavoring by rectifiers.[29]

Look for Kentucky bourbon. If *Kentucky* is in the name, the bourbon must have been produced in Kentucky from grains cooked, fermented, and distilled in Kentucky and aged for "a period of not less than one (1) full year." It can still be removed and aged or bottled elsewhere, but then the name *Kentucky* cannot be used, at the risk of license revocation.[30]

Purity is pure marketing. *Pure* is a term that was more important in the late 1800s and early 1900s than it is today, due to rectifiers, and the courts helped define the term as being "free from

> **TASTING NOTES**
>
> **Heaven Hill**
>
> *Louisville, Kentucky (distillery)*
>
> *Jefferson and Nelson Counties, Kentucky (warehouses and bottling)*
>
> Elijah Craig Small Batch Kentucky Straight Bourbon Whiskey
>
> Age: Unstated
>
> Proof: 94 proof
>
> Cost: $30.00
>
> Notes: Elijah Craig Small Batch bourbon is one of the best readily available value bourbons, combining affordability with fantastic flavors and finish, but it is also an example of drama associated with age statements. Elijah Craig traditionally included an iconic bright-red numeral 12 on its label, but in 2015 it was removed and replaced with an image of a barrel next to the words *Small Batch*, and text was added on the back label explaining that it had been aged for twelve years. Many enthusiasts saw this as a precursor to removing the age statement entirely, and in early 2016 those concerns were realized. Regardless, Elijah Craig starts with full, fantastic aromas and rich, balanced flavors of caramel, cinnamon apples, vanilla, butterscotch, cocoa, and a swell of oak.

extraneous matter; separate from matter of another kind; free from mixture, unmixed."[31] Since the early 1900s, courts held that adding neutral spirits to whiskey could not be called "pure" and that advertising it as pure was "grossly to deceive the public." Some brands, like Pure Kentucky xo, still use the term, which is uncontroversial today.

What's the proof? While bourbon must be bottled at a minimum of 80 proof,[32] there is no maximum proof, and in recent years consumers have demanded bourbon uncut by water, as if it were straight from the barrel. *Barrel strength* (e.g., Four Roses Private Selection Single Barrel),

> **TASTING NOTES**
>
> **Four Roses**
>
> *Lawrenceburg, Kentucky (distillery)*
>
> *Cox's Creek, Kentucky (warehouses and bottling)*
>
> Four Roses Single Barrel Kentucky Straight Bourbon Whiskey

(Continued)

Age: Unstated

Proof: 100 proof

Cost: $30.00–$40.00

Notes: Four Roses uses its obsv recipe for its standard single barrel bourbon, which, when decoded, means that it uses the highest rye recipe among all Kentucky distillers (60% corn; 35% rye; 5% malted barley) and a proprietary yeast strain that brings delicate fruitiness to the distillate. The high rye and fruitiness is a perfect pair, resulting in a full-bodied bourbon that shines with ripe dark fruits, caramel, vanilla, cocoa, balanced with expressive oak and maple.

barrel proof (e.g., Elijah Craig 12-Year Barrel Proof), and *cask strength* (e.g., Maker's Mark Cask Strength) refer to bourbon that is not diluted with water before bottling. It can range from single barrels (like Four Roses) to large batches (like Wild Turkey Rare Breed).

Small batch is almost meaningless. *Small batch* is an extremely popular phrase, but it is pure marketing, and it means different things for different distillers and bottlers. On the one hand, some bourbon is bottled in ridiculously large batches or even continually dumped into massive tanks, which in many cases results in more flavor continuity. Some distillers or bottlers consider two to five barrels a small batch. Others use fifteen to twenty barrels. Still others use forty barrels or more. The lesson here is that the term *small batch* tells the consumer nothing at all, unless the actual number of barrels is disclosed. One of the more popular brand examples is Elijah Craig Small Batch.

Single barrel is slightly more meaningful. *Single barrel* should be obvious, but it is undefined, legally. For example, there is no regulation that would prohibit the mingling of bourbon from separate original barrels into one barrel and then bottled as coming from a "single barrel." Bottle numbering ("bottle___of___") can be extremely helpful here to ensure that the total number of bottles is consistent with expected production given barrel age and evaporation loss. Wild Turkey's Russell's Reserve used the combined term *small batch single barrel* until 2015, causing some confusion because while neither term is legally defined, there is at least consensus that they mean different things. Four Roses Single Barrel is one of the more popular brands and is an excellent example of transparency because its label provides handwritten barrel and warehouse details.

But *craft* is totally meaningless. *Craft* is another undefined term that has become meaningless. To some producers *craft* is meant to signify artisan qualities, small production, and "farm to bottle" old-world techniques. To other producers it can be a marketer's dream to be able to recast a high-volume, mass-produced brand as something not made in a factory. The Distilled

Spirits Council (discus), a national trade association for the major distilled spirits producers in the United States, sets a cap of 84,000 cases annually to qualify as a "small distiller," the American Distilling Institute uses a 52,000 annual case cap, and the American Craft Spirits Association uses a whopping 315,000 annual case cap. Even the world's largest producer of bourbon, Beam Suntory, uses *craft* in its Jim Beam Signature Craft series.

The use of the term *finishing* is the latest trend. "Finished in_____barrels"—examples of which have included port, Pinot Noir, Cabernet Sauvignon, Zinfandel, Cognac, and sherry barrels—has long been used with other whiskies and is now a growing trend with bourbon. There are no regulations to govern finishing; therefore, open questions remain about whether whiskey is proofed down before finishing or whether it is blended with other barrels before finishing, and often there is no information about the provenance of finishing barrels, their prior use, or the length of finishing. Plus, some bourbon purists contend that finishing violates the core requirements for being called "bourbon" in the first place. But ttb has allowed use of the word bourbon so long as a label explains how it was finished. A popular brand example has been limited gift shop releases of Heaven Hill Select Stock, finished in Cognac barrels.

TASTING NOTES

Heaven Hill

Louisville, Kentucky (distillery)

Jefferson and Nelson Counties, Kentucky (warehouses and bottling)

Heaven Hill Select Stock Kentucky Straight Bourbon Whiskey

Age: Varies, often finished in other barrels

Proof: Varies but often barrel proof

Cost: $150.00–$250.00

Notes: Heaven Hill releases gift shop–only bourbon and some private barrels under the Select Stock label. A particularly unique spring 2014 release was aged eight years before finishing for two additional years in Cognac barrels and sold at barrel proof (130.2 proof) for $250.00. The Cognac influence shines in this wheated bourbon, combining to give it sweet dessert qualities, especially when enjoyed with the right amount of water to reduce the alcohol level.

Finally, *handmade* should be ignored. *Handmade* is one of the more interesting marketing terms for bourbon. At one level bourbon cannot be literally handmade because distillation happens in a still, aging happens in barrels, and bottling happens on an automated line. On another level human hands still control the process and the barrels selected for bottling. Perhaps it was this tension that has led to class action lawsuits against, for example, Maker's Mark for using the term *handmade* on its labels. In the end any consumer who believes that *handmade* literally means "made by hand" is insincere, and courts in Florida and California have dismissed the claims asserted against Maker's Mark.[33]

Combine all of these facets, and the complexity of bourbon makes it all the more American. Bourbon has even been called "America's Native Spirit" after Congress declared it to be "a distinctive product of the United States" in 1964:

Bourbon Whiskey Designated as Distinctive Product of U.S.

Whereas "Bourbon whiskey" is a distinctive product of the United States and is unlike other types of alcoholic beverages, whether foreign or domestic; and

Whereas to be entitled to the designation "Bourbon whiskey" the product must conform to the highest standards and must be manufactured in accordance with the laws and regulations of the United States which prescribe a standard of identity for "Bourbon whiskey"; and

Whereas Bourbon whiskey has achieved recognition and acceptance throughout the world as a distinctive product of the United States:

Now, therefore, be it

Resolved by the Senate (the House of Representatives concurring),

That it is the sense of Congress that the recognition of Bourbon whiskey as a distinctive product of the United States be brought to the attention of the appropriate agencies of the United States Government toward the end that such agencies will take appropriate action to prohibit the importation into the United States of whisky designated as "Bourbon whiskey."[34]

Bourbon is unique, but America has always had its share of imitators. Bourbon takes time and patience to mature, but it is the American way to innovate and cut production time. Bourbon is strictly defined, but Americans always find ways to test boundaries and argue about the details. That's bourbon.

Endnotes

1. Even the spelling makes a difference—maybe. The spelling of *whisky* versus *whiskey* is typically attributed to a distinction between Scottish (without the e) and the American versions (with the e), but as seen in statutes and lawsuits through the mid-twentieth century, American courts used the Scottish spelling. In fact, *current* federal statutes still use the Scottish spelling,

as does Maker's Mark, one of the world's most recognizable brands of "Kentucky Straight Bourbon Whisky." On the other hand, almost every other brand of American whiskey uses the—ey spelling, so the best advice may be to use *whiskey* when referring to American spirits distilled from grain but to accept the *whisky* spelling without being overly dogmatic. *See also* Maker's Mark Distillery, Inc. v. Diageo North Am., Inc., 679 F.3d 410, 414, n.1 (6th Cir. 2012).

2. 27 C.F.R. § 5.22(b).

3. *See* 27 C.F.R. § 5.22(b)(1)(i).

4. 27 C.F.R. § 5.22(l)(1).

5. *See, e.g.,* North American Free Trade Agreement, U.S.-Can.-Mex., Dec. 17, 1992, 32 I.L.M. 289, 319 (1993) ("Canada and Mexico shall recognize Bourbon Whiskey ... as [a] distinctive product[s] of the United States. Accordingly, Canada and Mexico shall not permit the sale of any product as Bourbon Whiskey unless it has been manufactured in the United States in accordance with the laws and regulations of the United States governing the manufacture of Bourbon Whiskey"); Council Regulation 1267/94, 1994 O.J. (L 138) 1 (ec); United States–Australia Free Trade Agreement, U.S.-Austl., May 18, 2004, Side Letter, Distinctive Products ("Australia shall not permit the sale of any product as Bourbon Whiskey ... unless it has been manufactured in the United States according to the laws of the United States governing the manufacture of Bourbon Whiskey and complies with all applicable U.S. regulations for the consumption, sale, or export as Bourbon Whiskey").

6. Rare Breed Distilling v. Heaven Hill Distilleries, No. c-09-04728 edl, 2010 wl 335658, *1 (N.D. Cal. Jan. 22, 2010).

7. United States v. 50 Barrels of Whisky, 165 F. 966, 967 (D. Md. 1908).

8. *See, e.g.,* Levy v. Uri, 31 App. D.C. 441, 445 (D.C. Cir. 1908) ("It is well understood that bourbon whiskey is a Kentucky product made principally out of corn, with sufficient rye and barley malt added to distinguish it from straight corn whiskey"); W. A. Gaines & Co. v. Rock Spring Distilling Co., 226 F. 531, 539 n.3 (6th Cir. 1915) ("Assuming that, at that date [1870], 'Bourbon' fairly meant a corn whisky from somewhere in Kentucky, even if not from Bourbon county").

9. Niels Christian Ortved, "The Making of Fine Kentucky Whisky," *Wine and Spirit Bulletin*, 19, no. 5, May 1, 1905, 20.

10. *See, e.g.,* In re Majestic Distilling Co., 420 F.2d 1086, 1087 (C.C.P.A. 1970) (citing *Webster's Third International Dictionary* [1966] for its definition of *bourbon whiskey* as "a whiskey distilled from a mash containing at least 51 percent corn, the rest being malt and rye, and aged in new charred oak containers").

11. Brown-Forman Corp. v. Merrick, No. 2014-sc-000717-dg, 2017 wl 4296968, *1 (Ky. Sept. 28, 2017) ("Before being labeled bourbon, the distilled spirit must be aged a minimum of two-years in new charred-oak barrels" [citing 27 C.F.R. § 5.22]).

12. 27 C.F.R. § 5.22(b)(1)(iii).

13. 27 C.F.R. § 5.11.

14. 27 C.F.R. § 5.40(a).

15. 27 C.F.R. § 5.40(a)(1), (e)(1), (e)(2).

16. 27 C.F.R. § 5.40(a)(1), (e)(1), (e)(2).

17. See The Beverage Alcohol Manual (bam): A Practical Guide, Basic Mandatory Labeling Information for distilled spirits, vol. 2 (Washington DC: Department of the Treasury, 2012), ch. 7, 10 (disallowing harmless coloring/flavoring/blending materials for "Whisky [Bourbon]").

18. 27 C.F.R. § 5.23(a)(2).

19. E. H. Taylor, Jr. & Sons Co. v. Marion E. Taylor, 27 Ky. L. Rptr., 124 Ky. 173, 85 S. W. 1085, 1086 (1905).

20. Ch. 3915, 34 Stat. 768 (1906).

21. United States v. 50 Barrels of Whisky, 165 F. 966, 970 (D. Md. 1908).

22. 50 Barrels of Whisky, 165 F. at 970.

23. Krauss v. Jos. R. Peebles' Sons Co., 58 F. 585, 593–94 (S.D. Ohio 1893).

24. Maker's Mark Distillery, Inc. v. Diageo North Am., Inc., 679 F.3d 410, 416 (6th Cir. 2012), citing H. Parker Willis, "What Whiskey Is," McClure's Magazine 34 (1910): 687, 699.

25. Maker's Mark, 679 F.3d at 416.

26. Maker's Mark, 679 F.3d at 416.

27. Maker's Mark, 679 F.3d at 416.

28. 27 C.F.R. § 5.22(b)(1)(iii); 27 C.F.R. § 5.23(a)(2).

29. W. A. Gaines & Co. v. Rock Spring Distilling Co., 226 F. 531, 545 (6th Cir. 1915).

30. Ky. Rev. Stat. Ann. § 244.370.

31. Levy v. Uri, 31 App. D.C. 441, 445 (D.C. Cir. 1908).

32. 27 C.F.R. § 5.22(b)(1)(i). See also Federal Bureau of Alcohol, Tobacco, and Firearms Ruling 79–9 (1979).

33. Salters v. Beam Suntory, Inc., Case No. 4:14cv659-rh/cas, 2015 wl 2124939 (N.D. Fla. May 1, 2015); Nowrouzi v. Maker's Mark Distillery, Inc., Civil No. 14cv2885 jah (nls), 2015 wl 4523551 (S.D. Cal. July 27, 2015).

34. S. Con. Res. 19, 88th Cong., 78 Stat. 1208 (May 4, 1964).

Unit II: Post-Reading Questions

Directions: Refer to what you learned in this unit to respond to the questions and prompts below..

1. What was the political philosophy that the people who founded the current American system mostly believed? How are its major features represented in the way in which our current government works? In what ways have these features been altered as the size of the country, its population, and its position in the world changed over time?

2. What is federalism? What kinds of federalism has the United States experienced during its history? What are the benefits to such a system, and what are its drawbacks? Could you provide examples of things that states are doing currently that show one of the key advantages of a federal system?

3. In what ways have the powers of the federal government grown in response to the nationalization and globalization of the economy? How is bourbon an example of both the growth of federal power and the need for federal regulation to keep consistency in the marketplace and a product?

4. What is common law? In what ways is the American system based on common law? What are advantages and disadvantages of the common law system?

5. How did the Great Depression and World War II change the American government in terms of size, power, relationships, and public expectations about what it will do? In what ways are will still living with the results of these changes?

Messaging and Marketing in American Politics

Unit III: Introduction

Americans see and hear more of and from their politicians now than they ever have. Prior to the 20th century, a few people might have seen or heard a president by attending a speech, many more might have read what was said in the speech, and some might even have attended a session of Congress. However, communication was slow, and travel was difficult, and that meant the experience of seeing the nation's political leaders in action was extremely limited.

During the last century and a half, advances in transportation and communication changed this situation gradually from one in which the nation's politician leaders and institutions were hardly seen to one in which they are constantly on display. The result has been a movement from a reality in which few Americans ever dealt with the national government to one in which the national government touches most aspects of their daily lives. The role of government and the ease with which Americans saw politicians have changed to the point that the situation would be unrecognizable to Americans who lived a century and a half ago.

The 20th century was one of continuous innovations in communications technology. One of the biggest changes in the relationship between citizens and the government has been the development of communications technologies that made it easy for citizens and leaders to communicate with each other. The result has been the nationalization of much of our political life. Politics has turned into more of a contest about market research, messaging, and branding than one about ideas or regional control that was the case in the long ago past. These major innovations are quite familiar to us: radio, television, and social media. Each gave politicians a new platform and a new way to reach the American public. Each one stressed different skill sets and empowered various kinds of politicians.

A lesser known but equally important innovation was the rise of a marketing model and extensive databases that allowed politicians and parties to engage in the same kinds of targeted consumer marketing that companies use to sell their products.

The marketing and media universe with which we are familiar began to develop in the industrial revolution's aftermath. As there were more products made and more manufacturers making products, it was[1] important to teach the public about them, how they worked and the unique features of each manufacturer's version of product to differentiate them and encourage sales (O'Reilly and Tennant, 2009).

The media that we know started to take shape in the late 19th century with the rise of cheap, sensational news outlets that appealed to a mass audience. These outlets practiced "yellow" journalism, a style that featured sensational stories and headlines designed to catch the eye and sell papers (Bryson, 2013) (Collins, 2011). Such papers were financed by advertising and sales. This was different than the model that existed in the early Republic. That was the era of the party press so named because journals were rewarded with patronage from political parties in return for supporting its candidates.[2] The yellow news outlets eventually produced a backlash that led to the era of so-called objective media with which we are familiar.

The age of marketing, advertising, and branding in which we live began around the same time that the media we know developed. While politicians might not have been the first to figure out how media could be used to sell themselves, there were some people who understood the possibilities quickly.

For example, Edward Bernays identified the uses of commercial marketing techniques to help governors understand their constituents and vice versa. Bernays' major works are entitled *Propaganda* (1923) *Engineering Consent* (1928), and *Crystalizing Public Opinion* (1945)—orientations that nicely sum up his work. He pointed out that people were not always logical and that many of the same techniques that were coming into use to sell commercial products could be used to sell politicians and public policies.

Among his earlier efforts, Bernays worked to humanize the image of "Silent" Calvin Coolidge by surrounding him with celebrities, thus introducing that emerging element into political communication (Tye, 2002). Political advertising increasingly came to resemble commercial advertising, a transformation that has continued up to the present. Politicians now sell themselves like any other commercial product and aim to reach specific subsets of customers just like any other commercial producer. As refinements were made in advertising techniques, the kinds of ads that appeared to "sell" politicians changed as well.

As technology changed, the skills it advantaged politicians changed too, as Neil Postman (1985) has noted. Politicians, like Abraham Lincoln, who lived in the age of the printed word and speeches, were great orators. As communications became electric, involving audio and video, then multi-platform-based skills came into vogue. Radio advantaged a president who could speak well like Franklin D. Roosevelt, while television placed a lot more emphasis on visual images. Just as the media that we know developed gradually, so too did the type of political marketing with which we are familiar. This allowed politicians to aim their messages at specific audiences.

The first president to significantly use television advertising was Dwight D. Eisenhower in 1952. One of his earliest ads was entitled "The Man from Abilene". The spot included Ike's biography, noted his experience, and included a question that he answered directly. His ads included that included longer videos themed as "Eisenhower Answers America" and shorter musical themed spots like "Ike for President" that stressed repetition.[3] It was John F. Kennedy who really figured out how to use advertising. Kennedy very much adopted an advertising model to run for president and was extremely public relations oriented during his time in office (Hall-Jamieson, 1996). This was the way in which politicians was sold until Ronald Reagan added a marketing focus that has remained ever since.

The Reagan Administration made cable television available to all Americans by changing the regulations around its deployment during the 1980s. Initially, this gave people access to more sports and entertainment channels, and then to one news program channel: the Cable News Network (CNN). Through the development of satellites and cable television, signals could be received anywhere there was a receiver, and the number of channels was limited to the number of transponders on the satellites in orbit. Cable television eliminated the need for cumbersome terrestrial and satellite antenna equipment for the home user.

The proliferation of these technologies meant that there could be many more outlets presenting different versions of the same event. Television fragmented into broadcast and cable television. This meant that the number of outlets presenting politics and the number of different presentation and interpretation of the same event that Americans were exposed to increased dramatically. It also meant that Administrations became continually scripted.

Through consumption of different media, Americans came to experience realities that were different from each other. People ended up living in highly sorted environments in which most members were more similar than different from them. CNN lost its monopoly in the mid-1990s when two other outlets emerged: a joint venture of Microsoft and TV network NBC, henceforth called MSNBC, and the Fox News Channel. Fox's rise shows how branding can be used to position a product as representing a unique offering in a competitive marketplace. To set itself apart from its rivals, Fox stressed that its news coverage would be "fair and balanced," something that tapped into longstanding conservative complaints about liberal bias in news coverage. Fox's success eventually pushed MSNBC in a leftward direction to find an audience and left the more centrist CNN struggling for ratings until Donald Trump became president.

The major political communications innovation of the late 20th century was the internet. The internet allowed people from around the world to be in touch with each other and exchange ideas easily. It became a key means through which people learned about news in their own country and around the world. This produced an explosion of new outlets that covered public affairs and undermined the role that the objective media once played in deciding what was and was not an acceptable national news as well as what ideas and individuals were acceptable in the national political discussion.

At first, a problem with the internet was that it could only be accessed with a physical connection. As mobile phone technology improved, this problem too was solved. Mobile platforms like Twitter and Facebook became key communications tools for politicians and news organizations. They were also vehicles through which anyone could get their story out to the public. This meant that the quality of information Americans saw became a lot more variable than it had been when there were fewer outlets.

Previously, the political conversation was shaped by those in the media exclusively, rather than as a two-way conversation between producers and consumers. The internet changed this. For example, Trump's personal campaign allowed him to thwart the will of the people who ran the Republican Party and showed that party elites might face a more limited future in terms of being able to pick their standard bearer than had been the case in all earlier eras of American history. Trump showed how internet technology allowed an upstart to launch their own campaign.

In the space of a few decades, Americans went from reading a newspaper and seeing or hearing a few minutes of daily news coverage about national politics to a world in which the news is covered 24 hours a day. We now live in a world in which narratives shaping the way people see an event have become at least as much of the coverage's focus as the facts surrounding the event. The line between opinion and fact-based news coverage that had developed in response to the yellow journalism of the late 19th and early 20th centuries likewise became blurred. In many ways, American politics is covered now in ways that would be more familiar to a person who lived a century ago than someone who lived 50 years ago. Highly segmented 24-hours-a-day blended news coverage and opinion journalism have become the norm.

One can argue that objective media was undermined by the rise of social media, partisan cable television outlets, and partisan talk radio shows in the time in which we live. Where once there was only one or two producers in each product category, now there are many, each making specific appeals to audiences that they understand very well. As is true for politicians, producers must say and do things that generate attention from the customer that they are seeking to reach, even if it pushes away others. This works because as Bishop (2009) notes, Americans are socially sorted in ways that have never been true before.

There are fewer broad-based aspects to American life than there have been before. People live, work, and consume like others in their own group. Further, as Joseph Turow (1998) has noted, marketers can use data-based research to figure out who their best customers are, where they are located, and how best to reach them. The emphasis on advertising and marketing has remained, but the places where these activities occur have changed to match the above-noted media revolution.

The way in which politicians learn about voters has changed a great deal. Where once voters were members of organized labor, political operations, or social groups that could be pitched for political purposes, contemporary voters are much more like consumers for commercial products. As a result, politics has become more of a marketed activity rather than the kind of activity that people have traditionally thought of it being in this country.

Political marketing takes place using the same kinds of marketing data bases, tracking cookies, and algorithms that are used by companies seeking to increase sales for everything from soap to streaming music. Politicians know with whom they are trying to speak, where these people can be found and what language to use when trying to talk with them. Political marketing has come to subsume the elected branches of government and many of the federal agencies. Campaigns around nominations to court and agency held positions have also become the subject of determined marketing campaigns. On the other hand, the functioning of the federal courts themselves have been much less impacted by this transformation.

As Frances Lee shows in *The Rise of the Partisan Message Vote*, much of what goes on in Congress is undertaken for reasons of political marketing. Lee defines the partisan message vote as being a measure that the members of one-party support, the other opposes and it has little chance of becoming law. It allows the parties to position themselves as supporting or opposing specific things and that can be fodder for future marketing and relationship building campaigns.

Lee notes that the use of the message vote is to make the case for a change in partisan control of the institution. It is also much easier for Senators to engage in this kind of activity than it is for House members, simply because the Senate's looser amending rules facilitate it. These rules allow a minority of Senators to hold a bill hostage to get the partisan messaging vote that they would like to have onto the agenda.

This kind of activity was pioneered by Senator Jesse Helms (R-NC) in the 1970s and this is a logical extension of the growing role of media in American politics. Before becoming a senator, Helms was a media figure in his home state of North Carolina. He understood the potential public relations value in holding such votes even though they were doomed to failure. These kinds of votes have become more common as Congressional elections have become more competitive nationwide, thus making the race for control of Congress more competitive. This is logical given that marketers tend to compete more when they have a chance to win or lose market share and customers than they do in less competitive environments.

While Lee notes that the measures that were most likely to pass have been sponsored by political moderates, much of the goal of the activity is to send marketing messages from the elected to the electorate. Policy success, under that framework, is more of an added benefit than a core function of the activity.

This kind of marketing activity runs throughout the political world. One useful way to consider the Trump Administration is through class and segmentation. Trump, as F. H. Buckley notes in *Trump vs. The New Class: The Donald Is a Liberal—Just like Ronald Reagan Was,* did not just take on the Democrats, he took on the upper-class elites in the Republican Party and earned their ire in the process. Trump sought to inject a working-class oriented populism into the party, something that makes sense given the size of that market, via the sheer force of his personality and marketing skills. This caught the GOP establishment, much of which was a product of the same institutions and resided in the same socioeconomic universe as did their Democratic opponents, off guard.

Trump spoke to a working-class America that did not feel that it had benefitted from the policy innovations that the elite held sacrosanct. Further, Trump resonated with voters who supported traditional institutions, values like arduous work, respect for the rule of law and patriotism, and were the folks who either fought the nation's wars themselves or saw their spouses and kids to go off to do so (and possibly not come back whole or at all).

As the 2020 election shows, the Trump phenomenon proved durable beyond the period in which Buckley wrote. Trump made significant inroads with working class people in general but especially with working class people of color. Trump tapped into the same sense that Bernie Sanders and Barack Obama reached in the electorate that only a few people were benefitting from the economic status quo. Trump's real insight was that they were in both parties and that class was an important way through which the electorate could be sliced up differently (segmented) than what was being discussed in Washington, academia, or the media.

While progressives have focused on economic inequality as the major problem of our age, Lee argues that the real problem is economic mobility that has set social classes in stone and policies favored by this elite (whom Lee terms the "New Class") that provide benefits to them at the cost of those lower down on the socioeconomic scale (whom he terms "Ragged Dicks" based on a hardworking 14-year-old protagonist of a Horatio Alger story who improved his lot in life). Trump, according to Buckley, was a liberal in that he tried to produce more social mobility and produce an economy that worked for more people as liberals in both parties have in the last century. He was not, Buckley argues, a conservative ideologue, Texas Senator Ted Cruz who sticks rigidly to the conservative message and ideology regardless of the situation in the country. Trump more saw an opportunity to reach people who felt the system was stacked against them in favor of new class professionals and sought to build an economy that worked for the former thus earning the enduring ire of the latter.

The need to market politics and politicians that we have seen involving Congress and the Presidency extends to the ways in which Supreme Court and other judicial nominees, as well as the heads of bureaucratic agencies, are chosen. Interest groups also do a great deal of marketing around themselves and their causes. These nominations are both a way to build awareness of and support for the group, but also to shape public policy for decades to come.

In *Interest Groups and Judicial Confirmations: A View from the Senate*, Amy Steigerwalt examines the way in which interest groups play a role in shaping senate confirmation of such nominees. Interest groups have played a key role in providing testimony about and rating systems around nominees. As Steigerwalt shows, their testimony has been more restricted in recent decades meaning that they moved onto other forms of activity to continue influencing the process. Interest groups have come to occupy this role because of the more limited amounts of information provided about nominees through the formal process, the murkiness of the Senate confirmation process, and because the courts are perceived to be doing more things now than they have in the past.

Now, all senators are expected to have a position on each nominee. Often the information they have about a nominee depends on what interest groups they have heard from and which media they have consumed. These groups play a key role in picking which Senators to lead the public fight and which information to use in that fight over a judicial nominee. Steigerwalt shows that senators not on the committee are more likely to be swayed by interest groups and that there is more public relations coordination between the Republican Party and conservative interest groups regarding messaging than is the case for Democrats and progressive interest groups. Given the events of the Brett Kavanaugh nomination to the Supreme Court, this might be a topic worth revisiting because progressive groups played a significant role in the messaging around that nomination.

The kinds of decisions a court makes can become fodder for marketing campaigns from interest groups, social movements, politicians, states, and bureaucratic agencies. In *MoveOn.org and the Tea Party*, Victoria Carty looks at two American groups: MoveOn.org and the Tea Party. Both groups are social movement organizations, meaning that they excel in getting people engaged and activated on behalf of a set of issues, candidates, and parties. Move On is a left-leaning organization, while the Tea Party is a right-leaning organization, but both share an activist orientation and have made excellent use of communications technologies to engage their fellow citizens.

Move On started out as a small petition regarding the Clinton Impeachment and a much bigger one in the aftermath of September 11, 2001, then has morphed into the model of a grassroots organization in the digital age. It engaged average citizens and made their voices heard in Washington. It leveraged the power of celebrity to build public awareness around and engagement with its agenda in a way that has become increasingly familiar during the first two decades of the 21st century. It combined online and physical events in a way that engaged people. It did all of this so well that it eventually encouraged a conservative counterpart: The Tea Party.

The Tea Party shows another way in which technology can lead to more political engagement. It started in a response to CNBC reporter Rick Santelli's suggestion, in response to tax and regulatory changes in the early days of the Obama Administration, that the traders on the floor of the Chicago Board of Trade start a Chicago Tea Party in response. The Tea Party movement was structured differently than Move On because it was both a loose collective and had close ties to Washington organizations like Americans for Prosperity. There was a long struggle in the conservative movement over control of the Tea Party. Like Move On, it successfully engaged some parts of the public, and it used a similar mix of online and in-person events, policy and celebrity, and strong emotional appeals. Both organizations not only show how technology can engage the public but also show how the targeted, emotional appeals that they make can be said to have increased the polarization found in the United States at present.

Candidates often use similar techniques to engage the public and differentiate themselves from their rivals. These techniques attract some voters while repelling others. Additionally, market conditions can change dramatically in a brief period as happened in 2008 and 2020 to the detriment of the party in power both times. This set up a situation in which the ways in which the voters align with the parties can change.

The Framers did not anticipate the rise of political parties as we understand them thus, they would be surprised to learn about the shifting fortunes of our two national political parties that J. K. White discusses. While White argues that Barack Obama's election might have signaled the end of the Reagan era, one could argue that it signaled more of an unfavorable marketplace for Republicans than it did a sea change in the way in which people identify with parties. John Kenneth White's examination of Barack Obama and the 2008 election in A *Transforming Election: How Barack Obama Changed American Politics* raises several issues worthy of consideration. The first of these is whether people vote for the party or vote for an individual candidate. The emphasis in White's (and many other authors') work on Obama places a great deal of emphasis on personal traits. In this construction, Obama was a unique figure capable of transforming the electorate in ways that few others could. On the other hand, White's work also notes the historically unfavorable market for Republican candidates in 2008. George W. Bush had won barely in 2000 and won a much bigger victory in 2004 premised on his success in launching a response to the events of September 11, 2001, and a strong economy.

By 2008, the response to 9/11 had come to include a war in Iraq based on faulty intelligence that was going badly combined with a major economic downturn. In that environment, any opposition candidate would have been advantaged. On the other hand, this market-based advantage did not necessarily amount to an electoral endorsement of the Democratic Party's policies, as the Obama years would eventually show.

It could also be argued that the Obama election signaled the beginning of a shift in the way people identify with the political parties. Part of the reason for this is found in the period after White authored this article. Donald Trump adjusted the Republican product to be more focused on race, class, and cultural nationalism than it had been during its Reagan incarnation. While this might have worked to elect Trump in 2016, it ended up making the party's problems with some parts of the electorate that had turned away from it during the Bush years worse and did nothing to appeal to people who did not remember why Ronald Reagan had been elected in the first place. White's piece was also written during a period in which the broad social sorting that Bill Bishop wrote about in *The Big Sort* (2009) was still taking place. Americans, as Bishop noted, had organized themselves into communities that were like-minded clusters more than truly diverse integrated environments and this impacted all aspects of American life, politics included. Americans tend to live among people like themselves and this sorting has significant implications for the state of our national political life. Polarization has developed because of sorting that limits the amount of exposure Americans have to people who do not think, act, or look like they do, because many of the institutions that help Americans understand politics like newspapers or television news have become both focused on the national level and more ideologically aligned with one or the other of the two major parties. Thus, our political parties are in flux in terms of their relative strength much of the time as are the relative strengths of the branches that they seek to control. White's piece articulates the "rising demographics" and "demography as destiny" thesis that has been popular among Democrats for much of the early 21st century.

As John Judis (2015) has argued geography counts for a lot in the American system. If the rising demographic audiences are clustered in a few states than their impact will be lessened because the federal system represents states because it was the states that created the national government, thus setting in motion the previously noted fights over relative power than have gone on throughout the history of the Republic. As the 2016 and 2020 elections also show, demographics can consist of things like age, education level, and occupational category not just racial, ethnicity, and gender, meaning that it is possible that a candidate could become President by only trying to persuade a few big and well-spaced parts of the American electorate instead of trying to appeal to all of it.

Further, as Richard Alba (2020) has noted, the extent to which American racial demography itself is changing may be as much a matter of statistical definition as real-world behavior. The extent to which the demographics is destiny thesis is valid remains an open question but what is not in question is that political parties understand how to target the audiences that they seek to reach very specifically, and this will be one of the major themes of the next section of our book.

Obama himself might have been popular, but the policies associated with Ronald Reagan that White notes captured a generation of voters also remained popular. This presented Obama with a governing problem in terms of building support for his policies and generated a Congress full of Republicans within two years. Obama's real significance might be closer to Reagan's in two ways. First, he built a much broader descriptive coalition than had been seen before in American politics. Second, he captured the imagination and earned the support of a generation of voters. The Obama legacy continues to play out in the electoral arena.

One could argue that the most important endorsement Joe Biden received during his 2020 campaign was that of President Obama and that, in this, Biden is more representative of a party in the White House than he is an empowered individual actor as Americans commonly believe the modern president to be in office. Biden's election shows the power of the party brand, organization, and coalition in a polarized America.

Biden's election produced a different kind of presidency from that of Obama or Donald Trump. Both of those leaders stressed their personal efforts and branding much more than does Biden, who more closely resembles a 19th century president. That is to say that he is the head of a partisan organization in the White House much more than a personal leader who takes responsibility for all aspects of governing, as presidents from Franklin Roosevelt to Donald Trump tended to do.

The Obama and Trump elections are important indicators of the ways in which the national electoral map has changed and, as White points out, how much the Republican Party has become a Southern regional party. After White's writing, there has been a notable change in the parties with which several types of voters identify. Donald Trump intentionally set out to add more working-class voters to the Republican Party coalition to hold it together as the governing coalition in response to the Obama challenge of which White wrote. Trump helped the Republican Party make inroads with some working-class voters, especially regarding employment and cultural issues, but cost the Republican Party support among college-educated White voters who once formed a key part of the party's support in the electorate.

This matters for two reasons. First, as the Trump campaigns, administration, and reaction to him show distinct groups of voters make decisions for distinct reasons. Some voters support candidates based on personal traits, others on economic policies, and still others on nonmaterial issues like cultural values or a combination of all three. Understanding how people make these decisions and the ways in which party coalitions can change is a keyway to understanding what kinds of policies government choses to or refrains from adopting.

Endnotes

1. O'Reilly and Tennant, 2009
2. David Bula "Party Press Era". Brittanica online https://www.britannica.com/topic/party-press-era
3. These spots can be seen at "The Living Room Candidate" online exhibition hosted by the American Museum of the Moving Image. http://livingroomcanidate.movingimage.us/exhibitions/2020/09/30/detail/the-living-room-candidate-presidential-campaign-commercials-19522020/
4. John B. Judis. "The Emerging Republican Advantage." *National Journal.* January 31, 2015.

The Rise of the Partisan Message Vote

By Frances E. Lee

> Every vote is about the next election. As soon as the last election is over,
> those who lost are thinking, "What can I do to get back in power?" And those
> who won are thinking, "What can I do to stay in power?"
> —Sen. Lindsey Graham (R-SC)[1]

Leaders are now expected to coordinate the use of the floor to advance partisan messages. Concurrent with the institutionalization of partisan communications, the partisan message vote—meaning a recorded vote deliberately crafted to dramatize party differences—has proliferated. Contemporary members of Congress regularly refer to "message" or "messaging" bills, "message votes," "message amendments," and "show votes." Message votes stand out from other votes not just because they are purposively framed to influence public perceptions. They are also distinct because they are not expected to change public policy. They are aimed at communication, not lawmaking. The goal is to "move the dial." These votes are a form of position taking, as defined by Mayhew (1974, 62): The "position taker is a speaker rather than a doer. The electoral requirement is not [to] make pleasing things happen but [to make] pleasing judgmental statements. The position itself is the political commodity."

Members are quite clear about how message votes differ from other votes that occur as a normal part of the legislative process. For example, during one 2011 colloquy with the Democratic leader discussing an upcoming vote, Republican Leader Mitch McConnell (R-KY) said, "The exercise we are going to have later today has nothing to do with making laws and making a difference. It is about making a point. We both know how to do that. We both know how to make points and make laws. What we are doing later today is not about making laws."[2] Drawing the same distinction in 2006, Sen. Robert C. Byrd (D-WV) said, "Instead of working to pass necessary legislation … we are engaged in yet another leadership-driven message dance."[3] "This is not real," stated Sen. Max Baucus (D-MT) in 2004. "It is not real legislation. … I am getting tired of message amendments. Mr. President, I want to legislate. I do not want to give messages."[4] On another occasion, Sen. Rick Santorum (R-PA) proposed to senators across the aisle, "We would be happy to give you a vote on your message amendment in exchange for you giving us a vote on something that is actually going to help people."[5] Members of both parties use the "message vote" terminology and distinguish between message votes and actual lawmaking.

This [reading] argues that once control of Congress became more insecure and two-party competitive, parties sought to make better use of the floor as a platform for communicating partisan campaign messages. This [reading] first lays out the strategy and tactics entailed, drawing upon perspectives from interviews, the *Congressional Record*, and various news sources. Second, the [reading] presents an analysis of amendments that receive recorded votes on the Senate floor, one of the most common ways message votes are staged. Examining floor amendments receiving roll-call votes in the Senate between 1959 and 2013, I offer evidence that senators make significantly more use of floor votes for purposes of partisan communications in the post-1980 period than did senators of the 1960s and 1970s. The implication is that there is more party-line voting in the contemporary Congress in part because floor votes have been enlisted as a weapon in the battle for party control of Congress.

HOW MESSAGE VOTES WORK

The logic behind partisan message votes is simple. A party brings to the floor an attractive-sounding idea with the following characteristics: (1) its members support it, (2) the other party opposes it, and (3) it is not expected to become law. Former Sen. Olympia Snowe (2013, 27) offers a more detailed explanation: "Much of what occurs in Congress today is what is often called 'political messaging.' Rather than putting forward a plausible, realistic solution to a problem, members on both sides offer legislation that is designed to make a political statement. Specifically, the bill or amendment is drafted to make the opposing side look bad on an issue and it is not intended to ever actually pass."

In the lead-up to the 2012 elections, for example, House Republicans sought to dramatize party differences on energy policy by bringing to the floor the "Congressional Replacement of President Obama's Energy Restricting and Job-Limiting Offshore Drilling Plan." Republicans were under no illusion that this bill would gain any traction in the Democratic-controlled Senate or win a presidential signature (Harder 2012). During the debate, Rep. Chris Van Hollen (D-MD) observed, "Here we are for the eleventh time in the past eighteen months wasting valuable floor time on another drill bill that has absolutely zero chance of becoming law."[6]

The failure of the attractive proposal is key to the strategy, because failure is precisely what argues for a change in party control. When the attractive idea is blocked from adoption, it offers a reason voters should elect more members of the proposing party so as to break the logjam. Republicans in 2012 hoped that Americans wanting development of more domestic oil and gas resources would get the message that they needed to elect Republicans. Such bills or amendments will only serve this political purpose when they go down to glorious defeat. If the legislative proposal became actual law, it would no longer be useful for electoral mobilization. "All we are doing today is having what we call message votes, show votes," observed Sen. Jim DeMint (R-SC). "They are set up to fail."[7]

As with the Republicans' 2012 drill bills, a party may opt to take repeated votes on the same basic policy idea. Just as congressional communicators coordinate members in repeating the same message, contemporary parties may stage failed roll-call votes on the same issues over and over. Holding votes on multiple occasions elevates an issue in the news repeatedly. Doing so also allows members to build a roll-call record that would enable a campaign to claim, as one senior Senate staffer explained, that "someone voted against X thirty-seven times."[8] Of the House's thirty-first attempt to repeal the 2009 Affordable Care Act, one journalist (Frates 2012) wrote, "If the definition of insanity is doing the same thing over and over again and expecting a different result, House Republicans are indeed certifiable. … But in an arena that rewards repetitive messaging, the laws of sanity don't hold."

Interviews with contemporary staffers confirm that both parties acknowledge the intentional staging of message votes. As one veteran Senate aide explained, "The leadership has spent a great deal of time working on how to control the floor agenda to help our message. … Particularly where we are not going to get legislation, we just focus on clarifying the differences between the parties. As part of this agenda, we have forced votes on the minimum wage, paycheck fairness, student-loan reforms, the Hobby Lobby decision. … It creates appealing messages for us, and it creates unappealing messages for the Republicans. We are consciously using the floor for this."[9] Discussing the amendments Republicans sought to offer, one Republican leadership aide said, "Those votes can be used against members in ads: 'You voted against this or that.'" He went on to note that these message amendments can cause political difficulty, even if they are tabled or otherwise handled via procedural motions: "The votes used in these [campaign] ads are often on procedural matters, so it doesn't matter how you handle them; they can always cause some trouble."[10] "All they're trying to do is come up with votes designed to make people look bad," said a senior Democratic staffer of the amendments Republicans had recently offered.[11]

Message amendments are not necessarily insincere, even though they are proposed in the recognition that they are not going to pass. One longtime former aide explained his party's message votes as follows: "With respect to the minimum wage, we think it's good policy, and we want to increase it. So we sincerely want to do it. But there are times when you realize it's not going to go forward, so you're holding votes to put people on the record, to embarrass the opponents of it, and to create fodder for the attack ad."[12] In such circumstances, "members aren't trying to legislate, aren't trying to work things out," said one veteran aide. "You're just out there jamming the bad guys. You're not trying to figure out what kind of deal can be done."[13] There are times when a party or a member will bring up bills in hopes of raising the visibility of an issue and building support for its eventual passage. One can use messaging as "a starting point. You raise awareness of a problem; you get people talking about it."[14] [...] however, party messaging is generally aimed at drawing clear "us versus them" lines. As such, negotiated legislative language that might potentially be acceptable to both parties does not work well for party messaging. "We're not putting things up there that are legislatively achievable," said another longtime leadership aide. "The hardest votes [for the other side] are often to vote against something moderate, but that's usually not what we're giving them with message votes."[15]

Because message amendments and bills are not expected to pass, there is little need to subject the legislative language to hearings, committee deliberation, or careful scrutiny. As Baucus pointed out during a 2001 debate, "We are in message amendment time. Nobody has looked at the substance. There have been no hearings on this."[16] To serve a messaging purpose, a legislative proposal need not be workable or carefully designed. A messaging bill "can't survive a real legislative process, to say nothing of passing it," said a former House staffer.[17] All that is necessary is that it sound good to constituencies outside Congress and clearly define the differences between the parties. "If your amendment is just to get a vote [and not to shape legislation]," said one former Senate aide, "it's likely to be short, simple, and pointed."[18]

Parties have many ways of staging message votes. Given their control over the agenda, a majority party can simply bring up bills it has no expectation of being able to move through the other chamber and/or get the president to sign (Groseclose and McCarty 2001). Unsuccessful party-line cloture votes in the Senate also effectively communicate what a majority party stands for and dramatize being blocked by the opposition.

The House minority party, however, does not have many opportunities to force message votes. The majority party's control over the House agenda restricts minority members' opportunities to bring matters to the floor. The House majority will screen the specific amendments the minority seeks to offer, disallowing many of the minority's best messaging opportunities. House minority parties can and do use the motion to recommit for messaging purposes, though rarely with much effect (Green 2015).

The Senate's open amending process affords unique opportunities for a minority party to force message votes. Formally, "the Senate's amending rules enable senators to offer any and as many amendments as they please to almost any bill" (Sinclair 2006, 186). Although the Senate majority leader possesses some cumbersome tools to restrict amending activity (Beth et al. 2009), in practice senators' ability to offer amendments is primarily regulated by informal bargaining processes (Ainsworth and Flathman 1995; Rawls 2009; Wallner 2013). Generally speaking, senators who are determined to force a vote on an amendment have both latitude under the rules and bargaining leverage to do so.

Hostage taking is the Senate minority party's primary bargaining chip for influencing the Senate floor agenda. Given the supermajority threshold for cutting off debate in the Senate, a Senate minority party can usually credibly threaten to block a bill the majority wants to consider and pass. In exchange for permitting a measure to clear the needed supermajority for consideration and/or passage, a Senate minority can induce the majority party to permit votes on amendments, even when those amendments will be politically painful for majority senators. Assuming the minority party holds its ranks together procedurally to engage in this kind of collective bargaining, the majority leadership will be forced to give minority-party senators opportunities to offer amendments if it wants to move forward legislatively. This type of bargaining occurs even on must-pass matters, such as appropriations (Hanson 2014a; Rawls 2009, 47–81).

The minority party may even take bills hostage that most of its members support. For example, Democrats demanded many roll-call votes on amendments to the 1995 Congressional Accountability Act, an uncontroversial measure that extended a variety of nondiscrimination rights to employees of the legislative branch. Democrats tied up the Senate for days forcing votes dealing with such matters as an across-the-board congressional pay cut and regulations on congressional frequent-flier miles—message amendments aimed at making the case that Republicans were not serious about ethics reform. None of these amendments were adopted. In the end, the Congressional Accountability Act still passed the Senate with ninety-eight yea votes. In other words, even though Democrats supported the underlying measure, they still forced the majority Republicans to take unpleasant votes on floor amendments that would potentially be useful for Democrats' electoral purposes. If the majority wanted to pass the bill, the minority expected to be compensated. "Hostage taking is baked into the process ... and it happens day in, day out on the Senate floor," said one Senate staffer.[19]

One might characterize the basic negotiation simply as follows: Whenever the majority wants to bring up and pass bills, the Senate minority party can exploit the occasion as an opportunity to force message votes. In this sense, the Senate minority party imposes a routine political tax on the majority's exercise of power. Virtually any time the Senate majority wants (or needs) legislation, the minority will likely demand the opportunity to offer amendments, and many of these amendments will be designed to cause political pain for the majority. One longtime former Senate staffer said that he and other aides used to call the process "the spanking machine," meaning "all the roll-call votes that the minority is going to demand if you're going to actually get a result." But, he continued, "you're prepared to go through that if you're going to be able to achieve something that you really want to do."[20] In Republican Leader Mitch McConnell's (R-KY) words, "The price of being in the majority is that you have to take bad votes."[21] Democratic Leader Harry Reid (D-NV) concurred with McConnell's characterization: "I agree with the minority leader that the deal around this place is the majority sets the agenda and the minority gets to offer amendments."[22] Meanwhile, Reid conceded that Republicans had devised some "great message amendments, causing a lot of pain over here."[23]

Senate bargaining over amendments may break down. The minority loses its leverage to demand votes on amendments if it will not allow the majority to pass bills. Bargaining will also fail when the majority party deems the minority's asking price too high. The majority leader may, for example, simply opt not to bring regular appropriations bills to the floor so as to avoid the painful amendments the minority will demand (Hanson 2014b). One former Senate aide observed, "As amendments become more pervasively pointed and less substantive, the leadership wants to crack down [by using procedures to limit the opportunity to offer any amendments]."[24] By historical standards, the Senate took few votes on amendments during the 112th (2011–12) and 113th (2013–14) Congresses.[25] In part, the cause was that the Democratic majority was sufficiently worried about losing control of the Senate that it was not prepared to pay a political price for trying to legislate, particularly when the prospects for getting its favored bills through the Republican-controlled House were so dim. "If we spent more time on things that were legislatively possible," one senior staffer explained, "we would also have to give the opportunity to Republicans to force votes, which they would use to damage marginal members. This is a conscious decision on our part."[26]

Bargaining had also broken down because the majority had lost confidence that the minority would ever permit the desired legislation to pass. As one former staffer stated, the majority leader is "not going to give these guys votes on controversial stuff just to see them obstruct the legislation in the end."[27] Or as another staffer put it, "We're not going to take a bunch of crappy political votes just to lose."[28] Despite the possibility that bargaining can break down, the minority's leverage to force amendments makes the Senate floor uniquely porous to message politics.

THE PREVALENCE OF PARTISAN MESSAGE VOTES

Message votes are by no means a new strategy. [...] Sen. Jesse Helms (R-NC) was a pioneer in their systematic use. He would repeatedly force the Senate to take votes on hot-button issues, knowing in advance that he would be unsuccessful but that he and his New Right allies could nevertheless use these votes for purposes of campaign fundraising and political mobilization. Helms, however, was an individual political entrepreneur, not a Republican Party leader. A difference between the Congress of the 1970s and that of the present is that the parties' incentives to use Helms-style tactics themselves grew stronger once the prospect for change in majority control of Congress appeared likely.

These expectations are intuitive. After all, it makes a lot more sense for parties to invest time, energy, and other resources in coordinated messaging when the majority is up for grabs. However, there are many challenges involved in testing these expectations empirically. It is simply not possible to offer a precise count of the number of bills and amendments intentionally framed for partisan messaging purposes. Little about the legislative language itself indicates that a bill or amendment was designed for messaging, with the exception of (increasingly common) bills with partisan taunts for titles, such as "Repealing the Job-Killing Health Care Law Act."[29] Members and leaders will not announce or publicly acknowledge that a particular legislative initiative is intended as a messaging vehicle.

Below, I attempt to gauge the prevalence of the partisan message vote first by turning to perceptions of longtime Beltway insiders. Then I offer a systematic analysis of Senate floor amendments over time that offers evidence consistent with the thesis that partisan messaging constitutes a larger proportion of the Senate floor agenda in the post-1980s era than it did in the 1960s and 1970s.

Perceptions

Hill insiders with long experience uniformly stated that they believed the use of partisan message votes was more common in the contemporary Congress than it had been in the past. Interview subjects specifically cited Helms as an important influence on the development of congressional message politics. "Helms was an innovator. The basic idea is losing to win," recalled a longtime Republican Senate aide. "You hold votes knowing you will not be successful. But then the losses on these key issues ... you can then use in elections."[30] Another Senate aide with decades of experience also reflected back to Helms as a pathbreaker: "He'd bring up a series of amendments—all hot potatoes. ... Today there's a heightened state of awareness of this strategy among leaders. It'd be leadership malpractice if you didn't allow some of that."[31] "Virtually single-handedly, Jesse Helms [brought] down the high wall that had separated the Senate from the outside world of partisan warfare," wrote former Senate aide Ira Shapiro (2012, 214).

When interview subjects were queried about the extent of messaging in the contemporary Congress, they saw it as a dominant activity. One senior Senate staffer characterized 90 to 100 percent of the issues that had come to the Senate floor from January through the summer of 2012 as oriented toward messaging.[32] Another former Senate aide said in 2014, "The only type of legislation on the floor these days is message related."[33] A longtime former high-level congressional staffer working as a lobbyist expressed concern that members' legislative skills had atrophied. "I worry about the current crop there," she said. "There's a class of members in there who only know messaging. They haven't had real legislative experiences. They haven't faced the hard choices, and they lose that skill set."[34] Another longtime leadership aide recalled, "Once setting up votes in this way was seen as a clever thing, but it is now a natural or expected thing. It is just routine."[35]

One can find numerous stories in national and Beltway news outlets about the increased use of the partisan message vote.[36] One such story (Kane 2011) quotes former Senate Republican Leader Trent Lott (R-MS). "I guess I did show votes," Lott said, though he indicated that the practice had become much more prevalent by the end of his congressional service. "There were a couple of votes I was actually ashamed of," he said. "I was getting cynical, and that's not my nature." Interviewed by a reporter about the changes he'd seen in Congress over the course of his career (1969–2011), former Rep. David Obey (D-WI) offered a colorful description of the growth in message votes (Rogers 2010): "I always tell people this [place] used to be 50 percent legislative and 50 percent political. Now it's 95 percent political because you didn't have these 'gotcha' amendments. … When you turn every damn bill into a gotcha vote, and when the parties are feeding every roll call to the campaign committees within the hour so they can blast facts to people in the marginal districts and distort what the hell the votes were, it just makes members far more ditzy and makes it harder for them to cast rational votes." Another longtime Washington journalist's history of negative campaigning (Mark 2006, 107) describes the emergence of the message vote technique with Helms in the late 1970s and concludes, "Tactics of campaigning-by-legislation are now a permanent fixture of congressional operations."

One other way of gauging the prevalence of messaging is to look for politicians themselves making explicit references to the strategy. Searches in the *Congressional Record* indicate that *message votes, message bills, show votes,* and *message amendments* are relatively new terms. The first example of this usage I was able to uncover via ProQuest's Congressional Publications Database was in 1997 when Sen. Paul Wellstone (D-MN) commented, "This amendment that I have offered isn't going to win. Maybe this is what you call a message amendment."[37] The second occurrence was Rep. Jim Moran (D-VA) in 1998 stating, "We do not need show votes in the Congress. What we need is people who are willing to make the tough choices. This constitutional amendment is not the right thing to do. It is at best a politically expedient 'show vote.'"[38] Note that both of these early references to message votes assume that the audience is already familiar with the terminology. The earliest example of a senator (that I have found) explicitly discussing partisan message votes in news reporting was, ironically, Helms himself, complaining about the amendments that Democrats had been forcing to increase social-welfare spending during consideration of the Reagan budget. "That's just what the Democrats call some of their proposals to increase spending—November amendments. ... They're walking down the aisle chuckling and saying, 'Well, we've got 'em on the spot'" (Tolchin 1982).[39]

Changing Patterns in Floor Amending

To assess whether an environment of intense competition for control of the chamber has driven a rise in partisan messaging activity, I analyze patterns in senators' success on the Senate floor across an extended time period, 1959–2013. As discussed above, Senate floor amending offers a particularly opportune outlet for the minority party's message purposes.

The expectation is that Senate floor amendments are more likely to be deployed for purposes of partisan messaging during the post-1980 era of intensified competition for majority-party control than had been the case during the 1960s and 1970s. Regardless of the two parties' competitive circumstances, however, one would expect senators to offer amendments for many varied policy and political purposes. Members will use amendments to adjust legislative language in accordance with their policy preferences. They will also offer amendments to cultivate a "legislative portfolio" (Schiller 2000), meaning a personal reputation for activism on particular issues. As senators aggressively pursue diverse personal goals, one might even see a flowering of Senate "individualism" (Loomis 1988; Sinclair 1989). But when majority control is in doubt, one would expect to find far more floor votes framed to advance partisan messages.

Given that partisan messaging is a losing-to-win strategy, its use should result in a higher failure rate, as senators propose amendments for the purpose of showing how their attractive ideas cannot advance in the current legislative context. If this is the case, one would expect to find that amendments offered by the minority party are disproportionately likely to fail in the post-1980 period. To test such a thesis, however, requires that one control for changes in the distribution of senators' policy preferences. Obviously, the polarization of Senate parties along ideological lines would also depress the minority party's success in floor amending. Under conditions of party polarization, the majority party ought to routinely outvote the minority party. The question, then, is whether minority senators in the post-1980 context are less successful than one would expect, after controlling for party polarization.

To test these expectations, I have estimated a multivariate probit model of amendment success. The dependent variable is *amendment success* (coded as 1 when the amendment is adopted, 0 when not). The key control variable in the model, *distance from the chamber median*, is the distance between the DW-NOMINATE position of the amendment sponsor and the chamber median, with the expectation that senators more distant from the chamber median are likely to be less successful on the floor than senators close to the median. This control should adequately account for how ideological polarization depresses the ability of minority-party senators to succeed on the floor. Beyond this, the model also includes a control for seniority, on the expectation that more senior members should have a higher likelihood of success. Two models are estimated: before and after the emergence of two-party competition for Senate control.[40]

The results of these models are displayed in table 3.1.1. All three explanatory variables have the expected, statistically significant effect on the success or failure of amendments in both time periods.

TABLE 3.1.1   Analysis of Amendment Success in the Senate, 86th–112th Congresses

	MODEL 1 (PRE-1980) 86TH–96TH CONGRESSES	MODEL 2 (POST-1980) 97TH–112TH CONGRESSES
Majority party (+)[a]	.13*	.55***
	(.06)	(.05)
Difference from chamber median (−)	−.97***	−.66***
	(.14)	(.14)
Seniority (+)	.08**	.05*
	(.02)	(.02)
Constant term	−.43**	−.85***
	(.12)	(.09)
N	5,172	6,095
Log-likelihood	−2904.65	−3524.26

Note: *The unit of analysis is the amendment, with the dependent variable coded 1 when the amendment is successful, 0 if not. Fixed effects are included for Congresses (not shown). Probit models are estimated with robust standard errors, clustering on the senator sponsoring the amendment. The number of clusters is 213 for model 1 and 251 for model 2.*
[a]*A test of the difference in the coefficients for majority party across the two models rejects the null of no difference* $(\chi^2 = 24.8, p < .001)$.
*$p < .05$; **$p < .01$; ***$p < .001$*

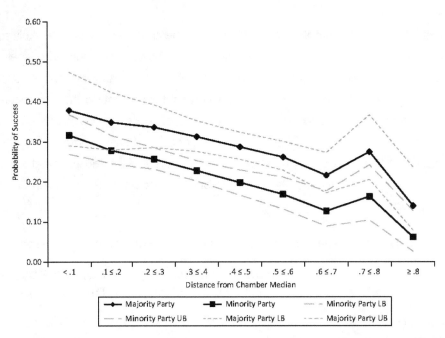

FIGURE 3.1.1. Pre-1980 majority- and minority-party amending success, by distance from the chamber median

Note: Predicted probabilities calculated based on the coefficients shown in table 3.1.1 holding all other independent variables in the model at the observed values. Confidence intervals were calculated via statistical simulation.

Majority-party amendments are modestly more successful than minority-party amendments, controlling for the sponsor's distance from the chamber median. But more importantly, centrist senators are more successful than extremist senators, regardless of party.

Based on these model results, figure 3.1.1 displays the predicted probabilities that an amendment will be successful in the 1959–80 period by party and across the ideological continuum, along with confidence intervals around the estimates.[41] As is evident here, amendments offered by centrist senators of both parties during this era were markedly more likely to succeed than amendments offered by more ideologically extreme senators. For both parties, centrist senators were more than twice as likely to see their amendments adopted on roll-call votes than were senators in the most extreme category. Party also had a small effect on amending success. Majority-party senators were slightly more successful at equal distances from the chamber median than minority-party senators. However, the confidence intervals around the estimates for the majority and minority party overlap during this period, raising questions about how different the two parties' success rates really were, especially among centrists and extremists for whom the amount of overlap is the most extensive.

Figure 3.1.2 presents the predicted model results for the 1980–2013 period. The contrast with the previous era is stark. Party has a powerful association with amending success in the contemporary era. Majority-party senators' amendments are 83 percent more likely to be adopted than those sponsored by minority-party senators, after controlling for the effects of party polarization. As in the previous era, amendments offered by centrists of both parties are more likely to succeed than amendments offered by extremists. But across the full range of ideology, majority-party senators are much more successful than are minority-party senators. Indeed, the most extreme members of the majority party are more successful than the most centrist members of the minority party.[42] To put this result in terms of the 112th Congress, a majority-party senator with the preferences of Bernie Sanders (I-VT) was more successful in the amendments he offered than a minority-party moderate with the preferences of Susan Collins (R-ME). A majority-party senator with the preferences of Tom Harkin (D-IA) was more likely to see his amendments adopted than was a minority-party centrist like Olympia Snowe (R-ME).

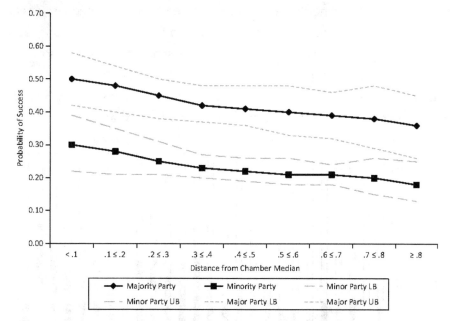

FIGURE 3.1.2. Post-1980 majority- and minority-party amending success, by distance from the chamber median

Note: Predicted probabilities calculated based on the coefficients shown in table 3.1.1 holding all other independent variables in the model at the observed values. Confidence intervals were calculated via statistical simulation.

Minority-party amendments are far less successful than majority-party amendments, controlling for the sponsor's distance from the chamber median. The most extreme majority-party members are more successful than the most centrist minority-party members.

These findings comport well with a theory that minority-party senators use floor amendments for different purposes during the contemporary era of competition for majority-party control. In the pre-1980 period, senators' success or failure in amending activity was largely a function of their individual policy preferences, with centrists more likely to succeed on the floor than extremists were. Party had little effect on amending success after *distance from the chamber median* was controlled for. Looking to these pre-1980 Congresses, it is clear why earlier research on the Senate politics of the 1950s, 1960s, and 1970s had identified no consistent pattern in which majority-party senators were more likely to succeed in floor amending (Sinclair 1989; Smith 1989).

In the post-1980 period, minority-party senators are dramatically less successful than majority-party senators, controlling for their individual policy preferences. The analysis reveals that party polarization as measured by DW-NOMINATE cannot account for this shift. But this pattern does make sense in light of the emergence of "message politics" on the Senate floor. As the two parties compete for majority control of the Senate in the contemporary era, a larger share of the minority party's amendments are crafted to highlight the differences between itself and its opponent. In short, minority-party senators' amendments succeed less often, because a larger proportion of their amendments are designed to fail. When the majority party rejects the minority's appealing amendments, the minority party scores political points as it constructs a message to take to the voters in the next election.

The patterns revealed by these analyses have clear implications for the Senate majority party's agenda control. As a window into the overall Senate floor agenda, figure 3.1.3 displays

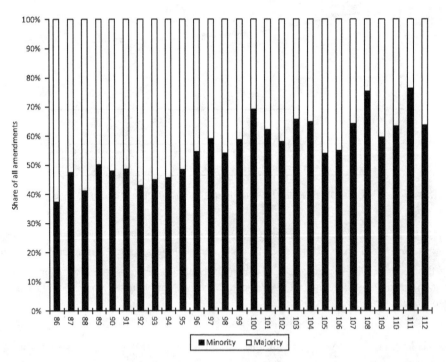

FIGURE 3.1.3.   Share of all Senate amendments receiving recorded votes, by party, 1961–2013 Message politics creates difficulties for the majority party's agenda control. After 1980, a larger share of all the amendments granted recorded votes in the Senate were proposed by minority-party senators than during the pre-1980 period.

the share of all amendments receiving recorded votes that had been offered by majority- and minority-party senators.[43] Although recent scholarship has shown that majority parties rarely lose on final passage votes in the Senate (Den Hartog and Monroe 2011; Smith 2007), the ability of the Senate minority party to extract amendment votes in exchange for permitting the consideration or passage of legislation forces the Senate majority party to allocate a tremendous share of floor time to considering amendments sponsored by the minority party. As shown in figure 3.1.3, the minority party's share of amendments has grown along with the development of partisan message operations. In fact, the Senate minority party has offered at least 54 percent of all the amendments considered on the Senate floor since the 96th Congress, even though there are by definition fewer senators affiliating with the minority party.[44] In many recent Congresses, the minority's share has exceeded 60 percent or 65 percent of all amendments receiving roll-call votes. Although the majority party is rarely "rolled" on the passage of legislation, it obviously cannot exercise the sort of control a majority party would like to have over the content of the political messages conveyed to the public out of floor debate.

THE PERMANENT CAMPAIGN ON THE FLOOR

The real question is, how is the Senate going to find a path to move beyond just trying to score points, trying to score political points, and getting to the substantive questions? ... What are you going to do with this hugely important position ... other than scheming to keep it?—Senator Ron Wyden (D-OR).[45]

In the midst of the lengthy "Vote-o-Rama" that concluded the debate over health-care reform in 2010, Sen. Jon Kyl (R-AZ) conceded, "It's very partisan, and it's not fun, and it's not productive." But when a journalist asked why the minority party nevertheless insisted on all those futile roll-call votes, Kyl replied, "You hope for a better day."[46]

The argument advanced here is that members' hope for "a better day" has changed floor politics in Congress. With the emergence of intense competition for majority-party control, an increased share of floor time is consumed with message politics. The intensification of party competition has given members powerful incentive to exploit their institutional resources in the quest for partisan advantage. [...] members have beefed up their party's capacities for outreach and public relations. As shown here, they have learned to use floor debate and votes in tandem with their electoral efforts. The interview subjects consulted for this project, along with a variety of other sources culled from the public record and news reporting, testify to the pervasive, deliberate use of the floor for partisan messaging purposes. On all sides, members and staffers concede that votes are explicitly crafted so as to put the other party in a negative light. This strategy turns on staging legislative failures. Parties define themselves against their opponents by inducing the opposition to block their attractive-sounding proposals. In message politics, a party wins politically when it loses legislatively.

These changes in floor politics cannot be explained simply by ideological polarization. Instead, message politics consumes a larger share of the Senate floor agenda in the post-1980 era. With the growth of message politics, minority-party senators have become much less successful than similarly situated majority-party senators. Indeed, the most centrist senators of the minority party have a lower rate of amending success than the most extreme members of the majority party. If contemporary minority-party senators are using floor amendments more for the purpose of communicating partisan differences to external constituencies, then it is hardly surprising that they are less successful in getting their amendments adopted. The whole point of offering amendments for partisan message purposes is to draw a sharp line between the parties, and when the minority party succeeds in doing so, it necessarily loses.

The perceptions and data presented in this chapter also offer insight into the rise of partisan conflict in Congress. Most of the work investigating the causes of increased partisanship in Congress has emphasized ideological changes in the party coalitions. The qualitative and quantitative evidence presented here offer evidence that party strategy plays a key role. If members are staging votes to highlight differences between the parties more frequently in the contemporary era than in the past, then not all the growth in partisan conflict represents genuine ideological polarization, a widening disagreement between the parties on basic questions of public policy. Instead, some share of the increased party conflict is simply an artifact of the changed strategic behavior. Put differently, a substantial amount of partisan conflict in the contemporary Congress is engineered for public consumption. In that sense, not all party conflict is "polarization," a widening difference in the two parties' policy preferences. Instead, driven by electioneering in a more party-competitive context, a considerable amount of party conflict in the contemporary Congress is position taking for partisan public relations.

Endnotes

1. Quoted in Hulse (2009a).
2. *Congressional Record*, November 3, 2011, S7094.
3. Ibid., August 1, 2006, S8506.
4. Ibid., March 26, 2004, S3217.
5. Ibid., April 1, 2004, S3530.
6. Ibid., August 3, 2012, E1441.
7. Ibid., May 25, 2011, S3342.
8. Interview 27.
9. Interview 3.

10. Interview 30. For confirmation that procedural votes are often used in campaign ads, see Smith et al. (2013).
11. Interview 8.
12. Interview 19.
13. Interview 27.
14. Interview 8.
15. Interview 3.
16. *Congressional Record*, March 17, 2001, S5090.
17. Interview 14.
18. Interview 26.
19. Interview 19.
20. Interview 11.
21. *Congressional Record*, October 6, 2011, S6317.
22. Ibid., S6319.
23. Ibid., S6316.
24. Interview 26.
25. The Senate only took 209 votes on amendments in the 112th Congress and 218 in the 113th Congress, as compared to an average of 400 amendment votes per Congress since 1980 and an average of 440 per Congress since 1960.
26. Interview 3.
27. Interview 19.
28. Interview 9.
29. H.R. 2, 112th Congress.
30. Interview 27.
31. Interview 11.
32. Interview 33.
33. Interview 19.
34. Interview 17.
35. Interview 3.
36. For a few representative examples, see Barbash (2011), Editorial (2014a), Harder (2012), Pierce (2008), Raju (2008), and Stanton (2008).
37. *Congressional Record*, September 10, 1997, S9055.
38. Ibid., April 22, 1998, H6394.
39. Searches in the *Congressional Record* for the term *November amendments* did not yield any hits. I have not been able to identify other synonyms for the tactic beyond those listed here.
40. The models do not include a control for the amendment sponsor's party (Republican or Democrat) in addition to the variables indicating majority or minority status because there

are no Republican Congresses between 1959 and 1980. If a party variable is included in the post-1980 models, it has no statistically significant effect and does not change the other model results.

41. Predicted probabilities are calculated holding all other independent variables in the model at the observed value for each case, and confidence intervals were calculated via statistical simulation (Hanmer and Ozan 2013).

42. Amendments offered by the most extreme group of majority-party senators (those with distances from the chamber median of .8 or greater) have a probability of success of .36. Amendments offered by the most centrist group of minority-party senators (those with distances from the chamber median of .1 or less) have a probability of success of .30. This difference is statistically different from zero ($p < .01$).

43. Note that the total number of amendments receiving recorded votes on the Senate floor rose and then fell over the time period examined. The number of amendments considered on the Senate floor increased dramatically over the 1960s and 1970s with the rise of a more activist Senate style (Sinclair 1990; Smith 1989). During the 1980s, however, there was a steady decline in the number of amendment votes back to 1960s levels (Lee 2012, 113–16). The number of amendments receiving recorded votes held steady at 1960s levels through the 1990s and the first decade of the 2000s, before dropping to levels characteristic of the late 1950s.

44. Through an analysis of all Senate amendments offered to landmark legislation (whether or not they received a recorded vote), Madonna and Kosar (2015, 7–8) show that amendments sponsored by minority-party senators have constituted a steadily escalating share of the total amendments offered since the 1970s.

45. "The State of the U.S. Senate: Understanding the Filibuster and the Emergence of the 60-Vote Majority," transcript, Brookings Institution, May 17, 2010, 7–8, http://www.brookings.edu/~/media/Files/events/2010/0517_senate/20100517_wyden.pdf.

46. Quoted in Senior (2010).

References

Ainsworth, Scott, and Marcus Flathman. 1995. "Unanimous Consent Agreements as Leadership Tools." *Legislative Studies Quarterly* 20 (1): 177–95.

Barbash, Fred. 2011. "Divided Government Could Result in Stalemate." *CQ Weekly*, January 10, 96–97.

Beth, Richard S., Valerie Heitshusen, Bill Heniff Jr., and Elizabeth Rybicki. 2009. "Leadership Tools for Managing the U.S. Senate." Paper presented at the Annual Meeting of the American Political Science Association, Toronto, Canada, September 3–6.

Den Hartog, Chris, and Nathan W. Monroe. 2011. *Agenda Setting in the U.S. Senate: Costly Consideration and Majority Party Advantage*. New York: Cambridge University Press.

Editorial. 2014a. "Congress's Plan to Get Nothing Done." *Washington Post*, September 7, https://www.washingtonpost.com/opinions/congresss-plan-to-get-nothing-done/2014/09/07/2358684e-347c-11e4-a723-fa3895a25d02_story.html.

Frates, Chris. 2012. "Health Care Repeal Votes—It's All about Messaging." *National Journal*, July 11, http://www.nationaljournal.com/blogs/influencealley/2012/07/health-care-repeal-vote-it-s-all-about-messaging-11.

———. 2015. *Underdog Politics: The Minority Party in the U.S. House of Representatives*. New Haven, CT: Yale University Press.

Groseclose, Tim, and Nolan McCarty. 2001. "The Politics of Blame: Bargaining before an Audience." *American Journal of Political Science* 45 (1): 100–119.

Hanmer, Michael J., and Kerem Ozan Kalkan. 2013. "Behind the Curve: Clarifying the Best Approach to Calculating Predicted Probabilities and Marginal Effects from Limited Dependent Variable Models." *American Journal of Political Science* 57 (1): 263–77.

Hanson, Peter C. 2014a. "Abandoning the Regular Order: Majority Party Influence on Appropriations in the U.S. Senate." *Political Research Quarterly* 67 (3): 519–32.

———. 2014b. *Too Weak to Govern: Majority Party Power and Appropriations in the U.S. Senate*. New York: Cambridge University Press.

Harder, Amy. 2012. "GOP Escalates Messaging Battle on Energy Issues." *National Journal Daily*, July 25.

Hulse, Carl. 2009a. "As Aisle Gets Wider, Arms Get Shorter." *New York Times*, December 28, A18.

Kane, Paul. 2011. "Partisanship Is No Longer Something to Hide on the Hill." *Washington Post*, December 8, A6.

Lee, Frances E. 2012. "Individual and Partisan Activism on the Senate Floor." In *The U.S. Senate: From Deliberation to Dysfunction*, ed. Burdett A. Loomis. Washing-ton, DC: CQ Press, 110–31.

Loomis, Burdett. 1988. *The New American Politician: Ambition, Entrepreneurship, and the Changing Face of Political Life*. New York: Basic Books.

Madonna, Anthony J., and Kevin Kosar. 2015. "Could the Modern Senate Manage an Open-Amendment Process?" R Street Policy Study No. 42, October 15, http://www.rstreet.org/wp-content/uploads/2015/10/RSTREET42.pdf.

Mark, David. 2006. *Going Dirty: The Art of Negative Campaigning*. Lanham, MD: Rowman and Littlefield.

Mayhew, David R. 1974. *Congress: The Electoral Connection*. New Haven, CT: Yale University Press.

Pierce, Emily. 2008. "Red Meat on Senate Agenda." *Roll Call*, April 24, 1.

Raju, Manu. 2008. "Campaign for White House Takes Reins on Capitol Hill." *The Hill*, June 12, 4.

Rawls, W. Lee. 2009. *In Praise of Deadlock: How Partisan Struggle Makes Better Laws*. Washington, DC and Baltimore: Woodrow Wilson Center Press with Johns Hopkins University Press.

Rogers, David. 2010. "Obey Surveys the House Then and Now." *Politico*, July 23, 8.

Schiller, Wendy J. 2000. *Partners and Rivals: Representation in U.S. Senate Delegations*. Princeton, NJ: Princeton University Press.

Senior, Jennifer. 2010. "Mr. Woebegone Goes to Washington." *New York*, April 4, http://nymag.com/news/politics/65239/.

Shapiro, Ira. 2012. *The Last Great Senate: Courage and Statesmanship in Times of Crisis*. New York: Public Affairs.

Sinclair, Barbara. 1989. *The Transformation of the U.S. Senate*. Baltimore, MD: Johns Hopkins University Press.

———. 2006. *Party Wars: Polarization and the Politics of National Policy Making*. Norman: University of Oklahoma Press.

Smith, Steven. 1989. *Call to Order: Floor Politics in the House and Senate*. Washington, DC: Brookings Institution.

———. 2007. *Party Influence in Congress*. New York: Cambridge University Press.

Smith, Steven S., Ian Ostrander, and Christopher M. Pope. 2013. "Majority Party Power and Procedural Motions in the U.S. Senate." *Legislative Studies Quarterly* 38 (2): 205–36.

Snowe, Olympia J. 2013. "The Effect of Modern Partisanship on Legislative Effectiveness in the 112th Congress." *Harvard Journal on Legislation* 50 (1): 21–40.

Stanton, John. 2008. "Election-Year Rhetoric Trumping Legislation." *Roll Call*, June 12, 3.

Tolchin, Martin. 1982. "Senate Turns Back Efforts to Modify Tax Cuts for 1983." *New York Times*, May 21, A1.

Wallner, James I. 2013. *The Death of Deliberation: Partisanship and Polarization in the United States Senate*. Lanham, MD: Lexington Books.

Trump vs. the New Class

The Donald is a liberal—just like Ronald Reagan was

By F. H. Buckley

The falcon cannot hear the falconer, wrote William Butler Yeats. Political leaders, like the falcon, were meant to obey their minders, but Yeats's falcon had soared above them and loosed mere anarchy on the world. Today, Donald Trump's campaign soars above our conservative elites, who in their foundations, their little magazines, their think tanks, define what conservatives may do or say. Trump ignores them, they tell us, and disorder and chaos must follow.

Mere anarchy is a fair description of the state of the Republican Party, at least amongst those who purport to be its falconers. Mimicking the vulgarity they decry in Trump, they employ every vile epithet to describe him and his followers. *National Review's* Rich Lowry enthused that Carly Fiorina had "cut his balls off." For Lowry's colleague Kevin Williamson, Trump is a "witless ape … not just an ass, but an ass of exceptionally intense asininity." As for Trump's followers, George Will calls them "invertebrates," while John Hood describes them as "a motley crew of simpletons, bigots, and cynical manipulators." In their hatred of Trump, they have come to resemble the man they despise.

It's not hard to see a little wounded self-love in all this. The conservative elites thought they had ownership rights to the Republican Party, at least to its thinking component, and it's a psychic shock to be quite ignored. Trump boasts that he is a winner, but the party had settled into a comfortable second-class status, more concerned with the purity of its policies than with winning anything. In 2012 George Will said that if the Republicans lost that year's election they should get out of the business, but that showed that he didn't understand the party of beautiful losers. Romney lost, but let's not forget that he had a very pretty 59-point plan.

There is, I fancy, one more thing that troubles our falconers. Worse still than Trump is the fact that so many Americans like him, ripping apart the imagined America of the elites, a preppy, mid-Atlantic country south of Iceland and east of *The New Yorker*. Their America has no monster-truck races, no hip-hop, no reality TV, no Donald Trump; and yet Trump is authentically American. He is *Sam Slick the Clockmaker*, Thomas Chandler Haliburton's fast-talking, Yankee peddler, whom Haliburton's Canadian and British readers saw as the archetypal American. He is, like Johnny Cash and Muhammad Ali, a person who could only be American, and whom Americans will recognize as one of their own. At some level, our elites must recognize this too, and in their anger experience the rage of Caliban seeing his face in the mirror.

The Republican race is far from over, and the choice seems to have settled between Trump and Ted Cruz, between raw emotion and pure reason, between the heart and the head. Cruz is the perfect intellectual embodiment of deep conservatism, of free-market policies championed by the Republican Party every two years and betrayed just as often. This time it's different, promises Cruz. With me we'll return to a constitution of separation of powers and of libertarian principles, and we'll not surrender.

Trump attracts—and repels—voters through his remarkably forthright personality. By contrast, Cruz's appeal is based upon everything but his personality. He inspires little affection and has made enemies of all of his colleagues in the Senate, Democrat and Republican alike. A Bush alumnus explains why people take an instant dislike to Cruz: "It just saves time." Psychologists tell us that he is unable to reproduce the Duchenne smile that signals sincere amusement and friendship. As with Nixon, you wouldn't want to buy a used car from this man.

For the flint-eyed ideologues on the right, none of that matters. Cruz is a true conservative and Trump a liberal in disguise. In truth, Trump's policies are not a little flexible, to use his word. So too is conservatism, however, and the conservative champions of today might do well to remember how closely their policies resemble those of yesterday's liberals. I am thinking here not of the McGovern liberals but of an earlier generation of Democrats, the party to which Ronald Reagan said he belonged before it left him. This was the party of the Americans for Democratic Action, of Arthur Schlesinger Jr. and of Lionel Trilling. They were strongly anti-communist and fought hard to expel the Marxists from their party. Of economics they were ignorant as swans, but then so too were the Republicans of the day. During the Eisenhower administration the highest marginal income tax rate was 91 percent, and it took Democrat John F. Kennedy to recognize that "a rising tide lifts all boats" and propose a tax reform that brought marginal rates down. Before Arthur Laffer, it was JFK who said that "it is a paradoxical truth that tax rates are too high and tax revenues are too low and the soundest way to raise the revenues in the long run is to cut the rates now."

My good friend Bob Tyrrell wrote a great book called *The Death of Liberalism.* He was half right. Liberalism did die, but only in the Democratic Party. There it became progressivism, the bastard child of the New Left and identity politics, the perversion of liberalism's every noble instinct. But liberalism itself did not die. Instead, it was incorporated into the Republican Party, through leaders such as Reagan, and now is almost mainstream conservatism. Like Reagan, today's conservatives are yesterday's liberals. What they are not are yesterday's conservatives.

In Kennedy's day, Republicans worried more about budget deficits than economic growth and therefore opposed his tax cuts. When the legislation came up for a final vote in the House of Representatives, only 48 Republicans supported it and 126 voted against it, and it passed only because 223 liberal Democrats voted for it. Remember, we are talking about a top marginal rate of 91 percent, which the bill reduced to a still very high 65 percent.

In the 1960s, conservative Southern Democrats aligned themselves with Republicans in voting against Kennedy's tax cuts and also opposed civil-rights legislation aimed at ending racial segregation. So too did many conservative thinkers of the time, including William F. Buckley. But for the support of liberal Republicans in the House and Senate, the 1964 Civil Rights Act would not have passed, and we can thank Ripon Society types in the Republican Party for this. They were right, the conservatives were wrong, and only the strictest of today's "constitutional conservatives" such as Rand Paul and Ted Cruz would question the law. No one would dissent from Martin Luther King's vision of racially neutral laws, except today's progressives with their race and gender triumphalism.

Kennedy's Democratic Party was the natural home for ethnic voters, who felt uncomfortable in a white-shoe Republican Party. Ronald Reagan helped change that, but African-American and white ethnic Republicans will tell you that much of the older party remains. Of the recent success of Ted Cruz, Marco Rubio, Ben Carson, and John Kasich, Republicans have much to be proud. And Trump, while he is not the poster child of inclusiveness when it comes to immigrants, has nonetheless revived the old Reagan coalition by bringing formerly Democratic voters to the voting booths to support him. They have left a Democratic Party whose leaders think them ignorant rednecks who cling to their guns and religion, and they're not made to feel especially welcome when Cruz supporters call them invertebrates and bigots: that's a good way to win an election, said no one ever.

If Donald Trump is something of a liberal, then perhaps that's not so bad. Indeed, it's his departures from liberalism that are more troubling.

While I've not read it, I believe that Mitt Romney's 59-point plan was every bit as good as anything Ted Cruz has come up with. I wouldn't fault the 2012 nominee for having left anything out—for failing to come up with a 60- or 61-point plan. But then nobody paid any attention to the plan. Here's what they heard instead:

> There are 47 percent of the people who will vote for [Obama] no matter what. All right, there are 47 percent who are with him, who are dependent upon government, who believe that they are victims, who believe the government has a responsibility to care for them, who believe that they are entitled to health care, to food, to housing, to you-name-it.

Romney's talk, to a group of right-wing donors, became the defining moment of the campaign when it was published in *Mother Jones*. It revealed a contempt for ordinary Americans and seemingly conceded the election. The 59-point plan was ignored, and what voters listened to was Obama's 2011 Osawatomie speech. America's grand bargain, the president said, was that those who contribute to the country should share in its wealth. That bargain had made the country great, the envy of the world, but now it was betrayed by the "breathtaking greed" of the super-rich.

> In the last few decades, the average income of the top 1 percent has gone up by more than 250 percent to $1.2 million per year. … And yet, over the last decade the incomes of most Americans have actually fallen by about 6 percent. … Some billionaires have a tax rate as low as 1 percent. One percent. That is the height of unfairness. It is wrong.

In a troubled economy, Obama told voters that he had their back. Romney came across as the boss about to hand you the pink slip. And Obama won.

What Obama had spoken to were the classically liberal themes of equality and mobility, of the promise of a better future. The Republicans weren't interested in inequality—but inequality was interested in them. The conservative elite told us that we were a center-right country, that we didn't do class warfare, that envy was un-American. But the voters, invertebrates that they are, disagreed. In fact, they thought Obama was on to something when he said that secretaries shouldn't have to pay a higher tax rate than their billionaire bosses.

While the left had complained of inequality, the far greater problem is immobility, especially the idea that it results from a set of unjust rules that advantage a new class of aristocrats. We might be prepared to accept the fact of deep income inequality if we thought that everyone stood the same chance of getting ahead and that people were sorted out by their abilities. That indeed is the American Dream. But now the countries of high mobility are Denmark and Canada. Must we then speak of the Danish and not the American Dream? If so, the core understanding of American exceptionalism will have been lost.

Table 3.2.1 reports on how countries rank on a measure of mobility, the correlation between the earnings of fathers and sons. With a ranking of zero there is perfect mobility, and perfect immobility with a ranking of one. It will come as a surprise to realize that the U.S. is one of the most immobile countries in the developed world, that children in other such countries are better able to climb the economic ladder. Through a broken educational system, insane immigration laws, a regulatory state on steroids, a disregard for the rule of law, we have created an aristocracy and betrayed the promise of America.

TABLE 3.2.1

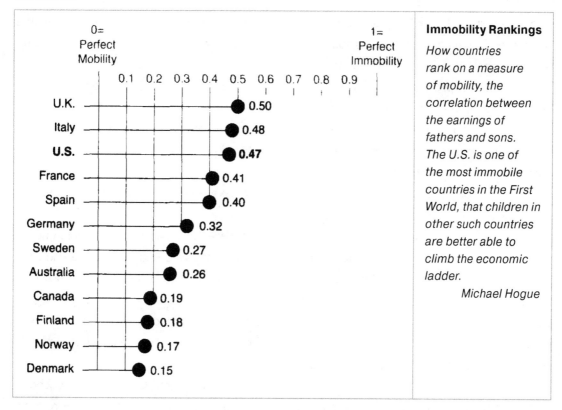

Immobility Rankings

How countries rank on a measure of mobility, the correlation between the earnings of fathers and sons. The U.S. is one of the most immobile countries in the First World, that children in other such countries are better able to climb the economic ladder.

Michael Hogue

Presented with these findings, the conservative intellectual is apt to deny that anything can be done to make us more mobile. It's all because of the technological revolution, he tells us, and we're not about to give up our iPhones. Or else it's a result of globalization. Or maybe there's a genetic explanation. If Lady Gaga was born that way, why not the rich?

It takes but a moment, however, to realize that none of these explanations can account for cross-country differences in mobility. The technological revolution? People like Robert Gordon tell us it's an illusion, and in any event it can't explain why other countries are more mobile. The Danes aren't exactly living in the Stone Age.

Our conservative elites would have us believe that none of this matters, that only socialists worry about income equality and mobility. That gives the issue away to the left, and is a good way to lose elections. The left would only make things worse, however. They want higher taxes, but we're already one of the most highly taxed countries. When we compare our income, capital gains, and corporate tax rates with those of other countries, we have nowhere to go but down. As for our welfare policies, we're among the most generous countries in the world. But that's not to say that we have to leave things as they are. Instead, conservatives should begin by admitting that income mobility is the defining political issue of our time, that we lost the 2012 election because we ignored it, that anger at the class society we have become explains the rise of Donald Trump, and that the way back lies in the pursuit of socialist ends through capitalist means.

Our mobility problem results from departures from and not our adherence to capitalism. Rising inequality in America has been blamed on the "1 percent," the people in the top income centile making more than $400,000 a year. They alone don't explain American income immobility, however. Rather, it's the risk-averse New Class—the 1, 2, or 3 percent, the professionals, academics, opinion leaders, and politically connected executives who float above the storm and constitute an American aristocracy. They oppose reforms that would make America mobile and have become the enemies of promise.

The New Class is apt to think it has earned its privileges through its merits, that America is still the kind of meritocracy that it was in Ragged Dick's day, where anyone could rise from the very bottom through his talents and efforts. Today's meritocracy is very different, however. Meritocratic parents raise meritocratic children in a highly immobile country, and the Ragged Dicks are going to stay where they are. We are meritocratic in name only. What we've become is Legacy Nation, a society of inherited privilege and frozen classes, and in *The Way Back* I explain how we got here and what we can do about it.

The most obvious barrier to mobility is a broken educational system. Our K-12 public schools perform poorly, relative to the rest of the advanced world. As for our universities, they're great fun for the kids, but many students emerge on graduation no better educated than when they first walked in the classroom door. What should be an elevator to the upper class is stalled on the ground floor. Part of the fault for this may be laid at the feet of the system's entrenched interests: the teachers' unions and the higher-education professoriate. Our schools and universities are like the old Soviet department stores whose mission was to serve the interests of the sales clerks and not the customers. Why the sales clerks should want to keep things that way is perfectly understandable. The question, however, is why this is permitted to continue, why reform efforts meet with such opposition, especially from America's elites. The answer is that aristocracy is society's default position. For those who stand at America's commanding heights, social and income mobility is precisely what must be opposed, and a broken educational system wonderfully serves the purpose. As such, the New Class will oppose school choice, vouchers and parochial schools, anything that smacks of competition to a broken system.

America prides itself on being the country of immigrants. There's a bit of puffery in this, since there's a much higher percentage of foreign-born residents in Australia and Canada, and America ranks only a little ahead of Great Britain and France. Still, the country historically has been the principal haven for waves of immigrants. Before the Immigration Reform Act of 1965, the new arrivals added immeasurably to the country's economy, culture, and well-being. Since then, however, the quality of the America's immigrant intake has declined. We're still admitting the stellar scientists of years gone by, but on average immigrants are less educated than they were in the past, or even than Americans are today—not the highest of bars. We're also incurring the opportunity costs of a broken immigration system in the high-quality immigrants we don't admit and who either stay home or move to more immigrant-friendly countries. That burdens the country and makes us more unequal, but it's heaven for an American aristocracy that can hire cheap household labor without worrying about competition from high-skilled immigrants.

For the Ragged Dicks who seek to rise, nothing is more important than the rule of law, the security of property rights, and sanctity of contract provided by a mature and efficient legal system. The alternative—contract law in the state of nature—is the old-boy network composed of America's aristocrats. They know each other, and their personal bonds supply the trust that is needed before deals can be done and promises can be relied on. We're all made worse off when the rule of law is weak, as it is in today's America, when promises meant to be legally binding are imperfectly enforced by the courts. But then the costs of inefficient departures from the rule of law are borne disproportionately by the Ragged Dicks who begin without the benefit of an old-boy network.

Image 3.23

For all these barriers to mobility we can thank the members of the New Class, who dominate America's politics and constrain our policy choices. It is they who can be blamed for the recent run-up in American income inequality. The economy has become sclerotic, and the path to advancement over the last 40 and 50 years has been blocked by a profusion of new legal and regulatory barriers, all of which they have supported. They tell us they're upset by inequality and immobility, but we shouldn't believe them. You can't suck and blow.

The falcon, that bird of prey, knows not to foul its own nest. But then for our New Class, the falconers, it's not their own nest. It's the nest of the invertebrates, the bigots, the Other.

Interest Groups and Judicial Confirmations

A View from the Senate

By Amy Steigerwalt

W hile considerable media and popular attention has been concentrated on the role outside interest groups play in the modern-day federal judicial confirmation process, in reality, we know relatively little about the activities of these groups. Conventional wisdom suggests that outside groups drive the process itself, setting the terms of the debate and dictating the activities of like-minded senators. For example, the cover of the April 8, 2002, edition of the *National Review* featured a picture of then Judiciary Committee chair Patrick Leahy attached to marionette strings with the headline, "Strings Attached: How Liberal Interest Groups Control Senate Democrats." Similarly, Judge Charles Pickering stated, in response to a question about why he was filibustered in 2005 but unanimously confirmed to a district court seat in 1990, "During this period of time these far-left special interest groups gained power and they had control of Democrats on the Judiciary Committee, and through the Senators on the Committee they gained control of the entire Democratic apparatus" (Giachino 2006).

[...], however, that other factors might be at work in explaining why some nominees face long delays: nominees may be blocked by their home-state senators through the exercise of senatorial courtesy or their nominations may be turned down the private political track through the use of holds. Most important, [...] revealed that the capture of nominations by private political tactics is usually incidental to the actual disputes: nominations are captured by these parliamentary procedures out of convenience or because of their bargaining significance. Thus, senators do not merely trap nominees to appease like-minded interest groups.

Nonetheless, we do know interest groups play an influential role in the lower court confirmation process. Since the start of the second Reagan administration, interest groups have been major players in the process as they, along with presidents and senators, have increasingly recognized the far-reaching and long-term consequences of who sits on the federal bench. While groups have historically recognized the importance of Supreme Court vacancies (see, e.g., Abraham 1999; Frank 1991; Maltese 1995; Silverstein 1994), only recently have they turned their attention to lower court selection. In the mid-1980s and early 1990s, judicial watchdog groups formed on the left and the right, and other groups began monitoring lower court nominations as well. For groups concerned with policy issues in which court decisions play a prominent role—issues such as gay marriage, abortion rights, discrimination, and the death penalty—the Senate confirmation process affords one more arena in which to pursue their goals.

[...] explore what roles interest groups play in the lower court confirmation process and the impact of these activities. I begin by examining the different functions interest groups perform. Interest groups historically participated formally in the judicial confirmation process by testifying at confirmation hearings. Previous studies focus on assessing when groups testified and whether, through testifying, these groups influenced a lower court nominee's likelihood of confirmation (Bell 2002a; Cohen 1998; Flemming, MacLeod, and Talbert 1998). Since the early 1990s, however, Judiciary Committee chairs have restricted the formal involvement of groups, so groups have turned to more informal mechanisms of participation.

We know relatively little about groups' informal activities. Seminal studies examine informal interest group activity in the context of particular, highly contested nominations (Bell 2002a; Caldeira, Hojnacki, and Wright 2000; Caldeira and Wright 1995, 1998), but no study to date has examined the full extent of the functions groups perform in the lower court confirmation process, including whether groups play any role in uncontested nominations.

This [reading] adds a different perspective to the debate over interest group activity by asking those who are most likely to be affected—senators and their staffs—what functions they believe interest groups perform. Senators and Senate staffers recognize that outside groups are a formidable force in the modern legislative arena. But are groups essential players in the lower court confirmation process, or are they a necessary evil that must be dealt with? Are groups the puppet masters of like-minded senators, or do they fill roles senators and their staffs cannot? This [reading] aims to answer these questions by examining the results of interviews with thirty-two Senate staffers and one former senator.

Before I turn to the interview results, I will briefly lay out what we do know. Studies find that interest groups play an important role in influencing members of Congress generally (see, e.g., Austen-Smith 1993; Cigler and Loomis 1998; Denzau and Munger 1986; Hojnacki and Kimball 1999; Schlozman and Tierney 1986; Wright 1996). In the judicial confirmation process, groups perform a crucial information-transmission role (Caldeira, Hojnacki, and Wright 2000; Caldeira and Wright 1995, 1998; Scherer 2003; Scherer, Bartels, and Steigerwalt 2008). Groups used to fulfill this role by testifying at confirmation hearings about the nominee's background and perceived views, and by providing reports from group members who resided in the nominee's home state. When formal participation was curtailed, groups turned to informal information-transmission mechanisms, such as written reports and lobbying (Bell 2002a). The question, however, is why such a task for outside groups is even necessary. The next two sections explain why information on judicial nominations is both essential and lacking, and provide an overview of what formal and informal sources of information are available to senators and their staffs.

THE NEED FOR INFORMATION ON JUDICIAL NOMINATIONS

Collecting and analyzing information on nominees is a crucial component of the judicial confirmation process. During every presidential term, hundreds of lower court vacancies need to be filled. Presidents need information about potential nominees for each vacancy, and senators and their staffs need information about each nominee once the nominations are formally sent to the Senate.

Members of the Judiciary Committee require considerable amounts of information, as they must determine whether every nominee is suitable for the federal bench. The Senate's committee structure requires committees to do the brunt of the work on bills and nominations related to their specific areas; as a result of this specialization, other senators depend on the committees to provide them with detailed information once a bill or nomination makes it to the Senate floor (Gilligan and Krehbiel 1989, 1990; Krehbiel 1991). With dozens of nominees awaiting Judiciary Committee attention at any one time, committee members and their staffs must try to determine which nominees require a more thorough investigation and which nominees can be quickly vetted. The quandary is that information gathered about one nominee does not help senators assess other nominees. As Caldeira, Hojnacki, and Wright (2000) explain, "Nominations strain the resources of Senators, for no two nominations are alike. Whatever information or expertise senators acquire about one nominee is not transferable to the next. On each nomination, senators must learn about a nominee's policy views and any controversial decision made by the nominee" (67).

As the nation has expanded in population and in size, the number of federal judgeships has multiplied, and the need for information about potential nominees has grown accordingly. In addition, as lower court confirmations have become the new battleground, the Senate's need for information has grown as well. Finally, "the demand for information on controversial nominees is high *and* constant" (Caldeira, Hojnacki, and Wright 2000, 54). Senators must therefore rely on both formal and informal sources of information to effectively vet judicial nominees.

Formal Sources of Information

Senators rely on four main sources of formal information on lower court nominees. First, every nominee completes a Judiciary Committee questionnaire. Nominees provide information about their background, education, financial interests, and work experiences, including information about any significant cases they have litigated. Nominees who have previously served as judges, whether at the local, state, or federal level, are asked to supply copies of their ten most significant decisions, as well as data on the number of times their decisions have been reversed by a higher court. Nominees are also asked to make available copies of all other published materials, such as books or articles, and any public speeches. The Judiciary Committee may also make other requests, such as asking for copies of a judge's unpublished opinions.[1] This information is available to every senator who serves on the committee.

The committee's investigatory staffers then vet each nominee by reviewing this information. The week prior to a nominee's confirmation hearing, the nominations counsel prepares a report that is sent to the members of the committee and any other senator who requests it.[2] This memo provides information about the nominee, with the aim of highlighting facts or cases of interest. As the chief nominations counsel explained in 2002, "It's usually just very straight information with an eye to what I know they will be concerned about. They're going to be concerned about the death penalty, abortion rights, civil liberties, and labor because these are Democrats. That's what they are very concerned about, so I let them know that. But it's not an opinion piece."

Second, the Federal Bureau of Investigation (FBI) conducts a background check on each nominee. This investigation takes place at the request of the White House prior to the formal nomination, and the report is initially sent only to the White House. The FBI's investigation consists of interviews with friends, family, co-workers, and employers, as well as inquiries into employment and arrest records. The FBI's investigation focuses on ensuring that the prospective nominee does not have any personal issues that may disqualify him or her from holding a lifetime appointment, such as substance abuse, serious financial problems, or potentially illegal or unethical activities. Once a person is formally nominated, a copy of the report is forwarded to the Judiciary Committee. Because of the confidential nature of the information collected by the FBI, only senators serving on the committee plus one staff member in each of the chair's and ranking minority member's offices are authorized to view this file. It is understood that information contained in a nominee's FBI file will not be discussed publicly, even if a senator objects to a nominee based on something discovered during the FBI's investigation.[3]

Third, the American Bar Association (ABA) conducts an in-depth investigation of each nominee. Lower court nominees are asked to fill out a lengthy questionnaire and to provide the ABA with copies of all previous writings or speeches. Confidential interviews are then conducted with at least forty individuals who have knowledge of the nominee's professional experiences and behavior. The ABA's investigation focuses on assessing nominees' professional competence and qualifications, as well as their integrity and judicial temperament (American Bar Association 2007; Grossman 1965). The ABA then rates each nominee as either "well qualified," "qualified," or "not qualified" for the position to which the candidate is nominated. The ABA publicly announces the rating given to each lower court nominee, as well as whether the rating was unanimous. The ABA does not, however, release any other information or a summary of these investigations to the White House, Senate, or public. If a nominee receives a "not qualified" or a split "not qualified/qualified" rating, the ABA may be asked to testify at the nominee's committee hearing and explain the reason for the "not qualified" rating.[4]

From the mid-1940s until March 2001, the ABA's investigation took place during the presidential selection phase, at the request of the White House. The ABA's rating would then be forwarded to the Senate post-nomination. In March 2001, President George W. Bush decided to discontinue the ABA's role at the presidential selection phase in response to growing complaints that the ABA's ratings were biased against conservative-leaning nominees.[5] Then Judiciary Committee chair Patrick Leahy determined that the committee would send the names of nominees to the ABA for evaluation, and wait to proceed on each nomination until a rating was received (Hudson 2001). While Republican senators did not necessarily agree with the initial decision, Orrin Hatch continued the practice once he regained the chairmanship in 2003 (Davidson 2003). Then, on March 17, 2009, newly inaugurated President Barack Obama announced the restoration of the ABA to its traditional pre-presidential-selection role.

The ongoing dispute over whether the ABA's ratings are biased against conservatives (see, e.g., Vining, Steigerwalt, and Smelcer 2009) only serves to illuminate the considerable impact these ratings have on judicial confirmations. Regardless of political affiliation, ABA ratings are the benchmark by which actors in the judicial selection process determine whether a particular nominee can be considered qualified to serve on the federal bench. Presidents use the ABA's ratings to determine which proposed candidate should receive a nomination; a low rating prior to presidential selection may prevent candidates from being formally nominated (Goldman 1997; Hall 1979). Once a nomination is sent to the Senate, senators look to ABA ratings to provide a clear signal as to the nominee's level of professional qualifications and fitness to be confirmed to the federal bench. Although a high ABA rating does not ensure a successful confirmation, it does generally shield nominees from facing an overly contentious path to confirmation (see, e.g., Martinek, Kemper, and Van Winkle 2002).

Finally, the nominees themselves provide further information in two ways. First, each nominee testifies at a Judiciary Committee hearing and answers oral questions from committee members.[6] Hearings may last a few hours or may continue for days—Robert Bork testified for five days—and the committee may ask a nominee to return for a second hearing, as they did in the summer of

2002 with Fifth Circuit Court nominee Charles Pickering. Nominees renominated in successive Congresses by the same president may also be subjected to additional committee hearings in the later Congresses, though this is not a hard-and-fast rule. These hearings are open to the public, and hearing transcripts are published by the Senate. Supporters and opponents of the nominee may be invited to testify as to the nominee's fitness for the bench. However, Judiciary Committee chairs have generally not allowed such outside testimony since the late 1980s (Bell 2002a, 87). Second, the nominee may be asked by senators to answer a series of written follow-up questions.[7]

There are thus four sources of formal information that the Senate Judiciary Committee receives. Committee members use these formal information sources to assess each nominee and determine whether the nominee should be confirmed. Most of this formal information is also available to the other senators and their staffs.

Informal Sources of Information

The conundrum is that these formal sources of information do not alleviate the enormous resource constraints confronting senators. Given the sheer number of nominations made each congressional term, senators and their staffs lack the time and resources to cull the mountain of information produced on every nominee; this is especially true if a nominee has a substantial written record from previous experience as a judge or law professor. When Senator Edward Kennedy became chair in 1979, he began the practice of hiring investigatory staffers to allow the committee to independently vet judicial nominees. However, as of 2002, as noted by the then current nominations counsel, the majority staff had only two staffers whose full-time job was to vet nominees.

Senators also require more than just raw information about the nominee and his or her background; they need information that can help them distinguish between the dozens of nominations pending at any one time and determine which nominees are acceptable and which require additional scrutiny. Senators additionally seek information about what Caldeira and Wright term "the 'politics' of nominations" (1995, 45). Senators must ascertain not only whether a nominee may hold troubling views but also how mobilized groups and voters in their home states view the nominee: since senators cannot fight every nomination, they need to determine which fights their constituents will support. As a result, senators and their staff rely heavily on a more informal source of information, interest groups.

Interest groups help senators identify which nominees require additional attention. Leading judicial watchdog groups provide senators and their staffs with information on nominees. Many times groups send detailed reports on a nominee's background and views, with special attention to potentially problematic judicial decisions or writings; the report may also highlight important political information about the nomination and home-state support. In this way, groups fill the gap left by the formal information sources by providing information designed specifically to help senators differentiate among the multitude of nominations pending each congressional term.

Currently we lack empirical, systematic evidence about the extent of groups' information-transmission role. I therefore interviewed Senate staff to determine how often groups send information, to whom they send it, and how this information is used by its recipients. The results of these interviews are detailed below.

TABLE 3.3.I Descriptive Statistics on Senate Staff Members Interviewed

	TOTAL INTERVIEWED	TOTAL CURRENT STAFF	TOTAL FORMER STAFF	TOTAL SENATE JUDICIARY COMMITTEE STAFF
DEMOCRATS	18	14	4	12
REPUBLICANS	14	9	5	9
TOTAL	32	23	9	21

THE INTERVIEWS

During the summer of 2002, I interviewed thirty-two current and former Senate staff members (table 3.3.1).[8] I also interviewed former senator Howard Metzenbaum (D-OH), who served on the Judiciary Committee between 1977 and 1994. I interviewed current and former staffers for the Judiciary Committee as well as current staffers who handled judicial confirmations for senators not on the committee. At the time of the interviews, twelve of the individuals interviewed worked for the Judiciary Committee and another nine interviewees were former committee staffers. The remaining eleven interviewees worked at the time as staff for senators who served on other committees. Eighteen individuals interviewed worked for Democrats and fourteen worked for Republicans. Many of the current staffers held the same position during the Clinton administration and thus could provide observations about the role of interest groups during both the Clinton and George W. Bush administrations. The nine former committee staffers provided an institutional memory dating back to the Reagan administration.

The interviews probed each interviewee's view of the role of interest groups in the judicial confirmation process. The interviewees were asked specifically about the types of information they received from interest groups and how often they received such information, their relationships with different interest groups, and the role they believed interest groups played in making particular confirmations contested. Finally, staffers who worked in the Senate during multiple presidential administrations were asked about any variations they observed in the functions played by outside groups during the different administrations. Most of these interviewees asked not to be directly quoted; these staffers are identified in the text by their political party and whether they worked for a senator on or off the Judiciary Committee.

I used a combination of structured and semistructured interview techniques. First, to provide a more systematic examination of how those in the Senate view outside interest groups, I posed the same series of questions to the interviewees. I then examined their answers much as John Kingdon did in his seminal study, *Congressmen's Voting Decisions* (1989). Kingdon asked a set series of questions of all his interview subjects. He then quantified their answers by counting how many interviewees gave similar answers to the same question. This approach allowed him to uncover systematic answer patterns across subjects and within discrete groups. I used this method for questions about the overall role of interest groups, as well as their information-transmission role. As a result, I was able to draw conclusions about the views held by my interview subjects, as well as to discover important differences between subgroups of interviewees. Second, I utilized semistructured interview questions to probe more broadly into the interviewees' view of interest groups and the confirmation process overall. I then analyzed these answers looking for broad, consistent themes. Three primary questions drove these interviews: (1) How important is interest groups' information-transmission role in the lower court confirmation process? (2) What other functions do interest groups perform in the lower court confirmation process? (3) Are there noticeable differences in the roles liberal and conservative groups play in the lower court confirmation process?

INTEREST GROUPS AND INFORMATION

Thirty interviewees were asked, "What do you see as the role of interest groups in the judicial confirmation process?" If a staffer described multiple roles for interest groups, each of the roles was recorded as a separate response. Therefore, the total number of responses in table 3.3.2 is more than the total number of staffers who were asked the question. In response to this question, 83 percent of those interviewed (twenty-four staffers and Senator Metzenbaum) answered that the main function interest groups performed was providing research and information about the nominees (table 3.3.2). Staffers described the reports they received from interest groups as "invaluable" and an "easy" and "huge" source of information.

All of the staffers seconded the arguments advanced in previous studies that information is a vital commodity lacking in the judicial confirmation process overall and that the Judiciary Committee is not equipped to acquire or provide the information senators and staff both on and off the committee require. All of the participants voiced a desire for complete information on

TABLE 3.3.2 Senate Staff Responses Concerning the Roles of Interest Groups in Lower Court Confirmations

	RESEARCH AND INFORMATION (%)	SET AGENDA (%)	MEDIA AND PUBLIC RELATIONS (%)	GRASS-ROOTS MOBILIZATION (%)	SUPPORT SENATORS IF IS A BATTLE (%)	INFLUENCE SENATORS' VOTING DECISIONS (%)	NOT MUCH AT ALL (%)
DEMOCRATS	19 (63)	5 (17)	2 (7)	2 (7)	1 (3)	0 (0)	0
CURRENT STAFF	13 (43)	4 (13)	2 (7)	2 (7)	1 (3)	0 (0)	0
FORMER STAFF	5 (17)	0	0	0	0	0	0
COMMITTEE STAFF	14 (47)	2 (7)	2 (7)	2 (7)	1 (3)	0	0
REPUBLICANS	6 (20)	1 (3)	4 (13)	2 (7)	1 (3)	1 (3)	2 (7)
CURRENT STAFF	3 (10)	1 (3)	2 (7)	1 (3)	0 (3)	1 (3)	1 (3)
FORMER STAFF	3 (10)	0 (7)	2 (7)	1 (3)	1 (3)	0	1
COMMITTEE STAFF	3 (10)	0 (10)	3 (3)	1 (3)	1 (7)	0	2
TOTAL	25 (83)	6 (20)	6 (20)	4 (14)	2 (7)	1 (3)	2 (7)

Note: The numbers reported for "Democrats total" also include responses given by former senator Howard Metzenbaum.

each nominee's background and views. A common complaint expressed during the interviews was the dearth of available information; information on nominees frequently was described as not forthcoming or readily available.

Even staffers serving on the Judiciary Committee felt they often lacked necessary information on each nominee. The week of a confirmation hearing, all committee members receive the memo composed by the chief nominations counsel and a copy of the nominee's completed questionnaire.[9] For nominees viewed as noncontroversial, this information is generally sufficient. However, when questions arise as to a nominee's fitness for the federal bench, staffers reported that these items lacked the substance needed to help them make an informed decision about the nominee. Staffers also noted their inability to conduct their own investigations. Each staffer must therefore find ways to augment his or her knowledge. Not surprisingly, many turn to interest groups to fill this gap.

Judiciary Committee staffers also frequently mentioned that they were responsible for numerous other issues beyond judicial confirmations, and so the research provided by interest groups freed them to focus on other priorities. As a Democratic committee staffer explained, "It's knowing that the groups are doing [research] that we are able to focus our energies on other things. If they didn't, we probably would make an effort, but we have to focus on all the other things the Committee does. ... I can devote less of my staff time to reading every case, if we're going to be getting very detailed reports from interest groups. Obviously, you have to take them with a grain of salt, and review what they've done, but it's a very good starting point."

The workload and the importance of judicial nominations also vary by office. A staffer working for a more junior member of the Judiciary Committee explained that information received from the committee and from interest groups the week of the hearing is invaluable, especially as she is the only staffer in her office working on judicial nominations. She further noted her approach to using the various sources of information. If the nomination is somewhat contentious, she relies mostly on the committee's memo; however, if the nomination is contested, she looks more closely at the interest groups' evaluations. Overall, she relies more on the interest groups' research, since interest groups generally can devote more resources to vetting each nominee than the committee can.

In comparison, many of the committee Republicans said conservative interest groups were not a significant source of information for them (see table 3.3.2). These staffers explained they received little to no information from interest groups (though many of them wished they did), and many further commented that any information they did receive from groups was usually information they already possessed, whether it came from then chairman Leahy's office, the Department of Justice, or their own research. As noted throughout this [reading], the more conservative a senator, the less likely he or she was to receive information from interest groups, and especially from groups on the left, who primarily fulfilled the information-transmission role during the 107th Congress.

Thus, overall, groups transmit needed information to committee members and their staff. Partisan differences emerge when this information-transmission function is examined more closely, as conservative offices rarely receive information from interest groups (and this was true even during the Clinton administration), while more liberal offices receive such information frequently and rely on it a great deal.

For those not serving on the Judiciary Committee, the formal information available through the committee was also viewed as inadequate for assessing nominees. There are a number of reasons why this might be so. The Judiciary Committee does not customarily send information about every nominee to every senator; rather, it does so only when asked. The vast majority of staff members I spoke with said that the amount of material they received from the committee was usually insufficient for their needs. As one moderate Republican explained, often he receives "only superficial or no information" on a nominee from the committee. Consequently for non-committee members, the information provided by interest groups fills this crucial gap. A Democratic staffer observed, "Especially with controversial nominees, [interest groups] provide information on that nominee that you may not get from the White House or the Judiciary Committee which is considered 'official information,' so the interest groups rely a lot on 'unofficial information.'" A moderate Republican staffer noted that "there are so many nominations that there is not the time or the resources to check out each and every one, [and] you don't have all the information you need, so interest groups play a crucial role in providing background information, and pointing out who are the potential controversies." Interestingly, this same staffer also maintained that one must look to information from interest groups because information from the majority and minority offices of the committee is "inherently unreliable to rely on because it has a biased view." As judicial nominees are not usually on a non-committee staffer's radar before they hit the Senate floor, interest groups play a large role in bringing attention to worrisome nominees (see Table 3.3.2). Thus, many staffers reported relying heavily on interest groups both to provide them with basic information and to alert them to problematic nominees (see also Scherer, Bartels, and Steigerwalt 2008).

Information from the Judiciary Committee was also found to be lacking in "insider information." Staffers expressed frustration at not knowing the status of nominees from their states and commonly said they did not know what was blocking their nominees' progress. When asked about her biggest frustrations, one staffer replied, "Information. I wish it could get to us faster. … I just want to know, so I can pass it on or know what's going on and know what to do. … You know those email alerts you get from CNN? I'd like to get one of those from the committee. 'Alert: there's a hold,' or 'Alert: your nominee is coming up.' ... But they have so many. ... When you call [the committee staff is] really friendly. ... But I have to call them." Interest groups thus appreciably augment formal information sources for non-Judiciary Committee members.

Where You Sit Determines What You Read

Beyond providing information about a nominee's background and views, interest groups also supply necessary information about the politics of particular nominations. However, one of the most interesting interview findings that emerged is that constituency concerns do matter, but only for certain senators. Overall, key differences in the types of information senators find useful exist between senators serving on the Judiciary Committee and those not currently serving on the committee.

For those serving on the committee, constituent concerns matter little. Committee staffers all dismissed the impact of constituent concerns on their bosses' decision-making calculi when determining whether to vote for a particular judicial nominee. A former Republican committee staffer explained, "We don't pay attention to any letters, as [Senator X] has such a safe seat. A lot of times the mail criticizes him for not being conservative enough, and that just doesn't matter on nominations."[10] Similarly, a current Republican committee staffer, when asked whether constituency concerns influenced his boss's vote, said, "Probably not. It's useful for us to see how many resources we need to dedicate to defending a nominee or explain [Senator X's] position on a nominee." While home-state nominees invoke constituent considerations, for the vast majority of nominees, committee senators focus on the nominee's background and views rather than on home-state political calculations.

Therefore, the groups with the greatest access to committee members and their staff are the leading judicial watchdog groups. As of 2002, these were the Alliance for Justice and People for the American Way on the left, and the Judicial Selection Monitoring Project on the right. These three groups monitor federal judicial selection on behalf of hundreds of smaller groups. They focus mainly on providing analyses of the nominees and their views rather than on offering more strategic or constituency-based information.

Many of the committee staffers I spoke with also specifically noted that they relied more heavily on information from national groups than on information from local groups. As one current committee staffer explained, he believes the national groups are more "plugged in," and he knows the "groups do a lot of legwork to check how local people feel." Moreover, since he "know[s] those at the national interest groups personally," he trusts them when they report local reactions. Other staffers reported similar views. Thus, for those senators on the Judiciary Committee, reelection concerns are not the primary impetus for granting an interest group access and influence. The question then arises, what is the primary concern of senators on the Judiciary Committee?

Simply put, many committee staffers felt that the decision of whether to support a judicial nominee was one "removed from politics." Staffers on both sides of the aisle argued that their senators were concerned with the role of the federal courts and the individual impact each nominee might make, rather than how each vote might affect their reelection chances. As one committee staffer explained, in a statement echoed by many, "The Judiciary Committee members … have a role to play in reviewing nominations that is completely separate from their constituents, and they take that role seriously, and they want to know what those who have concerns on substance think, whereas a Senator who's not on the Committee and not involved in the state or Circuit, when they cast their vote they're more concerned about how it's going to play at home. … [The committee members] make their decisions on their own judgment. They've taken on this responsibility, and they want to carry it out seriously."

Much like Fenno's (1973) conclusions in his seminal study, *Congressmen in Committee*, about why senators choose to serve on the Senate Foreign Relations Committee, the Judiciary Committee staff all agreed that senators join the committee out of a concern for the creation of public policy through the courts. Consequently, the policies (expected) to be created by those serving on the federal courts take center stage in these senators' deliberations. As a result, those groups that focus on providing such information—the primary actions of the leading judicial watchdog groups—play a central role in aiding committee members in making their decisions. Conversely, membership groups that primarily transmit information about constituency concerns and potential electoral ramifications play a much lesser role in influencing the views of committee members. Some staffers on the committee expressed skepticism about constituent contacts and views: "I think that there is a real sense that a lot of people who call are activated by these networks and in the end they won't actually know what the result is anyway. … I don't think that we have a huge concern about how [Senator X] votes on a particular nominee is going to get those folks upset with him because they probably won't know" (Republican committee staffer).

On the other hand, for those senators not serving on the committee, constituent concerns take priority. One staffer commented, "It's the constituents who drive the decision making, and how the Senator is going to respond to the nominee." A Republican staffer explained that for his office, an interest group's biggest influence was the likelihood that it could affect who was voting for his boss: "If [the interest group] got a lot of responses from [our] constituents, then we watch that very closely." Senators not on the committee therefore listen more closely to the objections of membership groups tied to their states and issues of importance to them. For example, for senators active on women's issues and abortion, the objections of membership-based groups such as the National Organization for Women and NARAL on the left and Concerned Women for America on the right—and the mobilized constituents they bring with them—are extremely important. These findings, at least for non-committee members, bolster the arguments made by Scherer (2003, 2005) that groups are able to exert influence because of senators' fears of electoral retribution.

Non-committee senators and their staffers are much more worried about constituent interests and less trusting of national groups than their counterparts on the Judiciary Committee. What the national interest groups can do is round up local constituents for senators and staff to talk with: "We use them [the national groups] as a source to get to our local constituents. We don't just take their word for anything, because sometimes the local constituents differ." This Democratic staffer continued, "You always want to quote the local office. ... You always want to be able to say I talked to Mrs. Jane Smith and this is what she thinks." Similarly, a Republican staffer suggested that national groups should always bring local constituents with them. He related that the meeting he had immediately following our interview was with the president of the League of Women Voters. While he was personally excited (and flattered) to meet with her, he explained that her visit would be much more powerful politically if she brought along local members from the state, as "the message is clearer if the group is from [our state]," especially as that transmits unmistakable constituency (and, consequently, electoral) cues.

Thus, constituency and reelection concerns predominate on both sides of the aisle for senators not serving on the Judiciary Committee. These staffers are less interested in the reports coming from national groups and more interested in letters and phone calls from their constituents. That said, not all constituent responses are valued equally: "The ways in which people contact are varied, and they are not equal in their effectiveness" (Verba 1993, 678). Many staffers explained that much of the correspondence they receive on judicial nominations is generated through interest groups. Groups send out "alerts" or bulletins that encourage their members to call or write their senators. To aid these efforts, interest groups have created mechanisms that allow interested members to send emails and faxes to senators directly from their Web sites.

Referred to as "Astroturf lobbying," this mechanism of manufactured grassroots activity can generate considerable action, but it can also be a deterrent to true debate, as offices are forced to determine where the calls are coming from and how much they actually reflect home-state concerns.[11] Thus, while senators and their staffs are highly responsive to constituent concerns, they also make clear distinctions between different types of constituent contacts, such as weighing 100 handwritten letters more highly than the same form letter with 100 different signatures. One staffer said he would speak to anyone who calls, but he also recognized the difference between the people who read an editorial on a situation affecting nominations to their circuit court and have "honest questions" versus the people who call to say "vote for candidate X" and know only the talking points generated by a particular interest group. He further explained, "On lots of controversial issues we get millions of calls because someone is spending money, and they just don't matter that much as they are not a good reflection of the state's views." He added that if a local mayor or community leader or worker in the state or local chapter of an interest group calls, those are the contacts that he relates to the senator, but 100 phone calls from "John Smiths" that were generated by a group's phone tree do not carry nearly the same weight: "They may not be totally ignored, but it's just different." Thus, while non-committee senators assess constituency concerns when making their decisions on judicial nominees, they have also learned to distinguish between the types of constituency contacts and their corresponding import.

Finally, a former Judiciary Committee staffer highlighted how committee members do rely on local chapters of national organizations. Mark Gittenstein, chief counsel under Senator Biden when he was chair, explained that interest groups could help committee senators lobby non-committee senators. He commented, "The [groups] in Washington were not nearly as effective as the ones in the field talking to members … Because they knew the members. The local NAACP or something like that more likely than not knows the members" (2002).[12] Thus, committee staffers find local organizations useful as a means of shoring up support from other senators once a nominee moves to the Senate floor, but not as an instrument to help their senators determine how to vote for a nominee in committee.

In sum, whom a senator listens to is highly dependent on where the senator sits. For senators not on the Judiciary Committee, electoral concerns dominate, and local membership groups exert enormous influence. These staffers want to hear from those in their home state. Oppositely, committee senators take their role of staffing the federal bench seriously. For these senators, the desire to make good public policy, much like the senators Fenno interviewed thirty years ago, dominates their decision-making processes, rather than the need to appease constituents at home. National groups provide these senators with important substantive information they can use to determine how to vote on a nomination, but grassroots lobbying efforts serve only to alert committee senators to how much time they need to devote to defending their positions.

OTHER INTEREST GROUP ROLES

Interviewees noted two other key functions interest groups perform, with an interesting split along party lines (see table 3.3.2). Twenty percent of respondents—four Democratic staffers, Senator Metzenbaum, and one moderate Republican staffer—stated that groups help set the agenda by identifying which nominees should be targeted for defeat, while another 20 percent of respondents—four Republicans and two Democrats—maintained that interest groups mainly played a public relations role.

Staff members I spoke with, especially those not on the committee, noted their reliance on interest groups to help determine which nominees were most vulnerable: "The role of interest groups is pretty huge, especially for a non-Senate Judiciary Committee member, because we pay attention when groups bring us information, because unless the nomination is pretty egregious, it is not even on our radar screen until it hits the floor. Thus, the role of the interest groups is to bring attention to a nomination before it hits the floor, to call and tell us which ones to be concerned about" (Democratic staffer not on the committee). The role of interest groups as strategists can go even farther. As one Democratic staffer explained, "interest groups are good about picking [senators] to lead the fights," as they are knowledgeable about who might be willing to be a lead spokesperson or put a hold on a nominee. Alternatively, numerous Republicans pointed to the important task they believe interest groups fulfill in terms of media and public relations.

This party division with respect to the secondary role of interest groups is not entirely surprising. First, because the interviews were done during a period of Democratic control of the Senate and Republican control of the presidency, liberal groups were the ones determining which of George W. Bush's nominations were viable targets for defeat. Conservative groups in turn had their greatest impact on the presidential selection process rather than the Senate confirmation process.[13] Similarly, since Republicans were focused on supporting President Bush's nominations to the federal bench, their view of interest groups as useful conduits for media relations is also not unexpected. However, the interviews also revealed that conservative interest groups play much less of a public and organized role than liberal interest groups, and this was true even during the Clinton administration. In fact, two of the Republican committee interviewees (7 percent) said they did not believe groups played much of a role at all in the judicial confirmation process.

Interviewees who highlighted the information-transmission role of interest groups were asked how often they received such information from groups. Interesting partisan distinctions again appeared, as well as differences based on whether the staffer served on the Judiciary Committee (table 3.3.3). Of the twenty-one staffers asked how often they received information from groups, 57 percent answered that they received information only on contentious nominees, though many of these staffers further commented that they received information "all the time" about these contested nominees. This dual response was usually given by those working on the Judiciary Committee. Eight staffers (38 percent) replied that they received information "rarely" or "never." Strikingly, seven of these eight staffers were Republican. The three Republican staffers who "never" received information from groups all served on the committee and worked for rather conservative senators. Thus, while Democratic staffers receive a considerable amount of information from interest groups, the groups do not seem to send Republicans similar levels of information, and this was especially true of Republican committee staffers. The Republican staffers who did report receiving a decent amount of information from groups all worked for senators not on the committee. The lone Republican who "almost always" received information from outside groups worked for a moderate non-committee senator known to reach across the aisle on a number of issues.

TABLE 3.3.3 Senate Staff Responses Concerning How Often They Received Information From Interest Groups

	ALMOST ALWAYS (%)	ONLY ON CONTROVERSIAL NOMINATIONS (%)	RARELY (%)	NEVER (%)
DEMOCRATS	7	8	1	0
	(33)	(38)	(5)	
CURRENT STAFF	6	6	1	0
	(29)	(29)	(5)	
FORMER STAFF	1	2	0	0
	(5)	(10)		
COMMITTEE STAFF	6	5	0	0
	(29)	(24)		
REPUBLICANS	1	4	4	3
	(5)	(19)	(19)	(14)
CURRENT STAFF	1	3	4	3
	(5)	(14)	(19)	(14)
FORMER STAFF	0	1	0	0
		(5)		
COMMITTEE STAFF	0	1	2	3
		(5)	(10)	(14)
TOTAL	8	12	5	3
	(38)	(57)	(24)	(14)

Finally, with regard to groups' information-providing role, eighteen interviewees were asked, "Do you ever receive information from interest groups on the opposite side of the aisle?"[14] This question was asked of eleven Democrats and seven Republicans, all of whom had stated earlier that they at least sometimes received information from outside groups (table 3.3.4). Overall, 67 percent of respondents stated they received information from groups across the aisle. However, when we look at these results by party, we discover that all eleven Democrats received at least some information from conservative groups, while only four of the seven Republicans received information from liberal groups.

The results in table 3.3.4, combined with those shown in table 3.3.3, indicate that groups are cognizant of the need to use different strategies when targeting committee senators versus non-committee senators. Groups also seem to recognize the utility of targeting various senators. Those who did not receive any information from groups and those who had never been targeted by groups across the aisle were all staffers who worked for conservative committee members who were highly supportive of all of President George W. Bush's nominees. On the other hand, those who received information constantly and from groups on both sides of the aisles were all either Democratic committee staffers or staffers working for moderate, swing-vote senators.

These findings afford an important glimpse into one of the unique features of lower court confirmation politics vis-à-vis the role of interest groups: groups must lobby their friends. In a significant study of the effect of interest group lobbying on the outcome of Robert Bork's nomination to the Supreme Court in 1987, Austen-Smith and Wright (1994, 1996; but see Baumgartner and Leech 1996) find that groups engage in "counter-active" lobbying of their friends on Supreme Court nominations only to offset the effects of lobbying by opposition groups. However, the above results illuminate the fact that, with regard to lower court nominations, groups spend quite a lot of time lobbying their friends. The question is, why?

TABLE 3.3.4   Senate Staff Responses Concerning Whether They Received Information From Interest Groups Traditionally Aligned With the Other Party

	YES (%)	FEW TIMES/ONCE (%)	NEVER (%)
DEMOCRATS	8	3	0
	(44)	(17)	
CURRENT STAFF	8	2	0
	(44)	(11)	
FORMER STAFF	0	1	0
		(6)	
COMMITTEE STAFF	5	3	0
	(28)	(17)	
REPUBLICANS	4	0	3
	(22)		(17)
CURRENT STAFF	3	0	2
	(17)		(11)

FORMER STAFF	1	0	1
	(6)		(6)
COMMITTEE STAFF	1	0	3
	(6)		(17)
TOTAL	12	3	3
	(67)	(17)	(17)

Simply put, the historical deference given to presidents and home-state senators to select lower court judges deters senators from voting against nominees without ample cause. Groups must assume that each senator will vote yes on a given nominee unless sufficient evidence becomes available to provide the senator with an acceptable reason to vote no (see also Scherer, Bartels, and Steigerwalt 2008). Interest groups therefore must devote much of their resources to convincing even their friends to vote no. Consequently, liberal groups routinely targeted liberal senators such as Charles Schumer and Barbara Boxer in order to galvanize opposition to particular Bush (43) nominees. Given this reality, groups opposed to a nominee recognize that spending time lobbying one's opposition (i.e., a member of the president's party) diverts precious resources, as the chance that these senators will vote against one of the president's nominees is extremely small; only in situations where groups lobby a member of the president's party who is known to be receptive to the views held by the group might such a strategy work (and only once opposition party senators have joined the fight). Thus, Lincoln Chaffee, a moderate Republican, was lobbied heavily by liberal interest groups during the 107th Congress, while conservative senators Jon Kyl and Jeff Sessions received no contact from any liberal groups.

Partisan Differences among Group Activities

The final notable finding from the staff interviews was the emergence of clear partisan differences regarding the amount and character of interest group lobbying. As of 2002, there existed a widespread belief that few conservative groups were consistently involved in the lower court confirmation process. A Republican staffer with leadership ties expressed a need to "create the groups" on the right. He felt conservatives such as Ralph Reed and Pat Robertson concentrated on nominations during the Reagan and Bush (41) administrations, but not more recently. He continued, "You would think the corporations would pay attention, but generally they are too busy doing business. We have to ask for help, the other side gets volunteers, and so we fight an uphill stream."

More important, all of the Republican interviewees claimed there was a "dearth" of interest groups on the right that provided information on nominees; instead, conservative groups were seen as playing mainly a media and public relations role (see table 3.3.2). For example, one Republican staff member commented that he could not think of a single group on the right from which he received information, while another stated that conservative groups had "never" provided any type of legal analysis or background information that his office did not already have. Several staffers noted that one group, Judicial Watch, sent numerous blast faxes, but the staffers then all reiterated that they could not think of any group that sent information, and especially not consistently. As one current Republican committee staffer commented, "[I] get nothing" on the nominees from conservative groups, and it is "frustrating." What he really wished for was an extra hand: "If there are a hundred cases and someone can say, 'Really look at these five especially,' that would be a lot of help. We're not getting it, and I really wish we did! It's just not there … or not being done." One moderate non-committee Republican commented, "It's not a matter of wishing for groups on the right but a matter of getting information on all sides. I get more from the left, perfected, they know how to do it, are just more effective. I think the right feels an inherently liberal bias in the media and so would not listen to them, and [do] not feel they get a fair hearing, so that may be partly why I appreciate information from all sides because the groups can slant information in any way." Similarly, another non-committee Republican stated, "I wish there were more sources of information to look through. I can't think of a single group on the right that I get information from. There are splinter groups who care only about one single issue, but there is not any one general group that sends information."

Instead, many staffers argued that the main function of conservative groups was media and public relations, another crucial lobbying tactic. Former Republican staffers indicated that conservative groups in earlier periods also concentrated more on media-related strategies. One former Republican committee staffer who had served during the Reagan administration described how conservative groups took the lead in convincing the public that Reagan's nominees were really no different from Carter's, Ford's, or Nixon's. Conservative groups did not provide information or lobby members; instead, he described how these groups worked to target the media and project the message of the Reagan administration. Similarly, another former Republican committee staffer said conservative groups did not conduct independent research but rather provided grassroots support once committee senators had made their decisions. He believed conservative groups had "zero influence" on the choices senators made and instead were used after the decision was made to mobilize elite and grassroots support for the senators' positions. Many times these groups actually received their information from the committee staff.[15] However, one Republican committee staffer expressed his wish for more help from conservative groups in "projecting their message."[16]

The activities of conservative groups and Republican offices are often highly coordinated. A former committee staffer explained how his office would work with the head of the Project for the Judiciary, a conservative think tank, on op-ed pieces about the Republican position on judges.

If their office had certain positions they wanted broadcast, they would feed arguments to the columnist, which he would then write up in opinion pieces published in key newspapers. Likewise, a senior administration official in the George W. Bush White House spoke in a 2002 interview about weekly strategy meetings attended by administration officials, Senate and committee leadership, and the leaders of key conservative groups. Thus, conservative groups do perform an important function in the judicial confirmation process, but it is a very different one from the role played by liberal groups.

CONCLUSION

Interviews with Senate staff revealed that interest groups play different roles in the judicial confirmation process. Because Senate staff and senators are those most likely to interact with groups and be affected by their actions (as they are the main targets of group lobbying activities), I asked these key players where they felt groups fit into the process. I then compared their answers with some of the main theories offered by other scholars vis-à-vis the role of outside groups in politics in general and in the judicial confirmation process in particular.

These interviews with current and former Senate staff produced four main findings. First, the overall role interest groups, especially liberal groups, play in the judicial confirmation process is to provide information. Although this function has been noted previously, the interviews uncovered the degree to which groups provide information because the committee cannot meet the information needs of those serving on and off the committee, whether the senator desires nominee-based information or more process-oriented information.

Second, senators who serve on the committee have very different information needs than non-committee senators. Committee senators desire objective, substantive information about the nominee, while non-committee senators crave strategic information about constituent views. And while committee members focus on the public policy aspects of staffing the federal bench, non-committee senators primarily pay attention to how their votes on nominees may affect their reelection chances.

Third, the lobbying strategies interest groups utilize differ in the context of judicial confirmations as opposed to other policy arenas. Because senators are predisposed to vote for a president's nominees, groups must lobby everyone, including their friends, to ensure an outcome in their favor. More lobbying must be done, and it must be directed at more friends than usually occurs in other policy arenas.

Finally, from the point of view of those in the Senate, the interviews illuminated significant partisan differences as to the role interest groups play in the confirmation process. Liberal groups primarily provide information, while conservative groups principally perform a media and public relations function. Democrats thus rely on liberal groups to identify the most problematic nominees, while Republicans rely on conservative groups to wage the necessary public relations campaigns.

This [reading] focused predominantly on groups' information-transmission role, which takes place early in the process as groups provide senators and their staffs with information on nominees to help them cull the large number of judicial nominations pending at any given time. This information helps senators and their staffs identify which nominees need to be scrutinized more carefully.

However, groups also perform another important task, that of publicly objecting to nominees they believe will be harmful to their goals if seated on the federal bench. Once a particular nominee begins to move through the confirmation process, groups must decide whether they will publicly object to the nominee and wage a campaign to defeat him or her. Because of limited resources, groups cannot oppose every nominee, and so they strategically and sparingly oppose objectionable nominees. These objections raise a "fire alarm" and send valuable ideological and institutional cues to senators about the nomination (Scherer, Bartels, and Steigerwalt 2008). [...]

Endnotes

1. During the 107th Congress, Charles Pickering and Dennis Shedd were asked to provide copies of any unpublished opinions they had written as district court judges (Democratic staffer 2002).

2. The report is available to all members on the committee. The minority staff may prepare a separate report, but during the 107th Congress, this occurred rarely (Republican staffer 2002).

3. On May 12, 2005, a minor scandal erupted when Minority Leader Harry Reid stated during the floor debate over Sixth Circuit nominee Henry Saad that "there is a problem there" in his FBI file; Republicans argued that these comments unfairly maligned Saad (Hulse and Lewis 2005; Hurt 2005; York 2005).

4. The ABA testified at Roger Benitez's hearing (nominated to the Southern District Court of California) on February 25, 2004, as well as at Dora Irizarry's hearing (nominated to the Eastern District Court of New York) on October 1, 2003, concerning their respective majority "not qualified" ratings. Both nominees were eventually confirmed.

5. There have been numerous complaints over the years that the ABA's ratings are not impartial, especially for more conservative nominees (Bronner 1989b; Lindgren 2001; Seckora 2001; but see Saks and Vidmar 2001). These allegations gained power when Robert Bork received a split rating of "well qualified/not qualified" by the ABA when he was nominated to the Supreme Court in 1987 owing to his "judicial temperament" (Greenhouse 1987; Stuart 1987). To many, the addition of judicial temperament as a criterion allows the ABA to make

political judgments about the views nominees hold, rather than merely assessing professional qualifications. More recently, Vining, Steigerwalt, and Smelcer (2009) find evidence of bias against more conservative nominees, at least with respect to whether a nominee will receive a "well qualified" rating.

6. There is considerable debate over what types of questions are suitable to pose to the nominees and whether nominees must answer questions that delve into their personal political views or views on issues they may confront once on the bench. This issue arises especially with the nomination of so-called stealth nominees who lack public records on key controversial issues. D.C. Circuit Court nominee Miguel Estrada's refusal to answer questions about certain issues posed by Democratic senators was a key reason for the filibuster mounted against his nomination during the 108th Congress (Stolberg 2003).

7. Staff commented that the nominee's answers to written questions were a significant source of information. One committee staffer interviewed in 2002 said, "Hearings are not always the most useful exercise, as there is not enough time to question nominees thoroughly and it takes a lot of work to get a Senator fully prepped such that he can do a back-and-forth dialogue with the nominee, especially on subtle legal points."

8. All interviews took place in Washington, D.C., between June and August 2002. Interviews with current staff took place in the office in which each worked, while interviews with former staff took place at their current places of business. The interviews were semistructured and lasted approximately one hour, with the longest lasting three hours and the shortest thirty minutes.

9. Given the other duties of the committee staff, preparation rarely begins before the week of the hearing. Hearings on judicial nominees usually occur no more than twice a month, and the general practice is for one circuit court nominee to testify, along with four to six district court nominees. In addition to judicial nominations, the committee also has jurisdiction over many other issues, such as changes to criminal laws, terrorism, and immigration, as well as appointments to be U.S. attorneys, non-career lawyer Department of Justice positions, and judgeships on the "local" District of Columbia courts.

10. In fact, a rift emerged between Republican committee members and leading conservative activists over whether Republicans did enough to stop Clinton nominees and to support George W. Bush's nominees. Thomas Jipping wrote a number of articles criticizing Orrin Hatch's stewardship of the committee during the Clinton administration ("Democrats Fight for Activist Judges, GOP Caves" 2000, liberally quoting Jipping as to the failings of the Lott and Hatch's leadership; see also Jipping 2000).

11. "The spontaneity of the grassroots gets replaced by Astroturf. ... Some citizen contacting is in response to carefully organized campaigns with little spontaneity" (Verba 1993, 679).

"Astroturf lobbying" refers to individuals or groups who do not directly lobby themselves but rather generate grassroots lobbying campaigns. Thus, for example, NARAL often does not have its Washington staff lobby but instead encourages its grassroots members to contact their representatives.

12. For a firsthand account of the Robert Bork Supreme Court confirmation fight, see Gittenstein (1992).

13. Many have discussed the suspected role played by conservative groups in George W. Bush's selection process, especially the Federalist Society, a conservative-leaning organization of law students and lawyers (Lichtblau 2002; Nemacheck 2008a, 23–24; see Volokh 2001 for an insider's description of the society and its beliefs). The Federalist Society attracted attention because of the number of executive and judicial nominees Bush selected who were believed to have belonged to the organization (Lewis 2001). However, as DeParle (2005) highlights, even this simple statement of fact is difficult to confirm, as many of these same nominees have tried to distance themselves from the society or have denied belonging (see also *New York Times* 2005). Scherer and Miller (2009) explore whether Federalist Society members are more conservative on the bench than their non-society counterparts; one issue they confronted was how to accurately identify society members. The Federalist Society did, however, play a prominent public role in helping confirm George W. Bush's Supreme Court nominees John Roberts and Samuel Alito (Savage 2005).

14. This question was asked only of staffers who indicated they received information from interest groups.

15. The leading conservative activist, Thomas Jipping, attested that he would research Clinton nominees when others (including senators and staff) brought them to his attention.

16. This same staffer also wished for more conservative media outlets: "Democrats are more successful at projecting their message because the press helps them, and their groups are better organized and funded. ... There is no question that the three conservative media outlets are the *Washington Times, Wall Street Journal,* and Fox News, and they help tremendously, but their circulation is much lower. Even more important is television—we have Fox News, but the Democrats have the rest."

References

Abraham, Henry J. 1999. *Justices, Presidents, and Senators: A History of the U.S. Supreme Court Appointments from Washington to Clinton.* 4th ed. New York: Rowman and Littlefield.

American Bar Association. 2007. *Standing Committee on the Federal Judiciary: What It Is and How It Works.* http://www.abanet.org/scfedjud/home.html.

Austen-Smith, David. 1993. "Information and Influence: Lobbying for Agendas and Votes." *American Journal of Political Science* 37:799–833.

Austen-Smith, David, and John R. Wright. 1994. "Counteractive Lobbying." *American Journal of Political Science* 38:25–44.

———. 1996. "Theory and Evidence for Counteractive Lobbying." *American Journal of Political Science* 40:543–64.

Baumgartner, Frank R., and Beth L. Leech. 1996. "The Multiple Ambiguities of 'Counteractive Lobbying.' " *American Journal of Political Science* 40:521–42.

Bell, Lauren Cohen. 2002a. *Warring Factions: Interest Groups, Money, and the New Politics of Senate Confirmation.* Columbus: Ohio State University Press.

———. 2002b. "Senatorial Discourtesy: The Senate's Use of Delay to Shape the Federal Judiciary." *Political Research Quarterly* 55:589–607.

Bronner, Ethan. 1989b. "ABA Role in Selection of Judges Questioned." *Boston Globe,* May 6, National Section, 3.

Caldeira, Gregory A., Marie Hojnacki, and John R. Wright. 2000. "The Lobbying Activities of Organized Interests in Federal Judicial Nominations." *Journal of Politics* 62:51–69.

Caldeira, Gregory A., and John R. Wright. 1995. "Lobbying for Justice: The Rise of Organized Interests in the Politics of Federal Judicial Nominations." In *Contemplating Courts,* ed. Lee Epstein, 44–71. Washington, DC: CQ Press.

———. 1998. "Lobbying for Justice: Organized Interests, Supreme Court Nominations, and United States Senate." *American Journal of Political Science* 42:499–523.

Cigler, Allan J., and Burdett A. Loomis. 1998. *Interest Group Politics.* 5th ed. Washington, DC: CQ Press.

Cohen, Lauren M. 1998. "Missing in Action: Interest Groups and Federal Judicial Appointments." *Judicature* 82:119–23.

Davidson, Lee. 2003. "Utahns Play Key Roles in D.C." *Deseret News,* January 8, B1.

"Democrats Fight for Activist Judges, GOP Caves." 2000. *NewsMax.com,* August 30. http://www.newsmax.com/articles/?a=2000/8/28/223819.

Denzau, Arthur T., and Michael C. Munger. 1986. "Legislators and Interest Groups: How Unorganized Interests Get Represented." *American Political Science Review* 80:89–106.

DeParle, Jason. 2005. "Nomination for Supreme Court Stirs Debate on Influence of Federalist Society." *New York Times,* August 1, A1.

Flemming, Roy B., Michael C. MacLeod, and Jeffrey Talbert. 1998. "Witnesses at the Confirmations? The Appearance of Organized Interests at Senate Hearings of Federal Judicial Appointments, 1945–1992." *Political Research Quarterly* 51:617–31.

Fenno, Richard F., Jr. 1973. *Congressmen in Committee.* Boston: Little, Brown.

Frank, John. 1991. *Clement Haynsworth, the Senate, and the Supreme Court.* Charlottesville: University Press of Virginia.

Giachino, Renee. 2006. "Interview with Judge Charles Pickering." *Your Turn: Meeting Nonsense with Common Sense.* WEBY 1330 AM. Posted online March 23. http://www.cfif.org/htdocs/freedomline/ current/in_our_opinion/Pickering.htm.

Gilligan, Thomas W., and Keith Krehbiel. 1989. "Asymmetric Information and Legislative Rules with a Heterogeneous Committee." *American Journal of Political Science* 33: 459–90.

Gittenstein, Mark. 1992. *Matters of Principle: An Insider's Account of America's Rejection of Robert Bork's Nomination to the Supreme Court.* New York: Simon and Schuster.

_____. 2002. Interview by the author. Tape recording. June 25. Washington, DC.

Goldman, Sheldon. 1997. *Picking Federal Judges: Lower Court Selection from Roosevelt through Reagan.* New Haven, CT: Yale University Press.

Greenhouse, Linda. 1987. "Court Vacancy Renews Debate on A.B.A. Role." *New York Times,* December 27, A24.

Grossman, Joel B. 1965. *Lawyers and Judges: The ABA and the Politics of Judicial Selection.* New York: John Wiley and Sons.

Hall, Kermit. 1979. *The Politics of Justice: Lower Federal Judicial Selection and the Second Party System, 1829–61.* Lincoln: University of Nebraska Press.

Hojnacki, Marie, and David C. Kimball. 1999. "The Who and How of Organizations' Lobbying Strategies in Committee." *Journal of Politics* 61:999–1024.

Hudson, Audrey. 2001. "Democrats Want ABA to Vet Judges; Will Put Holds on Confirmations Until Legal Group's Checks Are Completed." *Washington Times,* March 28, A4.

Hulse, Carl, and Neil A. Lewis. 2005. "Senators Wrangle as Panel Approves Judicial Nominee." *New York Times,* May 13, A18.

Hurt, Charles. 2005. "Reid Cites FBI Files on Judicial Pick." *Washington Times,* May 13, A1.

Jipping, Thomas L. 2000. "Will Republicans Fight as Hard as the Democrats Did?" October 9. http:// www.enterstageright.com/archive/articles/1000judges.htm.

Kingdon, John W. 1989. *Congressmen's Voting Decisions.* 3rd ed. Ann Arbor: University of Michigan Press.

Krehbiel, Keith. 1991. *Information and Legislative Organization.* Ann Arbor: University of Michigan Press.

Lewis, Neil A. 2001. "A Conservative Legal Group Thrives in Bush's Washington." *New York Times,* April 18, A1.

Lichtblau, Eric. 2002. "Debate Club's 'Secret Handshakes' Turn into Public Grins." *New York Times,* November 17, A26.

Lindgren, James T. 2001. "Examining the American Bar Association's Ratings of Nominees to the U.S. Courts of Appeals for Political Bias, 1989–2000." *Journal of Law and Politics* 17:1–40.

Maltese, John Anthony. 1995. *The Selling of Supreme Court Nominees.* Baltimore: Johns Hopkins University Press.

Martinek, Wendy L., Mark Kemper, and Steven R. Van Winkle. 2002. "To Advise and Consent: The Senate and Lower Federal Court Nominations, 1977–1998." *Journal of Politics* 64:337–61.

Nemacheck, Christine L. 2008a. *Strategic Selection: Presidential Nomination of Supreme Court Justices from Herbert Hoover through George W. Bush.* Charlottesville: University of Virginia Press.

Saks, Michael J., and Neil Vidmar. 2001. "A Flawed Search for Bias in the American Bar Association's Ratings of Prospective Judicial Nominees: A Critique of the Lindgren Study." *Journal of Law and Politics* 17:219–55.

Savage, Charlie. 2005. "GOP Rift Looms over High Court Nominations: Some Want Evangelicals to Keep Quiet During Fight." *Boston Globe,* June 26, A1.

Scherer, Nancy. 2003. "The Judicial Confirmation Process: Mobilizing Elites, Mobilizing Masses." *Judicature* 86:240–50.

———. 2005. *Scoring Points: Politicians, Political Activists, and the Lower Federal Court Appointment Process.* Stanford, CA: Stanford University Press.

Scherer, Nancy, Brandon Bartels, and Amy Steigerwalt. 2008. "Sounding the Fire Alarm: The Role of Interest Groups in the Lower Court Confirmation Process." *Journal of Politics* 70:1026–39.

Scherer, Nancy, and Banks Miller. 2009. "The Federalist Society's Influence on the Federal Judiciary." *Political Research Quarterly* 62:366–78.

Schlozman, Kay Lehman, and John T. Tierney. 1986. *Organized Interests and American Democracy.* New York: Harper and Row.

Seckora, Melissa. 2001. "Courting Prejudice: The ABA's Just Another Liberal Interest Group." *National Review Online,* March 21. http://www.nationalreview.com/nr_comment/nr_comment032101b.shtml.

Silverstein, Mark. 1994. *Judicious Choices: The New Politics of Supreme Court Confirmations.* New York: Norton.

Stolberg, Sheryl Gay. 2003. "Battle over Judgeship Tests Congressman's Loyalties to People and Party." *New York Times,* March 15, A14.

Stuart, Reginald. 1987. "Bork Backers: ABA Ratings Are 'Political.'" *Philadelphia Daily News,* September 22, 6.

Verba, Sidney. 1993. "The 1993 James Madison Award Lecture: The Voice of the People." *PS: Political Science and Politics,* December, 677–86.

Vining, Richard L., Jr., Amy Steigerwalt, and Susan Navarro Smelcer. 2009. "Bias and the Bar: Evaluating the ABA Ratings of Federal Judicial Nominees." Paper presented at the 2009 Annual Meeting of the Midwest Political Science Association, Chicago, April 2–5.

Volokh, Eugene. 2001. "Our Flaw? We're Just Not Liberals." *Washington Post,* June 3, B3.

Wright, John R. 1996. *Interest Groups and Congress: Lobbying, Contributions and Influence.* Boston: Allyn and Bacon.

York, Byron. 2005. "Harry Reid Steps Over the Line—Again." *National Review Online,* May 13. http://www.nationalreview.com/york/york200505130859.asp.

MoveOn.org and the Tea Party

By Victoria Carty

This [reading] examines two SMOs or, as we will see, what can more accurately be described as **social movement communities** (a term that Wollenberg et al. 2006 use). They are on opposite ends of the political spectrum: MoveOn.org, which is a left-wing organization that advocates for progressive causes, and the Tea Party, which is a conservative entity that is more reactionary in its agenda.

In a snapshot, MoveOn.org is known as one of the original and most successful digital public policy advocacy groups. It has been hailed for its pioneering tactics in support of progressive issues, and it raises large amounts of money to support Democratic candidates. MoveOn.org is made up of MoveOn.org Civic Action, which is a 501(c)(4) nonprofit corporation, and MoveOn Civic Action, which focuses on education and advocacy as they pertain to national issues. It also has a federal political action committee that contributes to the campaigns of many candidates across the country.

The Tea Party arrived later on the scene and in some ways, like MoveOn.org, resembles a social movement community more than a formal social movement in the typical sense, though its structure is more disparate and harder to classify. In essence, the Tea Party is an umbrella organization, an amalgam of somewhat loosely connected groups that consist mainly of libertarians, religious conservatives, independents, and some citizens new to politics who are frustrated with the contemporary political landscape. What unites the various groups is a shared, yet loosely held, set of beliefs. They are sometimes linked to national organizations such as the Tea Party Express and the Tea Party Nation, though they mostly operate independently (Williamson, Skocpol, and Coggin 2011). Other associated groups operate exclusively online, such as the National Tea Party

Federation, whose goal is to enhance and facilitate communication among the various groups affiliated with the Tea Party.

These two very different organizations give us some important insights into contemporary forms of social movement organizing in the United States that cut across both contentious and institutional politics. Both groups rely on some traditional methods that have been used in previous social movements, while concomitantly adopting other more innovative tactics. They demonstrate that what is often perceived as a zero-sum game between new and old activism is a false dichotomy: online and offline activism often reinforce each other. There are strong similarities between the organizational structure of MoveOn and the Tea Party as well as the combination of online and offline strategies they employ—they are both hybrids of sorts when it comes to promoting social change. This [reading] invites us to think theoretically and conceptually about what constitutes a social movement in the digital age, which subsequently raises questions as to how to best theorize the tactics and strategies of nuanced groups such as these.

Furthermore, a central concern of this chapter is how online sharing of information and e-activism lead to mobilization on the ground, or the spillover effect. We consider whether virtual activism replaces, complements, or has no effect on concrete forms of participation for social and political change.

A comparison of the two groups also raises the question of how to define grassroots organizations and their relationship to the public sphere, or communicative action, as posed by Habermas (1993, 1989). [...] his concerns about the shrinking role of the public sphere with the onset of television and the encroachment of professional experts (elites in the media and

MoveOn's model for electronic recruitment shows how "weak" virtual ties can lead to activism in the streets.

other major corporations) and contended that they have come to dominate public dialogue and debate, and civil society in general. However, the arrival of the Internet and digital technology prompts us to update his theory as the old top-down and hierarchal structures and modes of communication are being challenged, in some ways, by grassroots entities. MoveOn and some of the Tea Party groups are examples of Castells's (2001) informational politics that result in the electronic grass-rooting of democracy.

MOVEON.ORG

MoveOn emerged in the late 1990s in cyberspace via an online petition. In 1998, during the height of the Monica Lewinsky scandal, Silicon Valley computer entrepreneurs Wes Boyd and Joan Blades created an online petition that called on Congress to censure but not impeach President Clinton. Boyd e-mailed it to thirty friends, and within two weeks more than half a million people had signed the petition (Bennet and Fielding 1999). A few years later he heard from Eli Pariser, who had created an online petition urging moderation and restraint in responding to the September 11 terrorist acts. This petition also exploded in popularity, and at Boyd's suggestion the two merged their websites, and MoveOn.org was born (Markels 2003). The organization currently has more than 5 million members, and its running slogan is "Democracy in Action."

MoveOn's main strategy is to activate people on a few different issues at a time, often for short durations as legislative battles change, and this model allows it to play an important role as a campaign aggregator—inviting people in on a particular issue and then introducing them to additional issues (Markels 2003). According to Boyd, what unites MoveOn activists is support for progressive issues and a different type of politics, and the Internet is an essential tool for staying politically connected.

The organizational features of MoveOn are representative of contemporary social movements as theorized by new social movement theorists such as Melucci (1996): they are constituted by loosely articulated networks that permit multiple memberships and part-time participation, and there is little if any distinction between leaders and rank-and-file members, members and nonmembers, and private and public roles. MoveOn is often members' first step into political action, and what brings them to take that step is typically an e-mail message sent from one of the organizers or forwarded from a family member, friend, or colleague. This resonates with Castells's (2001) concept of informational politics and Giugni's (1998) research on the importance of electronic forms of communication among trusted sources that would-be participants in a social or political cause may not receive otherwise. For many members contributing money to a candidate or a political ad in response to an e-mail is the first time they participate in politics outside of voting (Boyd 2003).

MoveOn's success also highlights the importance of flexible and contingent forms of (wired) collective identity that developing theories of new media address, in particular Giugni's work noted above. Pariser explains:

> Every member comes to us with the personal endorsement of someone they trust. It is word-of-mouth organizing in electronic form. It has made mixing the personal and political more socially acceptable. Casually passing on a high-content message to a social acquaintance feels completely natural in a way handing someone a leaflet at a cocktail party never would. The "tell-a-friend" phenomenon is key to how organizing happens on the Net. A small gesture to a friend can contribute to a massive multiplier effect. It is a grassroots answer to the corporate consolidation of the media. (Boyd 2003)

As the statement shows, the way information is sent, received, and accessed represents a more pluralistic, fluid, and issue-oriented group politics among many contemporary activists that theories of new media, as well as theories of new social movements, recognize. Members and organizers of contemporary forms of collective behavior increasingly operate outside of state-regulated and corporate-dominated media and rely on innovative actions mainly mediated across electronic networks. These in turn enable new forms communicative action that assist in recruitment efforts and can result in concrete forms of mobilization. This exemplifies the grassrooting of civil society that Castells (2001) describes, and it is also illustrative of H. Jenkins's (2006) conceptualization of the importance of civic media in participatory democracy and the spillover effect. These new outlets for organizing can help update resource mobilization theory and illustrate how collective identity is established in new ways, thus calling for a modification of cultural theories to account for weak ties that lend to activism in the streets.

New Technology Campaigns

In terms of campaigns, from its inception, MoveOn's website has distributed e-mail action alerts that inform its members of important current events and has provided petitions and contact information of members' elected officials so that members can respond to those events. Its first campaign supported candidates running against impeachment backers. In 1999, in less than twelve weeks, it signed up over 500,000 supporters and received pledges of $13 million (Burress 2003). As a great example of e-activism, in June of that same year it set records for online fundraising by collecting more than $250,000 in five days, mostly in individual donations under $50 (Potter 2003).

Once the Clinton impeachment trial ended, MoveOn centered much of its energy on the peace movement in the wake of the 9–11 attacks. It hosted the online headquarters for the Virtual March on Washington—an act of online civil disobedience to protest the imminent invasion of

Iraq. It was sponsored by the WinWithoutWar Coalition, which serves as an online umbrella organization for the peace movement. Using e-mail connections to coordinate and organize a protestor base, on February 26, 2003, more than 200,000 individuals signed up and made more than 400,000 phone calls and sent 100,000 faxes to every senate office in the United States with the message DON'T ATTACK IRAQ! (MoveOn 2004). Every member of the US Senate also received a stream of e-mails, clogging virtual mailboxes in Washington, DC.

Another tactic MoveOn has used repeatedly as part of its repertoire is candlelight vigils, organized completely online. The March 16 vigils against the pending invasion of Iraq involved more than one million people in more than 6,000 gatherings in 130 countries and were organized in six days by MoveOn over the Internet (Stewart 2003). The online resource Meetup made the event possible, speeding the flow of politics, what Bimber (2003) refers to as accelerated politics. MoveOn's fundraising ability also contributed to the antiwar effort. In less than one week, members raised $37,000 over the Internet to run an advertisement in the *New York Times* on December 11, 2002, thus using alternative media to infiltrate mainstream media in an effort to influence public opinion. In February 2003 MoveOn solicited donations to raise $75,000 in just two hours to place an antiwar advertisement on billboards in four major American cities with a similar message (Stewart 2003).

Although resource mobilization theory has always directed attention to the need for financial backing for political mobilizing efforts, typically the assumption was that most of this would consist of large sums of money from organizations or wealthy individuals. With new technology, however, organizers of a political campaign can instead, as this example shows, raise large sums of money through relatively small donations, and quickly, through word-of-mouth sharing of information online. This beckons us to modify resource mobilization theory to account for these new digital tactics for garnering resources.

After the invasion of Iraq began, MoveOn members petitioned their congressional representatives to continue the inspections for weapons of mass destruction. More than one million signatures were collected in less than five days and were delivered to the UN Security Council. Signatory names and comments were also sent to the petitioners' respective congressional representatives. Additionally, on a single day 200,000 people called their representatives, and, in the run-up to the Senate vote on the Iraq resolution in October of 2003, MoveOn volunteers met face to face with every US senator with "Let the Inspections Work" petitions (Utne 2003). The organization also started to more aggressively engage in political campaigns, urging its supporters to donate money to Democratic House and Senate members who had opposed the Iraq resolution.

In sum, during the above campaigns MoveOn excelled at garnering available resources, people, and computer skills to increase sociopolitical awareness, influence public opinion, mobilize citizens and network with other SMOs, and help elect progressive candidates. It did so by using new technology to tap into submerged networks that could participate in Internet-mediated forms of civic engagement. Therefore, theories of new media best explain the success of MoveOn. Resource mobilization theory also informs our understanding of new groups such as MoveOn. org with its attention to traditional resources that activists have at their disposal such as labor power, financial backing, and support of allies and influential elites.

Cultural and Symbolic Tactics: Combining New and Traditional Media

Cultural and symbolic forms of political expression, as advocated by cultural theorists of social movements and certain strands of the new social movement school of thought, are viewed as key variables to a social movement's success. These tactics played another central role in MoveOn's repertoire of contention.

For example, the group used celebrities for political purposes. One of the group's first interactions with Hollywood came when filmmaker and cofounder of Artists United to Win Without War Robert Greenwald organized celebrities to join the Virtual March on Washington (Brownstein 2004).

Over one hundred celebrities joined as members of this group, including Matt Damon, Martin Sheen, and Mike Farrell. One of the most direct and visible forms of protest occurred when filmmaker Michael Moore spoke out against the war at his acceptance speech at the 2003 Oscars only a few days after the invasion: "We live in a time where we have a man sending us to war for fictitious reasons. Whether it's the fictitious duct tape or the fictitious orange alerts, we are against this war. Mr. Bush. Shame on you. Mr. Bush, shame on you" (Zakarin 2013). That same night at the Oscars ceremony, Susan Sarandon and Tim Robbins flashed peace signs to photographers. Actor Sean Penn went even further in resisting the war by traveling to Iraq in 2002. On his return he commented, "I cannot conceive of any reason why the American people and the world would not have shared with the Iraqis the evidence of the claim to have weapons of mass destruction. I think that the more information we push for, the more information we are given, the better off we are all going to be, and the right thing will happen" (Zakarin 2013).

Other celebrities who traveled internationally also spoke out against the impending invasion. For example, actor Dustin Hoffman publicized his displeasure during an awards ceremony in London, claiming, "This war is about what most wars are about: hegemony, money, power and oil." In Berlin actor Richard Gere spoke out as well, saying, "We have to say 'stop,' there's no reason for a war. At the moment, Hussein is not threatening anybody" (Zakarin 2013). Perhaps the most radical departure from the US government's agenda was the country music trio the Dixie Chicks at a concert in London. Lead singer Natalie Maines opined that she was "ashamed" that President Bush was also from Texas, where she was born and raised. Upon return to the United States, several country stations refused to play the Dixie Chicks' music in retaliation for her remarks.

MoveOn also has given substantial financial support to a number of Greenwald's films and documentaries to promote more independent and critical voices outside of mainstream and corporate-dominated media. Its website offered his *Uncovered: The Next War on Iraq* DVD as a premium to members who pledged thirty dollars or more, and approximately 8,000 individuals made pledges within the first three hours. More than 2,600 members hosted screenings in their homes and at community venues, and the movie was ultimately distributed in theaters across the country (Deans 2004).

House parties are another innovative tactic MoveOn uses to broaden the public sphere and the realm of civil society by combining the private and public spheres. It also adds to the explanatory power of theories that focus on the importance of collective identity (for example Snow et al. 1986; Benford 1993) and of morally and ethically based reasons for participation in collective behavior that some of the new social movement theories recognize (Giddens 1991; Tomlinson 1999; Johnston 1994). A few years later MoveOn provided free copies of Greenwald's *Iraq for Sale* and *The Ground Truth* documentaries for members to show at house parties. After viewing the films attendees made phone calls and wrote letters to voters. MoveOn also helped Greenwald finance *Outfoxed: Rupert Murdoch's War on Journalism*. Taking advantage of the mainstream media, it also took out a full-page ad in the *New York Times* declaring, "The Communists had *Pravda*. Republicans have Fox" (Deans 2004).

House parties are an innovative tactic MoveOn uses that broadens the public sphere and the realm of civil society by combining the private and public spheres.

In other cases various directors and film producers helped MoveOn construct homemade advertisements once sufficient funds were raised by its members. The "Real People" ads, for instance, were created by documentary filmmaker Errol Morris and featured ordinary members of the Republican Party explaining why they were crossing party lines to vote for Democratic nominee John Kerry (Deans 2004). This was the first time both the content and the funding for an ad campaign came from the grassroots membership of an organization, typical of social movement communities operating without an established vanguard (Wollenberg et al. 2006). The "Bush in 30 Seconds" ads challenging administration policies were shown during his State of the Union address. Grammy-nominated musician Moby helped to design them, held a competition for members to submit ads, and recruited a panel of celebrity judges that culminated in an awards show in New York City to raise funds for other anti-Bush television ads (Stevenson 2004).

This example shows us that the roles of leaders, spokespersons, formal SMOs, and elite allies—all of which played a prominent role in the development of the resource mobilization framework—are less relevant for many contemporary mobilizations. Theories of new media and some components of the new social movement school of thought are more useful because they highlight the decentralized and more egalitarian structure of today's contentious politics (Melucci 1996 most directly brings this to our attention). Also helpful is Mann's (2000) conception of the interstitial location, where activists promote their agendas outside the formal political system and traditional institutions.

The organization and its supporters also combatted infringement of corporate and elite domination of the cultural sphere in the fight against censorship when theaters across the United States were being pressured by right-wing groups to bar *Fahrenheit 9/11,* Michael Moore's controversial film. It asked members to pledge to see the film on opening night with other members to send a message to theater owners that the public supports Moore's message of peace (Moveon.org, e-mail to all members). Bridging the offline and online worlds and combining entertainment with serious political discussion, more than 4,600 parties were thrown across the United States, and at each Moore spoke to members over the Internet about his movie and his hope they would each bring at least five nonvoters to the polls for the upcoming November 2004 election (Brownstein 2004). This novelty bridges entertainment, activism, and institutional politics.

During the ten-week Don't Get Mad, Get Even! events preceding the 2004 election, MoveOn and America Coming Together held rallies and rock concerts that incorporated celebrity appearances by artists, authors, and actors. As part of the Rock the Vote tour, they jointly held a concert in New York City right before the Republican National Convention that featured rock stars such as Bruce Springsteen, the Dave Mathews Band, Pearl Jam, REM, the Dixie Chicks, Jackson Browne, and John Mellencamp. Some MoveOn members threw house parties to watch the concert, at which members wrote letters to swing-state voters. Additionally, relying on mainstream media platforms, "Don't Get Mad, Get Even!" television advertisements featured celebrity activists such as Matt Damon, Rob Reiner, Woody Harrelson, and Al Franken (Carty 2010).

Thus, MoveOn combines conventional forms of organizing with more nuanced tactics. Rock concerts that support their cause, pledging to view Michael Moore's film, and throwing house parties each serve to open up the public sphere more broadly to ordinary citizens (which Habermas feared we are losing to corporate and elite control) and are also displays of symbolic forms of protest. With this in mind, we can modify some of Habermas's theory to account for new tactics, many of them aided by new technology (for example, the organization of house parties through web-based tools). Parts of new social movement theories help in our assessment of how MoveOn operates as these kinds of activities also serve to politicize new areas of social life.

Bridging Online and Offline Activism

MoveOn continued its grassroots mobilization during the 2006 midterm election. Recognizing the essential role of on-the-ground (public) efforts to complement e-activism, it trained and supported volunteers on the ground to organize rapid responses to events and to hold news conferences, editorial board meetings, and rallies to target vulnerable Republican incumbents. As both political-process and political-mediation scholars would suggest (for instance Meyer 2005; Tarrow 2001; Soule and King 2006), politicians are vulnerable during election years and swaying public opinion is key, and these two theories assist us in clarifying MoveOn's strategizing. According to a Yale University study, the emphasis on face-to-face voter mobilization through social networks increased turnout by seven percentage points (Middleton and Green 2007). Prior to the election MoveOn members held more than 6,000 actions in these districts and organized 7,500 house parties (MoveOn 2007 annual report).

Members also donated enough money to establish the Call for Change program that used web-based tools and a call-reporting system to reach voters. Once again circumventing professional pollsters (and once again Mann's [2000] interstitial locations is fitting here), the web-based "liquid phone bank" allowed MoveOn members to call from wherever they lived into wherever they were needed within a day or two. Middleton and Green (2007) found that the phone bank was the most effective volunteer calling program ever studied and that it increased voter turnout by almost 4 percent.

Also during the 2006 election, a successful framing approach allowed MoveOn to combine parody and serious political discourse. Cultural as well as new social movement theories (Gamson 1992) that evaluate the effectiveness of social movement activity by their framing of issues are applicable here. For example, activists deployed the metaphor of being caught red-handed by displaying giant foam red hands and signs as they followed their representatives to town hall meetings, appearances, and fundraisers, questioning their allegiance to special interests. In

Virginia Beach, members attended every Coffee with Thelma event that Representative Thelma Drake held and asked questions about her allegiance to special interests. In Louisville, Kentucky, members rallied at a gas station to tell voters about Representative Ann Northup's ties to big oil with flyers describing war profiteering. Members in Fayetteville, North Carolina, attended a defense contractor tradeshow that Representative Robin Hayes sponsored. During this campaign alone local media wrote more than 2,000 stories about MoveOn's actions (MoveOn.org 2008 annual report), and, of the nine long-shot races members targeted, five won. As an overall tally, in 2006 Democrats supported by MoveOn lost four and won eighteen races, which helped build a Democratic majority in the Senate (Center for Responsive Politics 2006).

The red-handed campaign represents what MoveOn does best—framing issues in a way that resonates with voters and taps into their frustration, using humorous and innovative techniques by employing diagnostic and prognostic framing (Snow et al. 1986). Its success at harnessing popular entertainment to broadcast alternative voices, whether in the form of rock concerts, fundraisers, Bush-bashing ads, publicity stunts, or supporting alternative forms of media, and doing this jointly with representatives of the artistic community, is something MoveOn has excelled at.

The Importance of Social Media

As MoveOn evolves and relies on new resources and tactics, new media are becoming increasingly important to understanding how it now operates. The group still uses e-mail extensively but now also relies heavily on other forms of social media. In response to the negative ads against President Obama by Republican Super PACs that played out on television during the 2012 elections, for example, MoveOn stated in a March 1 e-mail,

> Over the last year we've been quietly developing a groundbreaking plan to counter these lies through social media sites like Facebook and Twitter—where millions of people now get their news, bypassing the corporate media. The results so far have been amazing. There have been 65 million views in the last year. We increased our web traffic tenfold. And we tripled our audience of Facebook fans who can spread the word. But to counter Fox's lies this election we need to raise $200,000 to pay for the researchers, editors and developers necessary to ramp up.

A link was included at the end of the e-mail asking members to chip in fifteen dollars to help fund the efforts.

MoveOn's recent strategizing has some theoretical implications for our understanding of contentious politics. It illustrates that people are now receiving news through sources outside of corporate-dominated media, and the news that they are receiving through digital outlets such as Facebook and Twitter is being shared in a horizontal fashion, through peer-to-peer networks. Therefore, SMOs' direction of social movement activity and dispersion of information is being complemented by these informal and decentralized hubs of activity, informing us how we can update resource mobilization theory put forth by Tilly (1978) and McCarthy and Zald (1973). We can complement this work with recent analyses that incorporate theories that focus on new media. Most prominently, Castells's (2001) notion of an explosive informational politics and grass-rooting of democracy, McAdam and Paulsen's (1993) recognition of the importance of weak social ties forged in the virtual sphere that spread information about mobilization efforts in support of a cause, Bimber's (2003) reference to accelerated pluralism, and Kahn and Kellner's (2003) emphasis on the importance of virtual public spheres in initiating and sustaining momentum for social movement activity all come into play.

Another e-mail read, "This is the strategy. Every day, a team of 50 of MoveOn volunteer editors will collect the most timely and persuasive progressive news and opinion from around the web. Graphics debunking Republican lies about the economy. Live video coverage of the Occupy movement. ... Then we'll push the most timely and persuasive stuff out to hundreds of thousands of people, who share it with millions more. We believe that people-powered media, funded by people like us, can be a secret weapon against the conservative noise machine" (March 9, 2012). This statement further indicates how reliant social movement actors are on web-based tools to share information, create a critical mass of support through peer-to-peer sharing, and create new sources of collective identity and community, thus broadening the public sphere on which much of Habermas's (1989, 1993) theorizing is based. It also supports Bennett and Iyengar's (2008) claims that new forms of grassroots civic engagement though online forms of communication can be resistant to state and corporate regulation.

MoveOn continued its distribution videos that spoof serious political challenges during the 2012 presidential election. It launched a video, "Mitt's Office," in which actor Justin Long played Mitt Romney—depicting him as caring only about the 1 percent. The e-mail that disseminated it asked members to share the video with friends and family on Facebook or via e-mail (December 26, 2012). That same month it asked members to protest laws that would restrict voter registration drives and early voting and require voters to present photo IDs at the polls, and it urged them to donate money to try to prevent the laws from passing (January 13, 2013). Supporters protested outside of federal courthouses to contest the ruling on *Citizens United* (which allowed corporations, as well as unions, to donate undisclosed and unlimited amounts of money to candidates running for office), and MoveOn sent a petition to call on President Obama to sign an executive order that would require corporations that do business with the government to disclose their political spending and declare support for a constitutional amendment to get big money out of politics permanently.

After President Obama announced a federal investigation into Wall Street in his January State of the Union address, an e-mail from MoveOn stated, "This is truly a huge victory for the 99% movement. Hundreds of thousands of us signed petitions, made calls, and held signs outside in the cold to make this issue something that President Obama couldn't ignore. Here's some of what MoveOn members and our allies did to bring about this victory" (January 26, 2012). It went on to note that members engaged in Facebook and Twitter activity, and it included a link where readers could post a message of thanks on the White House Facebook wall. It then stated, "And, we need to keep pushing for more wins for the 99%, including our campaigns to get big money out of politics and tax the rich fairly. ... MoveOn doesn't get big checks from ban CEOs! So please click here to donate to keep the momentum going" (January 24, 2012).

MoveOn is not as grassroots as it may appear, however. For instance, it works in collaboration with powerful progressive groups such as the American Civil Liberties Union, America United for Change, and United for Peace and Change. Though it does not receive any funding from corporate donors, it has received substantial financial support from international financier George Soros, who spent millions of dollars opposing President George Bush's re-election in 2004 (Drehle 2008). One difference from those funding Tea Party organizations, as we shall see later in the [reading] is that his motivation, as a peace activist, is to support a cause rather than to influence a political party.

In conclusion, MoveOn perhaps can best be conceptualized as a hybrid in terms of its status (part insider/part outsider) and a chameleon in terms of tactics (disruptive yet also engaged in the institutionalized side of the continuum of contentious/institutional politics). Though the social movement organization, or community, emerged as a dissident organization, it eventually evolved into more of a political advocacy group that supports pinpointed candidates for office and operates in an ad hoc fashion without a traditional organizational structure. The case of MoveOn also illustrates that nuanced ICTs have not replaced traditional models of organizing nor replaced activism in the material world. Rather, they have altered the contours of mobilizing strategies and participatory democracy in important ways that vary along the spectrum of contentious and electoral politics. What makes this entity additionally intriguing is the way its online operations allow it to not only straddle the virtual and material spheres in terms of collective identity, organization, and mobilization, but to also engage in both protest and institutional politics.

The case of MoveOn.org leads to the logical question of whether this new type of SMO is an anomaly or can we expect other SMOs to adopt similar ways of organizing and mobilizing. To address this query the next section provides an analysis of the Tea Party, which many view as the conservative counterpart to MoveOn (though it has a more institutionalized structure and forms of financial and strategic backing). An examination of this group allows us to draw some

The multiple groups that constitute the Tea Party have been able to take advantage of current political trends, in part by forming networks with other constituencies.

comparisons to, and differences from, MoveOn in terms of agenda and organizational style, and it poses similar theoretical questions that can aid our understanding of contemporary forms of collective behavior.

THE TEA PARTY

The Tea Party has been compared to MoveOn.org in terms of its organizational structure and the tactics it employs (though as we will see some of these comparisons are not accurate). In fact, FreedomWorks and other groups behind the Tea Party have long declared their intention to create the equivalent to MoveOn. Broadly, TEA (taxed enough already) Partiers hope to spearhead a movement that aims to reduce government spending and taxes, through an umbrella organization made up of various politically conservative groups and factions. It is this ideological connection that fosters a sense of collective identity among the disparate groups and individuals.

The Tea Party is also flexible and at face value, at least, leaderless, as it is composed of unconnected collections of local chapters with varying agendas. This organizational structure clearly resembles that of a new social movement: an assembly of roughly affiliated groups consisting of supporters rather than members in the traditional sense. Wollenberg et al. (2006) refer to these types of organizational structures as "social movement communities" rather than SMOs, and these are also at the forefront of Khan and Kellner's (2003) research on virtual public spheres as well as Bimber's (2003) work on the accelerated pluralism that new ICTs allow for. Therefore, as with MoveOn, we are encouraged to revise and update resource mobilization theory in some ways to account for these new types of horizontal structures, and we should also update cultural theories to understand what constitutes collective identity and how it is created.

In addition to the Tea Party Nation and Tea Party Express affiliations mentioned earlier in this [reading] there are other core groups that represent the interests of Tea Partiers. For example, Tea Party Patriots is a for-profit organization that organizes national conferences. It was born out of resistance to the Wall Street bailouts and what members view as runaway government spending. At the center of its agenda is an endeavor to restore the founding policy of the constitution, limited government control, and a free market economy (Kroll 2012).

Tea Party Express is a political action committee that actively campaigns in support of specific candidates. It is extraordinarily successful in this capacity. According to the Federal Election Committee, it raised $6.6 million during the 2010 midterm elections, making it the single biggest independent supporter of Tea Party candidates (Williamson, Skocpol, and Coggin 2011). Similar to MoveOn's success in the 2006 and 2008 elections, the Tea Party's influence was undeniably decisive in the 2010 elections, as supporters propelled Republicans to huge gains in the House, helped secure Senate victories for some barely known candidates such as Rand Paul, and captured seven hundred seats in state legislatures (Tanenhaus 2012).

The Tea Party's Impact on Electoral Politics

Political process theory (Tarrow 1996; McAdam 1982; C. Jenkins and Per-row 1977) argues that social movement agents have an advantage when the existing political system appears to be vulnerable to challenges, and this is especially true during times of electoral instability. This advantage is further enhanced when opponents can manipulate competition between key figures in the polity. The multiple groups that constitute the Tea Party have been able to take advantage of current political trends, in part by forming networks with other constituencies, and therefore resource mobilization theory is particularly relevant to grasping and assessing the success of the Tea Party.

For example, joining forces with the Campaign to Defeat Barack Obama (a Tea Party–linked political action committee), the Tea Party entered Governor Scott Walker of Wisconsin's recall fight in the wake of his attempt to curtail collective bargaining rights for public workers. Copying MoveOn's example, Tea Party groups used both digital and mainstream media to pursue the cause. Through e-activism it blasted several e-mails to supporters and launched a $100,000 money bomb fundraiser to help defend Walker, and it ran television ads defending his policies (Kroll 2012). In the summer of 2011 Tea Party Nation, together with Tea Party Express, launched a four-day bus tour across Wisconsin defending six Republicans facing recall elections for their roles in the collective bargaining battle (the Walker recall election will be discussed in more detail in a later [reading]). Just like MoveOn, the Tea Party groups' use of new information and media technologies is often complemented by contentious politics in the material world.

One of the Tea Party's first successes was when barely known Republican Scott Brown ran a grassroots campaign in the Massachusetts special election to win the seat vacated by Ted Kennedy, which had been held by Democrats since 1978. Resource mobilization theory contributes to our understanding of this victory given the financial backing provided by wealthy Tea Party advocates who used digital means to fundraise. They emulated some of MoveOn's tactics by organizing an online money bomb (raising more than $1 million online in twenty-four hours) and orchestrated an "on the ground" get-out-the-vote campaign (Stauber 2010). This again combined online and offline activism, and it forged institutional and extrainstitutional political activity. In another simulation of MoveOn's approach, through its Take America Back website it offered a web-based call center through which members could talk to voters from anywhere.

Allies as a Key Resource

One of the distinctions between the Tea Party and MoveOn is the Tea Party's reliance on powerful allies (as already noted, the Campaign to Defeat Barack Obama was key to the struggle in saving Walker's job)—though this is not to deny that MoveOn also has some wealthy financial backers. One of the major groups funding and organizing the Tea Party is FreedomWorks (formerly chaired by Dick Armey, former Republican Speaker of the House). This SMO provides abundant resources in terms of money, advice, knowledge, and personnel to invigorate and sustain the

Protesters rally against government taxation and spending policies at the US Capitol on September 12, 2009.

movement. It helped to organize the first Tea Party March on Washington on September 12, 2009, in conjunction with Glenn Beck's 912 projects and the Tax Day Tea Party campaign (such as Fox News) for the event (Bai 2012). It also utilized mainstream media to try to influence public opinion and promote civic engagement. On May 13 Beck launched this project on his Fox News program. He also mobilized it through a social networking site built by his production company, Mercury Entertainment Group (Rose 2010). The 912 demonstrations were planned over the Internet, with local chapters coordinating activities through digital tools such as Meetup.com and Ning.com. The occasion was designed to build national unity around his stated nine principles and twelve values rooted in commitment to the United States and good morals and ethics (labeled the "Take America Back" convention).

Americans for Prosperity, another core group behind the Tea Party, together with FreedomWorks provided funding for the ensuing eight hundred Tea Party protests held across the United States during the Tea Party Express bus tour (Bai 2012). Fox News gave extended coverage of the cross-country caravans that appealed to the media through the use of historical costumes, props, and catchy slogans (Rose 2010). The unpredictable protests, accompanied by symbolic displays of rebellion and disruptions of town hall meetings, as part of the Tea Partiers' repertoire, were also media friendly in their spontaneity and entertainment value. These symbolic forms of political protest parallel some of the tactics that MoveOn uses, and new social movement theories and constructionist theories can help us make sense of them. The use of symbolic displays of grievances and demands, and framing issues in a clear way that resonates with disgruntled citizens is something that both groups have mastered. They also open up the public sphere for more discussion and innovative forms of communicative action (using Habermas's 1993 terms).

The events that the Tea Party hosted and the rhetoric they engaged in are good examples of both frame alignment and frame amplification as promoted by social movement theories that focus on cultural aspects of social movements at the micro level (Snow et al. 1986 in particular). This is a tactic that activists can use to tap into deeply held morals, values, and beliefs that are congruent with other SMOs and that are embedded in the general population. Participants also used frame bridging to resonate with other organizations calling for resistance to the federal government. They also situated diagnostic framing in a way that promoted a critique of what they perceived to be the radical socialist agenda of the Obama administration. Other prognostic and motivational frames were embedded in a call to arms, with slogans such as "take your country back" and "what we need is revival and revolt!" (Rose 2010).

How to Define the Tea Party: Astroturf or Grassroots?

Some of the organizations that are affiliated with and support the Tea Party are corporate, while others are more grassroots in nature, and this led to some criticism of the Tea Party.

Critics argue that its attempts to frame itself as a grassroots and ad hoc popular uprising are contrary to the reality of how the Tea party is structured and funded. For example, the supposed spontaneous interruptions and heckling of both Democrats and moderate Republicans during the 2009 town hall meetings were not entirely unrehearsed. Much of this was orchestrated and funded by well-established insider groups such as FreedomWorks and Americans for Prosperity. It is the Koch brothers (David and Charles) who provide most of the funding for both of these groups. They own 84 percent of Koch Industries, which is the second-largest privately held US company, and they financially back a number of libertarian and conservative organizations and think tanks, such as the Cato Institute, as well Tea Party candidates, through their political action committee (Fisher 2012).

The Tea Party groups that participated in the caravans also received advice and encouragement from Beck's (no longer available) national website (912project.com), and other conservative leaning websites such as ResistNet.com (also no longer in service) provided talking points. FreedomWorks suggested particular questions Tea Party representatives should ask at the town halls and maintained a link detailing how members could infiltrate the meetings, spread inaccurate information, and harass members of Congress, and thus the strategy was actually very top down. Although most supporters consider the movement to be populist, FreedomWorks, as mentioned earlier, is a well-funded, well-connected, DC-based think tank. The organization spent more than $10 million on the 2010 elections on campaign materials alone and set up a Super PAC through which it donates hundreds of thousands of dollars to politicians (Coffey 2012).

Despite these top-down tactics, Tea Party participants assert that the movement is a mainstream resurgence among powerless, ordinary citizens. Detractors, however, view their primary agenda as one attempting to preserve their collective privileges, as most activists are middle-aged, middle class, and white. They contend that the Tea Party engages in reactive rather than progressive politics, responding to threats to their sense of entitlement and sometimes engaging in racist or xenophobic rhetoric. An example of this is displayed in an e-mail sent out in August 2010 by Tea Party Nation to its 35,000 members, asking them to post their "horror stories" about undocumented immigrants on its (now taken down) website (Young 2010).

Thus, although Tea Partiers brand the movement as a grassroots uprising, others view it as a tool of the Republican Party that has been used and co-opted by powerful political actors connected with the political establishment in the Beltway (Pilkington 2011). MSNBC talk show host Rachel Maddow describes the movement in the following way: "They're called Fox News Channel tax day Tea Parties because all the big Fox News Channel personalities appeared at tax day Tea Party events. They were Fox News endorsed and promoted and, in some cases, hosted events. They didn't just cover the Tea Party protests. They ran ads for them. They used Fox News Channel staff production time and ad time on the air to promote the events. They ran tea party promotions" (MSNBC 2006). This free access to traditional media helped catapult the movement into national consciousness and related it to public sentiment of frustration with the government. MoveOn had done this earlier; however, it relied more on the Internet and digital media as a resource, as it does not have the connections to, or much support from, corporate-owned media.

Hybrid SMO

Regardless of these differences and criticisms, each organization extensively employs both e-activism and contentious street protests as a part of its repertoire, and both straddle electoral and contentious politics by taking advantage of the shifting political context to influence public opinion, which political mediation theory highlights the relevance of (Soule and King 2006). In sum, although the 2012 election did not bode well for Tea Party candidates and it appears that the organization may have lost its momentum, it is important to acknowledge that social movements ebb and flow, and the Tea Party might very well bounce back in the next election. Regardless of what the future brings, through their framing devices Tea Partiers have been able to persuade many citizens that the issues they raise are urgent, that alternatives are possible, that they have the moral high ground, and that citizens can be invested with agency. This has served well as a recruitment mechanism. Their injustice frames explicitly appeal to moral principles for organizational outreach by resonating with deeply held values and beliefs among the general population and linking them to movement's causes. Framing their grievances as a threat to the very existence of "everyday Americans" helps to create a sense of collective identity among Tea Partiers and their supporters who see changes in the economic, political, cultural, and social spheres—and specifically the changing demographics—as a threat to their entitlements. Although different groups work on different issues, there is a very strong emotional thread that holds them together, which indicates that a vehement sense of solidarity cuts across the various segments of participants. Th is is typical of Mann's (2000) conceptualization of contemporary social movements within the rubric of the new social movement theories that focus on forms of collective behavior that bring diverse groups together to support emotionally charged issues and promote new sets of values in a collaborative way.

THEORY TOOLKIT

Moveon and the Tea Party

We can apply a few of the theories discussed [...] to the emergence and evolution of MoveOn.org and the Tea Party:

- **New social movement school of thought, cultural theories, resource mobilization theory, and political process theory.** These theories are all very useful in aiding our understanding of these new hybrid types of organizations. Each in some way informs us about how these two groups operate in both the realm of institutional politics (challenging vulnerable candidates for office; i.e. political process theory) and extrainstitutional politics (rallies, marches, the use of celebrities, house parties, etc.; strands of new social movement theories). Most important and applicable to these two cases are cultural theories that address the critical role of collective identity and framing.

- **Theories of new media.** As used in a complementary fashion to resource mobilization, these theories demonstrate (1) the importance of the peer-to-peer sharing of information within these two groups and across broader spectrums of society without heavy reliance on the mainstream media, (2) ways in which recruitment may be easier for contemporary social movement actors, (3) how weak ties forged in cyberspace can develop into strong ties with on-the-ground mobilization efforts and protest activity, and (4) nuanced forms of organizational flexibility that allow for more grassroots forms of participation and a broader spectrum for conversation and discussion.

The Internet and digital technology were essential resources for the emergence and outburst of Tea Party activism because it was in the virtual world that ordinary citizens first began to spread their message. By establishing weak ties in cyberspace, like-minded people were able to communicate with one another and show support for the causes that the Tea Party supports. This shows how the public sphere and sources of connectivity are changing because of the digital revolution, which allows for information to be created, disseminated, commented on, and circulated through diffuse networks. It also demonstrates how these in turn lead to on-the-ground local forms of participation in political and social issues. Therefore, theories of new media are important supplements to resource mobilization and cultural theories, in particular, their attention to what H. Jenkins (2006) calls the spillover effect.

CONCLUSION

Although different in their ideologies, tactics, and funding, what MoveOn and the Tea Party have in common is that they both take advantage of new ways of organizing and mobilizing their devotees through digital means. They both also rely heavily on different types of media in the hopes of influencing public opinion. Each has raised abundant amounts of money for advertisements and political campaigns. To impact the realm of institutional politics, MoveOn and the Tea Party have also pressured officeholders through e-mail and face-to-face lobbying efforts, and they have taken advantage of the vulnerability of politicians during election years. And, finally, both entities successfully used framing to pitch their concerns in a way that resonated with frustration among voters and citizens on both sides of the political spectrum.

MoveOn's and the Tea Party's mobilization endeavors therefore represent the growing symbiotic relationship between e-activism and local organizing, as they both work in the blogosphere as well as in real communities to impact institutional and extrainstitutional politics. Their strategies underscore the need to expand conceptualizations of Habermas's conception of the "public sphere" and participatory democracy.

References

Bai, Matt. 2012. "The Tea Party's Not-So-Civil War." *The New York Times,* January 15. Available at http://www.nytimes.com/2012/01/15/magazine/tea-party-south-carolina.html?pagewanted=all. Accessed June 5, 2012.

Benford, Robert. 1993. "Frame Disputes Within the Nuclear Disarmament Movement." *Social Forces* 71(3): 677–702.

Bennet, Daniel, and Pam Fielding. 1999. *The Net Effect: How Cyber-Advocacy Is Changing the Political Landscape.* Washington, DC: Capitol Advantage.

Bennett, William, and Shanto Iyengar. 2008. "A New Era of Minimal Effects? The Changing Foundations of Political Communication." *Journal of Communication* 58(4): 707–731.

Bimber, Bruce. 2003. *Information and American Democracy: Technology in the Evolution of Political Power.* Cambridge, MA: Cambridge University Press.

Boyd, Andrew. 2003. "The Web Rewires the Movement." *The Nation,* August 4. Available at http://www.thenation.com/article/web-rewires-movement. Accessed March 30, 2004.

Brownstein, Ronald. 2004. "MoveOn Works the Hollywood Spotlight to Amplify Its Voice." *Los Angeles Times,* July 4, p. B7.

Burress, Charles. 2003. "Making Their Move." *San Francisco Chronicle,* February 9, p. A23.

Carty, Victoria. 2010. "Bridging Contentious and Electoral Politics: How MoveOn Is Expanding Public Discourse and Political Struggle." In *Engaging Social Justice: Critical Studies of the Twenty-First Century Social Transformations,* edited by David Fasenfest, 58–81. Boston: Brill.

Castells, Manuel. 2001. *The Internet Galaxy: Reflections on the Internet, Business and Society.* Malden, MA: Blackwell.

Center for Responsive Politics. 2006. "Moveon.org Independent Expenditures." *Opensecrets.org.* Available at http://www.opensecrets.org/pacs/indexpend.php?cycle=2008&cmte=C00341396. Accessed April 7, 2009.

Coffey, Brenda. 2012. "Koch Brothers Exposed." Available at http://www.kochbrothersexposed.com/protest_movement_starts_rebranding_billionaire_koch_brothers. Accessed December 8, 2012.

Deans, Jason. 2004. "Fox News Documentary Tops Amazon Sales Chart." *Guardian Unlimited News.* Available at http://www.film.guardian.co.uk/news/story/012589/html. Accessed August 1, 2004.

Drehle, David. 2008. "Obama's Youth Vote Triumph. *Time*, January 4, pp. 15–17.

Fisher, Daniel. 2012. "Inside the Koch Empire: How the Brothers Plan to Reshape America." *Forbes*, December 5. Available at http://www.forbes.com/sites/danielfisher/2012/12/05/inside-the-koch-empire-how-the-brothers-plan-to-reshape-america/2. Accessed July 8, 2012.

Gamson, William. 1992. *Talking Politics.* New York: Cambridge University Press.

Giddens, Anthony. 1991. *Modernity and Self-Identity. Self and Society in the Late Modern Age.* Cambridge, MA: Polity.

Giugni, Marco. 1998. "Was It Worth the Effort? The Outcomes and Consequences of Social Movements." *Annual Review of Sociology* 98:371–393.

Habermas, Jürgen. 1989. *The Structural Transformation of the Public Sphere.* Cambridge, MA: MIT Press.
———. 1993. *Justification and Application: Remarks on Discourse Ethics.* Cambridge, MA: Polity Press.

Jenkins, Craig, and William Form. 2006. "Social Movements and Social Change." In *Handbook of Political Sociology: States, Civil Society and Globalization,* edited by Thomas Janoski, Robert Alford, Alexander Hicks and Mildred Schwartz, 331–349. Cambridge, MA: Cambridge University Press.

Jenkins, Craig, and Charles Perrow. 1977. "Insurgency of the Powerless: Farm Worker Movements (1946–1972)." *American Sociological Review* 42: 249–296.

Johnston, Hank. 1994. "New Social Movements and Old Regional Nationalisms." In *New Social Movements: From Ideology to Identity,* edited by Enrique Larana, Hank Johnston, and Joseph Gusfield, 267–286. Philadelphia, PA: Temple University Press.

Kahn, Richard, and Douglas Kellner. 2003. "Internet Subcultures and Oppositional Politics." In *The Post-subcultures Reader,* edited by D. Muggleton, 299–314. London: Berg.

Kroll, Andy. 2012. "The Tea Party Plan to Save Scott Walker." *Mother Jones*, February 1. Available at http://motherjones.com/politics/2012/01/scott-walker-recall-tea-party. Accessed June 5, 2012.

Mann, Michael. 2000. "Has Globalization Ended the Rise of the Nation-State?" In *The Global Transformations Reader: An Introduction to the Globalization Debate,* edited by David Held and Andrew McGrew, 136–147. Cambridge, MA: Polity Press.

Markels, Alex. 2003. "Virtual Peacenik." *Mother Jones*, May 5. Available at http://www.MotherJones.com/news/hellriiser/2003/05/ma_379_01.htm. Accessed April 7, 2006.

McAdam, Doug. 1982. *Political Process and the Development of Black Insurgency 1930–1970.* Chicago: University of Chicago Press.

McAdam, Doug, and Ronnelle Paulsen. 1993. "Specifying the Relationship Between Social Ties and Activism." *American Journal of Sociology* 99(3): 640–667.

McCarthy, John, and Mayer Zald. 1973. *The Trend of Social Movements in America: Professionalization and Resource Mobilization.* Thousand Oaks, CA: General Learning Press.

Melucci, Alberto. 1996. *Challenging Codes of Collective Action in the Information Age.* Cambridge, MA: Cambridge University Press.

Meyer, David S. 2005. "Social Movements and Public Policy: Eggs, Chicken, and Theory." Introduction to *Routing the Opposition: Social Movements, Public Policy and Democracy,* edited by David S. Meyers, Valerie Jenness, and Helen Ingram, 1–26. Minneapolis: University of Minnesota Press.

Middleton, Joel, and Donald Green. 2007. "Do Community-Based Voter Mobilization Campaigns Work Even in Battleground States? Evaluating the Effectiveness of MoveOn's 2004 Outreach Campaign." Yale University. Available at www.yale.edu/csap/seminars/middleton.pdf. Accessed January 19, 2009.

MSNBC. 2006. "The Rachel Maddow Show." Transcript. Available at http://www.nbcnews.com/id/36260269/ns/msnbc-rachel_maddow_show/. Accessed September 22, 2014.

Pilkington, Ed. 2011. "Koch Brothers: Secretive Billionaires to Launch Vast Database with 2012 in Mind." *The Guardian,* November 7. Available at http://www.guardian.co.uk/world/2011/nov/07/koch-brothers-database-2012-election. Accessed June 6, 2012.

Potter, Trevor. 2003. "Internet Politics 2000: Over-hyped, then Under-hyped, the Revolution Begins." *Election Law Journal* 1(1): 25–33.

Rose, Lacey. 2010. "Glenn Beck Inc." *Forbes.com,* April 8. Available at http://socialtimes.com/gaza-flotilla-sparks-social-media-debate_b13926. Accessed June 6, 2012.

Snow, David A., Burke Rochford, Steven K. Worden, and Robert D. Benford. 1986. "Frame Alignment Processes, Micromobilization, and Movement Participation." *American Sociological Review* 51: 464–481.

Soule, Sarah, and Brayden King. 2006. "The Stages of the Policy Process and the Equal Rights Amendment, 1972–1982." *American Journal of Sociology* 111(6): 1871–1909.

Stauber, John. 2010. "Tea Party Money-Bomb Elects Scott Brown, Blows-Up Obamacare." *PRWatch,* January 19. Available at http://www.prwatch.org/node/8841. Accessed March 2, 2010.

Stevenson, Seth. 2004. "Not-So-Amateur Night." *Slate Magazine,* January 13, p. 27.

Stewart, Ian. 2003. "Anti-War Group Revives 'Daisy' Ad Campaign." *Common Dreams.* Available at http://www.commondreams.org/headlines03/0116–06.htm. Accessed September 4, 2004.

Tanenhaus, Sam. 2012. "History vs. the Tea Party." *The New York Times,* January 15. Available at http://www.nytimes.com/2012/01/15/sunday-review/gop-history-vs-the-tea-party.html?pagewanted=all. Accessed June 5, 2012.

Tarrow, Sidney. 1996. "States and Opportunities: The Political Structuring of Social Movements." In *Comparative Perspectives in Social Movements,* edited by Doug McAdam, John D. McCarthy, and Mayer N. Zald, 41–47. New York: Cambridge University Press.

_____. 2001. "Transnational Politics." *Annual Review of Political Science* 4(1): 1–20.

Tarrow, Sidney, and Charles Tilly. 2006. *Contentious Politics.* Boulder, CO: Paradigm.

Tilly, Charles. 1978. *From Mobilization to Revolution.* Reading, MA: Addison-Wesley.

Tomlinson, John. 1999. *Globalization and Culture.* Chicago: University of Chicago Press.

Utne, Leif. 2003. "MoveOn.org Holds Virtual Primary." *Utne,* June 23. Available at http://www.utne.com/community/moveonorgholdsvirtualprimary.aspx#axzz3FTg6jkX1.

Williamson, Vanessa, Theda Skocpol, and John Coggin. 2011. "The Tea Party and the Remaking of Republican Conservatism." *Perspectives on Politics* 9(1): 25–43. Available at http://scholar.harvard.edu/files/williamson/files/tea_party_pop.pdf. Accessed January 2, 2013.

Wollenberg, E., M. Colchester, G. Mbugua, and T. Griffiths. 2006. "Linking Social Movements: How International Networks Can Better Support Community Action About Forests." *International Forestry Review* 8(2): 265–272.

Young, Patrick. 2010. "Tea Party Wants Your Illegal Immigration Horror Stories." Long IslandWins.com, August 4. Available at http://www.longislandwins.com/news/detail/tea_party_wants_your_illegal_immigration_horror_stories. Accessed November 17, 2014.

Zakarin, Jordan. 2013. "How Hollywood Fought Against the Iraq War." *Hollywood Reporter,* March 19. Available at http://www.hollywoodreporter.com/news/iraq-war-anniversary-hollywoods-anti-429697. Accessed September 25, 2014.

A Transforming Election

How Barack Obama Changed American Politics

By John Kenneth White; ed. William J. Crotty

> We are the ones we've been waiting for.
> —Barack Obama

E lection night 2008. At 11:00 p.m. eastern standard time, the television networks universally declared that Barack Obama had acquired more than the 270 electoral votes necessary to become the 44th president of the United States. Obama had done the extraordinary, winning a majority of the popular vote (52.63 percent)—something Democrats had been unable to accomplish since Jimmy Carter's minimalist 50.08 percent victory in 1976 over Gerald R. Ford.[1] And unlike 2000—when popular vote loser George W. Bush beat Al Gore by four votes in the Electoral College—this time the electors reflected Obama's strong popular showing: 365 votes for Obama to 173 for McCain.[2] The red state–blue state stasis that had bedeviled the country during the George W. Bush years was finally broken, as former red states that twice backed Bush—including Virginia, North Carolina, Ohio, Florida, Indiana, Colorado, and Nevada—switched to Obama.[3]

Clearly, voters were searching for someone very different from the president they had come to know (and dislike). The editors of the New Republic captured this prevailing sentiment when they implicitly observed that Obama had become the antithesis of the incumbent he sought to replace: "On the whole, he has turned in one of the most impressive performances in recent political history—demonstrating an ability to explain complex ideas in plainspoken English, impeccable managerial skills, evenness of temper, avoidance of sloppy errors, and pragmatism, not to mention that he can really deliver a speech" ("Obama for President" 2008). Most Americans

John Kenneth White, "A Transforming Election: How Barack Obama Changed American Politics," Winning the Presidency 2008, ed. William J. Crotty, pp. 185-208, 209-232. Copyright © 2009 by Taylor & Francis Group. Reprinted with permission.

agreed, and they largely set aside the cultural and values differences that created the partisan paralysis that began with Bill Clinton's impeachment in 1998 and subsided only with Barack Obama's victory a decade later.[4]

"PARTY LIKE IT'S 1964"

The un–George W. Bush–like qualities discerned by voters (and *The New Republic*) in Barack Obama prompted most Democrats to rhapsodize about their new president. Introducing Obama, talk show host Oprah Winfrey recalled reading *The Autobiography of Miss Jane Pittman*, which described how the enslaved Pittman searched for "the one" who would lead her to freedom. Winfrey told rapt audiences that she had discovered "the one" in Obama: "Well, I believe, in '08, I have found the answer to Ms. Pittman's question. I have fo-o-u-u-nd the answer! It is the same question that our nation is asking: 'Are you the one? Are you the one?' I'm here to tell y'all, he is the one. He is the one. *Barack Obama!*" (Thomas 2008, 48).

It had been a long time since Democrats were so giddy about a presidential contest. Not since Lyndon B. Johnson's 1964 landslide had Democrats so thoroughly routed Republicans on a given election night.[5] Several weeks before the Obama-McCain contest reached its final denouement, *Washington Post* columnist Richard Cohen (2008) forecast that when all the votes were counted, jubilant Democrats would "party like it's 1964" (2008, A17). In fact, the comfortable Democratic victories achieved by Obama and his ticket-mates made it seem like a political déjà vu experience. In the Senate, Democrats added eight new members to their once-slender 51-seat majority—a result that gave the remaining band of Republican senators pause in employing any filibusters against President Obama and his Democratic allies.[6] In the House, Democrats added 21 new members—making for a total of 51 additional seats won in 2006 and 2008.[7] Together these gains nearly equaled the 54 seats that House Republicans gained in their 1994 triumph that gave them the Speaker's gavel for the first time in 40 years.

Conservative columnist George F. Will observed that the 2006 and 2008 congressional results were the worst for the Grand Old Party since the Great Depression–era elections of 1930 and 1932, when Republicans also suffered back-to-back election night losses (Will 2008b). Particularly stinging was the defeat of Connecticut Republican Christopher Shays—a loss that reduced the number of House Republicans from New England to zero. When New York State is added to the mix, only three Republicans would take their places in the 111th Congress. And when the universe is broadened even further to include all of the Northeast, only eight of 64 congressional districts are controlled by Republicans. Even Staten Island (a district long held by a local Republican machine) was surrendered to the Democrats. As a consequence, no urban area of more than 500,000 inhabitants would have a Republican member in the new Congress. When state legislatures are included, the results are equally dismal: north of Virginia, Republicans do not have a majority in any legislative body, with the sole exception of the Pennsylvania state senate.[8]

These tallies reflect the toxic political environment in which John McCain and his fellow Republicans found themselves. Democrats won because voters officially pronounced the George W. Bush presidency dead and they wanted a new direction—a message the electorate attempted to deliver in 2006, and one that Bush ignored to the everlasting ire of both Democrats and independents alike.[9] As the campaign approached its predictable result, Democrats became competitive in congressional, state, and local districts that were once the exclusive province of the Republicans (e.g., Staten Island). Consequently, Republicans were reduced to their southern base, where McCain beat Obama by a solid margin of 54 percent to 45 percent (Edison 2008). McCain's southern support was buoyed by the 68 percent backing he received from southern whites, who remain a mainstay of the GOP (Edison 2008). Republicans also maintained their grip on Dixie's congressional seats. In the upcoming 111th Congress, 65 percent of senators from the Old Confederacy will be Republicans, while 52 percent of House members from Dixie will belong to the GOP. This means that Barack Obama has become the first Democratic president to assemble a governing coalition that *does not* include the South. Conservative southern Dixiecrats who used to vote with the GOP have been consigned to history's relics.

A SOUTHERN LOCK BECOMES A SOUTHERN CAGE

For decades, a "southern lock" ensured GOP dominance of the presidency. Ever since Richard M. Nixon made his Faustian bargain with South Carolina's J. Strom Thurmond in 1968—namely that Nixon, as president, would go slow on civil rights and appoint "strict constructionists" to the federal courts—both Richard Nixon and Ronald Reagan won near-unanimous southern support in their presidential outings.[10] Moreover, the Republican lock on the Old Confederacy strengthened each time Democrats placed a northerner at the top of their ticket (Hubert H. Humphrey in 1968, George S. McGovern in 1972, Walter F. Mondale in 1984, and Michael S. Dukakis in 1988). Bill Clinton was the only Democrat who could pick the Republicans' southern lock, and even that took some luck (a poor economy in 1992) and lots of extra effort (choosing Tennessee's Al Gore to be his vice president).[11]

But by 2008, the southern lock had turned into a southern cage. John McCain's best showings included these states of the Deep South: Alabama (60 percent), Louisiana (59 percent), Mississippi (56 percent), and South Carolina (54 percent). In each state, Barack Obama's overwhelming black vote was offset by a deluge of white votes: 88 percent for McCain in Alabama, 88 percent in Louisiana, and 84 percent in Mississippi (Edison 2008). Similarly, McCain performed well in the southern reaches of Appalachia, where he won 366 of its 410 counties; and he prevailed in Arkansas (59 percent), Kentucky (57 percent), Tennessee (57 percent), and West Virginia (56 percent).[12] Once more, McCain's victories were due to his strong base among white voters: Arkansas (68 percent), Kentucky (63 percent), Tennessee (63 percent), and West Virginia (57 percent). Ironically, the home states of the last successful Democratic ticket of Bill Clinton and Al Gore, Arkansas and Tennessee, were solidly in McCain's corner and remain firmly ensconced in the Republican camp.[13]

Yet the more John McCain and his fellow Republicans experienced solid victories in the Old Confederacy and Appalachia, the worse it was for the GOP everyplace else. Today, the Republican Party largely occupies territory once controlled by the Democrats following William McKinley's party-realigning triumph in 1896. Back then, Republicans dominated in the electoral-rich Northeast and Midwest, while Democrats retained their Civil War–era legacy strength in the South along with populist support in the interior West. McCain's chief strategist, Steve Schmidt, decries the shrinking of the GOP: "The party in the Northeast is all but extinct; the party on the West Coast is all but extinct; the party has lost the mid-South states—Virginia, North Carolina—and the party is in deep trouble in the Rocky Mountain West, and there has to be a message and a vision that is compelling to people in order for them to come back and to give consideration to the Republican party again" (Cox 2008). Minnesota governor Tim Pawlenty, a prospective 2012 presidential candidate, concurs: "We cannot be a majority governing party when we essentially cannot compete in the Northeast, we are losing our ability to compete in Great Lakes States, we cannot compete on the West Coast, we are increasingly in danger of competing in the mid-Atlantic States, and the Democrats are now winning some of the western states. This is not a formula for being a majority governing party in this nation" (Cooper and Robbins 2008).

The financial crisis that blossomed in October only sealed the Republicans' fate. That month, the Dow Jones Industrial Average experienced a massive 6,000-point fall from its 14,000 peak a year earlier. More than *$8 trillion* in stock value was lost in just a few short weeks. On a single day, October 10, 2008, the market had a 1,000-point swing, a first. In the ensuing days, the market was extremely jittery—rising 900 points one day and losing 700 points the next. To ensure financial stability, the Bush administration proposed a massive $700 billion Wall Street rescue plan—the largest government intervention in the private markets since Franklin D. Roosevelt's National Recovery Administration efforts of the 1930s. Despite rapid congressional passage of the federal bailout (after an initial false start), Wall Street's financial crisis hit Main Street. October unemployment rose to 6.5 percent (with two million described as being "long-term unemployed"—i.e., not having a job for 27 months or more) (Bureau of Labor Statistics 2008). From January to October 2008, 1 million jobs evaporated.[14]

And these were not the only bad economic tidings. Millions of otherwise employed citizens who joined what pollster John Zogby once called the "investor class" (and had been staunch supporters of George W. Bush) were shocked to open their 401(k) statements and discover that their retirement savings had been sharply reduced (Zogby 2005). Home foreclosures reached record levels, as the combination of unemployment and bad credit meant that millions of Americans had to surrender their personal palaces to the banks. In the three-month period from July to September 2008, foreclosures totaled 765,000, and six states (Nevada, California, Florida, Ohio, Michigan, and Arizona) accounted for 60 percent of the lost homes.[15]

The result was a consumer crisis of confidence. In October, retail sales fell 2.8 percent, as would-be customers pared their spending in the wake of gloomy financial headlines (Jack Healy 2008). The prevailing mood was captured in the Consumer Confidence Index, as it fell from 61.4 in September 2008 to just 38.0 one month later—the lowest number since 1967.[16] Jerry Mills, an Ohio welder and former Bush supporter, was among those fearing foreclosure and fretting about the future, and he blamed Bush: "I voted for Bush, and I can't believe it. I don't want to admit to it, I'm not happy with where he put us" (Wallsten and Hook 2008). Mills backed Obama, as did 51 percent of his fellow Ohioans.

Not since 1933 had a new president assumed office under such dire circumstances: an economic implosion combined with two wars in Iraq and Afghanistan. Economic anxiety remained palpable and further government action was required; Iraq was a source of danger and no political solution to the war had been reached; and there was a growing consensus that Afghanistan was slipping away and more U.S. troops would be needed to succeed there. A *New York Times* editorial endorsing Obama captured the exegesis of the moment: "It will be an enormous challenge just to get the nation back to where it was before Mr. Bush, to restore its self-confidence and its self-respect" ("Barack" 2008). Voters agreed, and they concluded that they could no longer afford the luxury of having an election dominated by social and cultural issues—such as guns, gay marriage, abortion, Willie Horton, William Ayers, or even the Rev. Jeremiah Wright. According to the exit polls, only 30 percent cited "shares my values" as the most important candidate quality (and 65 percent of them backed McCain), whereas 34 percent mentioned "can bring about needed change" as the most important attribute they sought (and 89 percent of them supported Obama).[17] For the moment, the clanging culture wars had reached a tentative truce.

Other October straws in the wind also pointed toward an inevitable Democratic victory, including these:

1. George W. Bush recorded a 21 percent job approval rating—a number three points *lower* than Richard M. Nixon's on the eve of his 1974 resignation, and one point below the previous record set by Harry S Truman in February 1952, when the U.S. was beset by stalemate in the Korean War and a host of other Cold War–era challenges.[18]

2. Only *9 percent* pronounced themselves satisfied with the direction of the United States, the lowest recorded response ever to that question in the history of the Gallup Poll (Newport 2008).

3. September fund-raising totals (reported in mid-October) showed Obama raised a record $150 million. Overall, the Democratic candidate had 3.1 million contributors (with 630,000 added in September alone), whose average contribution totaled $86.00. This treasure chest allowed Obama to blanket the airwaves with paid advertisements (including a 30-minute infomercial) and financed an enormous get-out-the-vote campaign.[19]

Tommy Thompson, a former Republican governor of Wisconsin, was asked by the *New York Times* in mid-October whether he was satisfied with the McCain campaign. He answered, "No, and I don't know anyone who is" (Nagourney and Bumiller 2008, 1). A dozen years earlier, the same Tommy Thompson told the *Times* on the eve of Bob Dole's defeat, "I thought George Bush's campaign [in 1992] was probably the poorest run presidential campaign—and I think this [Mr. Dole's campaign] is a close second" (Berke 1996, 1). Both times, Mr. Thompson expressed what many Republicans privately thought about their ticket's chances in November.

Despite all the good news for Obama and his Democratic ticket-mates, several questions remained unanswered until Americans gathered around their election night television campfires. Most involved race and whether the old shibboleths of politics still retained enough power to determine the outcome, including these:

- Would October's bad economic news be enough to elect a black man president of the United States? Even the very thought of an African American president was relatively new. In 1958, the Gallup Poll first asked its respondents whether they would support a "well-qualified" African American for president. Only 37 percent said yes; 53 percent, no.[20]

- Would the so-called Bradley effect create an election night surprise? The Bradley effect referred to the 1982 California gubernatorial race when Los Angeles Mayor Tom Bradley, who was black, lost to Republican George Deukmejian, who was white, despite Bradley's significant leads in the preelection polls.[21]

- Would any Bradley effect be offset by increased nonwhite (especially African American) turnout that would offset Obama's expected losses among whites?

- Would enough white, blue-collar, Joe-the-Plumber types come home to the Democratic Party after years of supporting Ronald Reagan and the two George Bushes (and in sufficient numbers) to make Obama president?

- Would younger, twenty-first-century voters show up at the polls and vote for Obama? And would these first-time voters form a portion of a new and enduring Democratic majority?

Barack Obama's comfortable win provided answers to each of these questions. For starters, 63 percent named the economy as the most important issue (and 53 percent of them supported Obama). Other concerns received scant mention: Iraq, 10 percent; terrorism, 9 percent; healthcare, 9 percent; energy, 7 percent. Second, Americans were more than willing to accept an African American as president. Only 9 percent said race was an important factor in making their voting decision (and of these voters, 53 percent supported Obama!). In fact, John McCain's age proved to be a more significant factor than race: 15 percent said age mattered (and 77 percent of these voters backed Obama).[22] Third, there was no significant Bradley effect, as the preelection polls consistently gave Obama a lead of six to seven points—exactly the scenario that played out on election night. The disappearance of the Bradley effect heartened historians, who noted that the long arc of the civil rights movement that began in the 1960s finally came to rest with the selection of an African American as president in 2008.[23]

These favorable headlines sent Republicans reeling. In many ways, their present-day funk is reminiscent of their despair following Lyndon B. Johnson's 1964 triumph. After the Johnson landslide, political scientist Nelson Polsby noted that efforts to revive the GOP "may be insufficient to prevent an effective shift in this country to a one-and-one-half party system" (Ladd 1978a, 24). But, for Democrats, all this good news did not cause them to compare Barack Obama to Lyndon Johnson. Instead, many Democrats believed (and hoped) that in Obama they had found their own modern-day version of the iconic Republican Ronald Reagan.[24]

There are many similarities between Ronald Reagan and Barack Obama: both were gifted writers and effective communicators, and both were covered with a durable Teflon coating that prevented attacks from sticking to them.[25] Years ago, U.S. Representative Pat Schroeder coined the term "Teflon president" to describe Reagan following the Democrats' failed efforts to make numerous accusations adhere to the popular chief executive (e.g., he's uncaring and callous toward the poor, and his tax and budget cuts were unfair).[26] More than two decades later, Republican vice presidential nominee Sarah Palin evoked fears about an impending Obama presidency, telling audiences: "This is not a man who sees America the way you and I see America."[27] The GOP ticket accused Obama of being unpatriotic and having "palled around with" (Palin's words) William Ayers, a man who was an "old washed up terrorist" (McCain's words) (McCain-Obama 2008). But repeated references to Ayers, a founding member of the Weather Underground who attempted to bomb the Pentagon as a protest against the Vietnam War, cost the Republican ticket votes. According to an October survey, 23 percent of registered voters thought less of McCain than they did at the start of the campaign.[28] The exit polls confirmed this result: nearly two-thirds thought McCain attacked Obama unfairly, while a minority believed Obama attacked McCain unfairly.[29]

1980 AND 2008: HISTORY REPEATS ITSELF

The comparisons between Ronald Reagan's 1980 victory and Barack Obama's triumph in 2008 are striking. Twenty-eight years ago, Reagan deplored the incumbent president, Jimmy Carter, telling Republican delegates: "Can anyone look at the record of this administration and say, 'Well done?' ... Can anyone look at our reduced standing in the world and say, 'Let's have four more years of this?'" (Reagan 1980). In 2008, Democrats euphemistically quoted Reagan's words back at another president, George W. Bush, and they made doubly sure that voters saw John McCain as Bush's stand-in. At one Democratic debate, Bush's name was invoked 47 times (all of them negatively), while at a comparable Republican debate, the president was mentioned just *twice* (and even one of these citations was negative).[30] As the months wore on, Barack Obama almost seemed uninterested in running against John McCain, the war hero, making "Bush-McCain" his preferred candidate of choice.

Writing in an election volume about Ronald Reagan's 1980 victory, political scientist Gerald M. Pomper summoned the ghost of Oliver Cromwell, who once famously told the British Parliament: "You have sat too long here for any good you have been doing. Depart, I say, and let us have done with you. In the name of God, go!" (1981, 65). Pomper believed Americans had channeled Cromwell's ghost to deliver the same message to Jimmy Carter and the Democrats. In 2008, voters channeled Cromwell once more, telling George W. Bush and his fellow Republicans to depart at once. Indeed, after all the gains made in party identification during the efflorescence of the Reagan years, Republicans unhappily discovered in 2008 that their advances were eviscerated. In 1980, 51 percent of voters called themselves Democrats, 30 percent were Republicans, and 19 percent were independents (Decision/Making/Information, 1980). By 1994—a high point of the Reagan Revolution when Republicans won control of Congress—the number of partisan identifiers stood at parity: Democrats, 34 percent; Republicans, 31 percent.[31] The partisan tug-of-war persisted for the rest of the Bill Clinton regime and into the George W. Bush years. But by 2008, the number of Republican partisans was virtually *unchanged* from that of 1980, while the number of Democratic identifiers soared: 51 percent of likely 2008 voters leaned Democratic; only 37 percent were aligned with the Republicans.[32] Exit polls also found a seven-point Democratic advantage, the largest two-party disparity since 1980.[33] Simply put, the pro-Democratic shifts that occurred during George W. Bush's second term were so powerful, it was as if the two terms of Ronald Reagan never happened.

"We Are Dying at the Box Office"

A year before Barack Obama's victory, California governor Arnold Schwarzenegger sounded an alarm. Noting that 370,000 registered California Republicans deserted his party from 2005 to 2007, Schwarzenegger analogized the GOP's plight to that of a failed motion picture: "In movie terms, we are dying at the box office. We are not filling the seats" (Schwarzenegger 2007).

Republicans were losing their audience, not only in California but nationally. The numbers tell the tale. Following George W. Bush's 2000 victory, the GOP enjoyed a 56 percent favorable rating; by 2008, its favorable figure fell (like the stock market) to just 40 percent.[34] Things became so dire that Virginia congressman Tom Davis told his colleagues that the GOP brand was "in the trash can," adding, "If we were a dog food, they would take us off the shelf" (Davis 2008).

Nowhere is the Republican collapse more evident than among independents. In 2007, only 33 percent expressed a favorable view toward the GOP; 55 percent held an unfavorable opinion.[35] Former Reagan pollster Richard B. Wirthlin noted in 2006 that GOP attempts to woo disillusioned independents were about as effective as "raking water up a hill" (Kirkpatrick 2006, WK-1). Wirthlin's observation held true again in 2008: only 44 percent of independents sided with John McCain—an especially low figure given that McCain ran well among independents in the 2000 and 2008 Republican primaries, giving him margins that provided victories in the primaries.[36] Other Republican notables—including Elizabeth Dole, John Sununu, Gordon Smith, and Ted Stevens—bid adieu to their Senate colleagues thanks to the one-two punch of overwhelming Democratic and independent opposition. (For the first time since 1952, neither a Bush nor a Dole would serve in an upcoming session of Congress.)

At the heart of the problem was the strong link between the Grand Old Party and George W. Bush. It was that word association game that proved fatal to Republican hopes (and one from which Republicans must disassociate themselves for a recovery to begin). In 2007, CBS News and the *New York Times* conducted a revealing survey that showed just how tarnished the Republican brand had become. When respondents were asked to name the first word that came to their minds when thinking about the Republican Party, the answers were the following:

Respondent used a negative word (12 percent);
Conservative (10 percent);
Liars/illegal/corruption (9 percent);
Good/positive word (5 percent);
Rich/upper class (7 percent);
George W. Bush (5 percent);
Confused/disorganized (5 percent);
Bad/the bad people (4 percent);
Business/big business (3 percent);
Neutral word (3 percent);
Strong/fights for its beliefs (2 percent);
Taxes/tax cuts/spending (2 percent);
Reasonable/unreasonable (2 percent);
Iraq war/wars/military (2 percent);

Other policies (2 percent);

Other words (10 percent);

Don't know/no answer (17 percent).[37]

Republicans preferred to counter the bad polling news by summoning the glory days of the Reagan years. But Ronald Reagan exited the White House two decades ago. In many ways, the GOP reaction to bad news is similar to that of the Democrats following their 1980 rejection at the polls. That year, the late political scientist Wilson Carey McWilliams wrote that Reagan's election signified the end of the New Deal era: "[T]he Roosevelt coalition has come to an end, as it was bound to. There are middle-aged voters today who were not born when Franklin Roosevelt died, and the youngest voters in 1980 were only a year old when John Kennedy was shot. We will remember Roosevelt and the Great Depression less and less, and—just as Truman has suddenly acquired cachet—[John F.] Kennedy will increasingly be the symbol whose memory excites Democratic partisans" (McWilliams 1981). Today, something similar is happening as memories of Reagan are steadily fading into the mists of history (and with them his potent political coalition), while the recent unhappy experiences of the George W. Bush years remain fresh—especially with the young (read 18-yearold voters born in 1990), whose political attitudes were almost exclusively shaped by the Bush years.

A Twenty-First-Century Hoover?

Near the end of the Reagan presidency, Richard Wirthlin sent a memo to Ronald Reagan. In it, he took stock of the president's standing, outlining three "conditions for greatness" that, he claimed, "have long served to underpin the 'can-do spirit' that has made America a leader among nations":

There must be strong public confidence and pride in America—belief in "the great experiment."

There must be trust in the government and a confidence that elected officials can deal effectively with problems.

The public view of the future must be hopeful and optimistic.[38]

In each category, Wirthlin argued that Reagan had successfully met these criteria, which, in turn, assured him of a positive assessment in the history books. And with each passing year, Wirthlin has been proven right.

Using Wirthlin's "conditions of greatness" as a present-day model, George W. Bush fails miserably. Confidence in the American experiment and in the institutions of government that keep the American Dream alive have fallen to all-time lows. In 2007, the Gallup Organization found public disenchantment had reached a level not seen since the dark days of Watergate:

51 percent trusted the federal government to handle international problems, the lowest percentage recorded since 1972.

47 percent had faith in the federal government to handle domestic problems, the lowest response since 1976.

43 percent believed in the executive branch of government, just above the 40 percent expressing support in April 1974, four months before a disgraced Richard Nixon resigned the presidency.

50 percent trusted the legislative branch, a decline from 62 percent in 2005.

55 percent trusted "the men and women in political life who are seeking office," matching the low-point reached in 2001. (Jones 2007a)

It is no surprise, therefore, that voters turned on George W. Bush. Two-thirds were dissatisfied with the way he was running the country; 70 percent said he had no clear plan for getting U.S. troops out of Iraq; 75 percent maintained he had acquired more power than his predecessors, and that this development has been bad for the country.[39] Most tellingly, when asked who was the better chief executive, George W. Bush or Ronald Reagan, more than three-quarters answered, "Reagan"—another reaffirmation of Wirthlin's "conditions of greatness."[40] Given this lack of public consent, it is fair to say that the United States did not have a fully functional president until Barack Obama took the oath of office on January 20, 2009.

Perhaps there was no greater commentary on George W. Bush's shortcomings than a John McCain television advertisement aired just three weeks prior to election day. In it, McCain stated the obvious: "The last eight years haven't worked very well, have they?"[41] But even that self-evident admission proved to be too little, too late. In his final debate, an exasperated McCain tried to shuck the "Bush-McCain" label Obama had so successfully pinned to his chest: "Senator Obama, I am not President Bush. If you wanted to run against President Bush, you should have run four years ago. I'm going to give a new direction to this economy in this country" (McCain-Obama 2008). But McCain's protestations suffered yet another setback the weekend before the balloting when Vice President Dick Cheney heartily endorsed McCain: "I believe the right leader for this moment in history is Senator John McCain. John is a man who understands the danger facing America. He's a man who has looked into the face of evil and not flinched. He's a man who's comfortable with responsibility, and has been since he joined the armed forces at the age of 17. He's earned our support and confidence, and the time is now to make him commander in chief" ("Endgame" 2008). Obama seized upon Cheney's words, cutting a commercial quoting Cheney, and sarcastically adding that McCain had really worked hard for the vice president's support since he had voted with the Bush-Cheney administration 90 percent of the time.

The reasons that John McCain sought to keep his distance from George W. Bush and that Barack Obama never failed to mention Bush and McCain in the same breath were obvious: Bush's job approval ratings had descended into the 20 percent range, especially as the financial crisis took discontented voters and transformed them into scared voters. The late Clare Booth Luce once said that every president gets one line in the history books. Thus, for George Washing-ton, "He was the Father of the Country." For Abraham Lincoln, "He saved the Union and freed the slaves." For Franklin Roosevelt, "He launched the New Deal and fought World War Two." For Ronald Reagan, "He helped end the Cold War." For George W. Bush, the line is not fully formed, but these words seem likely to appear: "terrorism," "September 11," "Iraq," "Afghanistan," and "financial crisis."

In his March 4 inaugural address in 1933, Franklin D. Roosevelt delivered a harsh assessment of his predecessor, Herbert Hoover: "Only a foolish optimist can deny the dark realities of the moment." During the next four years, one can only hope that a financial crisis, wars in Iraq and Afghanistan, and the "dark realities of the moment" will give way not just to brighter days, but to a sense of order—both in foreign and domestic affairs, something Americans deeply craved at the start of the Obama administration.

Elections that transform U.S. politics often happen because voters want a restoration of order. So it was in 1968. In his masterful book *Nixonland*, historian Rick Perlstein (2008) wrote that the nightly televised chaos was crucial to Richard Nixon's victory: "Turn on the TV: burning huts in Vietnam. Turn on the TV: burning buildings in Watts. Turn on the TV: one set of young people were comparing another set of young people to Nazis, and Da Nang was equated with Nagasaki" (Perlstein 2008, 14). Similarly, Richard Wirthlin advised Ronald Reagan in 1980 that he should "convey the clearest possible message that Reagan stands for leadership and control. The prevailing view in America is that no one is in control; the prevailing impression given by the [Carter] White House is that no one can be in control; and the prevailing view abroad is that the will to be in control is gone" (White 1990, 54). For both Richard Nixon and Ronald Reagan, their promises to restore order provided a powerful mandate.

A similar desire for order was evident in 2008. *New York Times* columnist David Brooks described how the proverbial "Patio Man"—a suburban male beset by falling home prices, job insecurity, credit card debt, and investments gone sour—was searching for order amidst financial chaos. Patio Man, who liked Richard Nixon and adored Ronald Reagan, was shifting his thinking "from risk to caution, from disorder to consolidation." According to Brooks, the cool, self-contained, and reassuring Barack Obama was poised to win lots of votes from suburban Patio Men because he seems like "the safer choice—socially moderate, pragmatic, and fiscally hawkish" (Brooks 2008). Exit polls proved Brooks right, as suburban voters backed Obama 50 percent to 48 percent (Edison 2008).

But it was more than the votes of discontented Patio Men (and women) that made Barack Obama president. A new demography had reshaped the political landscape and transformed old ways of thinking about politics.

THE REAL MAJORITY BECOMES A REAL MINORITY

In 1970, Richard M. Scammon and Ben J. Wattenberg published a book entitled *The Real Majority*. It was a tour de force that concluded the real majority consisted of those voters who were "*un-young*, *un-poor*, and *un-black*." This real majority of white, middle-aged, middle-income voters—who were also married with kids under 18 years of age residing in their suburban homes and who attended church regularly—had drifted away from the Democratic Party of Franklin D. Roosevelt and were about to enter a Republican Party led by Richard Nixon and Ronald Reagan who conjured memories of a happier, more orderly era of the 1950s.

These newly minted Real Majority Republican voters were decidedly middle-class and relatively prosperous—thanks to the *successes* of Roosevelt's New Deal, which transformed a generation of "have-nots" into "haves." According to Scammon and Wattenberg, what now concerned the Real Majority was an emerging "Social Issue"—a first explication of the culture wars. Scammon and Wattenberg (1970) listed crime, drug use, pornography, law and order, and race as voter priorities to be addressed by their leaders. Nixon speechwriter Patrick J. Buchanan was an avid fan of the book, and he sent it along to Nixon, who, in turn, encouraged his fellow Republicans to employ the Social Issue in their upcoming campaigns.[42] In 1971, Buchanan fired off a memo to Nixon entitled "Dividing the Democrats." In it, he argued that race was the ultimate Social Issue that could separate white Democrats from the party of Franklin D. Roosevelt. Buchanan urged the Nixon White House to take the following steps: "Bumper stickers calling for black Presidential and especially Vice Presidential candidates should be spread out in the ghettoes of the country. We should do what is within our power to have a black nominated for Number Two, at least at the Democratic National Convention." Such gambits, he added, could "cut the Democratic Party and the country in half; my view is we would have far the larger half" (Packer 2008).

Although Buchanan's bumper stickers were never printed (at least not to my knowledge), the emergence of the Real Majority with its emphasis on social and cultural issues transformed many Democrats from economic voters into values voters. That transmutation helped Richard Nixon to a narrow victory over Hubert H. Humphrey in 1968, and to a sweeping landslide in 1972, when his coalition was augmented by supporters of third-party candidate and former Alabama governor George C. Wallace. Watergate was only a temporary detour in the building of a new Republican coalition that encompassed large swaths of Scammon and Wattenberg's Real Majority. Ronald Reagan completed the work when he appealed to the Real Majority's conservative values of family, work, neighborhood, peace, and freedom—and its desire for order in an age when these old verities were under siege by the now-grown baby boomers of the 1960s.[43]

In 2008, the Real Majority remained strongly tilted toward the Republican Party and John McCain. McCain won majorities of the white vote and held on to a plurality of middle-aged voters, who themselves had come of age during the Reagan years. McCain also performed well among older whites who formed Scammon and Wattenberg's Real Majority in 1970. While middle-income voters (those making between $50,000 and $75,000) barely supported McCain (shaken as they were by the financial crisis that upset Wall Street and Main Street), other elements of Scammon and Wattenberg's Real Majority remained loyal to the GOP. These included married voters, those with children under the age of 18 living in their households, white Catholics, and regular churchgoers (see Table 3.5.1).

TABLE 3.5.1 McCain versus Obama: The "Real Majority" Decides (in percentages)

DEMOGRAPHIC GROUP	MCCAIN	OBAMA
Whites	**55**	43
Whites, aged 45–59	**56**	42
Whites, aged 60 and older	**57**	41
Aged 45–59	**49**	49
White Catholics	**52**	47
White Protestants/Other Christians	**65**	34
Southern whites	**68**	30
$50,000–$75,000 annual income	**49**	48
Suburbs	**50**	48
Weekly churchgoers	**55**	43
Married	**52**	47
Married with children	**51**	48
Nonworking women	48	**50**
Candidate that shares my values	**65**	32

Note: *Boldface type denotes winner.*
Source: *Edison Media Research and Mitofsky International 2008.*

What is especially noteworthy is the largely white template of the 2008 Republican coalition. Exit polls revealed that nearly 90 percent of John McCain's total vote was white (Associated Press 2008). This finding was reflected in the crowds that came to see McCain and Palin. Observing the GOP rallies, *New York Times* columnist Frank Rich wrote: "There are indeed so few people of color at McCain events that a black senior writer from the *Tallahassee Democrat* was mistakenly ejected by the Secret Service from a campaign rally in Panama City in August, even though he was standing with other reporters and showed his credentials. His only apparent infraction was to look glaringly out of place" (Rich 2008, WK-10).

But the influence of white voters is quickly waning. In 1976—the year Jimmy Carter was elected president and became the first southern white to hold that office since Zachary Taylor—whites constituted 90 percent of the electorate. By 2004, that figure had fallen to 77 percent.[44] And in 2008, the white percentage of the electorate fell once more to 74 percent, the lowest ever in the history of exit polling (Edison 2008). Recently, the U.S. Census Bureau estimated that by 2042, whites will be a minority throughout the United States—further proof that with every passing year the total percentage of white voters will continue to drop.[45]

Other portions of Scammon and Wattenberg's Real Majority are also on the wane. In 1970, the United States was still an industrialized nation with only hints of an emerging information age. Industrialization placed a premium on working with one's hands; the information age requires an active mind that is the means of production. Thus, a college education has become today's union card for employment. Many Americans are finding themselves not just in four-year college classrooms but also earning graduate degrees to advance their employment prospects. John McCain and Barack Obama were, in many respects, twentieth-century and twenty-first-century candidates, respectively. In the 10 states with the fewest number of residents aged 25 or older who had earned a bachelor's degree or more, McCain prevailed in eight (often by solid margins). Moreover, in all of these states except three (Nevada, Mississippi, and Indiana), McCain won solid majorities of those who were either high school graduates or had not finished high school (see Table 3.5.2).

TABLE 3.5.2 Top 10 States with Fewest Number of College Graduates and McCain Vote

STATE	PERCENTAGE OF POPULATION WITH B.A. DEGREE OR MORE	STATEWIDE PERCENTAGE OF MCCAIN VOTE	MCCAIN PERCENTAGE AMONG HIGH SCHOOL GRADUATES OR LESS
West Virginia	15.9	56 (Won)	58
Arkansas	19.0	59 (Won)	51
Kentucky	20.2	57 (Won)	55
Wyoming	20.8	65 (Won)	78
Alabama	20.8	60 (Won)	58
Nevada	20.8	43 (Lost)	38
Mississippi	21.1	56 (Won)	48
Louisiana	21.2	59 (Won)	54

| Indiana | 21.9 | 49 (Lost) | 47 |
| Tennessee | 22.0 | 57 (Won) | 58 |

Sources: Edison Mitofsky International 2008; http://www.census.gov/compendia/statab/tables/0850221.pdf.

Truly, the portion of the electorate that can be best described as un-young, un-poor, and un-black is waning. Scammon and Wattenberg's Real Majority could muster only 48 percent of the vote for George W. Bush in 2000 (and not even a plurality at that). Four years later, Bush garnered just 51 percent of the ballots (and he did so thanks to the 44 percent support he received from Hispanics). In 2008, John McCain won only 46 percent of the votes cast. The Real Majority is truly today's new Real Minority.

"WE ARE THE ONES WE'VE BEEN WAITING FOR"

On the night of Super Tuesday, after wrestling Hillary Clinton to a draw in the 24 Democratic primaries and caucuses held earlier that day, Barack Obama took to the stage and repeated his mantra of change. But this time Obama added a new twist: "Change will not come if we wait for some other person or if we wait for some other time. We are the ones we've been waiting for" (Obama 2008). In this speech, as in so many others, Obama implied that his supporters were just the sort of twenty-first-century denizens who could make change happen. Throughout the campaign, Obama attracted crowds that were both racially diverse and young. These twenty-first-century demographics proved crucial to his victory.

In 2008, youth mattered. Simply put, if a voter lived a majority of his/her life in the twentieth century, that person tilted toward John McCain. But if a voter was going to spend the majority of his/her life in the twenty-first century, that person was strongly inclined toward Barack Obama. Two-thirds of young people aged 18–29 voted for Obama. This represented a dramatic shift of youth toward the Democratic Party: in 2000, Al Gore carried 18- to 29-year-olds by two points; four years later, John Kerry won them by nine points; and in 2008, Obama beat McCain among this group by a whopping *34 points!* During the George W. Bush years, Republicans have continued to shed young voters, even while winning the presidency. These victories came at great cost, since no party can afford to lose so many of the nation's young without eventually wallowing in the sloughs of despair.

History teaches that once a political party captures a generation, it often remains loyal to it. During the 1930s, first-time Franklin D. Roosevelt voters stuck with the Democrats for a lifetime. Likewise, young voters who backed Ronald Reagan have remained largely loyal to the GOP, even during these difficult years. In 1984, 59 percent of those aged 18–29 supported Reagan; only 40 percent backed Walter F. Mondale. These young voters were born between the years 1955 and 1966. None experienced a successful presidency until Reagan: John F. Kennedy was assassinated in 1963; Lyndon B. Johnson and Richard M. Nixon left the White House as discredited public figures; Gerald R. Ford provided a brief, but not very consequential, interlude; and Jimmy Carter was a disappointment. Only Ronald Reagan conveyed a sense of optimism combined with accomplishment. When those formerly young Reagan voters are examined in 2008 (those aged 45–59), they split 49 percent for McCain and 49 percent for Obama. This proved to be John McCain's second-best age cohort (as older voters broke for McCain 51 percent to 47 percent) (Edison 2008).

College-educated voters likewise backed Obama, constituting yet another twenty-first-century component of his coalition. Just as states with few college-educated voters were more likely to back McCain, those with higher proportions of college-educated voters supported Obama. Of 10 states with the highest percentage of their populations 25 and older sporting a B.A. or some other advanced degree, all (save Kansas) voted for Obama (see Table 3.5.3). Many have advanced twenty-first-century information-age economies—including Massachusetts, Colorado, Connecticut, Vermont, Virginia, Washington, and Illinois. Most strikingly, those with postgraduate degrees were strong Obama supporters, often giving him two-thirds of their votes (see Table 3.5.3). In 2004 the collapse of Republican support among postgraduates has made the backing Democrats have received from today's new "creative class" a dominant feature of the electoral landscape.[46]

TABLE 3.5.3   Top 15 College-Educated States with Greatest Number of College Graduates and Obama Vote

STATE	PERCENTAGE OF POPULATION WITH B.A. DEGREE OR MORE	STATEWIDE PERCENTAGE OF OBAMA VOTE	OBAMA PERCENTAGE OF COLLEGE GRADUATES	OBAMA PERCENTAGE AMONG POST-COLLEGE GRADUATES
District of Columbia	49.1	93 (Won)	92	87
Massachusetts	40.4	62 (Won)	59	68
Colorado	36.4	54 (Won)	51	63
Connecticut	36.0	61 (Won)	55	62
Maryland	35.7	62 (Won)	54	70
New Jersey	35.6	57 (Won)	54	61
Vermont	34.0	67 (Won)	67	80
Minnesota	33.5	54 (Won)	49	67
Hawaii	32.3	72 (Won)	71	78
New York	32.2	62 (Won)	63	66
New Hampshire	32.1	54 (Won)	52	68
Virginia	32.1	53 (Won)	50	52

Kansas	31.6	41 (Lost)	40	51
Washington	31.4	57 (Won)	62	64
Illinois	31.2	62 (Won)	55	58

Sources: Edison Mitofsky International 2008; http://www.census.gov/compendia/statab/tables/0850221.pdf.

Another important component of the Obama coalition was the support he won from nonwhites, who represented a quarter of the electorate. In 2004, George W. Bush managed to snag 11 percent of African American voters; this time John McCain captured just 4 percent.[47] This was not surprising, given that Obama was the first African American ever to win a major party nomination for president. Still, this represented a low point for the Republican Party. As recently as the 1940s, Republicans continued to collect a substantial share of the African American vote. For example, in 1940, Republicans won 32 percent of the black vote, and 42 percent of African Americans called themselves Republicans.[48] Even in 1960, Richard M. Nixon was still holding on to a quarter of the black vote (Ladd 1978b). But after Lyndon B. Johnson signed the Voting Rights Act into law in 1965, and Republican lawmakers subsequently promised to go slow on civil rights and school busing cases, African American support for the GOP fell into the low double digits. Thus in 1972, Nixon won just 18 percent of the black vote against George S. McGovern in what otherwise proved to be a historic landslide.[49]

Reducing Republican support among African Americans to the *low single digits* is a prescription for disaster, one that is compounded by the poor GOP showing among Hispanics. In 2008, two-thirds of Hispanics voted for Barack Obama. This strong support for the Democratic ticket is in sharp contrast to 2004, when 44 percent of Hispanics backed George W. Bush. Bush won Hispanic votes for three reasons. First, he provided strong leadership following the September 11, 2001, terrorist attacks. Second, he strongly condemned anti-Hispanic ballot measures. During his 1994 campaign for the Texas governorship, for example, Bush opposed Proposition 187, a California initiative that would have made it illegal for state agencies to provide assistance to illegal immigrants. As president, he continued to oppose anti-Hispanic measures, including state-sponsored English-only laws. As he wrote in his campaign autobiography, *A Charge to Keep*, "Those who advocate 'English-only' poke a stick in the eye of people of Hispanic heritage. 'English-only' says me, not you. It says I count, but you do not. This is not the message of America" (Bush 2001a, 237). A final reason for Bush's Hispanic strength was his strident opposition to gay marriage. Hispanics have been largely unsympathetic to gay rights claims and were instrumental in defeating gay marriage ballot initiatives, including Proposition 8, which overturned the California Supreme Court's decision legalizing gay marriage. This ballot initiative passed by a slim 52–48 percent margin thanks to support from Hispanics and African Americans.

But in 2008, the Hispanic vote tilted strongly to Barack Obama. One obvious reason was continued Republican opposition to immigration reform. In 2006, George W. Bush and John McCain agreed on a measure that would have provided a path to citizenship for illegal immigrants. As a compromise, border security would be strengthened, thus stemming the flow of illegal immigrants into the United States. The bill failed thanks to a lack of Republican support—opposition that McCain tacitly acknowledged during the primary season when he backed away from immigration reform. To paraphrase George W. Bush, Hispanics got the message: "It's me, not you, that counts." And they took it out on the GOP. Of the 10 leading states with the greatest proportion of Hispanics, Obama won eight (see Table 3.5.4). Taken together, these states gave Obama 168 electoral votes (nearly half of the 365 electoral votes he accumulated).[50] The combination of overwhelming black and Hispanic support for Obama led Republican consultant Steve Lombardo to conclude, "Given the demographic trends in the country, the GOP is unlikely to win any future presidential election if it is losing 95 percent of the black vote and 67 percent of the Hispanic vote" (Broder 2008, B-7).

TABLE 3.5.4 Top 10 States with Hispanics Eligible to Vote and Obama Statewide Vote Total and Hispanic Vote

STATE	PERCENTAGE OF HISPANICS ELIGIBLE TO VOTE AS A TOTAL OF THE STATE POPULATION	STATEWIDE PERCENTAGE FOR OBAMA	HISPANIC PERCENTAGE FOR OBAMA
New Mexico	44.0	57 (Won)	69
California	35.9	61 (Won)	74
Texas	35.7	44 (Lost)	63
Arizona	29.2	45 (Lost)	56
Nevada	24.4	55 (Won)	76
Florida	20.1	51 (Won)	57
Colorado	19.7	54 (Won)	61
NEW YORK	16.3	62 (Won)	N/A
NEW JERSEY	15.6	57 (Won)	78
ILLINOIS	14.7	62 (Won)	72

Sources: Edison Mitosfsky International 2008; Taylor and Fry 2007.

CONCLUSION: STEPPING OFF A BRIDGE

Accepting renomination at the Democratic National Convention in 1996, President Bill Clinton observed that during his second term his administration would construct a "bridge to the twenty-first century" (Clinton 1996). But in the intervening years, Clinton's infamous bridge took its riders on several detours: the 1998 Monica Lewinsky scandal that resulted in Clinton's impeachment; the September 11, 2001, terrorist attacks; and the 2001 and 2003 wars in Afghanistan and Iraq, to name but a few. Now Clinton's bridge to the future seems complete with Barack Obama's election. Americans were motivated at the end of an inestimably long election season to finally step off Clinton's bridge and march into the future. Such motivation was hardly surprising. Nearly two centuries ago, Alexis de Tocqueville wrote: "People often manage public affairs very badly." But when they get genuinely engaged, he added, the engagement "is bound to extend their mental horizon and shake them out of the rut of ordinary routine" (Delbanco 2008, 8). The lethargy and fear that prevented the public from marching forward during the Clinton and Bush years have given way to a newfound sense of urgency that the United States must either enter the twenty-first century with both feet firmly planted in it, or risk becoming a *former* superpower that is enervated by memories of yesteryear.

Surely, the 2008 election represented a final public judgment on George W. Bush and his fellow Republicans. But it was also much more than that, for it represented a moment when a new demography caught up to a new politics. That fact, combined with an actively engaged public, has given Barack Obama and his fellow Democratic officeholders an enormous opportunity to make the policy changes they seek and consolidate their political gains. Four years from now we will know whether they succeeded in transforming these opportunities into an enduring majority. But this is what endures for the moment: after traipsing off Bill Clinton's bridge, we are entering a period of consequence.

Endnotes

1. Obama beat McCain by an impressive 8,366,077 votes—a far cry from the narrow vote margins separating the major party presidential candidates in 2000 and 2004. In 2000, Al Gore and Joe Lieberman out polled George W. Bush and Dick Cheney. The Gore-Lieberman ticket received 51,003,926 votes to Bush-Cheney's 50,460,110, a Bush deficit of 543,816 votes. Four years later, Bush and Cheney received 62,040,610 votes to John Kerry and John Edwards's 59,028,439 votes, a difference of 3,012,171 votes in Bush's favor.

2. In 2000, Bush received 271 electoral votes to Gore's 266 (one D.C. elector voted for another candidate to protest the District's lack of statehood). Barack Obama's 2008 electoral count included one electoral vote he captured from Nebraska, the only state other than Maine

to award its electoral votes by congressional district. Obama won the second congressional district in Nebraska, which includes the city of Omaha.

3. Iowa and New Mexico, which supported Al Gore in 2000 and George W. Bush in 2004, backed Obama in 2008.

4. For more on this see White (2003).

5. Of course, Democrats did enjoy an off-year landslide in the post-Watergate midterm election of 1974, which helped them cement their House majority for two more decades until the 1994 Republican Revolution.

6. After the 2006 midterm elections, there were 94 Republican-led filibusters in the Senate.

7. Democrats gained 31 House seats in the 2006 midterm elections.

8. See Cook (2008).

9. For more on this see White (2006).

10. The exceptions: in 1968, Hubert Humphrey carried Texas thanks to residual support for Lyndon B. Johnson and the Democrats there; in 1980, Carter won his home state of Georgia. Otherwise, Nixon and Reagan carried every southern state in 1968, 1972, 1980, and 1984.

11. In 1992, Clinton carried Louisiana, Georgia, Arkansas, and Tennessee. In 1996, Clinton won Louisiana, Arkansas, Tennessee, and Florida.

12. For the county results, see Nossiter (2008).

13. The Clinton-Gore ticket barely won Tennessee in 1996 (a two-point victory), and Gore lost his home state in 2000, a devastating blow since its 11 electoral votes would have given him an Electoral College victory without Florida.

14. See Grynbaum (2008) and Cho, Shear, and Rosenwald (2008).

15. See O'Connor (2008). Each of these states, save John McCain's home state of Arizona, voted for Barack Obama.

16. Grynbaum (2008). According to this survey, a reading of 100 represents the consumer outlook on the economy in 1985.

17. Edison Media Research and Mitofsky International (2008), exit polls, November 4. Text of question: "Which ONE of these four candidate qualities mattered most in deciding how you voted for President?" Shares my values, 30 percent (of these voters: Obama, 32 percent; McCain, 65 percent); can bring about needed change, 34 percent (of these voters: Obama, 89 percent; McCain, 9 percent); has the right experience, 20 percent (of these voters: Obama, 7 percent; McCain, 93 percent); cares about people like me, 12 percent (of these voters: Obama 74 percent; McCain, 24 percent).

18. See Zogby International (2008). See Gallup Poll, August 2–5, 1974. Text of question: "Do you approve or disapprove of the way Nixon is handling his job as President?" Approve, 24 percent; disapprove, 66 percent; no opinion, 13 percent. See Gallup Poll, February 9–14, 1952.

Text of question: "Do you approve or disapprove of the way Truman is handling his job as President?" Approve, 22 percent; disapprove, 65 percent; no opinion, 13 percent. For more on Truman's problems in 1952, see White (1997), 79–106.

19. See Mosk (2008c) and Luo (2008c), A21. John McCain accepted $84 million in public funding, and he could not match Obama either in paid advertising or in mobilizing his supporters to the polls.

20. Gallup Poll, July 30–August 4, 1958. Text of question: "Between now and 1960, there will be much discussion about the qualifications of presidential candidates. If your party nominated a generally well-qualified man for president, would you vote for him if he happened to be a Negro?" Yes, 37 percent; no, 53 percent; no opinion, 10 percent.

21. For more on this, see Tarrance (2008) and Khachigian (2008), B1.

22. These data are compiled from Edison Media Research and Mitofsky International (2008), exit polls, November 4.

23. See, for example, James M. McPherson, the renowned Civil War historian and professor emeritus of history at Princeton University, who said of Obama's victory, "It's an historic turning point … an exclamation point of major proportions to the civil rights movement that goes back to the 1950s." Quoted in Lewan (2008).

24. Some Republicans agreed. Jeffrey Hart, a former Reagan speechwriter, saw similarities between his old boss and Obama. Hart noted their similar temperaments and believed that Obama, like Reagan, would be a transformative president. See Hart (2008). Others compared Obama to John F. Kennedy, including the late president's daughter, Caroline. In a *New York Times* op-ed, Kennedy wrote, "I have never had a president who inspired me the way people tell me that my father inspired them. But for the first time, I believe I have found the man who could be that president—not just for me, but for a new generation of Americans." See Kennedy (2008).

25. For more comparisons between 1980 and 2008, see Zelizer (2008), 51.

26. See White (1990), 21.

27. See Edsall (2008).

28. CBS News/*New York Times* Poll, October 10–13, 2008. Text of question: "What is the main reason your opinion of John McCain has changed over the past couple of weeks?" Attacks on opponent, 23 percent; Sarah Palin, 22 percent; debate performance, 10 percent; economic policy/tax policy, 10 percent; healthcare policy, 10 percent; erratic/unsteady, 10 percent; handling attacks from opponent, 3 percent; not prepared/experience/knowledge, 2 percent; other, 8 percent; don't know/no answer, 2 percent. The same poll found by a two-to-one margin that voters believed McCain had spent more time attacking Obama than explaining his policies. Text of question: "What do you think John McCain has been spending more time doing in his campaign—explaining what he would do as president or attacking Barack Obama?" Explaining, 31 percent; attacking, 61 percent; don't know/no answer, 8 percent.

29. Edison Media Research and Mitofsky International (2008), exit polls, November 4. Text of question: "Did either of these candidates for president attack the other unfairly?" Barack Obama did, 49 percent; Barack Obama did not, 47 percent; John McCain did, 64 percent; John McCain did not, 32 percent.

30. See Nagourney (2007), 24. Of the two Republican citations, the one made by Representative Ron Paul, an antiwar candidate, was highly critical.

31. Gallup/CNN/*USA Today* Poll, November 2–6, 1994. Text of question: "In politics, as of today, do you consider yourself a Republican, a Democrat, or an independent?" Republican, 31 percent; Democrat, 34 percent; independent, 32 percent; other party (volunteered), 1 percent; don't know/refused, 2 percent.

32. See Pew Research Center (2008). The 27 percent who identified themselves as Republicans marked a low point in 16 years of polling by the center. According to the 2008 exit polls, 39 percent of voters called themselves Democrats, 32 percent were Republicans, and 29 percent were independents (Edison Media Research and Mitofsky International 2008).

33. See Connelly (2008).

34. Princeton Survey Research Associates International, poll, October 23–26, 2008. Text of question: "Would you say your overall opinion of the Republican party is very favorable, mostly favorable, . mostly unfavorable, or very unfavorable?" Very favorable, 10 percent; mostly favorable, 30 percent; mostly unfavorable, 27 percent; very unfavorable, 23 percent; can't rate, 10 percent.

35. Gallup Poll, "Democratic Party's Image More Positive Than GOP's." Independents are much more positive in their assessments of the Democrats: 47 percent have a favorable opinion; 40 percent do not.

36. Edison Media Research and Mitofsky International (2008). Fifty-two percent of those who classified themselves as independents or something else backed Obama; 44 percent supported McCain.

37. CBS News/*New York Times* Poll, March 7–11, 2007. Text of question: "When you think about the Republican Party, what is the first word that comes to mind?"

38. Memo from Richard B. Wirthlin to Ronald Reagan, December 16, 1988. Given to the author and reprinted in full in White (1990), 185–189.

39. See Gallup Poll, September 14–16, 2007. Text of question: "On the whole, would you say you are satisfied or dissatisfied with the way the nation is being governed?" Satisfied, 31 percent; dissatisfied, 67 percent; don't know/no answer, 2 percent. See CBS News/*New York Times* poll, December 2–6, 2005. Text of question: "So far, do you think George W. Bush has developed a clear plan for getting American troops out of Iraq, or hasn't he developed one?" Has developed a clear plan, 25 percent; has not, 70 percent. See Opinion Research Corporation poll, October 20–22, 2006. Text of question: "Do you think [the fact that George W. Bush

has more power than any other president in U.S. history] has been good for the country or bad for the country?" Has more power and that is good for the country, 21 percent; has more power and that is bad for the country, 75 percent; has more power and unsure if that is good for the country, 3 percent.

40. Associated Press/IPSOS–Public Affairs Poll, June 18–20, 2004. Text of question: "Who do you think history will remember as the better president? Former president Ronald Reagan, current President George W. Bush?" Reagan, 76 percent; Bush, 12 percent; both equally/neither (volunteered), 9 percent; not sure, 3 percent.

41. Kurtz (2008). John McCain shared a similar fate with Hubert H. Humphrey. On September 30, 1968, Humphrey made a televised address in which he broke with Lyndon Johnson over the Vietnam War and advocated a bombing halt. Humphrey's speech began a comeback that nearly won him the presidency. For more on this, see White (1969), 353–357.

42. See Scammon and Wattenberg (1992), 3.

43. For more on this, see White (1990).

44. See Will (2008a), A23.

45. See Passel and Cohn (2008), 9, and Roberts (2008).

46. See Florida (2004).

47. See Voter News Service (2004); Edison Media Research and Mitosfsky International (2008).

48. For more on this, see Ladd with Hadley (1978), 57–60.

49. See Connelly (2008).

50. This bears out the advice political scientist Thomas F. Schaller gave to the Democrats in 2006 when he advised them to forget about the South and concentrate on the Southwest, where a treasure trove of Hispanic votes could carry the party to victory. See Schaller (2006).

References

Associated Press. 2008. "Exit Poll Survey Confirms Partisan Shift." *New York Times*, November 8.

Associated Press/IPSOS–Public Affairs Poll. 2004. June 18–20.

"Barack Obama for President." 2008. *New York Times*, October 24, A26.

Berke, Richard L. 1996. "G.O.P. Leaders Doubtful That Dole Can Close Gap." *New York Times*, October 20, 1.

Broder, David. 2008. "Trending Away from the GOP." *Washington Post*. November 16, B-7.

Brooks, David. 2008. "Patio Man Revisited." *New York Times*, October 20.

Bureau of Labor Statistics. 2008. "Employment Situation Summary," press release, October 3.

Bush, George W. 2001a. *A Charge to Keep: My Journey to the White House*. New York: HarperPerennial.

CBS News/*New York Times* Poll. 2005. December 2–6, http://www.nytimes.com/packages/pdf/politics/20051207_POLL.pdf.

_____. 2007. March 7–11, http://www.cbsnews.com/htdocs/pdf/mar07a-dems.pdf.

Cho, David, Michael D. Shear, and Michael S. Rosenwald. 2008. "Obama Calls on Congress to Act Fast on Stimulus." *Washington Post.* November 8, A1.

Clinton, William. 1996. Acceptance Speech, Democratic National Convention, Chicago, August 29, 1996.

Cohen, Richard. 2008. "Party Like It's 1964." *Washington Post,* October 21, A17.

Connelly, Marjorie. 2008. "Dissecting a Changed Electorate." *New York Times,* November 8.

Cook, Charlie. 2008. "Obama's Short Coattails." *National Journal.* November 8, 100.

Cooper, Michael, and Megan Thee. 2008. "Poll Says McCain Is Hurting His Bid by Using Attacks." *New York Times,* October 15, A1.

Cox, Ana Marie. 2008. "McCain Campaign Autopsy." *Daily Beast,* November 7.

Davis, Tom. 2008. "Where We Stand Today," memo to Republican Leadership, May 14.

Decision/Making/Information. 1980. Survey for the Reagan for President Campaign, June.

Delbanco, Andrew. 2008. "A Fateful Election." *New York Review of Books.* November 6, 8.

Edison Media Research and Mitofsky International. 2008. Exit polls, November 4.

Edsall, Thomas B. 2008. "For GOP, Reliable Wedge Issues Suddenly Fall Flat." *Huffington Post*, October 16.

"Endgame: November 1." 2008. *New York Times,* November 1.

Florida, Richard. 2004. *The Rise of the Creative Class and How It's Transforming Work, Leisure, Community, and Everyday Life.* New York: Basic Books.

Gallup/CNN/*USA Today* Poll. 1994. November 2–6, http://www.pollingreport.com/trade.htm.

Gallup Poll. 2007. "Democratic Party's Image More Positive Than GOP's." http://www.gallup.com/poll/102745/Democratic-Partys-Image-More-Positive-Than-Republican-Partys.aspx.

Grynbaum, Michael M. 2008. "Rattled by Housing Slide, Consumers See Worse to Come." *New York Times,* October 29.

Hart, Jeffrey. 2008. "Obama Is the New Reagan." *Daily Beast,* November 4.

Healy, Jack. 2008. "A Record Decline in October's Retail Sales." *New York Times,* November 15.

Jones, Jeffrey. 2007a. "Low Trust in Federal Government Rivals Watergate Era Levels." Gallup Poll, press release, September 26.

Kennedy, Caroline. 2008. "A President Like My Father." *New York Times,* January 27.

Khachigian, Ken. 2008. "Don't Blame the Bradley Effect." *Washington Post*, November 2, B-1.

Kirkpatrick, David D. 2006. "Voters' Allegiances, Ripe for the Picking." *New York Times,* October 15, WK-1.

Kurtz, Howard. 2008. "Ad Watch." *Washington Post*, October 17.

Ladd, Everett Carll. 1978a. "Shifting Party Coalitions—1932–1976." In *Emerging Coalitions in American Politics,* ed. Seymour Martin Lipset. San Francisco: Institute for Contemporary Studies.

_____. 1978b. *Where Have All the Voters Gone? The Fracturing of America's Political Parties*. New York: Norton.

Ladd, Everett Carll, with Charles Hadley. 1978. *Transformations of the American Party System: Political Coalitions from the New Deal to the 1970s*. New York: Norton.

Lewan, Todd. 2008. "Historians, Too, Call Obama Victory 'Monumental.'" *Associated Press*, November 9.

Luo, Michael. 2008c. "Obama's September Success Recasts the Campaign Fund-Raising Landscape." *New York Times*, October 20, A21.

McCain-Obama Third Presidential Debate. 2008. October 15.

McWilliams, Wilson Carey. 1981. "The Meaning of the Election." In *The Election of 1980*, ed. Gerald Pomper. Chatham, NJ: Chatham House.

Mosk, Matthew. 2008c. "Obama's September Haul Provides Huge Advertising Edge." *Washington Post*, October 20, A2.

Nagourney, Adam. 2007. "A Year Still to Go, and Presidential Politics Have Shifted Already." *New York Times*, November 4, 24.

Nagourney, Adam, and Elisabeth Bumiller. 2008. "Republicans Voicing Concern after Rough Week for McCain." *New York Times*, October 12, 1.

Newport, Frank. 2008. "Americans' Satisfaction at an All-Time Low of 9%." Gallup Poll, press release, October 7.

Nossiter, Adam. 2008. "For South, a Waning Hold on National Politics." *New York Times*, November 11, A1.

Obama, Barack. 2008. Address to supporters. Chicago, IL, February 5.

O'Connor, Patrick. 2008. "U.S. Layoffs Mount, Home Foreclosures Rise." Inteldaily.com. October 24, http://www.inteldaily.com/?c=139&a=8531.

Opinion Research Corporation. 2006. Poll, October 20–22.

Packer, George. 2008. "The Fall of Conservatism: Have the Republicans Run Out of Ideas?" *New Yorker* (May 26).

Passel, Jeffrey S., and D'Vera Cohn. 2008. *U.S. Populations Projections: 2005–2050*. Pew Research Center report, February 11.

Perlstein, Rick. 2008. *Nixonland: The Rise of a President and the Fracturing of America*. Scribner.

Pew Research Center. 2008. "Fewer Voters Identify as Republicans," press release, March 20.

Pomper, Gerald. 1981. "The Presidential Election." In *The Election of 1980: Reports and Interpretations*, ed. Gerald M. Pomper. Chatham House.

Princeton Survey Research Associates International. 2008. Poll, October 23–26.

Project for Excellence in Journalism. 2007a. "Mike Huckabee Gets His Media Close-Up." www.journalism.org/node/8975 (accessed December 28, 2007).

Reagan, Ronald. 1980. Acceptance Speech. Republican National Convention, Detroit, July 17.

Rich, Frank. 2008. "The Terrorist Barack Hussein Obama." *New York Times,* October 12.

Roberts, Sam. 2008. "A Generation Away, Minorities May Become the Majority in U.S." *New York Times,* August 14.

Scammon, Richard, and Ben J. Wattenberg. 1970. *The Real Majority.* Howard-McCann.

———. 1992. *The Real Majority.* Donald I. Fine.

Schaller, Thomas F. 2006. *Whistling Past Dixie: How Democrats Can Win without the South.* Simon and Schuster.

Schwarzenegger, Arnold. 2007. Address to Republican Party Fall Convention. Indian Wells, California, September 7.

Tarrance, V. Lance, Jr. 2008. "The Bradley Effect—Selective Memory," *Real Clear Politics,* October 13.

Taylor, Paul, and Richard Fry. 2007. "Hispanics and the 2008 Election: A Swing Vote?" Pew Hispanic Center press report, December 6, 18.

Thomas, Evan, and Newsweek's Special Project Team. 2008. "How He Did It: The Inside Story of Campaign 2008." *Newsweek,* November 17, 48.

Voter News Service. 2004. Exit poll, November 2.

Wallsten, Peter, and Janet Hook. 2008. "Four Big Questions of the Presidential Election." *Los Angeles Times,* November 2.

White, John Kenneth. 1990. *The New Politics of Old Values.* University Press of New England.

———. 1997. *Still Seeing Red: How the Cold War Shapes the New American Politics.* Westview Press.

———. 2003. *The Values Divide: American Culture and Politics in Transition.* Congressional Quarterly Press.

———. 2006. "The Death of a Presidency." *Forum* 3 (4, January).

Will, George F. 2008a. "Kentuckian in the Breach." *Washington Post,* November 13, A23.

———. 2008b. "What Would Goldwater Do?" *Washington Post,* November 6, A21.

Zelizer, Julian E. 2008. "Here We Go Again—Maybe." *Newsweek,* October 20, 51.

Zogby International. 2008. "Survey Finds President's Job Approval Marks Hit a New Low of 21%." Press release, October 15.

Zogby, John. 2005. "Investors for Bush." *Wall Street Journal,* March 15.

Unit III: Post-Reading Questions

Directions: Refer to what you learned in this unit to respond to the questions and prompts below.

1. **Lee defines the term partisan message vote.**

   a.   What is the partisan message vote and what is it used for?

2.   Did Barack Obama really change American political campaigning? Or did his campaign take advantage of favorable market conditions for what he was selling?

3.   What role do interest groups play in shaping judicial and cabinet-level selection and Senatorial hearings?

4.   How do Moveon.org and The Tea Party reflect the way in which the internet has changed political activity? What are the consequences of these changes?

5.   In what ways did Donald Trump make a class-based appeal as a political candidate? For whom and against whom did Mr. Trump make this appeal?

UNIT IV

Modern America and Its Challenges

Unit IV: Introduction

The people who founded our system focused a great deal on questions of what the good government, good life, and good society should be. They derived a lot of their answers from philosophy, history, and religion. The Framers knew that they had to persuade people to support their ideas and proposed system but would have largely seen this as more of a philosophical rather than a commercial marketing argument. The Framers took the approach that their system would work well to prevent the tyranny that worried them and, as a result, would help people live a secure, good life.

While they probably gave little thought to the ways in which the country they were creating would change behaviorally in the future, they certainly understood that it was likely going to expand geographically. As James Madison noted in the *Federalist Papers (1961)*, this expansion would be a key roadblock against the establishment of an oppressive government because as people moved westward their interests would change to fit their environment and, as that happened, the concerns people brought to government would balance each other thus acting as a check on all of them. The Framers assumed that the country's geography would change but it isn't clear that they understood how much its population and values would change in a little over two centuries or how a new technology, the internet, would serve to shrink the intellectual space in which Americans live with the result of producing a much more nationalized political environment than has probably existed here before.

Political marketers are interested in better understanding what makes a voter support a candidate or party. This makes them like commercial marketers who are always interested in finding new ways to increase sales, keep loyal customers, and develop products that hold onto most existing customers while attracting desirable new ones. American politics has become a series of questions expressed using political marketing and mobilization techniques to find answers at the ballot box on a regular basis. What makes a voter buy one political product instead of another one? Is because of a candidate's personality? Is it because of the policies that the candidate or party promotes? Is it because of their geographic or demographic traits? Or is it the emotions that the candidate expresses? Or is it some combination of these factors? Do they do so because of their personality, their policies, the party that they represent, or some combination of these factors?

Another question that political marketers consider when selling a candidate is the extent to which values matter versus the extent to which policy performance matters when voters pick a candidate. A second question in this category is, if people vote based on policies, then do they vote based on their impact on them or what they think their impact would be on the broader society?

The political science literature has termed people who vote based on values "post-materialist" voters and those who vote on economic conditions to be "materialist" voters. Those who vote based on their own experiences are called "individualistic" voters, while those who vote based on perceptions of the wider society are called "sociotropic" voters. While a lot of Americans vote on economic policy alone, many others care about values. Given the shifting fortunes of the American economy in recent decades, it is entirely possible that Americans vote individualistically and materialistically at some points and by evaluating the broader society and post-materialistically at other points and so forth.

Thus, the kind of politics in which there is a battle between material and post-materialist issues that the political scientist Ronald Inglehart (1977) has written about in-depth is playing out before our eyes.[1] Inglehart argued that people's interest in voting on material versus post-material issues largely depended on their personal circumstances. As their physical needs were met, they moved onto to other concerns but, if those were not met, it was also possible for them to switch from voting on post-materialist issues back to voting on materialist issues.

Complicating this discussion is a question about what it means to be an American in a country that has changed significantly in recent decades. At least rhetorically, the United States has always had a deep commitment to the liberal philosophy's goals of life, liberty, and the pursuit of property as John Locke put it for all. In recent years, this commitment seems to be changing into more of a focus based on producing equitable outcomes based on group identity something that is not within the liberal tradition of which the United States has historically been a part. As we will see, an emphasis on equity differs from an emphasis on equality in a variety of different ways and these differences form the crux of our current national political debate. This is the kind of debate that philosophers have always taken on and, in this chapter, we will discuss the work of Allen Bloom and its relevance in our time.

This section examines these questions in-depth. The answers to these questions matter because they impact the way in which we understand the ways in which voters, parties, and individual politicians behave and this, in turn, impacts what the government does in all aspects of its functioning. It is important to understand the voters and the way in which political actors approach them to fully appreciate the way in which American politics works in the political marketing age.

This is an important topic to think about because the answer helps shape the way in which political actors' brand and market themselves, how they do so, and to whom they do so. If a candidate thinks that the thing that their likely voters want to hear about is a set of emotive values then they might build an emotional brand but if the candidate feels the voters have other concerns, then they might take another approach to branding.

Two cases in point of politicians who used such branding were Barack Obama (Yes, We Can!) and Donald Trump (Make America Great Again). Both used an emotional pitch to sum up a set of values appeals. These might have resonated with some voters but there were others with whom that didn't resonate and for those voters both campaigns had specific policy pitches intended to win their support. These candidates, and many other kinds of political producers, build brands around such emotional pitches, have policies that they can present through a variety of platforms to audiences that they understand very well through market research and segmentation.

Marketed politics focuses on how to define the audience, the customers, and the political product. Thus, focus groups, polling, and evaluative tools like sentiment analysis are important for the political marketer because they allow for regular measurement of what people are interested in and how interested they are exactly in it. American politics has become a battle between candidates and parties presenting wildly different values and policies to specific parts of the electorate. It is the party or candidate that understands more of the public mood in more places in a constituency that usually carries the day.

While this sounds wonderful, it has limitations in addition to its advantages. The market imperative means there must always be a new product to drum up interest from the voters. Thus, political marketing literally cannot solve all our problems, or it will cease to have a function. New crises must always be found. Further, this kind of political activity offers no prescriptions about how to live, what the best form of national government is, or many other subjective things. It can just tell us what people think and feel at a given moment in time. Shaping what people think and feel at a given time is an important undertaking in a system in which marketed politics exists, thus the theme of this chapter is at the center of how contemporary politics functions in this changing country.

The United States has changed a lot during the last century. It has become a demographically, geographically diverse society. Twentieth-century America became a largely industrial then a postindustrial country. Most of its residents live in urban and suburban settings and have access to a cornucopia of communications technologies. It is a much different place from the largely agrarian country in which the Framers wrote the constitution. The country has welcomed millions of immigrants and those people have developed their own definitions of what it means to be an American and changed the nation's identity to boot. The country went from a largely Judeo-Christian identity prior to World War II to a more secular identity in the decades after World War II. The American Government became much bigger, it came to deal with much more complicated topics and people expected to do much more in reaction to World War II and the Great Depression. The United States had never had a government before Franklin Roosevelt's time in office that it has always had since. Of course, the Framers would have had no idea about the interstate highway, internet, atomic weapons, or space exploration—things that the modern United States Government has been heavily involved in developing.

The New Deal set up an American government that worked along pluralist lines. Pluralism represents a version of what the Framers, especially James Madison (1961), thought would happen as the country developed. It argues that people identify with the world through some group category and that these groups vie for influence in shaping the way in which government makes policy and for whom it makes policy. This policy regime lasted for 48 years after which it was challenged directly by the Reagan Revolution's advocacy of more decentralized, individualistic, market-oriented policies.

While these have been called conservative, one could argue that they're nothing of the sort in the way that philosophical conservative like Edmund Burke would have understood the term. Reagan's hero was Franklin Roosevelt and as a slew of observers have noted he was a liberal in the classical sense of the term and in his advocacy for protecting key parts of the New Deal. His quibble was largely with the way government had grown more expensive and become more involved in regulating more aspects of American life over time. Writing during the period in which the American and French Revolutions occurred, Burke argued for a system in which the elected went off and voted their conscience, then submitted the results to the voters for their consideration at the next election in his "Speech to the Electors of Bristol[2]." All in all, Burke argued for the value of institutions, tradition, and incremental change (1969). Modern American conservatism has sometimes aligned with Burke's view on these matters but sometimes it has not.

Many modern American conservatives argued for a much stronger sense of individuality than what Burke had in mind. This was so much so that some argued that there was no such thing as society at all (a philosophy called objectivism most associated with the writer Ayn Rand), thus individuals were free to pursue their individual interests. Others stressed the value of traditional institutions and order and most agreed that market-oriented economics worked better than anything else. Instead of advocating for a kind of European conservatism in which individuals should know their place and stay within it, the Reagan era conservatives argued that the market would allocate resources most efficiently and it was important for people to try to compete within that using their own skills and innovation to succeed. This meshed with a broader trend in society that Robert Putnam picked up on his work *Bowling Alone*. Putnam argued that Americans had become much more individualistic and socially isolated during the prior couple of decades by the time his work appeared in 2000. The kind of conservatism that Ronald Reagan promoted had fit a society in which the arrangements of the New Deal had broken down.

In 1987, something odd happened: a book by an academic philosopher, Allan Bloom, hit the best seller list. Bloom's *The Closing of the American Mind* raised intellectually serious questions about what Americans should know and what they should be taught. Bloom was writing in response to a series of trends in education that are still with us today. As Patrick Dineen notes in *Who Closed the American Mind? Allan Bloom Was Brilliant, but Wrong About Burke and Multiculturalism*, Bloom was very concerned about the rise of relativism. Relativism means treating the world around us largely as being more the result of construction by a society than as a naturally occurring phenomenon. By this definition, social values can vary considerably, and nobody could judge a society to be good or bad, healthy, or unhealthy. Other commentators have taken Bloom's critique further to argue that relativism also means that no distinctions can be made between forms of cultural expression instead the value of one form of culture versus another is simply a matter of societal convention.

While this seems to have a lot of positives associated with it, there are many downsides. In such a society, it would not be possible to ever say why something is good or bad and the traditions that often provide social stability would be rendered meaningless because they could be so easy to change. As Dineen notes, a society without an established canon of knowledge is highly susceptible to radical change. In some ways, this is what Bloom was warning about and was a major concern of the people who wrote the U.S. Constitution. The Framers thought the country would change but most favored slow, gradual change, thus they set up a system to ensure that this would happen not the kind of radical change like the French Revolution, which ultimately ended in terror and the Napoleonic tyranny.

Bloom's focus was on higher education, partly because he worked in it but partly because he saw it as the training ground for the societal elite. Bloom, as Dineen notes, strongly disagreed with the idea that everything was just an opinion and that were no standards that should be upheld as having more value than others. We see the net result of going in the opposite direction in recent years in our politics within debates over "fake news" and "disinformation" in political campaigns and news marketing. In part, the lack of objectivity regarding facts has polarized society because if there are no objective truths than people are free to consume only the information and ideas with which they agree without ever having to confront the idea that their beliefs are objectively wrong.

A case in point of this is Donald Trump's assertions of electoral fraud in 2020 that led to the events of January 6, 2021. Trump's claims were credible to some of his supporters because they strongly believed in him but also because they lived within a specific information bubble in which facts are selectively presented. If all one saw were Trump's claims and the news analysis of his supporters in his favored channels, then these assertions appeared to be credible. This phenomenon repeated almost simultaneously with the COVID vaccine hesitancy that occurred later that spring. Those unwilling to take the vaccine could find support for their rationale in online outlets of varying editorial quality. Because there was no single authority on which everyone could agree or clearly set standards for information, it was possible for people to cherry pick the information that they liked best and political marketers to trot out a few theories to their audiences that those audiences would be predisposed to support based on their own lived experiences.

Bloom's argument is relevant to our own time as the Biden Administration promotes an agenda in part around the pursuit of equity. Equity is a different value than the equality that has been, at least partly for some Americans, embodied in the constitution and public policy for the much of the history of the republic. The Framers didn't anticipate a push for this kind of agenda but, as Dineen shows, Bloom's concern that multiculturalism could lead to an illiberal society through its emphasis on group identities can at least arguably be seen as coming alive in the present moment. Dineen argues Bloom railed against of a society in which the rights of individuals were about to be "displaced by the incipient warfare of identity tribalism and groupthink." Equity is an assumption of group membership being the defining category of a person's existence and it differs significantly from the construct of equality because equality assumes individuals have rights that are theirs alone and that they have agency over their own lives. Further, this emphasis will keep government at the center of everything forever and will make the United States a society based more on racial consociationalism than a liberal democracy because group membership is immutable and define characteristic of everything. Thus, regardless of a person's individual attributes, regardless of the workings of the largely market-based economy in the United States, the country will morph into something closer to the system Belgium or Northern Ireland have in which many things are allocated along group membership lines (the defining characteristic in that case is language). Bloom's philosophical point has, over time, morphed into a public policy debate, the result of which holds profound implications for every aspect of American society.

Part of the problem with an approach that seeks to allocate costs and benefits along group lines is that the members of the defined groups often don't see themselves and their interests as being monolithic. While Dineen suggested Bloom saw multiculturalism being used to allocate benefits based on group membership, he also noted how many of these benefits focused on elite institutions. Most Americans of all races and ethnicities will never worry about gaining admission to an Ivy League University or becoming a member of presidential cabinet. On the other hand, they are impacted by the things that their government does and who wins the opportunity to control those things.

In *Beyond Identity Politics: To Reach the White Working Class, Promise an Economy That "Works for Everyone,"* Ruy Teixeira and John Halpen show the importance of understanding the nation's diversity in-depth and that it's possible to take one thing a voter does or consumes (behavioral and psychographic segmentation), then link it to another thing in a voter's profile (age, race, education level, area or residence) in order to produce a specific voter profile that can be an important tool through which an election can be won or lost. Teixeira and Halpin aren't arguing that the Democrats will win a majority of White working-class voters with this approach, but they are suggesting that they could win just enough of them to be successful. To do it, their argument is that the Democrats should appeal to millennial age cohort voters and below rather than chasing all White voters. This is the kind of targeting strategy that we could expect in a politics dominated by political marketing techniques, including segmentation.

The 2020 presidential election can be considered to have been either a fluke or a template for a durable majority. The Democrats nominated the one candidate in their field who would resonate with White working-class voters: Joe Biden. Their analysis shows the importance of understanding the true diversity of all the nation's racial and ethnic categories because political campaigns that approach things with an eye toward this kind of diversity tend to be quite successful. As they note, White voters without college degrees made up around 45 percent of the electorate in 2016, about 40 percent in 2020, and Whites in total make up around 70% of the electorate and, as Richard Alba (2020) has noted elsewhere, their decline in importance as a share of the electorate may very well be being overstated because of the way in which the Census Bureau categorizes responses.

While such matters may seem arcane, they show the importance of understanding the composition and diversity of the electorate. In the case of the above-noted equity, an emphasis solely along racial lines will miss the class diversity that exists within the electorate. It would also make the Biden coalition susceptible to appeals from Republicans arguing that White people are being discriminated against in the name of equity as Republicans did for years around affirmative action policies.

While there has been a lot of emphasis on race in the public discussion of the Trump years and the two elections they cover, there has been far less discussion of the role class played in shaping this outcome. Class played a significant role in the 2016 Trump campaign's success and the 2020 Biden campaign shows how it could be used as Teixeira and Halpen suggested to elect Democrats. By alienating White college-educated voters, Donald Trump gave the Democrats an opening that they took advantage of since 2016 to win elections. The Democrats did this by stressing the kinds of cultural issues that resonate with college-educated voters like GLBTQIA+ rights and by making Donald Trump into the avatar of evil in their marketing. On the other hand, the 2020 Biden campaign made a point of reassuring most of them that their taxes would not be increased by setting a cut off at a vaguely defined income level of $400,000, a number few Americans make, and reflected the kinds of inclusive values and representation that form a core part of the contemporary American university education. Thus, college-educated voters who once voted for Republicans based on their market-oriented economic policies, including lower levels of taxation could be pitched to vote for Biden. In some ways, the Trump experience kicked off a class-based realignment in American politics.

Donald Trump was not wrong to try to expand the working class share of the electorate of all races that vote Republican. Much of the college-educated vote makes choices at least as much on post-materialist as materialist issues and many of them to do so with a specific rejection of traditional values like patriotism and religion. Trump made a cultural and economic argument to these audiences that resonated but it drove other audiences, especially college-educated voters, away in big numbers. While working class Whites vote overwhelmingly for Republicans, there are some that are susceptible to Democratic appeals. Teixeira and Halpen show that breaking these voters out by other categories (a technique called segmentation in the marketing world) can be more useful than simply relying on broad top-level categories to run campaigns and argue that within in the broader categories of White and working class, the category of age also matters. Both Obama campaigns, both Trump campaigns, and the Biden campaign all broke the top-level group categories down into smaller parts, meaning that they could then target specific voters in a focused way without other voters ever seeing these appeals.

Older working-class voters are more conservative than younger ones and therefore more less likely to vote for Democrats. On the other hand, a candidate like Joe Biden appealed to them because he could credibly argue that he understood their experiences and would govern with their interests in mind as he postulated on the campaign trail in 2020. For that reason, Biden was a difficult matchup for Trump's class-based campaign, but one could question how replicable this model is in case the Republicans don't nominate a similar candidate in the future. On the other hand, the Democrats' opportunity with younger White working-class voters might be more durable because they are more reliably liberal on the kinds of social issues with which Democrats work and are more supportive of an interventionist economic approach like the one advocated by Democrats.

Their piece is an outline of how a Democratic Administration could develop a product that would appeal to these voters via a focus on favorable economic policies. They outline what roughly amounts to the Biden Agenda when they argue that Democrats should promote policies that grow the middle class and that, by doing this, the Democrats could win just enough of the White working class vote to becoming a governing party for a long time. This would represent something like a return to the New Deal style of governance with its tax and spend policies conducted primarily by the federal government instead of at the state level or with an emphasis on balanced budgets and deficits. It should be noted that the other portion of the Harry Hopkins quote about FDR's policies that includes "tax and spend" is "and elect and elect." The point to building policies like this, in addition to setting up a more equalitarian economy, would be to produce a durable electoral coalition.

Frank Dobbins' *The Business of Social Movements* reminds us that politics is very much a business in terms of the way in which interest groups, social movements, political parties, and political campaigns structure themselves. Political organizations use market research to develop their products, figure out what their brand should stress in terms of values and policy content, who their customers are, and how to best make sales within these audiences. In this sense, political organizations are like the companies that produce and market bourbon.

Through the prism of corporatized and professionalized social movements, Dobbins raises the question of what this development means for the ways in which the citizens experience politics. The political organization is managed much as is any other organization. The existence of such professional organizations in what is supposedly a civic democracy raises its own questions on which he touches via the prism of social movements. We are currently in a moment in which the Republicans and Democrats are tweaking their product offerings in response to changing market conditions. The party as organization ensures that the Democrats and Republicans will exist. In other systems, it is possible that parties that see the market shift away from their core offerings might cease to exist. American political organizations are well suited for reinvention in this way because they are not rigidly run in a top-down way as are their Canadian and European counterparts. It's possible for an outsider movement to take over the party in the United States while keeping its organizational structure in intact, something that is not always possible in other countries and other systems.

If the goal of the political party is to win, then it will develop a product and brand that appeal to as many of the right customers as it feels it can reach. The brand is the emotional vehicle through which a political producer presents their product to potential customers. For example, Democrats favor higher taxes on corporations and wealthy individuals but almost always try to argue that this is so out of a desire to make these entities pay their "fair share" without ever defining what that is exactly. Republicans try to rebut this argument by pointing out that most federal taxes are paid by the top 25% of income earners in the United States, that huge numbers of Americans pay no taxes at all, and that the United States has the most progressive tax code of the major developed nations.

The Republican argument is data based but lacks the emotional punch that the Democrats get from pointing out that others, who probably have more than do the people their pitching, got away with paying an unfairly low amount of tax. Effective marketing usually gives the target audience a relatable example and, in this case, it is that Warren Buffett paid less in taxes than did his secretary. This sounds very unfair given that the billionaire is paying less than is the working-class person and will resonate with people who are not expert in the nuances of the tax code. Buffett's income is largely capital, his secretary's income is largely wages, and those are treated differently in the tax code. Thus, branding works with understandable examples and emotional appeals instead of simply facts or data nor does it worry about philosophical questions like the democratic linkage between rights and responsibilities and how having so few people pay most of the taxes breaks the link between rights and responsibilities for most of the population.

Most voters, like most customers of anything, make purchasing decisions for a variety of reasons. Some issues matter more to voters than do others. For example, Donald Trump in 2020 pitched the upper middle class, including those new class professionals we saw earlier who didn't like him, that given the Democrats proposal to change the way in which assets were treated to make investments taxed like wages, the value of many people's retirement accounts would fall thus making them either work many more years or retire into poverty. Thus, this is also an example of how segmentation could work to sell a political product. Not everyone has a retirement account like a 401 (k), thus not everyone would respond to this issue in this way and the people who did respond to this issue might also have other concerns to which they might respond more than this. In this case, Trump's theoretical negative impact was years away, whereas the voters' dislike of him was more immediate and concrete. In this case, the concrete and immediate likely trumped the far-off hypothetical outcome.

This section has shown how a philosophical question can become a policy question and how policy issues can resonate with some audiences but not with others. It has outlined how a change in philosophical values from equality to equity in government might have all sorts of knock on social and political implications for what the government does, who it does it for, and how campaigns seek election. It has examined the way in which political organizations in the United States have become professionalized structure like other kinds of corporate entities, and how this encourages them to do things that corporations do like build brands, segment the marketplace, and make targeted appeals to specific audiences.

Endnotes

1. See Ronald Inglehart and Pippa Norris Cultural Backlash: Trump, Brexit and Authoritarian Populism. (2019) for an in-depth discussion of the contemporary global applications of the trend.

2. https://vault.hanover.edu/~smithr/Burke.pdf

Who Closed the American Mind?

Allan Bloom was brilliant, but wrong about Burke and multiculturalism

By Patrick J. Deneen

O ne crisp morning 26 years ago I was walking across the campus of the University of Chicago, where I had just enrolled as a first-year Ph.D. candidate in the renowned Committee on Social Thought. While I had not yet met him, I had heard much about Allan Bloom, a legendary professor, teacher, and lecturer. I had read his translation of Plato's *Republic* as an undergraduate and had some notion that I would write my eventual dissertation under his direction.

As I crossed one of the campus quads, I saw a man sitting on a bench, swaddled under a heavy overcoat and his head topped by a fedora. A photographer was arranging his equipment across from him, while he bemusedly awaited some kind of publicity shoot. While I realized only a short time later that the man I had seen was Allan Bloom, it was a year later—a quarter-century ago—that I realized that I had witnessed the photo session that led to the headshot inside the hardcover jacket of Bloom's blockbuster book *The Closing of the American Mind.* By that time, I had left the University of Chicago, disillusioned by the program and put off by Bloom's circle of students. But I loved the book and credit it, at least in part, for my eventual return to the academy and a career as a professor of political philosophy.

I still assign the book with some regularity, especially in a freshman seminar on education that I've taught over the last half-decade. As the years have passed, I've noticed how the book has aged—many of its cultural references are long dated, while contemporary hot-button issues like gay marriage and religious liberty are altogether absent from Bloom's confident pronouncements on our likely future. Still, the book continues to excite new readers—today's students find it engaging, even if, unlike their elders, they don't get especially upset by it and almost unanimously have never heard of it before. And with every re-reading I invariably find something new that I hadn't noticed before, a testimony to the expansiveness of Bloom's fertile mind.

While I continue to learn much from Bloom, over the years I have arrived at three main judgments about the book's relevance, its prescience, and its failings. First, Bloom was right to be concerned about the specter of relativism—though perhaps even he didn't realize how bad it would get, particularly when one considers the reaction to his book compared to its likely reception were it published today. Second, his alarm over the threat of "multiculturalism" was misplaced and constituted a bad misreading of the *zeitgeist,* in which he mistook the left's tactical use of identity politics for the rise of a new kind of communalist and even traditionalist tribalism. And, lastly, most of his readers—even today—remain incorrect in considering him to be a representative of "conservatism," a label that he eschewed and a worldview he rejected. Indeed, Bloom's argument was one of the early articulations of "neoconservatism"—a puzzling locution used to describe a position that is, in fact, today more correctly captured by its critics on the left as "neo-liberalism."

What should most astonish any reader of Bloom's *Closing* after 25 years is the fact that this erudite treatise about the crisis of higher education not only sat atop the bestseller list for many weeks but was at the center of an intense, lengthy, and ferocious debate during the late 1980s over education, youth, culture, and politics. In many ways, it became the most visible and weightiest salvo in what came to be known as "the culture wars," and people of a certain generation still hold strong opinions about Bloom and his remarkable, unlikely bestseller.

Today there are many books about the crisis of higher education—while the nature of the crisis may change, higher education never seems to be out of the woods—but none before or since Bloom's book achieved its prominence or made its author as rich and famous as a rock star. It was a book that many people bought but few read, at least not beyond a few titillating passages condemning rock-and-roll and feminism. Yet it was a book about which almost everyone with some engagement in higher education held an opinion—indeed, it was obligatory to have considered views on Bloom's book, whether one had read it or not.

Bloom's book was at the center of a debate—one that had been percolating well before its publication in 1987—over the nature and content of a university education. That debate intensified with the growing numbers of "diverse" populations seeking recognition on college campuses—concomitant with the rise of departments of Women's Studies, African-American Studies, and a host of other "Studies" studies—leading to demands that the curriculum increasingly reflect contributions by non-male, non-white, non-European and even non-dead authors.

The Closing of the American Mind spawned hundreds, perhaps even thousands of responses—most of them critiques—including an article entitled "The Philosopher Despot" in *Harper's* by political theorist Benjamin Barber, and the inevitably titled *The Opening of the American Mind* by Lawrence Levine. Partly spurred by the firestorm initiated by Bloom's book, perennial presidential candidate Jesse Jackson led a march through the campus of Stanford University shouting through a bullhorn, "Hey hey, ho ho, Western Civ has got to go!" Passions for campus reform ran high, and an avalanche of words, articles, denunciations, and ad hominem attacks greeted Bloom's defense of the Western canon.

Yet the nuances of Bloom's qualified defense of the Western canon were rarely appreciated by critics or supporters alike. While Bloom was often lumped together with E.D. Hirsch—whose *Cultural Literacy* was published the same year and rose to number two on the *New York Times* bestseller list, just behind Closing—Bloom's argument was fundamentally different and far more philosophically challenging than Hirsch's more mundane, if nevertheless accurate, point that educated people increasingly did not have knowledge about their own culture. Hirsch's book spoke to anxiety about the loss of a shared literary and cultural inheritance, which today has been largely supplanted by references to a few popular television shows and sports televised on ESPN.

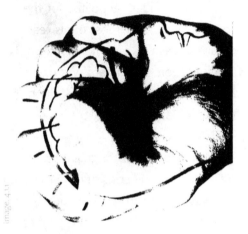

Bloom made an altogether different argument: American youth were increasingly raised to believe that nothing was True, that every belief was merely the expression of an opinion or preference. Americans were raised to be "cultural relativists," with a default attitude of non-judgmentalism. Not only all other traditions but even one's own (whatever that might be) were simply views that happened to be held by some people and could not be judged inferior or superior to any other. He bemoaned particularly the decline of household and community religious upbringing in which the worldviews of children were shaped by a comprehensive vision of the good and the true. In one arresting passage, he waxed nostalgic for the days when people *cared:* "It was not necessarily the best of times in America when Catholic and Protestants were suspicious of and hated one another; but at least they were taking their beliefs seriously …"

He lamented the decline of such true belief not because he personally held any religious or cultural tradition to be true—while Bloom was raised as a Jew, he was at least a skeptic, if not a committed atheist—but because he believed that such inherited belief was the source from which a deeper and more profound philosophic longing arose. It wasn't "cultural literacy" he wanted, but rather the possibility of that liberating excitement among college-age youth that can come from realizing that one's own inherited tradition might not be *true*. From that harrowing of belief can come the ultimate philosophic quest—the effort to replace mere prejudice with the quest for knowledge of the True.

Near the beginning of *Closing*, Bloom relates one telling story of a debate with a psychology professor during his time teaching at Cornell Bloom's adversary claimed, "it was his function to get rid of prejudices in his students." Bloom compared that function to the activity of an older sibling who informs the kids that there is no Santa Claus—disillusionment and disappointment. Rather than inspiring students to replace "prejudice" with a curiosity for Truth, the mere shattering of illusion would simply leave students "passive, disconsolate, indifferent, and subject to authorities like himself."

Bloom relates that "I found myself responding to the professor of psychology that I personally tried to teach my students prejudices, since nowadays—with the general success of his method—they had learned to doubt beliefs even before they believed in anything ... One has to have the experience of really believing before one can have the thrill of liberation." Bloom's preferred original title—before being overruled by Simon and Schuster—was Souls *Without Longing*. He was above all concerned that students, in being deprived of the experience of living in their own version of Plato's cave, would never know or experience the opportunity of philosophic ascent.

This core of Bloom's analysis seems to be not only correct, but, if possible, he may have underestimated its extent. Consider the intense response to Bloom's book as evidence against his thesis. The overwhelming response by academia and the intelligentsia to his work suggested anything but "indifference" among many who might describe themselves as cultural relativists. Extraordinary debates took place over what books and authors should and should not appear in the "canon," and extensive efforts were undertaken to shape new curricula in light of new demands of "multiculturalism." The opponents of Bloom's book evinced a deep concern for the formation of students, if their concern for what and whom they read was any indication.

In retrospect, however, we can discern that opponents to Bloom's book were not the first generation of "souls without longing," but the last generation raised within households, traditions, and communities of the sort that Bloom described, and the last who were educated in the older belief that a curriculum guided the course of a human life. The ferocity of their reaction to Bloom was not simply born of a defense of "multiculturalism" (though they thought that to be the case) but a belief that only a curriculum of the right authors and books properly shapes the lives of their students. Even in their disagreement with Bloom, they shared a key premise: the books we ask our students to read will shape their souls.

Today we live in a different age, one that so worried Bloom—an age of indifference. Institutions of higher learning have almost completely abandoned even a residual belief that there are some books and authors that an educated person should encounter. A rousing defense of a curriculum in which female, African-American, Latino, and other authors should be represented has given way to a nearly thoroughgoing indifference to the content of our students' curricula. Academia is committed to teaching "critical thinking" and willing to allow nearly any avenue in the training of that amorphous activity, but eschews any belief that the content of what is taught will or ought to influence how a person lives.

Thus, not only is academia indifferent to whether our students become virtuous human beings (to use a word seldom to be found on today's campuses), but it holds itself to be unconnected to their vices—thus there remains no self-examination over higher education's role in producing the kinds of graduates who helped turn Wall Street into a high-stakes casino and our nation's budget into a giant credit card. Today, in the name of choice, non-judgmentalism, and toleration, institutions prefer to offer the greatest possible expanse of options, in the implicit belief that every 18- to 22-year-old can responsibly fashion his or her own character unaided.

Bloom was so correct about the predictable rise of a society defined by indifference that one is entitled to conclude that were *Closing* published today, it would barely cause a ripple. This is not because most of academia would be inclined to agree with his arguments any more than they did in 1987. Rather, it is simply the case that hardly anyone in academe any longer thinks that curricula are worth fighting over. Jesse Jackson once thought it at least important to oppose Western Civilization in the name of an alternative; today, it would be thought untoward and unworkable to propose *any* shared curriculum.

Those who run institutions of higher learning tell themselves that this is because they respect the choices of their young adult charges; however, their silence is born precisely of the indifference predicted by Bloom. Today's academic leaders don't believe the content of those choices has any fundamental influence on the souls of our students, most likely because it would be unfashionable to believe that they have souls. As long as everyone is tolerant of everyone else's choices, no one can get hurt. What is today called "tolerance," Bloom rightly understood to be more deeply a form of *indifference*, the extreme absence of care, leading to a society composed not only of "souls without longing" but humans treated as utilitarian bodies that are increasingly incapable of love.

If this core argument of Bloom's seems prescient, a second major argument not only seems to me incorrect but in fact is contradicted by this first argument. It was because of his criticisms about the rise of "multiculturalism" that Bloom came to be readily identified with the right-leaning culture-warriors like William Bennett and Dinesh D'Souza and was so vilified on the academic left. Yet Bloom's first argument implicitly makes a qualified praise of "multiculturalism," at least as the necessary launching pad for the philosophic quest. In his praise of the belief structures that once inspired some students to disillusionment, he was singing the praises of a society composed of various cultural traditions that exercised a strong influence over the beliefs and worldviews of that culture's youth.

Such qualified praise led him to wax nostalgic about an age when Catholics and Protestants cared enough to hate one another. But at his most alarmist—and, frankly, either least perceptive or most pandering—Bloom portrays then-regnant calls for "multiculturalism" as a betrayal of the norms of liberal democracy and as the introduction of dangerous tribalism into the university, as well as the body politic. At times, Bloom painted a portrait in which the once-ascendant claims of American individual rights, enshrined in the Declaration of Independence, were about to be displaced by the incipient warfare of identity tribalism and groupthink.

At his best, Bloom sees through the sham of yesterday's "multiculturalism" and today's push for "diversity"—little of which had to do with enthusiasm for real cultural diversity, but which was then and remains today a way for individuals in under-represented groups to advance entitlement programs within America's elite institutions. Those individuals, while claiming special benefits that should accrue to members in a particular group, had no great devotion to any particular "culture" outside the broader American anti-culture of liberalism itself. Indeed, the "cultures" in question were never really cultures at all, if by a culture we mean an identifiable group of people who share a generational, geographical, and distinctive set of customs aimed at shaping the worldview and practices of successive generations.

By this measure, women, blacks, Hispanics, and so on were people who might once have belonged to a variety of particular cultures, albeit not specifically as women or blacks or Hispanics. These new categorical groupings came to be based on claims of victimhood rather than any actual shared culture; many cultures have been persecuted, but it does not follow that everyone who has been mistreated constitutes a culture. While in passing Bloom acknowledged the paucity of such claims to cultural status, too often he was willing to take seriously professions of "multiculturalism" and to lament the decline of the American project of universalist natural rights.

The stronger case would have been to expose the claims of multiculturalism as cynical expressions from members of groups that did not, in fact, share a culture, while showing that such self-righteous claims, more often than not, were merely a thin veneer masking a lust for status, wealth and power. If the past quarter century has revealed anything, it has consistently shown that those who initially participated in calls for multiculturalism have turned out to be among the voices most hostile to actual cultures, particularly ones seeking to maintain coherent religious and moral traditions.

Bloom was prone to obtuseness about this fact because, at base, Bloom himself was not an admirer or supporter of the multiplicity of cultures. Indeed, he was suspicious and even hostile to the claims of culture upon the shaping of human character and belief—including religious belief. He was not a conservative in the Burkean sense; that is, someone apt to respect the inheritances of tradition and custom as a repository of past wisdom and experience. Rather, he was at his core a liberal: someone who believes that the only benefit of our cultural formation was that it constituted a "cave" from which ambitious and rebellious youth could be encouraged to pursue a life of philosophy.

Reflection about Bloom's distaste for particular cultures suggests that the differences between Bloom and his apparent nemesis, the Cornell professor of psychology, are rather minimal. Both wanted to disabuse the youth of their "prejudices" in the name of openness: the psychology professor in the name of nihilisitic openness, and Bloom for the encouragement of philosophical inquiry, open to the possibility of Truth as well as the possibility of nihilism.

In fact, Bloom's critique of the "multicultural" left is identical to and drawn from the critique of the "multicultural" right advanced by his teacher, Leo Strauss. In his seminal work *Natural Right and History*, Strauss identified Burke's criticisms of the French Revolution as one of the lamentable responses to the "Crisis of Modern Natural Right," a crisis that arose as a reaction against the social contractarianism of "modern natural right." Burke's argument against the revolutionary impulses of social contractarianism constituted a form of conservative "historicism"—that is, in Strauss's view, the rejection of claims of natural right in favor of a preference for the vagaries of History. While today's Straussians concentrate their criticisms largely on left historicism (i.e., progressivism), Strauss was just as willing to focus his criticisms on right historicism, that is, the traditionalism of Burke and his progeny.

Ironically, because the left in the 1980s adopted the language (if not the substance) of multiculturalism, Bloom was able to turn those Straussian critiques of Burke against those on the left—though of course they were no Burkeans, even if they used some Burkean language. For this reason, Bloom was assumed by almost everyone to be a "conservative," a label that he not only explicitly rejected, but a worldview that he philosophically and personally abhorred.

Bloom's argument became a major touchstone in the development of "neoconservatism," a label that became associated with many fellow students of Strauss but which, ironically, explicitly rested on rejection of the claims of culture, tradition, and custom—the main impulses of Burkean conservatism. Bloom continuously invoked the natural-rights teachings of the Declaration and Constitution as necessary correctives to the purported dangers of left multiculturalism: rather than endorsing the supposed inheritance of various cultures, he commended the universalistic claims of liberal democracy, which ought to trump any identification with particular culture and creed. The citizen who emerged from the State of Nature, shorn of any specific cultural, religious, or ancestral limitation, was the political analogue for the philosopher who emerged from the Cave. Not everyone could become a philosopher, Bloom insisted, but everyone *could* be a liberal citizen, and ought rightly to be liberated from the limitations of place and culture—if for no other reason, to make them more tolerant of the radical philosophers in their midst.

Bloom's was thus not only an early salvo in the culture wars, but an incipient articulation of the neoconservative impulse toward universalistic expansion. Burke's willingness to acknowledge the basic legitimacy of most cultures—his "multiculturalism"—led him, in the main, to oppose most forms of imperialism. The rejection of multiculturalism, and the valorization of a monolithic liberal project, has inclined historically to a tendency toward expansionism and even imperialism, and neoconservatism is only the latest iteration of this tendency. While many of the claims about Strauss's influence on the Iraq invasion and the neoconservative insistence upon spreading democracy throughout the world were confused, there was in fact a direct lineage from Bloom's arguments against the multicultural left and rise of the neo-liberal or neoconservative imperialistic impulse. Bloom explicitly rejected the cautiousness and prudence endorsed by conservatism as a hindrance to philosophy, and thus rejected it as a political matter as a hindrance to the possibility of perfectibility:

> Conservatives want young people to know that this tawdry old world cannot respond to their demands for perfection. … But … man is a being who must take his orientation by his possible perfection. … Utopianism is, as Plato taught us at the outset, the fire with which we must play because it is the only way we can find out what we are.

Bloom here witheringly rejected "realism" as "the easy way out" of real inquiry; yet, in the wake of the Iraq invasion, one of Bloom's longstanding allies and admirers, John Agresto, lamented the overconfidence of the neoconservatives, and especially their neglect of the reality of culture, in a post-invasion book entitled *Mugged by Reality*.

Bloom's book remains a kind of liberation, an intellectually adventurous work written with a kind of boldness and even recklessness rarely to be found in today's more politically correct and cramped age. But it was, ultimately, more reckless than many of its readers realized at the time—not because it was conservative, but precisely because it rejected the conservative impulses to modesty, prudence, the genius of place, and tradition. It opened an era of "culture wars" in which the only combatant who seemed absent from the field was a true conservatism. Perhaps it is finally time for an opening of the American mind.

Image 4.12

Beyond Identity Politics

To reach the white working class, promise an economy that "works for everyone."

By Ruy Teixeira and John Halpin

In the last three presidential elections, the Democratic candidate lost among white working-class (non-college-educated) voters by an average of 22 points. The worst performance came in 2012, when Obama lost this group—once the bulwark of the Democratic coalition—by a staggering 26 points (62 to 36 percent).

The loss of this key demographic is mitigated to some degree by its shrinking size. The numbers of white working-class voters will probably dip to just 30 percent of all voters by 2020 and 44 percent of white voters. This is a dramatic decline from 1988, when white working-class voters were 54 percent of all voters and almost two-thirds (64 percent) of white voters.

Some observers argue that since the ranks of the white working class are declining, Democrats should simply rely instead on their rising "Obama coalition" of minorities, unmarried and working women, seculars, Millennials, and educated whites living in more urbanized states. Yet it would be a grave mistake for Democrats to count on this strategy.

For one, the Democrats' deficit with working-class whites was the key reason for the GOP landslide in 2010, and could hand the Republicans another big win in the upcoming midterm elections. Despite their declining numbers, white working-class voters will be an ever-present threat to progressives in elections and to progressive governance as long as so many remain so hostile to the party.

The Democrats don't need a majority of white working-class voters to come over to their side. But they do need to deny the Republican Party the supermajorities of white working-class voters that Republicans successfully mobilize today. Moreover, broadening the Democratic appeal to white working class voters should greatly reduce the threat posed to the party when other

The evolution of the post-industrial white working class as mirrored on TV: By the end of the 1970s, Archie Bunker no longer worked as a loading dock foreman, but rather as a taxi driver and bar owner Today, 2 *Broke Girls* try to make a go in the cupcake business without a patriarch in sight.

constituencies, such as Latinos or younger voters, exhibit only modest turnout—particularly a problem during off-year elections—or waiver in their support for Democrats. Furthermore—and this is critical—by depriving the GOP of its uncontested supermajorities among white working-class voters, Democrats would finally force today's intransigent Republican Party toward the center. It is only those supermajorities that allow Republicans to thumb their noses at the rising Obama coalition and dig in their heels at the smallest progressive change.

Take that advantage away, and the electoral arithmetic becomes so dire for Republicans that their strategy will have to change simply to remain competitive. True, a more moderate and reasonable GOP would attract more voters who now vote Democratic, but overall it would be a plus for progressive governance by improving the climate for legislation that actually addresses social problems.

Is there reasonable hope that such a coalition can be formed? We believe there is.

Start with the evolution of the white working class itself. Over time, we expect that generational change will make the white working class more liberal and open to progressive agendas. This will occur as white working-class Millennials gradually take the place of generally more conservative white working-class Baby Boomers and older Americans. Democrats generally receive greater support among Millennial white working-class voters than among older white working-class voters. This gap peaked in 2008 when Obama's margin was 30 points better among eighteen- to twenty-nine-year-old white working-class Millennial voters than among their older counterparts.

This generation gap is partially explained by the fact that white working-class Millennials are substantially more liberal on social issues. For example, in the 2012 National Election Study, 54 percent of white working-class Millennials thought that gay and lesbian couples should be allowed to legally marry, compared to just 34 percent of older white working-class voters. They are also more likely than older working-class Americans to be secular in orientation, another indicator of liberalism. In the 2012 Democracy Corps post-election survey, 33 percent of white working-class Millennials reported no religious affiliation, compared to 14 percent of their older counterparts.

And perhaps most important, today's young white working-class voters are notably more liberal on issues concerning the role of government, which have been an especially strong factor in moving the white working class to the right over time. (Most academic analyses agree that these issues were far more important in causing white working-class defection from the Democrats than were social/cultural issues.)

An example of how large a generation gap exists within the white working class on the role of government comes from a 2010 Hart Research/CAP survey. It found that 61 percent of Millennial non-college-educated whites favored a strong government to deal with today's complex economic problems, compared to just 38 percent of older working-class whites. White working-class Millennials are also very close to white college-educated Millennials in their views on this issue, in contrast to older white working-class individuals, who are more conservative than older white college-educated cohorts.

One might fear a growing, reactionary backlash among the white working class, young and old, as they find themselves contending with an increasingly diverse society. This is possible, but data from a 2013 CAP/PolicyLink/Latino Decisions poll suggests that the white working class is far less resistant to diversity than is generally supposed. The poll asked, for example, whether "Americans will learn more from one another and be enriched by exposure to many different cultures." Almost two-thirds (64 percent) of the white working class agreed. The same number agreed that "[a] bigger, more diverse workforce will lead to more economic growth." Similarly, 62 percent agreed that "diverse workplaces and schools will help make American businesses more innovative and competitive," while 58 percent agreed that "people will become more accepting of their differences and more willing to find common ground." Fifty-seven percent agreed that "with more diverse people working and living together, discrimination will decrease." Finally, 52 percent agreed that "the entry of new people into the American workforce will increase our tax base and help support our retiree population."

Further, as we would expect, white working-class Millennials are significantly more open to rising diversity than the white working class as a whole, so generational replacement will simply enhance these positive sentiments. For example, 75 percent of white working-class Millennials think Americans will be enriched by exposure to many cultures, and 73 percent believe a bigger, more diverse workforce will lead to more economic growth.

All this suggests that the white working class is likely to change over time in ways that should make it more receptive to progressive appeals. But which appeals? It is not enough to gain a somewhat more receptive audience; the sale must still be made. What, if anything, do progressives have in their portfolio that might particularly appeal to the white working class, while also appealing to the base groups of their rising coalition?

There is a burgeoning progressive narrative and policy focus that might be able to fulfill this role. This new narrative is based on the idea that rising inequality actually undermines rather than fuels growth. This "equitable growth" or "middle-out economics" school of thought points to a growing body of evidence that reducing inequality is not merely compatible with growth but also can be a significant contributor to both the quantity and the quality of growth. The broad argument is that the economy grows from the "middle out," and that the true heroes in our economic drama are not corporations and the wealthy but rather a robust and growing middle class. With such an approach, the economy can work for everyone, not just the wealthy few, as it does today.

Data from a 2013 CAP/Hart Research poll shows that this argument has strong support from the American public. Start with the idea that the economy should work for everyone, not just the wealthy few. In the poll, Americans identified this as the single most important goal for the nation's economic future. While voters also rated many other goals as priorities—job creation, a strong future for the next generation, a stronger middle class—none resonated nearly as strongly as having an economy that works for all Americans.

And note that this is more than a call for a larger economic pie. The final clause—"not just the wealthy few"—is what makes this phrase so resonant. It speaks to Americans' growing conviction that our economic system now benefits only the wealthy and corporations, while the deck is stacked against everyone else.

This approach offers a compelling contrast to the discredited conservative agenda of plying the rich with tax cuts and other goodies on the trickle-down theory that the wealthy will create jobs for the rest of us. Instead, it posits that a relentless focus on the economic health of the middle class, together with expanding opportunities for the poor and working class to move into the middle class, are the best ways to grow the economy.

This, in turn, points to a policy agenda heavy on investment in the middle class—its living conditions and sense of security, its skills, its entrepreneurial capabilities—and in the conditions that allow the middle class to succeed—modern infrastructure, cutting-edge scientific research, and dynamic new industries that can provide middle-class jobs. And it leads away from a policy agenda focused on deficit reduction, which has been a loser for progressives and simply reinforces already-existing antigovernment tendencies.

For most Americans, this is a moral as well as an economic story. The public believes that virtuous behavior (especially hard work) is not being properly rewarded today because of barriers erected by the wealthy and powerful. In the CAP/Hart poll, three-quarters of those surveyed agreed that "the rules in America have changed—hard work and sacrifice are not rewarded anymore." And 63 percent say a very high priority is providing more opportunity to those who work hard and struggle to provide for their families.

This approach draws strong support from the various elements of Obama's "coalition of the ascendant"—minorities, unmarried and working women, Millennials and more secular voters, and educated whites living in more urbanized states. But, crucially, this middle-out approach also draws solid support from white working-class voters.

For example, two-thirds of the white working class characterizes "an economy that works for everyone, not just the richest 1 percent" as exactly what America needs today (9-10 on a 10-point scale). And 82 percent of these voters agree that "the middle class is being squeezed and we are increasingly becoming a nation divided between the rich and everyone else." In addition, by a 2-to-1 margin (67 to 33 percent) white working-class voters agree more that "[g]overnment is too concerned with what big corporations and the wealthy want, instead of helping the middle class" than that "[g]overnment is doing too many things better left to businesses and individuals."

This data suggests that the middle-out approach is the most feasible way to fend off continued anti-progressive surges among white working-class voters, who are inclined to indict the government for their increasing economic insecurity. If they can provide these voters with upward mobility into an expanding and dynamic middle class, progressives will be able to capture more of their votes—not a majority, but a strong enough minority to stabilize the new progressive coalition and insulate it from right-wing backlash, as well as force the GOP to move toward the center. Conversely, leaving these voters in their current frustrated condition (Obama approval rating: 29 percent) is guaranteed to produce periodic meltdowns that will play havoc with progressives' ability to win elections and govern, while allowing extremists to continue to dominate the Republican Party.

How should this middle-out economic model be presented to white working-class voters? For starters, it's imperative that progressives begin framing their economic and social agenda in class-based terms that allow white voters to feel that they, too, are part of a movement to use government action to support working people. The toxic racially focused discourse about the social welfare state that underlies many contemporary and historical debates about the role of government serves no one's interests, particularly progressive proponents of an activist state. There's simply no reason for progressives not to broaden their appeals based on class lines.

The survey evidence is clear that white working-class voters are as supportive as other Americans of large-scale public action to address chronic joblessness, income disparities, and unequal education and social opportunities. A massive study on the fiftieth anniversary of the War on Poverty conducted by the Half in Ten Campaign and the Center for American Progress found that more than two-thirds of white non-college-educated voters supported all eleven out of eleven proposed policies to fight poverty—from an increase in the minimum wage and subsidized child care to an expanded Earned Income Tax Credit and even a national jobs program to combat unemployment. Support among these voters topped 80 percent for universal pre-K, expanded Pell Grants for low-income families, and affordable child care. White non-college-educated support slightly outpaced white college-graduate support in many cases and was basically on par with the views of African Americans and Latinos.

Before he was struck down by an assassin's bullet, Bobby Kennedy extolled this vision of an activist and supportive government that serves the values and interests of all working people across racial and ethnic lines. Today, the stars are aligned for progressives to resurrect his dream.

The Business of Social Movements

By Frank Dobbin; ed. Jeff Goodwin, James M. Jasper, and Francesca Polletta

[...] The paradigm they take issue with is a highly rational one, in which social movement activity proceeds much as business activity proceeds. It is spearheaded by ideological entrepreneurs, competing in markets for the allegiance of potential participants. It is based on the calculated employment of well-defined organizing and oppositional strategies. It depends on the use of these strategies during particular windows of political opportunity.

[...] challenge that vision of social movement activity. They sketch a different kind of social movement, driven by indignation, fear, hope, a sense of right and wrong. One might see the project as an effort to re-romanticize political activity, in that it recalls an era when social movements were self-consciously about ideology and right versus wrong—an era when the language of rational political calculation had not yet invaded either social movements or the social-science theories that described them.

These days, the prevailing social-science paradigm for understanding social movements emphasizes rational calculation among movement "entrepreneurs." [...] explore, conversely, how passion matters. In this brief commentary I sketch the transformation of passionate action into calculative interest-driven action not merely within social movements but across social realms. My aim is not to romanticize the past but to note a wider trend in which human action is increasingly framed as driven by interest and calculation, even in realms that were, not long ago, thought to operate on other principles.

Albert Hirschman, in *The Passions and the Interests* (1977), described how the process of modernization transformed the "passions" motivating social behavior into modern "interests" and thereby turned passionate behavior, rhetorically at least, into calculative behavior. [...] by suggesting that while "interest" is the new rhetoric of social movements (both in practice and in social theory), passions and emotions continue to be an alternative trope through which social movement actors make sense of their own behavior. Outward-looking descriptions of activity may have assumed the language of strategic management, but inward-looking descriptions still often assume the language of emotion and commitment.

My contention is simply that the ongoing substitution of interest for passion, in conceptions of human behavior, helped to generate the prevailing rationalist social-scientific paradigm. This change may also be leading social movements to depict themselves as oriented to rational calculation—as "managed" in the conventional sense, rather than as spontaneous, devotional, and charismatic. Until recently, theorists had described both social and religious movements as based on beliefs, ethics, and sentiment. Now, social and religious movements alike are seen as akin to business enterprises, and theorists describe individual behavior with metaphors borrowed from rational choice theory. Modern theories of political activity more generally depict the world in this way. This raises a question: Should we satisfy ourselves with constructing theories that mimic the rhetoric of actors themselves, or should we try to explain that rhetoric itself? Is it enough to develop a theory that treats social movement leaders as the strategic actors they describe themselves as?

The wider phenomenon that produces this dual change, in social movements and social-science theories describing those movements, is the rationalization and demystification of social life. The particular course that rationalization has taken in the West has been to exalt the individual and to envision all of her behavior from the vantage point of micro-economic theory. The rise of rational choice theory in political science is part and parcel of this process, for now modern political behavior is thought to be subject to narrow principles of calculation. Not only voting choices are calculated, but the color of candidates' ties and the force with which they kiss their wives on television. What has happened to social movement theory and practice has happened everywhere, and certainly to political theory and practice.

The power of the universal rational-actor model is abundantly clear in the sociological field of organizational studies and in the various practical fields of administration. As recently as the 1960s, organizational theorists held that different administrative models were appropriate for different realms. They argued that soup kitchens should be managed differently from stock brokerages, because organizational goals and individual motives vary between realms. But in all domains of management theory these days, actors are first and foremost rational. Thus it was not so long ago that public administration was a separate field from hospital administration, which was distinct from educational administration, social service administration, etc. (e.g., Clark 1956; Scott and Meyer 1983). Some of these realms were closer to one another than others, but there were broad differences across realms. Theories of administration were taught in distinct professional schools, each with its own ethic. Each was based in a distinct theoretical tradition and in a distinct empirical core of cases or studies, precisely because organizational goals, and the motives of workers in those organizations, were thought to differ radically. But this world has changed. Hospitals, social service agencies, and now social movement organizations hire MBAs who craft incentive and reward systems, career ladders and evaluation systems, based in the presumption that everyone is a rational actor. That no one acts out of passion.

The economics-based model of organizing diffused from business corporations to every imaginable realm of social activity (Meyer 1994). Churches and little leagues now buy into the notion that there are universal laws governing social behavior that demand a universal set of organizing principles. The distinct philosophies of management found in different sectors a generation ago have given way to a common model, based in micro-economic theory. What elicits the right behavior on Wall Street will work, as well, at Unicef. All sorts of organizations:

- Adopt strategic plans.
- Use internal labor markets to create long-term incentives.
- Write mission statements.
- Depict themselves as entrepreneurial.
- Appoint CEOs and presidents and human resources management vice presidents.
- Consider mergers to achieve economies of scale and spinoffs to help them focus on their core mission.

Management is management. Organizational goals, and the motives of members, no longer matter. Managing a social movement is no different from managing a bank because we are all in it, whatever it is, to pursue self-interest. Thus the models of how to organize collective endeavors—whether automobile plants, stock brokerages, or environmental movements—have converged on a single set of precepts, based loosely in economic theory. One obvious consequence of this shift is that people in all walks of life pay increasing attention to issues of remuneration, for our incentive-based, individualistic, rationalized management systems signal to us that this is what we should care about. "Show me the money" is the mantra everywhere. An unintended consequence of the economists' effort to incentivize work is a growing disparity in income—as doctors and HMO managers and United Way directors and even professors come under this system, those at the top of their professions get "incentivized" off the charts (Frank and Cook 1996). The incentives have become a legitimate reason for being and doing—everywhere and not only in executive suites.

Even entire organizations that were founded to proselytize or to do good works can legitimately abandon their missions if it seems rational to do so. The YMCA abandons religious evangelizing when the market for it dwindles, and runs health clubs (Zald and Denton 1963).

Community colleges give up on bringing college education to the masses and instead offer French cooking and remedial math (Clark 1956).

Rather than pondering this trend, most social scientists have taken it at face value. They increasingly treat people as self-interested, rational, and calculating. Theories of social services management, educational management, and indeed social movements themselves are increasingly rationalized. They reduce human motivation to the single dimension of rational calculation, for that is how the actors themselves describe their own motives. I don't mean to evoke a romantic past in which people, and theories about them, were driven by passion for life, altruism, and brotherly love. Most sociological theories have described actors as driven not by passion but by something much more mundane, namely habit and routine. Rather than romanticize the past, I simply mean to suggest that we might think of this shift itself as a sociological outcome to be explored.

This trend has so fully taken over social movement theory that management theorists are beginning to borrow back. When they look to social movement theory, lo and behold, they find precisely the same kinds of rational-actor models found in strategic management theory. In some cases, those models have been extended by social movement theorists, and their innovations have been embraced by management theory (Swaminathan and Wade 1999).

Social scientists cannot really be faulted for this. Theorists of modernity typically take actors at their word. To the extent that social movement activists frame their own behavior in terms of strategy, calculation, and prevailing principles of management (windows of opportunity, issue entrepreneurialism), it comes as no surprise that theorists use the same kinds of language. But of course, the language of rational calculation is, in social movements as in corporations, a lens through which actors see their own actions, retrospectively and prospectively. When you do what you do, you invent stories to tell that are highly rationalized. The president of Exxon does, but so does the president of Greenpeace. This is the point of the organizational theorist Karl Weick (1993), when he talks about the process as "sense-making"—the post hoc construction of meaning for behavior. In the organizational cases Weick comes into contact with, as in modern social movements, the accounts actors construct are calculative, rational, and strategic. Sense-making occurs within given cognitive frames, and actors construct rationales for their behavior based on the choice of frames. One can frame any single action in a multiplicity of ways. A demonstration against the abuse of laboratory animals can be framed in terms of the natural rights of those animals and in terms of the opportunity to build a coalition and expand membership in a social movement organization. Movement activists now supplement, or even supplant, the former sort of "sense-making" with the latter.

In *The Passions and the Interests* Hirschman did not argue that in the modern world only rational calculation exists. He argued that in the modern world interest and rational calculation are how people understand behavior. Where prevailing political/rational theories in the field of social movements fall short is that they are insufficiently skeptical about actors' own accounts. When anthropologists observe totemic societies in which local lore has it that frog spirits rule the universe, they do not conclude that frogs are inscribed in plows and circumcision mats because frogs indeed rule this domain. They conclude that the locals have developed a system of meaning that locates authority over social practices in the frog totem. Likewise, when we study modern social practices, we must do what we can to step outside of the frame of reference of the locals. We must try to see rationality as a system of meaning that locates authority in a set of universal social and economic laws—laws that have the same status as the frog totem.

What is perhaps regrettable about the expansion of the interest frame is that we all make sense of our own behavior through this lens, and it is, after all, the lens of the "dismal" science of economics. Would that we could choose the frame we use, for we might well choose to see our lives in terms of the pursuit of salvation or the liberation of house cats. Indeed, what is distinctly irrational about the rational choice model that we all now must live by is the very choice of this dismal model of action. Would we freely choose to orient our lives to the accumulation of German luxury sedans, however splendid, when we could substitute the glory of eternal salvation?

Because managers have been at the game of behaving rationally for quite a while, students of management developed cultural accounts of managerial rationality long ago. Weber emphasized the importance of verstehen in sociology, or grasping the actor's own understanding of his actions. On Weber's shoulders stand most of the constructionist theorists of organizations, from John Meyer (Meyer and Rowan 1977) and W. Richard Scott (1995) to Paul DiMaggio and Walter Powell (1991), as well as many of the network theorists, from Harrison White (1992) to Mark Granovetter (1985). They see rationality as a frame of action, which shapes action (to be sure) but which also shapes the accounts people give of their own action. In Weick's terms, rationality provides the framework within which sense-making happens. Anthropologists have long been in the business of parsing the meaning of human behavior, and they come to similar conclusions when they observe modern, rational, settings. Mary Douglas (1986) underscores this by noting that rationalized social systems carry very different logics of rationality that shape individual action. She thereby refutes the notion that individuals behave in ways that are rational in an absolute sense. Clifford Geertz (1983) treats the modern meaning system of lawyers as much like that of aborigines, in that it provides an interpretive framework for action.

Prevailing social movement theorists, like early management theorists, have perhaps moved a bit too far in the direction of taking actors' accounts as the gospel. They give too much credence to the stories their informants tell. Surmounting this problem is not easy, because if actors frame their behavior, both prospectively and retrospectively, in terms of rational calculation rather than in terms of emotions and sentiments, it may be empirically impossible to detect, much less prove, that their motives are otherwise. The typical sociological response under these circumstances is to assume that habits and sentiments, and not merely calculations, motivate actors. After all, for the average movement activist, there is little fame and glory and very little gold indeed in the pursuit of the rights of whales, or of women. Economists have long since learned to elide the question of whether we are primordially rational by declaring that they cannot predict people's preferences (this is the job of sociologists) but only the (rational) means by which people will pursue those preferences. That is, they hold no opinion about whether individuals will prefer to save whales or to accumulate BMWs, but they can predict the means once they know the preference. Of course, they are so well able to predict the means because those means are spelled out in economic theories that are, in varying degrees of precision, available to all. We all know that the carrot of a promotion is a strong incentive to work hard, even if we do not know the formula for the optimal size of that carrot.

The economic perspective suggests that preferences (for saving whales, or fighting abortion) are determined by arational sentiments, but that the means to achieving those preferences are determined by rational calculation. This approach insulates social movement theorists from having to address the question of motives, and indeed much of recent social movement theorizing has moved in this direction. But this approach is inadequate in social movement theory, just as it is in management theory. It has been shown to be inadequate in management theory by a host of studies demonstrating that rational courses of action are historically contingent and socially constructed. If rational action is not invariant and predictable, then problematizing the particular frame of rational calculation itself becomes important. To that extent, social movement behavior has, as it has embraced the frame of rational calculation, become part of the wider empirical universe of organizational theory.

There is every reason to believe that this focus on rationality, among movement "entrepreneurs" and among social-science paradigm-entrepreneurs alike, will decline over time. In organizational theory, the pendulum has swung back and forth during this century, with periods of extreme rationalism (in theory and in corporate practice) followed by corrective periods when "Theory Y" about the importance of the group, or some version of psychobabble, take over (Barley and Kunda 1992). Social movement theory has recently had its first big swing toward rationalism. The time is ripe for a swing back toward theories that take emotions, culture, narratives, metaphors, and norms into account.

If and when the field of social movements swings back toward passions and emotions, will the lesson be that social movement participants are really motivated by their hearts rather than by their heads? It seems to me that this isn't the lesson to be derived at all. Rather, if we make sense of the world through one of the cognitive frames available to us and if the rational actor model is but one of those frames, the passionate actor model is but another. To say that people *really* participate in movements because of their passions is little different from saying that they *really* act rationally. Perhaps the more important question before us concerns where these frames come from in the first place, and how we select among them in explaining our own behavior to ourselves.

References

Barley, Stephen R., and Gideon Kunda. 1992. "Design and Devotion: Surges of Rational and Normative Ideologies of Control in Managerial Discourse." *Administrative Science Quarterly* 37: 363–400.

Clark, Burton R. 1956. *Adult Education in Transition.* University of California Press.

DiMaggio, Paul J., and Walter W. Powell. 1991. "Introduction." In Walter W. Powell and Paul J. DiMaggio, eds., *The New Institutionalism in Organizational Analysis.* University of Chicago Press.

Douglas, Mary. 1986. *How Institutions Think.* Syracuse University Press.

Frank, Robert H., and Philip J. Cook. 1996. *The Winner-Take-All Society: Why the Few at the Top Get So Much More than the Rest of Us.* Penguin.

Geertz, Clifford. 1983. *Local Knowledge: Further Essays in Interpretive Anthropology.* Basic Books.

Granovetter, Mark. 1985. "Economic Action and Social Structure: The Problem of Embeddedness." *American Journal of Sociology* 91: 481–510.

Hirschman, Albert O. 1977. *The Passions and the Interests: Political Arguments for Capitalism before its Triumph.* Princeton University Press.

Meyer, John W. 1994. "Rationalized Environments." In W. Richard Scott and John W. Meyer, eds., *Institutional Environments and Organizations: Structural Complexity and Individualism.* Sage.

Meyer, John W., and Brian Rowan. 1977. "Institutionalized Organizations: Formal Structure as Myth and Ceremony." *American Journal of Sociology* 83: 340–63.

Scott, W. Richard. 1995. *Institutions and Organizations.* Sage.

Scott, W. Richard, and John W. Meyer. 1983. "The Organization of Societal Sectors." In John W. Meyer and W. Richard Scott, eds., *Organizational Environments: Ritual and Rationality.* Sage.

Swaminathan, Anand, and James Wade. 1999. "Social Movement Theory and the Evolution of New Organizational Forms." Paper presented at the annual meeting of the Academy of Management, Chicago.

Weick, Karl E. 1993. "Sensemaking in Organizations: Small Structures with Large Consequences." In J. Keith Murnighan, ed., *Social Psychology in Organizations: Advances in Theory and Research.* Prentice Hall.

White, Harrison C. 1992. *Identity and Control: A Structural Theory of Social Action.* Princeton University Press.

Zald, Mayer, and Patricia Denton. 1963. "From Evangelism to General Service: The Transformation of the YMCA." *Administrative Science Quarterly* 8: 214–34.

Unit IV: Post-Reading Questions

Directions: Refer to what you learned in this unit to respond to the questions and prompts below.

1. **Texiera and Halpin define the term segmentation.**

    a. What is segmentation, and how do Texiera and Halpin show how Democrats could benefit from using it to reach a specific subset of voters?

2. **Bloom defines the terms equality and equity.**

    a. What is the difference between equality and equity?

3. How did Allen Bloom's work outline the potential danger in this shift of emphasis from equality and equity?

4. In Dobbins argument, how do social movements become something like commercial corporations?

5. What is the impact of having a political party or social movement structure itself and behave like a corporation?

6. **Dobbin defines the term brand.**

    a. What is a brand?

7. How is "fair share of taxes" consistent with the impact of political branding and marketing on American politics?

8. What are the limits of adopting a political marketing model over a philosophical or religious orientation in public life?

CONCLUSION

The United States has changed a lot since the American Revolution. The country extends from coast to coast, whereas it was only 13 colonies along the Eastern Seaboard at its founding. There are no foreign powers sitting on its western frontier or are there European colonies adjacent to it as there were when independence was won. On the other hand, it is now a global military and economic colossus.

The United States has gone from a loosely related structure in which colonies made most of their own decisions to a continent-wide federal system in which the national, state, and local governments sometimes work cooperatively and sometimes fight each other over responsibilities and policy. The country now faces challenges both foreign and domestic. It has significant weaknesses as well. Its public life is fractious. Political consensus can be difficult to build, America's bureaucracy lacks transparency and has accountability problems, and finally, marketing and branding have encouraged people to look at the things that divide them rather than the things that they have in common and created a crisis of civic engagement.

The American political system has a marked tendency toward extended periods of gridlock and compromise. In the pre-Civil War period, the central issue that gridlocked the system—slavery—was dealt with through a compromise. Slaves were counted for representation in Congress as three-fifths of a person, and the number of free and slave states was balanced by admitting one of each simultaneously as the country expanded westward. For example, Maine was admitted to the Union as a free state, after leaving Massachusetts, as part of a deal to bring Missouri into the Union as a slave state.

Once the arrangements that fueled the compromise collapsed, the stage was set for the Civil War. That conflict ended slavery and clarified exactly what the United States was as new Constitutional Amendments secured rights for African Americans and created a category of national citizenship that did not exist previously. However, the Civil War did not end racial strife in the United States by any means. Within a few years, legal segregation had taken hold in many parts of the country while informal racial barriers were set up in others. It took until the 1960s Civil Rights Movement to dismantle legal racial barriers and much longer to dismantle the informal racial barriers that developed after the Civil War.

The end of the Civil War began a prolonged period of growth for the United States that only ended with the Great Depression. The country industrialized, its cities and towns grew rapidly, Americans moved off the farm into towns to work in factories, and that growth attracted people from all over the world. Growth was good but it also produced problems that the Framers could not have anticipated. Issues that came up like food and water quality, factory working conditions, and income inequality to name just a few. Also, the development of this type of economy changed the relationship between citizens. Fewer Americans became the small farmers and merchants that the Framers thought would safeguard the system, while more became wage workers and renters' groups whom the Framers believed would be less invested in their community and more dependent on government, thus putting the entire system in danger.

The genius of the Framers rested in the fact that their constitution was adjustable through amendment to current circumstances and the federal system that they created meant multiple layers of government could act to solve perceived problems. Still, issues around this ability to amend produced whole new issue categories and problems that the Framers could not have anticipated. Eventually, a movement arose that tried to use the government to promote public good through regulation.

This movement, called the progressive movement, believed in an expert and activist national government to solve the problems created by the new urban and industrial economy. The conflicts of the progressive era between private initiatives and social responsibility resemble those that we currently are experiencing, as this era is similar in terms of rapid technological and demographic changes. The progressive era set the stage for the massive expansion of the regulatory state that took place because of the Great Depression.

It is difficult to underestimate the extent to which the Great Depression shaped the country's future development. Programs like Social Security and an alphabet soup of federal agencies were established. Taxes were raised and the federal government's ability to collect taxes nationwide gave it a big fiscal advantage over the states. Gradually, the federal government began to use this advantage over time to implement public policy changes nationwide. The American government attempted to fine tune the swings of the market and regulate its activities. All of which was a long way away from anything that the Framers had ever contemplated.

The Great Depression coincided with the other great expansion of the national government: World War II. The United States had gradually become involved on the global stage in the late 19th and early 20th centuries, but it made its biggest splash with its entrance into World War I. The American military shrunk in size after World War I, but it grew again with the onset of World War II and has never quite shrunk again. The United States has been a leading power on the global stage for a century, and this has come at great cost but also great benefit for Americans. Americans wrote the rules of the international system and having most international transactions denominated in dollars. The United States has considerable structural advantages that other countries would like to have as well.

World War II ended with the United States and its allies victorious. That victory soon turned into an ideological conflict against communism as represented by the Soviet Union. The Soviets, given their history of invasion from the West, did seek a buffer zone in Eastern Europe, and sought immediate reparations for the horrors of World War II. The Soviet Union saw itself as an international headquarters from which communism might be exported around the globe. It had a Marxist perspective on capitalism and liberal democracy.

American political, military, and cultural leaders feared that the Soviets were on a mission to make the world communist, meaning the Cold War was about values, culture, and economics. The Soviets were acceptable allies in the fight against Hitler, but they were not desirable as a durable presence on the world stage. This conflict lasted from the late 1940s until 1991. During that time, the United States developed a permanent intelligence and military establishment. The United States also remains part of an alliance system that was established to fight against the Soviet Union in the Cold War and has continued even though the Soviet Union has ceased to exist. The alliance system shows how the world has changed since 1991 because it has struggled for years to find a central rationale for its existence.

The end of the Cold War did not end American defense or security establishments. Instead, the United States came to see itself as the "essential nation" and came to occupy a vital role in keeping global peace. At the same time, the country was trying to engage the People's Republic of China economically to encourage it to adopt liberal democratic values, and not paying enough attention to what was going on in Russia and the Middle East. Then, the United States suffered a major terrorist attack on September 11, 2001. The response was a lot more surveillance and security at home, two wars fought by volunteers abroad, and a singular focus on preventing terrorism. At the same time, the world was changing around us and, by the time Joe Biden was inaugurated, the country was confronted by a rising China, a resurgent Russia, and a great deal of domestic disquiet.

All the above shows the wisdom of President Eisenhower's warnings in his farewell address[1]. Eisenhower suggested that the military–industrial complex could exercise significant power over what the national and state governments did. Further, he pointed out that much of what the government did was now advanced technologically meaning that it was possible that a specific class of people would become dominant in American government and life[2]. The Framers did not anticipate the rise of an expert class and a permanent bureaucracy, nor did they anticipate that public policy would come to be made through the Court system. The people who founded the Judicial system could scarcely have imagined how their idea would evolve over time.

From the onset of the New Deal in the early 1930s during Franklin Roosevelt's administration to Ronald Reagan's election in 1980, the trend in American government was toward national government centralization. The Presidency gained power because of the above-noted crises, but also due to the emergence of electronic media that placed a premium on personalization. The president could respond to a crisis quickly or become the face of that crisis.

The modern presidency has a balance of power that is radically different from what the Framers had in mind as it advantages the president over all else in the system. The problem is that individuals seeking the presidency tend to overpromise versus what the powers of the office make it possible for them to deliver. Thus, they end up being perceived as either polarizing if they try to do what they promised or a failure if they compromise or scale back promises as Suri (2017) has noted. The Framers thought that Congress would be the key body in the system. The current situation is that the executive branch issues orders that expire when they leave office and the courts rule in ways that both establish accountability and let elected officials avoid taking controversial votes that might lead to their electoral defeat.

Reagan took steps to reverse the trend of centralization in the national government, especially in domestic policy. This has set up the current battle between Democrats claiming to act in accordance with FDR's legacy and Republicans pursuing the ideas Reagan brought to government. However, Reagan's ideas proved to be so successful that the first Democrat elected president after him, Bill Clinton in 1992, opined that "the era of big government is over." While Barack Obama had some success tinkering around the margins of it, he was not successful on those occasions where he took dead aim. Joe Biden is better positioned to take on the Reagan legacy as there are many people in the electorate who do not remember Reagan or why he was elected in the first place, the issues that Reagan was elected to solve have mostly been solved, and contemporary issues have appeared for which the Reagan approach is not appropriate.

The United States now has a postindustrial, service-based economy that is quite different from the agricultural and mercantile economy that it had when it won its independence. America's economy is highly innovative and its good are sold all over the world. As we saw in the case of bourbon, having international rules and regulations has significant advantages for the country's producers abroad, while having domestic rules and regulations is good for producers and consumers alike. The Framers would never have envisioned American bourbon whiskey becoming a global prestige product, but they would be pleased that the governmental system that they put in place would provide for an effective, orderly marketplace. On the other hand, the development of an economy in which many people work for others or in large companies has raised questions about what citizens owe to each other, who should benefit and who should pay, and how government can enforce these arrangements.

In our time, we hear much about the importance of science (but little about how science is done or why its findings can change the things we thought we knew into something else) and we have seen a series of American Presidents and Congresses do battle with federal bureaucrats over many scientifically advanced topics. The emphasis on technology and expertise has advantaged the presidency as an institution. It has advantaged presidents who support the establishment positions on the workings of government as they are rather than insurgents like Republicans

Nixon or Trump or the unconventional Democrat, Jimmy Carter, who sought to change those. This evolution of the American government away from the values the Framers envisioned toward the values that the progressive movement supported has serious implications for the system as Skowronek et al. (2021) noted. The gradual and uncoordinated changes that brought this situation into being also threatened to weaken the system's legitimacy. This is because many of the policies implemented by the government were not made by elected officials, and therefore, can differ significantly from public preferences.

One can argue that every president since Reagan has run on a promise to change Washington, but as Bachner and Ginsburg (2016) note, none of them have been able to do it. Donald Trump was a clear example of this phenomenon. For a long time, Americans have said they wanted less immigration overall and less tolerance of those who did not go through the standard immigration process for living in the country, but a combination of courts and bureaucracy fought Trump's proposals at every turn.

The people who implement these policies are not representative of the country's population nor do they seem to know much about what the public's policy preferences are or even what the public looks like (Bachner & Ginsburg, 2016). Instead, they assume that their own policy preferences mirror those of the public. The security state that the United States developed does much of its business in secret, fueling conspiracy theories about its activities. These conspiracy theories flourish partly because the people in elected positions are often not curious about these agencies' activities. This was especially true for the period from the mid-1950s to the mid-1970s. Some of the roots of today's conspiracy theories about the behavior of U.S. intelligence agencies can be traced back to the lack of transparency and Congressional oversight around these agencies during this era. It was only in the mid-1970s that this began to change as Congress began to ask questions about what the agencies did instead of just taking their word for it (Sundquist, 1981).

The security state itself developed incrementally and comprises several different agencies that have their own organizational missions, cultures, and relationships outside agency walls. The rivalries between these agencies came to be so intense that, even though American intelligence agencies may have had enough information to prevent the 9/11 plot, they failed to share information with each other. They have sometimes also fought with individual members of Congress or tried to limit the information that was shared with them.

This has produced several challenges for American democracy. The biggest one is in terms of transparency. With some of these agencies, it is difficult to know exactly what they are doing or why they are doing it. A second one is accountability. To whom are the unelected accountable? Congress? The president? Nobody? The answer to this question is not obvious, and it matters because, as Bachner and Ginsburg (2016) note, bureaucratic rule-making processes create more policy in the United States than Congress does. All this history also matters, because it shows how the United States has evolved away from the idea that the Framers had into a much different kind of system. This should give us pause to consider if these transformations have been for the good in terms of the representativeness and performance of the American political system.

Another way that policy can be made by the unelected is through court decisions. The Supreme Court is a legal body, but it is in many ways a political one. When Donald Trump complained about Obama judge's ruling against him, the Chief Justice of the Supreme Court shot back that such judges did not exist. If this is so, then why all the fights over who gets onto the Supreme and other federal courts?

The answer is because different judicial philosophies align with the two parties. The Democrats tend to take more of a "living Constitution" approach in which the document can be interpreted to fit current circumstances. The Republicans take an "originalist" position which argues that the constitution means exactly what the Framers said in the document.

How does this impact policy? Since the decision in the *Marbury v. Madison* case in 1803, the Supreme Court has had the right to review lower court rulings. This is frequently called the right to judicial review. In practice this means that the Supreme Court can make public policy and the fruits of it doing so have often been controversial.

Since World War II, the court has made controversial rulings on school desegregation, the right to free speech, reproductive rights, and same sex marriage. These rulings often become fodder for marketing campaigns from both parties. When the Supreme Court has a vacancy, there have come to be protracted battles over who fills the open seat. These battles are both good for business for political parties and interest groups because they raise a lot of money and engage people, but also important ways for parties and interest groups to express their policy preferences. Thus, there may not formally be Obama or Trump judges, but informally both parties assume that winning the White House will get their kind of justice onto the Supreme Court over time.

As Fiorina (1977) long ago noted, this system policymaking endures because Congress wants it to. Because the courts never have to face the voters, they can rule on controversial issues without fear of losing their jobs. Congress is an elected body and taking positions on controversial issues is one way to lose the next election. Thus, elected representatives are more than happy to let courts take the blame. Even in a case where the court decides something in a way that a member of Congress does not like, this has its uses. Election and fundraising campaigns can be waged in opposition to the decision and with a pledge to work to overturn it.

The problem with having courts play this role is that their decisions are not made legitimate in the way in which the output of the elected legislature and executive's output is legitimated. Instead, their decisions become fodder for never-ending marketing campaigns in which an outcome must be preserved or overturned through judicial rulings or by putting enough like-minded people on the court to achieve the desired result. Fights over controversial issues are good for marketing campaigns, but they provide Americans with a continuous sense that the entire system is polarized and gridlocked, and that their fellow citizens are opponents to be beaten not neighbors to be lived with.

One consequence of all this was the backlash it generated in the form of anti-elite politicians like Richard Nixon or Donald Trump who were publicly disdainful of elites and expertise even though they had difficulty governing without them. Not surprisingly, an entrepreneurial politician tapped into all of this and used it as the basis of a marketing campaign. While Skowronek et al. (2021) note that Donald Trump was not exactly right in his construction about the Deep State, he was not exactly wrong either. The incremental development of a permanent bureaucracy with its own goals insulated from public pressure was a goal of the earlier progressive movement. The permanent security establishment developed later but with a similar notion that experts could make better choices than could the average American.

The complex nature of the activities in which these agencies engage, the way much of their activities are conducted with a high degree of secrecy, and the way in which some of them are able to ignore public opinion for extended periods of time, raise fundamental questions about the representativeness of the American system. In the case of Trump, public polling had suggested ambivalence about the issues that he marketed himself with, including immigration, international engagement, the culture, and the way in which government involved itself in economic affairs and on whose behalf it engaged.

The Framers believed in a citizenry that was engaged in its community in a variety of ways. Contemporary observers fret that the contemporary American is much too interest in themselves and their private life to ever become the kind of citizen that the Framers envisioned. For example, Robert Putnam (2000) pointed out the decline of civil life in favor of more and more private orientation. Americans act like consumers, but states sometimes require their citizens to do things that are not in their personal interest because they are in the nation's interest. Government requiring citizens to do things, in a country this individualistic, is a difficult selling proposition. Americans have become accustomed to the fruits of a market system in which they are able to pay less and get more rather than a system in which civic responsibilities are undertaken for the good of society instead of individual interests. This raises basic questions about the choices the government makes too. Consumerism and political marketing have led to a focus on providing the customer with the best product at the best price, but this is not always something that government can or should do, or that the Framers envisioned it doing.

Another threat to American democracy is the concentration of power over daily living in private hands. Most Americans do not work for themselves today. Americans often work in large corporations, universities, or bureaucracies. Increasingly this means that they are subject to the rules that their employers make far more frequently than they are governed by rules made by the government.

As Elizabeth Anderson (2017) has noted, private organizations function in ways that would be authoritarian were an actual government to attempt them. People will put up with such authoritarian behavior for the simple reason that they need a paycheck. This plays itself out in a wide variety of ways, from elections over workplace representation to when voting should be allowed to accommodate the kinds of work schedules people have now versus the kinds that they had when the Framers wrote the constitution.

A different version of this is the amount of influence private social media companies have over free speech. While these are private companies, they use publicly funded infrastructure to provide their services. They also have a special legal position (Section 230 of the Communications Decency Act) because they are not supposed to exercise editorial functions as they now seem to be doing. The idea that a former American president can have his speech, no matter how distasteful, limited by private companies is something that should concern all Americans. If most of the public discourse takes place online through social media platforms, then a few private companies can exercise the kind of authority normally reserved for governments that is sharply limited in the United States by the constitution.

Political marketing and political consumerism have had very mixed results in American society. On the one hand, political marketing at its best can make tighter links between the governed and the governors. This sometimes does happen. It is also possible that it is producing ceaseless disquiet because without disturbance or unmet need there would be few ways to use it to sell politicians. Thus, Americans are subject to crisis without end—because crisis sells. This can also lead to overly emotive politicians as this kind of behavior gets attention in a crowded media landscape.

Political marketing techniques like branding and segmentation have combined to produce bubbles in which Americans can reside without seeing or hearing from people who are not like them or with whom they disagree. This has produced a situation in which politics has become about identity as Liliana Mason (2018) has noted. Politics involves meta identities that are deep, enduring, and difficult to change. People now follow politicians and political parties like they follow sports teams. This makes a system that is designed to force compromise and consensus have problems functioning.

Deep identities and thick bubble walls convince us that our view is the only possible right one and that to compromise would be to show weakness and undermine our faith in the political brand that we support. Meta identities flourish because political brands can now be distributed directly to the right consumers via social media and partisan channels on cable TV and YouTube. The development of customer databases that contain detailed information about citizens means that political marketers can hit just the right audience with just the right message. Every voter has a demographic profile, and the rise of tracking cookies gave political marketers a chance to see what citizens do as opposed to what they claim to do in survey data, and how citizens behave, meaning that individual marketers know which citizens to target with a specific political appeal. This means that, as Joseph Turow (1998) noted, we are given highly targeted messaging and we talk within but not across bubbles. Such is hardly the recipe for a functioning society.

Political consumerism has created a country with a serious civic engagement problem. Americans are not asking what they can do for their country as John F. Kennedy once asked them to do; American are asking what kind of deal the people seeking to run the country are offering them. The country has a voluntary military, routinely has trouble getting people to serve on juries, has a small tax participation rate, and a weaker sense of social connectedness and state legitimacy in comparison to similar countries. This is a direct outcome of the logic of the political marketing model: offer the consumer the best deal. The flaw in that is what is best for individuals might not be good for the collective.

We all want public services, a strong military, and a functioning jury trial system, but it might not be a good deal for us individually to serve on or pay for these things. It is a better deal for us if we can get these things at little or no cost to ourselves regardless of from whence they came. This was a sentiment that several of the Framers feared would develop. Why feared? Because it has the potential to undermine the civic values necessary to maintain a functioning democracy. Thus, this anthology closes with the United States at a key moment in its history.

Endnotes

1. Dwight D. Eisenhower. "Farewell Address" January 17, 1961. National Archives. https://www. archives.gov/milestone-documents/president-dwight-d-eisenhowers-farewell-address
2. Ibid.

CONCLUDING QUESTIONS

Directions: Refer to what you learned in this unit to respond to the questions and prompts below.

1. What caused the American Government to become more insulated from its citizens?

2. Is it possible to have government without politics? Would that be a better situation than what we have now in which seemingly everything is political?

3. What factors do you think have been most important in shaping the ways in which the United States developed from its founding to now? Why?

4. Is it better to compromise with one's opponents or should politics be like a sporting event in which one team wins and the other loses?

5. How has a focus on consumerism and political marketing changed the expectations citizens have of their government and those seeking to lead it?

REFERENCES

Alba, R. (2020). *The demographic illusion*. Princeton University Press.

Anderson, E. (2017). *Private government*. Princeton University Press.

Bachner, J., & Ginsburg, B. (2016). *What Washington gets wrong*. Prometheus.

Baker, P., & Glassner S. (2020). *The man who ran Washington*. Anchor.

Bernays, E. (2013). *Engineering consent. Public relations*. University of Oklahoma Press.

Bernays, E., & Ewen, S. (2011). *Crystalizing public opinion*. IG Publishing.

Bernays, E., & Miller, M. C. (2004). *Propaganda*. IG Publishing.

Berry, J. (1984). *The interest group society*. Little, Brown.

Bishop, B. (2009). *The big sort*. Mariner Books.

Bloom, A. (1987). *The closing of the American Mind*. Simon and Schuster.

Bryson, B. (2013). *One summer: America 1927*. Anchor.

Burke E., & Paine T. (1969) *Reflections on the revolution in France and The rights of man*. Anchor.

Collins, P. (2011). *The murder of the century: The gilded age crime that scandalized a city and sparked the tabloid wars*. Broadway

Fiorina, M. P. (1997). *The decline and resurgence of Congress*. Yale University Press.

Hall Jamieson, K. (1996). *Packing the Presidency: A history and criticism of presidential campaign advertising*. Oxford University Press.

Hamilton, A. Madison, J., & Hay, J. (introduction by Rossiter, C.) (1961) *The Federalist Papers*. Mentor.

Inglehart, R. (1977). *The silent revolution: Changing values and styles among Western publics*. Princeton University Press.

Mason, L. (2018). *Uncivil agreement: How politics became our identity*. University of Chicago Press.

Norris, P., & Inglehart, R. (2019). *Cultural backlash: Trump, Brexit and authoritarian populism*. Cambridge University Press.

O'Reilly T., & Tennant M. (2009). *The age of persuasion: How marketing ate our culture*. Counterpoint.

Postman, N. (1985). *Amusing ourselves to death: Politics in the age of showbusiness*. Viking.

Putnam, R. D. (2000). *Bowling alone*. Simon and Schuster.

Skowronek, S., Dearborn, J. A., & King, D. (2021). *Phantoms of a beleaguered Republic*. Oxford University Press.

Sundquist, J. R. (1981). *The decline and resurgence of Congress*. Brookings Institution Press.

Suri, J. (2017). *The impossible Presidency: the rise and fall of America's highest office*. Basic Books.

Tye, L. (2002) *The father of spin*. Picador.

Turow, J. (1998). *Breaking up America*. University of Chicago Press.

CPSIA information can be obtained
at www.ICGtesting.com
Printed in the USA
BVHW021345100323
660178BV00009B/985